MAYNOOTH MISSION TO AFRICA
THE STORY OF ST PATRICK'S, KILTEGAN

Thomas Kiggins

Maynooth Mission to Africa

The Story of St Patrick's, Kiltegan

Gill and Macmillan

Published in Ireland by
Gill and Macmillan Ltd
Goldenbridge
Dublin 8
with associated companies in
Auckland, Delhi, Gaborone, Hamburg, Harare,
Hong Kong, Johannesburg, Kuala Lumpur, Lagos, London,
Manzini, Melbourne, Mexico City, Nairobi,
New York, Singapore, Tokyo

© Thomas Kiggins 1991
Index compiled by Helen Litton
Print origination by Seton Music Graphics Ltd, Bantry, Co. Cork
Printed by Billing & Sons Ltd, Worcester

British Library Cataloguing in Publication Data
Kiggins, Thomas
Maynooth Mission to Africa : the story of St Patrick's Missionary Society
1. Africa. Catholic missions. St Patrick's Missionary Society
I. Title
266.396

ISBN 0–7171–1824–X

Contents

Preface

WHEN I was commissioned to write the story of St Patrick's Missionary Society, I was given for my bedsitter-cum-study the room in which Pat Whitney set up the first Society office in 1930. It has not been necessary for me to travel very far from this room in order to complete my task. The archives of the Society are nearby and all documentation, prior to 1960, was made available to me. Moreover, I had access to two important works of scholarship which helped me through these archives and unlocked the relevant secrets of more than twelve separate archives in Ireland, Paris, Nigeria and England. These are two dissertations written by Fr Colman Cooke. The first, presented for an M.A. in University College Cork in 1971, is entitled 'Irish Diocesan Priests in Southern Nigeria 1920–1942'. The second, entitled 'The Roman Catholic Mission in Calabar 1903–1960', is a thesis presented to the University of London for a Ph.D. in 1977. The story as I tell it is built, to a great extent, on the travels, researches and thorough-going scholarship of Fr Cooke and with his blessing and encouragement. I owe him a great debt of gratitude. The presence of a number of people who had direct contact with the early days of the Society was also a great asset. Some of these are living with me in Kiltegan while others are regular visitors. Interviewing them was for me a privilege and a pleasure.

For thirty years I have been listening to the story of St Patrick's Missionary Society; how a handful of young Maynooth priests went out to Nigeria in the 1920s to work with Bishop Shanahan and the Holy Ghost Fathers, and how they formed a Missionary Society of their own which eventually spread to more than twelve countries. It was a story read and re-read in *Africa*, the Society magazine and given colour and life by the anecdotes of my fellow Society members. I approached the present task with this colloquial picture in my mind and proceeded to measure it against the documents of the time, to check it out, where possible, with living witnesses and to sift for the real story in the midst of the legend.

The resulting book gives, in some detail, the background of the Society and the history of its first twenty-five years. Conscious of the fact that the story of the subsequent three decades is not likely to be told for a long time, I have added a postscript to bring the reader, rather by leaps and bounds, up to the present day. This final chapter does not set out to be inclusive of the events of the long period which it covers. Rather, it explores a few selected incidents and initiatives and seeks to find in them the strengths and struggles of the Society as it charted its course in the midst of a changing Church and a dramatically developing missionary world.

As this is a family history, I have used familial names throughout. Someone known as 'Paddy' within the Society is called so in the book. On the other hand, if a man was usually referred to in a more formal way, e.g. 'Father Hickey', I give him that title in the book. I have tried to avoid using the surname on its own as I feel it belongs to formal historical writing rather than to the present genre. Although not a scientific history, the book does make reference, in some detail, to the sources which were consulted in piecing the story together. Long lists of names have been omitted from the main text, in the interests of readability, but are given in the notes or in the appendix which includes the names of students and lay missionaries, between 1932 and 1957.

I wish to acknowledge the contribution of my fellow Society members to this book especially the priests and students living in Kiltegan. They gave me encouragement and support and many of them added to the story. A number of priests in Ireland, Kenya and Zambia read various drafts of the text and made suggestions. To mention all those I am indebted to would be outside the conventional bounds of a Preface. Those who gave formal interviews are listed elsewhere while the others are remembered in the heart.

I am grateful to the Holy Ghost Fathers, the Holy Rosary Sisters, St Patrick's College Maynooth and the Bishop of Ardagh and Clonmacnois for permission to publish archival material. I owe special thanks to Fr Desmond Forristal for giving me access to his book *The Second Burial of Bishop Shanahan*, long before it was published. I am also grateful to the office staff in Kiltegan, especially Mary D'Arcy for preparing the typescript with exceptional graciousness.

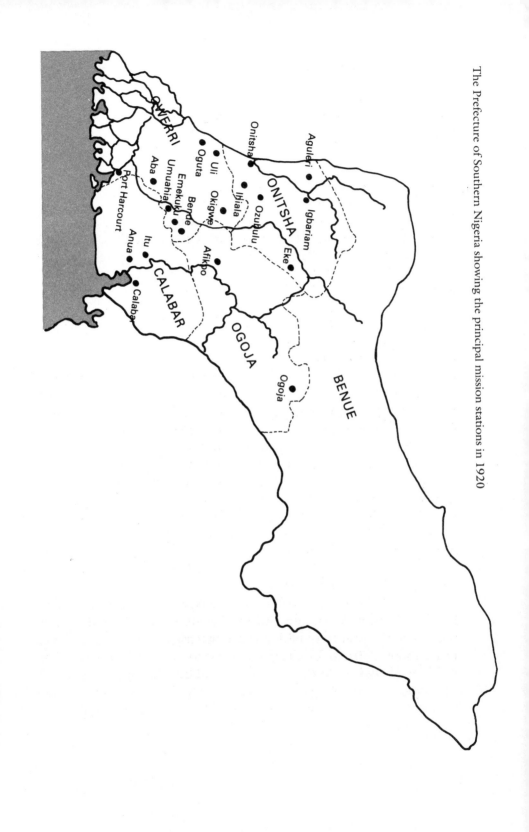

The Prefecture of Southern Nigeria showing the principal mission stations in 1920

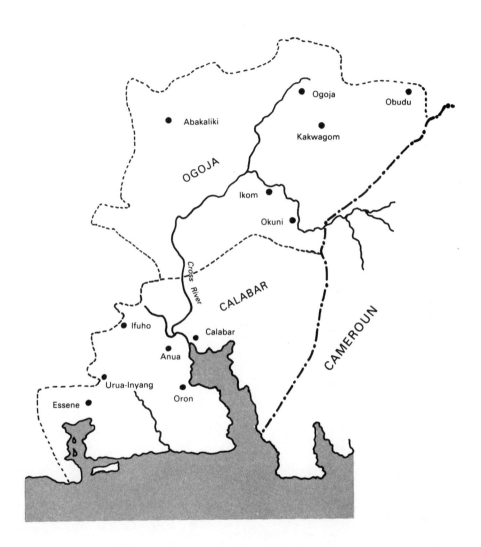

The Prefectures of Calabar and Ogoja showing the principal mission stations in **1940**

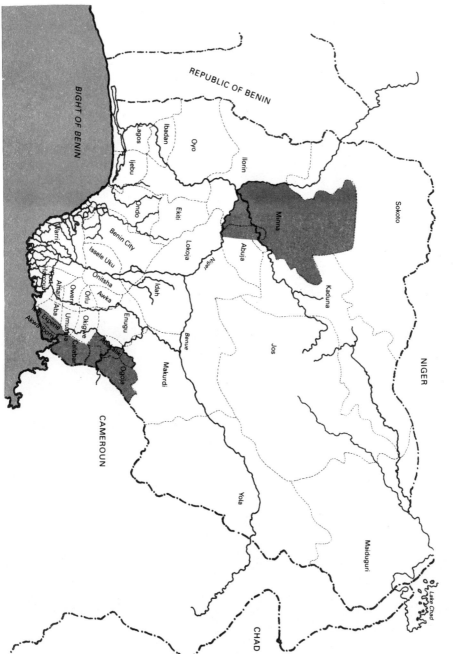

Catholic dioceses of Nigeria in 1990. Shaded areas represent the original mission territories entrusted to St Patrick's Missionary Society

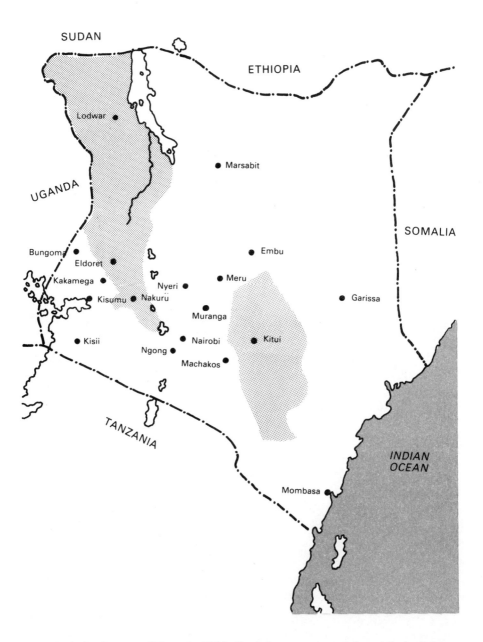

The Catholic dioceses of Kenya in 1990. Shaded areas represent the original mission territories entrusted to St Patrick's Missionary Society

1

Irish Diocesan Priests Volunteer for Nigeria

OUR story begins on 23 December 1921 in the village of Emekuku in Southern Nigeria. A young Irish priest is writing in his diary, a simple notebook to which he has regularly committed his thoughts since 1918, when he was a student in St Patrick's College, Maynooth, the National Seminary of Ireland. His name is Patrick Joseph Whitney and he is one of the priests working in a vast African diocese of some six million people. It is a Friday and his thoughts are with his family and friends whose Christmas letters have brought him up to date with news at home. While relaxing before the rush of Christmas confessions and Masses, he records his intention of making a remarkable suggestion to his bishop, as follows:

> I've thought out a stunt of a Maynooth Nigerian diocese, and I am going to submit it to his Lordship. If he approves we shall aim at getting an organisation set up at once in Ireland leaving things in Browne's direction. I wonder what will come of it.

The entry is remarkable for its brashness. Pat Whitney is twenty-seven and just over a year in Nigeria. He was ordained in June 1920, for Ardagh diocese and arrived in Nigeria the following December. He is now assistant to Daniel Walsh C.S.Sp. and is trying without much success to learn the Ibo language. By his own account, he is 'just a little lonesome sometimes and much too cross with the people'.

He is one of two Irish diocesan priests on temporary service in the Vicariate of Southern Nigeria. The other is Thomas Ronayne of Dublin who is stationed in the coastal town of Calabar. The other priests in the

Vicariate, with one exception, are Holy Ghost Fathers, less than a third of whom are Irish. The exception is Joseph Delaney, a former Christian Brother who came to Nigeria as a lay volunteer in 1909 and was ordained as a diocesan priest ten years later. Pat Whitney is thinking of a diocese staffed entirely by Irish diocesan priests with a back-up organisation in Ireland. He is about to submit concrete proposals to Bishop Shanahan, the head of the mission, who holds the position of Vicar Apostolic of Southern Nigeria. His hopes for an organisation in Ireland rest on a classmate and friend from Tuam diocese named Michael Browne, who is later to become Bishop of Galway. He calls the proposal a 'stunt' which is the word he uses again and again for any enterprising plan. It is an extraordinary proposal in the circumstances, but more extraordinary still is the fact that his 'stunt' would one day be realised in St Patrick's Missionary Society and would have an influence far beyond the borders of Nigeria.

Holy Ghost Mission
To understand how Pat Whitney came to be in Africa, it is necessary to go back to 1885, when the first Holy Ghost missionaries arrived in Nigeria. The Holy Ghost Congregation was in the forefront of modern Catholic missionary work in Africa which dates from 1842, when Rome established the Vicariate of the Two Guineas which stretched from Senegal to the Orange River. The Vicariate has five thousand miles of coastline and extended without limit into the interior. In 1848, the Holy Ghost Congregation came into being as a result of the merging of the tiny Congregation of the Holy Ghost, which went back to 1703, and the recently founded, and somewhat larger, Congregation of the Holy Heart of Mary. This newly-constituted missionary body was given responsibility for the immense Vicariate of the Two Guineas, which it proceeded to develop. Soon, it received assistance from the Society of African Missions which was established in 1856. The first missionaries in Nigeria were in fact, members of this Society which opened a mission in Lagos in 1868. In 1884, the Society of African Missions was given responsibility for another territory to the north of Nigeria which was called the Prefecture of the Upper Niger. A year later, the Holy Ghost Fathers moved into Southern Nigeria, which was to gain ecclesiastical independence as the Prefecture of the Lower Niger in 1889, and was to become, later, the Prefecture of Southern Nigeria.

The first Holy Ghost group consisted of two priests and two brothers, all in the prime of life. Before long, one of the brothers was dead and one of the priests had returned to Europe, broken in health by recurring malaria. It was to be the pattern for the early years of the Nigerian mission which were years of immense sacrifice and bitter failure. Nigeria lived up to its reputation as 'the white man's grave' and the mortality rate among the missionaries was very high. The work was confined to a few mission stations close to the Niger river, in towns and villages already influenced by British administration and trade. The early adherents were, for the most part, former slaves who had been ransomed by the missionaries or liberated by the British authorities. These were grouped together in villages where it was hoped they would live the Christian life and become bearers of Christianity to the surrounding countryside. The custom of grouping people in villages under the authority of the missionary existed in South America in the early sixteenth century and was used to great effect by Jesuit missionaries, especially in Paraguay, in the seventeenth and eighteenth centuries. In nineteenth-century Africa, the Christian village emerged again in Catholic and Protestant missions alike. Bishop Stephen Neil describes how it came about:

> No sooner had a settlement been effected, than the missionaries began to experience the difficulties of life in a tribal area. The last thing they desired was to create a new and separate Africa; yet again and again they found themselves the centre of a new settlement, made up of freed slave children, of men who for some reason had lost their identity with their tribe, of criminals fleeing from justice (murderers not excluded!) and of young men who wished to learn the skills that only the white man could teach.[1]

Inevitably, such villages and their inhabitants were held in very low esteem by the local population. It seemed to the latter that the missionary's concern was chiefly with the outcasts of society and that his religion was a religion for slaves. This was true in Nigeria as elsewhere and although the early Holy Ghost missionaries made overtures to the free population these were largely ignored.

Ordinary Africans saw little need for a new religion since they already perceived themselves as spiritually self-contained, in a life comprehensively regulated by custom and tradition. Although termed *pagan*, the people of Southern Nigeria followed a well-developed form of traditional religion. There were differences of belief and practice from tribe to tribe and often from village to village but there were many common elements such as the existence of a High God and a number of lesser deities. The predominant Ibo tribe called their High God *Chukwu* but also venerated, among others, a sun-god, a storm-god and an earth-goddess who was depicted in statues reminiscent of the Christian Madonna. There were simple hut-temples to various deities, and numerous shrines, many of them honouring family ancestors. There were oracles, too, which were used to settle disputes and provide direction in times of difficulty. The most famous of these was a sinister cave at Arochukwu known as the *Long Juju*. Ibos came from far and wide to consult this oracle and it became a symbol of unity and integration for the tribe.[2]

The Catholics were not the only Christian Church trying to evangelise Southern Nigeria; nor were they the first. Anglicans, Presbyterians and Methodists had been on the coast for up to 40 years and had made some headway there. They had made few inroads into Iboland, however, although the Church Missionary Society had a mission at Onitsha under the leadership of Bishop Samuel Crowther, a celebrated missionary pioneer and a native Nigerian. The Anglicans, too, adopted the Christian-village approach and were no more successful than the Catholics in establishing an influential presence. In 1900, the lot of the Catholics began to change with the appointment of Leon Lejeune as Superior of the mission and Prefect Apostolic of Southern Nigeria. This strong-minded priest from Normandy had already spent fifteen years as a missionary in Gabon and could be expected to make radical changes in a mission that had produced few results in fifteen years of effort and sacrifice. One of his most important decisions was a simple one. He decided to build in brick. As a result, the dwelling houses offered greater protection and that meant better health and longer life for the missionaries. He also saw the shortcomings of the accepted pastoral approach and began to explore ways of breaking away from the Christian village and bringing the message to the mainstream of the population. To this end, he established a mission in the coastal town of Calabar with schools which attracted the sons and daughters of the leading townsfolk. It was a foretaste of things to come although it was not Monsignor Lejeune who directed these developments. He returned to France in 1905 with terminal cancer and was replaced by Joseph Shanahan, a 34 year old Irishman who had arrived in Nigeria three years earlier.

The new Prefect Apostolic adopted the same approach as his predecessor and pursued it so singlemindedly as to initiate a mass movement of people into the Church, especially from among the Ibo tribe. He decided to penetrate deeply into Ibo country away from the river and the principal land routes to an area where people were untouched by

Christian missionaries of any denomination. He introduced a system of widespread contact in which the missionary staked his claim and moved on, leaving intensive instruction and development until later. He also made a firm commitment to education, having decided that it was possible to transform Ibo society by means of the school and to use all the resources of the mission to achieve such a transformation. These decisions laid the foundation for a phenomenal expansion of the Church among the Ibo people which was unparalleled elsewhere in Africa except in Uganda where the Baganda tribe made a similar, although less singularly Catholic, response.

The presence of a colonial power was an important factor in this progress. In 1900, the British, after nearly sixty years of trading on the Niger, began to establish a colonial administration in the area. This brought new ideas, new laws and a new authority which challenged traditional beliefs and values. The colonial authorities never set out to dismantle the traditional religion but nonetheless contributed to its eclipse. In a bid to establish law and order, the excesses of the powerful secret societies which had their origin in ancestor worship were curbed and the societies themselves considerably weakened. In 1901, government forces destroyed the organisation of the Long Juju because it had become a slave-trading ring. Gradually, traditional religion was robbed of much of its power and a void was created which Christianity was poised to fill. Initially, it was education which offered an entry point for the missionary. The Ibos developed an insatiable thirst for education which was seen as the way forward for the tribe in the new dispensation. Education opened the door to the employment opportunities offered by the colonial administration and became the focus of intense competition among rival clans and villages.

Every village wanted a school and was prepared to pay for it. The government, too, was keen to develop an educational programme and, in 1903, offered to assist education by means of grants and professional supervision. The Churches, as voluntary agencies involved in education, were eligible for these grants on condition that they guaranteed that religion would be an optional subject on the curriculum. The Anglican Church Missionary Society refused to accept this condition and had to forgo government aid for a time. Joseph Shanahan agreed to the condition, having judged rightly that the vast majority of parents would have no objection to their children being instructed in the white man's religion. He cooperated fully with the government and sat on a Commission for Education which was established in 1906. In 1908, the mission received £3,077 from the Government and had close to 2,500 pupils in the schools.[3]

When Joseph Shanahan made his commitment to education, he had only ten priests, two brothers and five sisters in his Prefecture. The sisters were members of the French Order of St Joseph of Cluny, whose involvement with Southern Nigeria dated back to 1888. With such a small number of personnel, Joseph Shanahan launched his education policy. H.J. Koren in a history of the Holy Ghost Congregation described how it worked:

> He accomplished his objective by stationing priests in a few strategic points where they would open a school and then use the best students of their school as temporary teachers for subsidiary bush schools in the surrounding areas. After a time these apprentices were replaced by other students. They would then return to finish their own training, whereupon they would go out to open new schools from which the snowballing process could continue in geometric progression. After a few years of this procedure the original mission became the vibrant centre of an enthusiastic Christian generation.[4]

The school finally broke down the barriers that had stood for so long between the missionaries and the Ibo people. Joseph Shanahan wrote in 1912, in a letter to Rome:

> So far we cannot but congratulate ourselves on the fidelity of the children, and on the goodwill of the pagans. The school keeps the missionary in contact with the people, because the children give him free entry into every house. He is no longer a stranger but a member of the family. This fact alone makes what he can effect, and what he can prevent, really incalculable. He is known everywhere, and he alone can go through the country without danger. Other Europeans dare not move about the country unescorted. But at the very moment of writing, our presence is being demanded in some fifty towns.[5]

The pupils themselves became enthusiastic evangelists and, before long, adults too were asking for baptism. This is borne out by the figures for 1917 which show that there were 32,448 catechumens while the number of schoolchildren stood at 20,900.[6]

Shortage of missionaries was the great stumbling block to the growth of the Church. Joseph Shanahan appealed repeatedly to the Holy Ghost

Superiors to send more priests and brothers. He felt, with some justification, that Southern Nigeria deserved to be given priority among the territories staffed by the Congregation. He looked to the Irish Province in particular for men who would be suitable to staff the Teacher Training College and the High Schools, which soon came into existence. No help was forthcoming, however, apart from an equal share of the small number of men who became available each year. In 1917, the numbers stood at sixteen priests and seven brothers. It was an improvement, but still a tiny number for the task in hand. John P. Jordan gives an interesting perspective to the task which faced the missionaries:

> To begin with, there was the great Ibo tribe, some three million strong, bulging inland from the River Niger; south and east of them the Effiks and Ibioios; north and east, a host of petty tribes governed from Ogoja; north, the Munchis, Igarras and many more—nearly twice the population of Ireland, and far more than twice the extent. To christianise and educate them he had exactly sixteen Fathers, with two on leave. Remove the rails and roads of Ireland; put two priests in Cashel to look after Munster; two in Portlaoise to deal with Leinster; two in Armagh to tackle Ulster— that gives you an exact idea of what he faced, and of the personnel at his disposal for the task.[7]

In 1917, as a result of the first world war, Joseph Shanahan was given charge of the Prefecture Apostolic of Adamawa in Cameroon because the German Holy Ghost missionaries who staffed the Prefecture had been interned by the British administration there. In four months, he trekked a thousand miles visiting the abandoned missions and afterwards he was so ill and exhausted that he had to go back to Ireland for a rest and for medical treatment.

Appeal to Maynooth Students

During his time in Ireland Joseph Shanahan went to Maynooth to appeal for diocesan priests to come to Southern Nigeria for a period of temporary service. It was not entirely his own idea, as the Superiors in Paris had suggested such an overture some time previously. He made contact with Maynooth through Father Malachy Eaton, a member of the College staff and a close friend of his sister's family, the Dawsons, who lived in Maynooth village. He was well received by the President, Monsignor J. McCaffrey, who had a genuine interest in the foreign missions and was to become a great friend of the Nigerian mission.

Later he recalled the circumstances in which he received the blessing of the Irish hierarchy:

> I became very friendly with the President of Maynooth and discussed with him my scheme for getting out secular priests to Nigeria. He was a great missionary. One day he said to me:
>
> 'Next week there will be a dinner here for all the bishops of Ireland and the Cardinal [Logue] himself will be at it. You come and I shall put you beside the Cardinal so that you can get him interested in your plan. But whatever you do, take a pinch of snuff if he asks you, and sneeze as hard as you can.'
>
> Well, I came to the dinner and was put beside the Cardinal. The meal progressed but no opportunity arose of talking about Nigeria for a long time. However, he turned to me at last and said:
>
> 'Where do you come from Father?'
>
> 'Nigeria,' I said.
>
> 'Hot spot,' he said. 'How long were you there?'
>
> I told him and then immediately he said:
>
> 'By the way, do you snuff?'
>
> 'I do, of course,' I replied.
>
> Thereupon, he produced the box and I took a large pinch which I snuffed as hard as I could and sneezed and sneezed 'til the tears ran down my cheeks. The Cardinal chuckled and said: 'Great stuff, it has the power of giving a hardened missionary a good shaking up.'
>
> After that we got talking and I unfolded my scheme. I offered to give any young priest who would volunteer to come back with me a three years' university course in the Apostolate and send him back to his diocese better for the schooling.
>
> 'Why not make it five years?' said the Cardinal and rising up he called for silence. He introduced me to the assembled bishops and told them I had something to say to them. Here was my chance, and standing up I faced all the bishops of Ireland and spoke as never before or since. When I had finished they agreed to my proposal, and gave me permission to meet all the Maynooth students and to seek volunteers among them.[8]

A few weeks later, in February 1920, he addressed the students. A number expressed interest including one who was to be ordained in June of that year. He was Pat Whitney and he wrote in his diary:

Father Shanahan pleaded for Africa—Nigeria. He will give a temporary mission there to priests from Maynooth. There is immense work to be done and the pagans are asking for Baptism. The appeal went to my heart. If I can I will go—God direct me. If I don't go there, Garret Pearce is asking for men for Minnesota. By Patrick's Day it will be decided. St Patrick pray for me.

Joseph Shanahan's appeal was only one of three appeals made to the students since their return from the Christmas holidays. The others were for India and China. Of the three missions, it was India which had the longest connection with Maynooth. The Maynooth mission to India sprang from a burst of missionary activity which occurred soon after Catholic Emancipation.[9] The annals of the College record the first manifestation of this taking place in February 1838. The account reads:

> . . . seven zealous students of the College renounced their prospects and exiled themselves from friends and country in order to devote their lives to the propagation of the Gospel of Our Lord in New South Wales under the jurisdiction of Right Rev. Dr Polding.[10]

In May, three priests went to Scotland and, in June, Dr Patrick J. Carew, a Professor of Theology in the College, was consecrated and appointed Coadjutor to the Vicar-Apostolic of Madras. Later in the year, he left for India with five priests including William Kelly, Professor of English and French. The Maynooth men had been recruited by the Irish Augustinian Vicar Apostolic of Madras, who had been recently appointed by Rome in an effort to dismantle the Padroado which was stifling the progress of the Church in India. (The Padroado was the 15th century agreement by which the Pope granted to the Kings of Spain and Portugal the right to create bishoprics in their respective territories.) Shortly afterwards, Bishop Carew became Vicar Apostolic and, three years later, was transferred to Calcutta. Once again, a staff-member of Maynooth—this time the Bursar, John Fennelly—was consecrated bishop and sent to Madras and, until 1911, Madras remained in the hands of Irish bishops. Three students from Maynooth accompanied Bishop Fennelly to India and a number of others went in the following years. Before long, however, the movement of Irish priests to India lost momentum and eventually stopped entirely. This was partly due to the fact that there was no organisation in Ireland to fuel interest in the Indian mission. Besides this, the Irish famine contributed to its decline.

After the famine, the pastoral care of the emigrants who had settled in the Americas, Australia and New Zealand became a priority for the Irish Church. Many of those ordained in the diocesan seminaries of Carlow, Kilkenny, Thurles, Waterford and Wexford spent their lives among the emigrants. Many others went from All Hallows College in Dublin, which had been established, in 1842, with the express purpose of training secular priests for work abroad. Maynooth accepted only students for the Irish dioceses but as the supply of priests became more plentiful a number were allowed to go abroad on temporary mission. After the extension of the college in the 1850s a greater number was ordained each year and more and more dioceses found themselves with a surplus of priests. At the beginning of this century, many priests could expect to spend the early years of their priesthood abroad. A man was generally left free to choose a particular diocese on the understanding that he would return home when his services were needed in his own diocese.

The next big missionary initiative of the Irish Church was closely associated with Maynooth. It was the foundation of The Maynooth Mission to China, later called the Missionary Society of St Columban.[11]

John Frazer, a Canadian priest, was the first to speak of the needs of the Chinese mission in Maynooth. He was recruiting and fund-raising on behalf of the French Lazarist Fathers and arrived in the college in June 1911. Professors and students assisted him with money but no volunteers came forward. It was in New York, a year later, that John Frazer got his first Irish volunteer. He was Edward Galvin, a priest from Cork who had been ordained in Maynooth in 1909, and was now coming to the end of a temporary commitment in Brooklyn diocese. He volunteered for China and spent the next four years there. He was a prodigious letter writer claiming to have written 'over two hundred and fifty letters' in one month alone. His many letters to Maynooth and to priests who had studied with him there kindled an interest in China. The outbreak of war had led to the withdrawal of many French missionaries who had been drafted into the army. The mission was in dire need of priests, a fact which Ned Galvin brought home to his correspondents. In December 1915 he was joined by two priests from Ireland, Patrick O'Reilly of Meath and Joseph O'Leary of Cork. At their urging, Ned Galvin returned to Ireland with the express purpose of launching an Irish mission to China.

Arriving in Ireland in August 1915, he first secured the backing of his own Bishop, Daniel Cohalan of Cork, who gave him letters of introduction for Cardinal Logue. It was part of Ned Galvin's plan to get a Maynooth professor to head the proposed mission as he felt that such a man would have the confidence of the bishops of Ireland. He told this to Tom Ronayne, whom he met in Dublin on his arrival. The latter wrote to his classmate and friend John Blowick, who was a Professor of Theology in Maynooth, inviting him to join the new movement, 'to head the organisation—as a Kitchener of the new army, so to speak'. Soon afterwards, John Blowick resigned his chair of theology to become the key figure in the work of organisation that was to follow. In October, the Bishops of Ireland, meeting at Maynooth, approved, in principle, an Irish Vicariate in China with a mission house in Ireland to provide priests and funds for the Vicariate. Other priests had joined the two Founders and an intense promotion campaign was launched.

The tremendous emotional appeal of this campaign is captured by historian Hugh McMahon as follows:

> With the help of friends on the Maynooth staff, in religious orders and in the dioceses, the first five members of the society wanted to bring the message to every bishop, seminary, parish and house in the country. They were determined to go to the cabins of the poor as well as the homes of the rich. Plans to make a house-to-house collection had to be abandoned as impractical. Instead they turned to the dioceses and parishes. Bishops welcomed them in their homes, planned visits to the churches and loaned them their cars. Beginning on a Monday morning they travelled around the parishes until ten or eleven at night. While they arranged times for parish appeals and the manner of taking collections, they shared their vision with the parish clergy. Later a magazine called *The Far East* was launched to keep the memory of China alive in homes after those who made the appeals moved on.

Most of the people were hearing about China for the first time. According to John Blowick 'it was a very common thing to have the people in tears in the course of a sermon given by the priest'. The response was phenomenal. Reflecting on it many years later, John Blowick mused that while Vatican II had drawn attention to the fact that 'all Christians are called to be missionaries' the implications of this had been understood and practised in Ireland from as long ago as 1916.[12]

Towards the end of 1917, the promotion campaign was extended to the United States. In January 1918, a college was opened at Dalgan Park in Galway diocese with nineteen students, most of whom had transferred from Maynooth. In June of that year, the mission was canonically erected as a Missionary Society by Bishop O'Dea of Galway. A Chapter was convened and John Blowick was elected Superior General. The Constitutions were careful to preserve the secular character of the new Society and to differentiate it from a religious order. The Society incorporated, as far as possible, the style of priesthood embodied in the Irish diocesan clergy. In March 1920, the first eleven missionaries set out for China. It was the beginning of a great missionary work which would spread to Australia, the Philippines, Korea, Burma, Japan and Latin America.

The foundation of the Missionary Society of St Columban marked a new flowering of the missionary spirit of the Irish Church. It was not a new departure within the Church however, as it belonged to the great missionary thrust of the Catholic Church which had been revived in the early nineteenth century and had gathered momentum as the century progressed with the personal encouragement of successive Popes. Before the Columban initiative, however, Ireland did not have very many missionaries in the so-called pagan lands. This was due to the urgent needs of Irish emigrants in England, the Americas and Australia. The priests, brothers and nuns who undertook this apostolate were also termed 'missionaries' and many of them operated under the jurisdiction of the Roman Congregation of Propaganda Fide which had responsibility for the Church's missions. It was not until 1908, for example, that the United States ceased to be under Propaganda and became a mission-sending Church. The Irish Church did, however, have some people on the 'pagan missions'. They belonged to the religious orders and in particular to the Holy Ghost Congregation and the Society of African Missions. The former had come to Ireland in 1859, and the latter in 1877. Both had gained considerable support and had recruited a number of Irish members. The new movement was different in that it had its origin within the ranks of the Irish diocesan clergy. It was also different in that it constituted a mass-appeal, stirring up enthusiasm for the 'foreign missions' in every parish in Ireland.

It is very likely that the 1916 rising contributed to the success of the Missionary Society of St Columban. The leaders of the rising had been executed only three months before Ned Galvin arrived from China to promote his idea of a new missionary society. There followed a venerations of these heroes—called 'martyrolatry' by one commentator—and a desire to emulate their spirit of self-sacrifice.[13] What they had done took on a religious significance and was compared frequently to the sufferings of Jesus Christ. Some sought to follow their example in the political arena while others looked further afield for opportunities to serve nobly and honourably. The needs of the poor benighted peoples of distant lands provided one such opportunity. This affinity between missionary work and the spirit of the age was not lost on John Blowick, Co-Founder of the Columbans. He wrote in a pamphlet, in 1916:

> Thousands of Irish today are as much inspired as their fathers were with the spirit of bravery, chivalry and sacrifice. They are looking for an outlet by which they may renovate the world by the frenzy of their soul and their religion. We have found such an outlet.[14]

The war, too, fuelled this urge to heroism, and the bravery of the young Irishmen who died at Ypres and the Somme contributed to the missionary revival. Once again, John Blowick was alive to the implications and wrote in the same pamphlet:

> In after years when little ones come to us and ask us what did we do when the great European war was on, let us be able to say we converted China.

While it is difficult to assess the extent of these influences, the fact remains that, in 1920, missionary idealism was in the air. It had been fanned into flame by the foundation of the Maynooth Mission to China and was now an enabling force for other missionary endeavours. It was embodied in the student audience which listened to Joseph Shanahan in Maynooth. Some of those present had already made a commitment to China; others were trying to make up their minds; all were sympathetic.

Joseph Shanahan's appeal in Maynooth had two unique elements which put his competitors, representing India and China, at a disadvantage. One was the extraordinary personality of the speaker. There was a kind of aura about him which impressed everybody and seemed to embody the ideal qualities of the listener. After the appeal, Pat Whitney described him, in his diary, as 'a fearless man who is at home before everyone yet humble as a saint'. Photographs of Bishop Shanahan exude integrity and spiritual depth while his writings bear witness to his warmth, honesty and rich humanity. The second element which favoured his appeal was the temporary commitment he asked of volunteers. He wanted men who would give a minimum of four years' service to the mission before returning to their home diocese. The Maynooth Mission to China, on the other hand, asked for a life-time commitment and did not accept volunteers on a temporary basis. A strong organisation was vital for the China mission as there was no body of Irish missionaries there to whom they could attach themselves. Furthermore, the pioneers were aware of the fact that the mission to India had failed because there was no organisation at home to back up the mission effort and to provide a continuity of men. So, they insisted on a strong organisation with total commitment from the members. Volunteers for Nigeria could function adequately without an organisation of their own as they had the Irish Province of the Holy Ghost Fathers to look after their interests. Language posed another obstacle to short-term service in China, where it was necessary to learn a difficult language before starting missionary work. The situation was different in Southern Nigeria. English was fast becoming a lingua franca and priests on temporary mission could be very effective without mastering a local language. The use of interpreters was acceptable, apart from the confessional, and it was not difficult to learn the limited vocabulary needed to hear confessions. Moreover, English was the principal language of the school, and Maynooth men, all of whom held University degrees, could expect to spend much of their time dealing with school matters.

Apart from the unique elements, certain widely held presuppositions of the day contributed to the attraction of missionary appeals. Chief among these was the conviction that missionary activity was of great advantage to those among whom it was carried out, especially in the spiritual sphere. To some it was simply a question of offering eternal salvation to people who were otherwise doomed to eternal perdition. Many Protestants subscribed to this view and had no great difficulty with it because of their belief that some people were not predestined to be saved. Among Catholics there was a lot of confusion. On the one hand there was the key doctrine that God wills the salvation of all mankind. On the other, there was the axiom 'no salvation outside the Church'. The latter teaching goes back to the early centuries. It was affirmed by Popes and Church Councils, most notably the fifteenth-century Council of Florence which stated:

> [The Holy Roman Church] firmly believes, professes and proclaims, that no one of those living outside the Catholic Church, neither pagans nor Jews nor heretics nor schismatics, can become sharers in eternal life, rather they will go into eternal fire prepared for the devil and his angels, unless they join the church before the end of their lives . . .'[15]

It was not until European explorers discovered that there were vast numbers of people who had never heard the Gospel and who, through no fault of their own, had never heard of the Church that Catholics became uneasy with this teaching. How could God who willed that all men should be saved exclude those multitudes who had no opportunity of joining the Church? Theologians argued that a desire to belong to the Church was sufficient for salvation. Later it was held that where an explicit desire was not possible, an implicit desire would suffice. The Church never officially endorsed this last viewpoint, and as a result the question of the salvation of non-Catholics remained a grey area in theology until well into the twentieth century when Pope Pius XII and, later, the Second Vatican Council made official statements on the subjects which clarified the traditional teaching and de-emphasised its exclusiveness.

It is probably true to say that few enough Catholics accepted this teaching in its most rigid interpretation. A few did, among them a group in Boston who were condemned by the Vatican in 1949. The vast majority adopted a benign if uninformed interpretation. Missionaries, in general, were ambivalent in their attitude but seldom adopted the stricter view on the subject. Bishop Thomas McGettrick, after a lifetime spent on the Nigerian mission, said in an interview given in 1988: 'We never fully bought the idea of outside the Church no salvation.' Yet, there was a great emphasis on baptising the dying whenever possible and there was an unease about the fate of the unbaptised after death. It was accepted that salvation was particularly precarious for those outside the Church and could, at best, be attained with great difficulty and in exceptional circumstances. The Church, on the other hand, had at its disposal powerful aids to the salvation of souls. The Gospel, the sacraments, Christian moral teaching and the support of the community put salvation within the reach of people who might otherwise fail to enter God's Kingdom. Nor was the Kingdom always thought of in terms of the next life. There was a deliverance from fear and evil which was attainable in this life as one missionary, writing in 1934, emphasised:

> The minds of those poor people are not elevated to Heavenly ideas. They are stuck in the mud of superstition—they centre around the power of evil. What a shame that the mind of man who was created for such noble things, should be steeped in such ignorance! What a shame that men would not love their most lovable God! *They* are not to blame; they have not been instructed. How could they have learned! The blame rests on us if we do

not raise them up; if we do not teach them to know, love and trust in God. Let us all do whatever we can to help them to trust in the power and goodness of God, and to cease to live in a continuous state of fear and evil.[16]

Similar arguments applied in the social and cultural sphere. European civilisation, insofar as it could be distinguished from Christianity, was thought to be of inestimable value to the Africans. There were a few dissenting voices but, in general, it was accepted that the education, law, technology and medicine which the European could bring would improve the lot of the African and constitute a service to humanity. To many sincere and well-meaning Europeans this service became a duty, a moral duty of the race, 'the white man's burden'. Priests and students for the priesthood were men of their time and arguments from such high moral ground obviously appealed to them.

In the light of these factors, it would be reasonable to expect an enthusiastic response from the Maynooth students, and Joseph Shanahan expected such a response. In the short term, he was not disappointed. Pat Whitney 'signed on for Nigeria' at the end of April after some resistance from his widowed mother. A number of students in the lower theology classes were interested and a small number went, over the next three or four years. In the longer term, however, the response fell far short of expectations. Over the next nine years only eleven Maynooth priests volunteered for Southern Nigeria.

There were two main reasons for this. Firstly, there was a reluctance to work in a completely alien culture. Those who were prepared to do so were already committed to China. Then, for temporary volunteers, who were happy to go to England or the United States, the health risk involved in an assignment in Africa was a big consideration. Much of the correspondence of the early Maynooth men in Nigeria was aimed at reassuring those at home that it was possible to live a healthy life on the missions. Pat Whitney came up with the knock-out argument that the wives of English colonial officers were able for it—why not Irish priests.[17] The risks to health were nonetheless real and were to remain unchanged for a long time. Bishop Moynagh recalls the risks in his memoirs:

In those days West Africa was regarded as really the worst health risk in the world. It was truly the white man's grave. It was assumed that up to 50% of men who went out would not survive. There was no answer to yellow fever which had 80% mortality and no full answer to malaria, blackwater fever etc. Remember in 1937 we lost three missionaries . . . The vaccine for yellow fever came in 1938.[18]

The third consideration was the reluctance of diocesan priests to go abroad under the umbrella of a religious order. The two groups had little contact with one another, especially since the foundation of Maynooth which trained only diocesan priests. The number of religious in Ireland after the Reformation was very small and they did not make a major impression on the life of the Church. In some dioceses, they worked very closely with the local bishop but more often they resisted his attempt to control them. Patrick Corish in a study of the Irish Church gives some examples:

> In 1793 Bishop Moylan of Cork demanded that the various religious orders in the city preach in his cathedral. His successor Bishop Murphy claimed they had a strict obligation to do so and when this claim was resisted he closed the novitiate the Franciscans had set up in the city. Other Bishops took a similar line. Bishop Abraham of Waterford tried to stop the Franciscans building a new Church, and when it was completed in 1834 he tried to stop them using it, as he wished all the friars in the town of his diocese to work in the parishes.[19]

There was often rivalry in parishes where religious and parish churches were situated. The result was lack of contact, lack of understanding and mild suspicion.

Moreover, many orders were more continental than Irish in style and traditions. This was especially true of newer orders. The Holy Ghosts were still very French. They were founded in France; the Motherhouse was in Paris; the majority of their missionaries in Nigeria were French; the bulletin of the congregation was published in French and there was a French flavour to their style of life. Maynooth students were understandably very wary about 'joining' such a group, if only for four years. In his diary Pat Whitney quotes from a letter he had received from the Vincentian James Downey who had been his spiritual director in Maynooth and was soon to become Coadjutor Bishop of Ossory: 'Father Downey also writes to say that temporary men won't come to work with an order; says we should do like Galvin.' The wisdom of this judgment is borne out by the early statistics. From 1920–1929, only eleven volunteers went to Nigeria under the auspices of the Holy Ghost Fathers. In the following ten years, 1930–1939, when the invitation came from the newly-formed Society of St Patrick, forty-four volunteer priests went to Nigeria and a further thirteen volunteered for support work at the Society headquarters in Kiltegan.

After making his appeal in Maynooth, Joseph Shanahan visited the Holy Ghost Motherhouse in Paris and went on to Lisieux to pray at the grave of the Little Flower whose cause for canonisation was gaining momentum at the time. On his way home, he received a letter in London from Tom Ronayne volunteering for Nigeria. The Prefect Apostolic was delighted to get the services of a priest who had already had seven years' pastoral experience, part of it in the United States. On arrival in Ireland he received Pat Whitney's final word. It seemed that Thérèse of Lisieux was doing her bit. Both Tom Ronayne and Pat Whitney were praying to her too and the latter wrote in his diary on 2 May: 'I can thank the Little Flower for getting to Nigeria.' Presumably, it was her influence on his mother or on the Bishop of Ardagh and Clonmacnois which he had in mind.

On 17 April, it was announced that the Prefecture of Southern Nigeria would become a Vicariate and that Joseph Shanahan was to be made a bishop. He chose to be consecrated in Maynooth in a move which was calculated to draw attention to his appeal and cement the link between his diocese and the Irish Church. Tom Ronayne and Pat Whitney were involved in the event as Master of Ceremonies and Deacon, respectively. It took place on 6 June. Bishop Shanahan attended Pat's ordination in Maynooth two weeks later and in November all set sail for Nigeria accompanied by seven Holy Ghost missionaries, of whom Edward Leen and Philip O'Connor were newcomers. The other five were Frenchmen who had already worked in Nigeria.

Maynooth Men on the Mission

On 15 December, the party came ashore at Calabar which was within the Vicariate of Southern Nigeria. It was the first of many landings to be made by Irish diocesan priests on the Nigerian coast. An enthusiastic welcome awaited the newly consecrated Bishop Shanahan and afterwards the whole group relaxed in Calabar until after Christmas. Then, before leaving for Onitsha, the headquarters of the Vicariate, Bishop Shanahan gave the priests their appointments. Tom Ronayne was to stay in Calabar town as one of the three priests attached to the mission. He was to have special responsibility for the schools. It was a dream come true for the cheerful bespectacled young man whose health was never very robust.

As a seminarian, he had been told by his doctor to walk only on level ground to avoid putting undue strain on his heart.

Tom Ronayne was born in Dunmore, Co. Galway and was educated by the Holy Ghost Fathers in Rockwell and Blackrock Colleges. He attended Maynooth as a student for Dublin diocese, and was ordained in 1913. He worked in Sioux Falls diocese in the United States and, on his return, was appointed to the parish of Monkstown, then one of the most exclusive suburbs in Dublin. It was there that he was contacted by Ned Galvin when the latter returned from China to promote his idea for a new missionary Society. Tom Ronayne became involved in the project and would have become one of the first members but for the opposition of his Archbishop, William J. Walsh, who did not share the general enthusiasm for the Chinese mission. He had no difficulty getting permission to go to Nigeria and, on arrival there, he was very pleased to be appointed to the town of Calabar which, on account of his poor health, was considered more suitable for him than a 'bush' mission.

Calabar was a steamy seaport situated at the mouth of the Cross river. In 1920, it was a prosperous if unprepossessing place. A contemporary account from the pen of British traveller Raymond Gore Clough, describes the town as seen from the estuary:

> At intervals along the foreshore were dotted the trading premises of the various companies. From the river each appeared as a large galvanised iron or timber shed with a 'T' shaped jetty jutting out into the water. On each jetty were fixed a few hand operated derricks which were used mainly for lifting puncheons or casks of palm oil from the canoes which clustered around them . . . From the decks of the *Munchi*, Calabar presented an attractive scene. Steep green hills rose from the river, some covered with palms and groups of tall mushroom shaped trees. To the left there were a few large bungalows, with wide canopied roofs, built in a clearing with shade trees and gardens around them; clearly these were the homes of the European Government officials. In a cleft between two hills lay Duke Town, one of the twin towns of old Calabar; the other Creek Town could be seen in a shimmering heat haze a little further up river . . . The waterfront was taken up by a long market and rising behind it Duke Town appeared from the river as tier upon tier of mud, thatch and corrugated iron hovels, all of an even burnt Sienna colour. A few large two storied buildings, with coloured glass panels in their gothic shaped windows stood out;

they were the homes of the chiefs and merchants. In the middle of the town stood a church of corrugated galvanised iron with a steeple of the same material slightly askew.[20]

Calabar had traded with Europe since the mid-seventeenth century. There were a number of tribes in the town but the dominant group was the Efik. They were the traders and they had established themselves over the years as the rulers of Calabar. They had prospered as middlemen in the slave trade, and after its abolition did equally well in the export of palm oil. When the area came under British rule in 1885, Calabar enjoyed a period of prominence as the headquarters of the Colonial administration. In the early years of this century, however, a decline set in. With various changes in colonial housekeeping, Lagos became the colonial capital; Enugu the capital of Eastern Province and Calabar merely the capital of one of the four sub-provinces of the East. Port Harcourt supplanted it as the major port of the East and robbed it of its trade with the interior. Nonetheless, it remained a prosperous town until the palm oil trade collapsed with the world recession in the 1930s.

The first Catholic missionaries visited Calabar in 1900 and found a tiny nucleus of Catholics among African, Lebanese and European immigrants. In spite of Protestant opposition, it proved easy enough to get permission to set up a mission and to secure a site. The fact that the Catholics would provide educational facilities was a major consideration as many of the administrators and the chiefs were dissatisfied with the education offered by the Church of Scotland mission which had been there since 1846. A mission was established in 1903. It took over an existing boys' school which had been set up by one of the chiefs and opened another boys' school and a girls' school. Most of the pupils were drawn from Protestant schools and this led to a bitter attack on the Catholic Church in *The Calabar Observer*, a newspaper run by the Church of Scotland Mission. This underlines the rivalry and intolerance that existed between various missionary groups at the time. Tooth and nail opposition was at once a God-given duty and an occupational hazard. Nonetheless, the Catholic mission came to enjoy great prestige although the growth of the Catholic community was slow compared to other parts of the Vicariate.

Pat Whitney was assigned to the parish of Emekuku, in the interior. It was a rural area at the heart of Iboland. The people lived in 'compounds'—fenced-in clusters of half a dozen huts—which were so close together as to form a kind of rural town. There was plenty of food, yams, corn and palm-oil. There was also a buzz about the place as an extremely talented and dynamic people set about taking advantage of the opportunities being offered by education. It was a wonderful first appointment for a missionary and Pat Whitney appreciated it to the full. It gave him a love for Africa and a conviction about the urgency of the missionary task which was to stay with him all his life.

The parish was small by Nigerian standards of the time. It was only 136 square miles in area but was very densely populated. The mission at Emekuku was opened in 1912 and had made great progress with 4,000 Catholics, 50 main stations and 350 catechists, in 1921.[21] The schools were crowded and there was a great clamour for baptism. Pat Whitney gives an idea of the numbers involved which, allowing for some exaggeration and a certain youthful optimism in his predictions, presented the two priests with a very daunting task. He writes:

> There are roughly two hundred schools in the parish. These contain, according to the latest returns, which were based on school and church registers, *forty thousand catechumens* . . . In other words, we have in this parish *ten thousand people who may be baptised before the end of 1922* . . . It is also true that if there was not a single conversion made during the next four years (which supposition is absurd) there could still be Baptism at the rate of four thousand a year during the time. We would only then have picked all who honestly wish for Baptism out of the present number in our schools, supposing there are ten thousand now attending who are really not going to toe the line. Imagine that mass of work that has to be got through in this one parish. The foregoing estimate is not meant to dazzle people at home. It is literally true. It is a truth which has almost an unnerving effect on the two priests who work the parish. In face of such numbers they realise their helplessness. They are already full-handed with their four thousand Christians. They still continue to baptise. In the year beginning July 1920, there were one thousand seven hundred baptisms. Who will take care of those whom these priests are now baptising? Who will baptise the ten thousand who are ready and fiercely importunate?[22]

Faced with this challenge, Pat thought of the many young men ordained in Maynooth every year and determined to enlist some of them—'going to launch a big offensive on Maynooth' as he put it in his diary. He wrote many letters to friends of Maynooth days. A number of articles which he had written appeared in the Holy Ghost magazine *The Missionary Annals*. Shortly before he submitted his proposal to the Bishop for a separate diocese for diocesan priests, he completed a manuscript intended for publication as a book and passed it on to Tom Ronayne for his comments. The book, entitled *An Irish Missionary in Central Africa* appeared in print, in 1923. It was aimed at winning support for the Nigerian mission, particularly from the ranks of the diocesan clergy, and described in 128 pages the opportunities for evangelisation and the conditions in which the missionaries lived and worked. In everything he wrote, Pat Whitney's primary concern was to entice more diocesan priests to volunteer for Nigeria. He knew in his heart, and the message was coming through from home, that a large number of Irish diocesan priests would never agree to work as associates of a Religious Order. Tom Ronayne agreed with him in that. The only alternative was some kind of independent status for the volunteers. And this was the substance of his proposal to Bishop Shanahan—his 'stunt' to evangelise Southern Nigeria.

According to Pat Whitney's diary, the Bishop's reaction was positive. He thought the idea was a good one and encouraged Pat to keep writing. The Bishop was very hopeful for the success of the volunteer movement. At the time he received Pat Whitney's proposal, two more volunteer priests were preparing to come to Nigeria. They were Patrick F. Whitney of Ardagh and Clonmacnois and Vincent Davey of Down and Connor. Patrick F. Whitney known as Frank, was Pat's second-cousin. Bishop Shanahan had no problem with the suggestion that the Vicariate of Southern Nigeria might one day be divided in favour of Irish secular priests. He was preoccupied with his responsibility to evangelise the area and had no desire to hold on to it for his own congregation. At the time, it seemed impossible that the Holy Ghosts would ever be able to supply enough priests. Bishop Shanahan saw a separate diocese for Irish secular priests as very much in the future but he saw it as a possibility. For the present, he was happy that Holy Ghosts and volunteers would work together, sharing fully in the life and responsibilities of the mission. However, neither the volunteers nor many of his confrères were happy, for long, with this situation.

2

The
Holy Rosary Sisters

THE story of the diocesan volunteers took an unexpected turn at the end of 1923 when Pat Whitney was given the task of raising funds for a congregation of sisters about to be founded by Bishop Shanahan. This congregation, called the Missionary Sisters of Our Lady of the Holy Rosary, was established the following year. The diocesan volunteer priests played a significant role in promoting the new venture in Ireland and this work, in turn, influenced the direction of their own movement.

The Prefecture of Southern Nigeria had the benefit of religious women from its earliest days. In 1889, only four years after the arrival of the first priests and brothers, a group of sisters belonging to the French Congregation of St Joseph of Cluny took up residence at Onitsha. This Religious Order, founded in 1807, was distinguished for its commitment to missionary work. The foundress was Blessed Anne Marie Javouhey, a great missionary pioneer who was once described by the King of France as 'a great man'. She is renowned for her efforts to establish an indigenous African clergy and, in 1924, she set up a seminary for African candidates in France with eight Senegalese students. She had sent sisters to Senegal in 1817 and, within twenty-five years, had 200 sisters on the missions, teaching in schools and working in colonial hospitals. The sisters who came to Nigeria ran a girls' school in Onitsha from the beginning and opened a similar school in Calabar, in 1905. Two of the sisters in Calabar worked in the European hospital for a short time but withdrew because of their lack of rapport with the hospital administration. The Onitsha convent was closed down in 1908, and there remained only the Calabar community. The sisters were plagued by ill-health and found it difficult to function in a non-French colony. Nonetheless, they continued to run the girls' school until March 1920, when the only English speaker among the three remaining sisters was hospitalised with heart trouble. She had been twelve years in Africa, without a break. Soon afterwards, all three were recalled to France, bringing to an end an association of more than thirty years between their congregation and the Prefecture of Southern Nigeria.

Some years before this crisis occurred, Joseph Shanahan had attempted to get other sisters for his Prefecture. He had always been impatient with the French Sisters whose rule of life confined them to the precincts of the convent and did not allow for the active apostolate which he considered necessary in Nigeria. He wanted sisters who would move out among the people, train and instruct the women, teach in schools and care for the sick. He envisaged sisters who would be qualified in these fields and who would be flexible enough to adapt to a pioneering life. He approached the Irish Sisters of Charity in 1914 and again in 1919 but, in spite of considerable interest among individual sisters, no help was forthcoming. An appeal to the Franciscan Missionaries of Mary brought a promise of six sisters, in 1920, but the promise was never fulfilled.[1] In the end he turned to lay women for temporary assistance. While he was in Ireland, he had met Marie Martin, an auxiliary nurse from a wealthy Dublin family. At the time she intended to join Lady Frances Moloney as a founder member of the Columban Sisters who were to work with the Columban priests in China. In 1921 she changed her mind and persuaded another prospective Columban, Agnes Ryan, to accompany her to Nigeria. Tom Ronayne was instrumental in bringing about this change of direction. It was he who introduced Bishop Shanahan to Marie Martin's mother who had been involved in fund-raising for the Columbans and was now to organise a circle of supporters for the Nigerian mission. Known at first as 'The Missionary Union for the conversion of Southern Nigeria', it later became an official lay association called 'The Holy Ghost Mission League' with Mrs Martin as President. It was her mother's interest in the Nigerian mission and her own friendship with Tom Ronayne, whom she had known since 1916, which influenced Marie Martin to change her allegiance from China to Nigeria. She had met Bishop Shanahan personally and it is certain that his considerable powers of persuasion played no small part in her decision.[2]

A New Congregation

The two women, 29 year old Marie Martin and 42 year old Agnes Ryan, arrived in Calabar in June 1921. They took over St Joseph's

Convent and the girls' school. To minimise the confusion caused by the change-over, they were to assume the title 'Sister'. It was to be a holding operation until nuns came. As there seemed to be little prospect of this, the idea of founding a new congregation emerged. The lay women—four more were to come in 1922 and 1923—were to form the nucleus of the new congregation. Marie Martin was to be the key figure. Her wealthy background and her personal qualities made her eminently suitable for the role of foundress. It was a role she accepted readily although she protested that she wished only 'to pave the way for someone more worthy'.[3]

Work on the Constitutions began during the Easter of 1922, in the priests' house in Calabar. Marie Martin was the only woman present as Agnes Ryan had returned to Ireland for health reasons and the others had not yet arrived. With her were Bishop Shanahan, another Holy Ghost priest Dr Edward Leen, and Tom Ronayne. Marie herself was working on a design for the religious habit and had suggested to her mother that the garments would be made by Brown Thomas, in Dublin. Meanwhile, a solitary Sister of Charity, Sister Charles Walker, who had met Bishop Shanahan when he called to her convent in Foxford, Co. Mayo, had petitioned the Pope for permission to leave her convent and to come to Nigeria. She was friendly with Marie Martin and it was the latter who had carried the message to Bishop Shanahan that Sister Charles was anxious to go to Nigeria in spite of the fact that her congregation was unwilling to send a team. The proposal was unusual and only the Pope himself could give her the necessary permission. Nevertheless, the Bishop was enthusiastic and urged her to go ahead and look for Papal approval. At first he intended that she would head the school in Calabar but when plans for a new congregation emerged, he thought of her for the post of novice mistress.

In August 1922, Bishop Shanahan returned to Ireland for medical treatment. He intended to use his time there to make final plans for the new Order of sisters. Before travelling to Ireland, he went to Paris and put the proposal to the Holy Ghost Superior General, Archbishop Le Roy. It was not very well received. The Archbishop had recently established an Order of sisters called the Holy Ghost Missionary Sisters. He was of the opinion that Bishop Shanahan should send his women volunteers to join this group with a view to setting up an Irish Province later. The Vicar Apostolic would not hear of it. His experience with the Sisters of St Joseph of Cluny had convinced him that certain French traditions of convent life were unsuitable for the missions. He also realised that he would have no control over the French Order and would have to be satisfied to share whatever personnel became available with other Holy Ghost missions throughout the world. He decided to press ahead with a separate organisation although this was to earn him a lot of criticism from members of his own Order.

The situation in Ireland was no more encouraging for Bishop Shanahan. After undergoing a successful operation, he began to look around for a house in which to base the new congregation. It proved more difficult than he had expected to get an Irish bishop prepared to accept such a house in his diocese. The bishops who were approached were put off by the financial demands which would be made on the local Church and by the drain on vocations to the diocesan convents which would ensue. Although it would be difficult to work without a base in Ireland, Bishop Shanahan decided to go ahead with the foundation and take the aspirants to Nigeria for their training. This possibility became a real option in June 1923, when Sister Charles got clearance to go to Nigeria. Now, there would be an experienced sister to train the aspirants on the mission field.

In July, Bishop Shanahan visited Rome and received the blessing of Pope Pius XI on the project. While this entitled him to found the congregation and was a boost to his morale, it did nothing to solve the practical difficulties of recruiting Irish girls for a convent in Nigeria. The Pope had emphasised that no girl should be sent to Nigeria or novitiate until her vocation was tested by experienced religious at home. To implement this, Bishop Shanahan approached the Dominican Sisters who had a prestigious boarding school in Cabra, Dublin. They agreed to accept the aspirants in Cabra and to give them a one-year orientation course prior to their journey to Nigeria. In October, the first four candidates took up residence in Cabra and were soon joined by four others. Then, an unplanned visit which Bishop Shanahan made to Bishop Patrick Finegan of Kilmore led to an invitation to found the congregation in Kilmore diocese. A large house was purchased at Killeshandra, near Cavan town, and the Dominican Sisters were persuaded to provide a staff of four nuns to run the novitiate. Those assigned to the task were Sr Francis Xavier, Superior, Sr Aquinas, Novice Mistress with Sr Ursula and Sr Anastasia to provide back-up services. Plans for a novitiate in Nigeria were abandoned and the aspirants left Cabra to take up residence at Killeshandra on 7 March 1924. The title of the new Congregation, 'Missionary Sisters of Our Lady of the Holy Rosary' was chosen after Rome had rejected 'Missionary Sisters of the Holy Ghost'.

Meanwhile, Marie Martin and another lay volunteer, Veronica Hasson, ran the school in Calabar until the arrival of Sister Charles Walker on 3 October 1923. Sister Charles had been renamed Magdalen to signify her new status outside her own Order and under the authority of the Vicar Apostolic of Calabar. Veronica Hasson sailed immediately for Ireland leaving Sister Magdalen and Marie Martin to run the school. The latter received a letter from Bishop Shanahan telling her that he would arrange for her to do her novitiate under Sister Magdalen. Soon, word came that new plans for the congregation were emerging and, in January 1924, Marie Martin was asked to return to Ireland to begin her novitiate in Killeshandra. She was to travel home with Tom Ronayne who had been ill and was badly in need of a break. She did as the Bishop asked but with some misgivings. On the one hand, she felt called to a contemplative life and, on the other, was interested in the medical apostolate. Neither of these aspirations would be fulfilled in the Holy Rosary Sisters which was to be an active congregation devoted to pastoral activity and school work. Nevertheless, she entered Killeshandra in June 1924 but left in March 1926 as the time to take her religious vows approached. Her departure was a great disappointment to Bishop Shanahan. He was losing the woman he had chosen to be the leader of the new congregation and he was also losing her dowry which was no small matter in view of the uncertain financial circumstances of the Holy Rosary Sisters.[4]

Role of the Volunteers
In Bishop Shanahan's plan for the new convent, the volunteer priests were to play a very important role. He was confident that their connection with the Irish Church and their contacts through former Maynooth students could be put to good use in the matter of raising funds for the convent. He had borrowed £5,000 from the Ulster Bank to purchase the property. This had to be repaid and the running of the convent had to be assured. This meant setting up a fund-raising system that would provide a steady income for the convent. The Mission League was already a point of contact but it needed to be promoted vigorously in order to bring in anything like the amount of money needed. He decided to put one of the diocesan volunteers in charge of the entire project. When he made this decision, in 1923, there were only three such priests in the Vicariate as Frank Whitney had already returned home unable for the rigours of missionary life. This left Pat Whitney, Tom Ronayne and Vincent Davey in Nigeria, and James

McGinley of Raphoe and Thomas Mulvaney of Meath about to leave Ireland to join them. Pat Whitney was chosen to promote the cause of the Holy Rosary Sisters and came to Ireland for that purpose towards the end of 1923.

Pat Whitney Fund-raiser

At first glance, there was little in Pat Whitney's family background to prepare him for a task which involved public relations and the management of money. He was born, in 1894, in an area where the three counties of Roscommon, Leitrim and Sligo meet. The townland of his birth was called Breenletter, Co. Roscommon and the Whitney homestead was a two-roomed house on fifteen acres of land. He was the oldest of seven children, four boys and three girls. He attended Dereenargon National School 'which in his day was just a thatched cottage with a leaking roof'.[5] His life as a boy followed the usual pattern of boyhood in rural Ireland—work in the fields, school, hunting for rabbits, fishing and football. A less common feature was an enthusiasm for drama which gained him parts in local amateur productions and led him to master many of the long poems or 'recitations' which were popular party pieces at the time.

Family ties were very important. Aunts, uncles and cousins kept in close contact. Two generations before, three Whitney brothers had come from Drumlish in Co. Longford and bought a piece of land in Breenletter which they divided equally among them. The price of the land had come from 'jobbing'—buying cattle and horses from farmers with a view to an immediate and profitable turnover. Like all 'jobbers', they relied on their skill in judging animals, their ability to read the market and an opportunism which rarely missed a bargain. Now, their descendants formed a large extended family in Roscommon-Leitrim, while contact with the relatives in Longford was maintained. One of Pat's uncles, also Patrick Whitney, had gone to England as a young man and was successful as a shopkeeper. He returned to his home area and bought two farms and a 'gentleman's residence' called Port House. He married a local teacher and, having no children of his own, took a great interest in the wider family, virtually adopting a whole family of relatives who were orphaned. Pat gives the impression in his diary that his uncle's wife was often a bit annoyed by her husband's generosity. Indeed, she would appear to have had considerable grounds for annoyance. Port House was always full of young people either living there or passing through. Some were looking for school fees; others for dowries;

all were enjoying Patrick Whitney's largesse. He was benevolent to nephews and nieces and also to distant cousins, all of whom referred to him as 'Uncle Rick'. When the time came for Pat to begin his secondary education, his uncle paid his fees as St Mel's College, Longford. He and his wife were pleased when Pat decided to go to Maynooth and they agreed to pay his 'pension' for the seven years he would spend there.

Pat Whitney entered Maynooth in 1913. His time there was not particularly distinguished. To have got in, in the first place, he would have had to be above average intelligence. He sat and passed the B.A. exam. but, at a time when there was no particular emphasis on academic achievement in Maynooth, he was happy to be an average student. Bishop Michael Browne, recalls him as 'a popular and respected member of my class . . . keen hurler, strong, straightforward, vigorous . . . little finesse but yet pleasant . . . a bare pass man academically'.[6]

Although Pat had a fine physique, he was not an outstanding sportsman nor was he as fanatical about sport as was the average Maynooth student in those days. This set him apart from the general run of students for whom total dedication to sport and a sceptical attitude to the academic life was the norm. It was not that Pat was especially dedicated to study but he was interested in drama and in anything that was a little out of the ordinary. For this reason, his classmates were not surprised that he should volunteer for Nigeria. The cynics among them suggested that if everyone had been volunteering for Africa, Pat Whitney would have gone to China. He took part in everything that was going on, however. He played hurling with 'the crocks' on a hurling pitch nicknamed 'Sinn Fein' and according to Bishop Browne he played 'with a certain ruthless ferocity'.[7] He won a set of pipes for coming second in an obstacle race during his Fourth Divine year and, although he enjoyed a smoke, he considered that there would be more fun and more profit in raffling off the pipes. The dramatic society was his big passion and he wrote in his diary, on 28 February, prior to his ordination: 'thinking of a play for St Patrick's Day: had a very successful one on Shrove Tuesday night'. Everything he did was done with great determination and without sparing any effort. This is borne out in a story told by a classmate, Bishop James Fergus. The Bishop recalled in a letter to Kiltegan, written in 1984, that in his first examination in public speaking, Pat gave a disastrous performance much to the enjoyment of his audience. He was humiliated and was determined to 'show them' the next time. When the next time came, and as a result of hours and days of practice, he delivered his set-piece flawlessly.

It was a quiet, reasonably contented student life. He showed deep compassion for people and his description of his visit to a neighbour, Mrs Molloy, who was dying of TB in Boyle hospital, is very moving. Her husband and young children had already died of the disease.

> Ah it was a sad awful sight to look at her wasted form and tear stained eyes, to watch her laboured breathing, to hear her choking cough, to try to catch the whispered words. To tell the honest truth I was afraid to stay . . . Ah but memory makes the present time more dark. I remember her a beautiful young bride as fair as eyes could dwell upon. I remember her dancing in our house; happy and radiant. I remember John a strapping young man tossing up in the lamp light the handkerchief that he was to give her as a wedding present and now there she is wasted and worn, having gone through the dark years of married life; having laid her husband and her children in the grave and praying for the day that God will permit her to join them in heaven. God grant it soon.

His faith, as expressed in his diary, was simple and unquestioning. He experienced difficulty and sorrow and writes:

> And yet those Maynooth years were years of the Cross—quasi ill-health which few knew about but God, and then the loss of father and John Joe [his brother]. I had pictured poor father, how he would enjoy ordination day—how he would go about with his hands behind his back, and admire the buildings and the grounds, how I'd point out things to him and enjoy his quiet talk. But it wasn't to be. God knows if my dream came true I'd be too happy and perhaps proud.

But he does not question God's providence or acknowledge that he has any doubts about his faith. He accepts God's presence and his care and expresses it in the language of the spiritual and theological manuals. During his pre-ordination retreat he writes:

> May I always have for Him the love of a little child, place in Him a child's confidence, not trust in myself for anything; may I always keep Him and He alone my friend; to consecrate to Him all my work; may I try to live and move in Him; may I look on others as the creatures of his hands, the vessels of his love, as men and

women and boys and girls for whom he died. May He and the B.V.M. and the Little Flower protect me from becoming cold and tepid in his service.

Such was the background of the 30 year old priest chosen by Bishop Shanahan to mobilise supporters for the Holy Rosary Sisters. The Bishop had been impressed by Pat's great enthusiasm for the mission and by what he had written in support of the work over the past three years. In these writings, he had demonstrated a common touch which would appeal to the people of Ireland. Pat Whitney knew how to touch the heart and relied more on emotive preaching than on theological argument. It was an approach which was to serve him well in his new work.

The fund-raising drive got under way while the aspirants to the sisterhood were still in Cabra. They helped Pat Whitney to post raffle tickets to various addresses and to acknowledge the receipts. They did the same from Killeshandra, taking care of the correspondence under the supervision of Sister M. Ursula until such time as they entered the novitiate, after which work of this kind was not allowed. Pat Whitney lived in the gate lodge at Killeshandra and toured the country giving talks and slide-shows to various groups. He made full use of his contacts from Maynooth days and through them gained admission to many parishes. He concentrated on the primary schools, gaining access to the homes through the children who delivered the literature, and became involved in collecting the pennies and sixpences which, added together, amounted to a lot of money. Through his efforts, the Mission League grew in numbers countrywide and a network of contacts was built up which was to serve the sisters well for many years. More than fifty years later, Bishop James Fergus, then retired Bishop of Achonry, recalled meeting Pat in Co. Galway on a typical fund-raising journey.

I remember one evening in the early twenties, when he was travelling the rough and dusty roads in Ireland collecting funds for the Killeshandra convent: the priests of Dunmore deanery were assembled in Williamstown for a wind-up station or some similar function. The clergy had finished dinner and were engaged in conversation, and it was getting on towards twilight when a tap came to the dining room window. I, being nearest the door was asked to go out and see who it was; it was P.J. on his rounds, in his riding gear all covered with dust. He was brought in and given a good meal. Where he slept the night I can only guess.

Indeed, where Pat lodged for the night was often a cause for comment among the Irish clergy. At a time when priests were expected to be reserved in manner, Pat's behaviour fell short of the norm. The lodgings he chose on his fund-raising tours were not always of the respectability befitting a member of the clergy. If not staying in the parochial house, a priest was expected to stay in the Railway Hotel or some similar establishment. Pat went for much cheaper accommodation, often with people who were supporters of his cause. There, he could meet potential supporters while keeping out of the way of the parish priest whom he liked to keep in the dark about the details of his campaign. The parish priest of one Limerick town was upset to hear that Pat was staying in a little pub run by a girl called Queenie Griffin who lived with her father, sold a few pints now and again and kept the occasional lodger. Operating part of his campaign in this way satisfied a certain leaning towards harmless intrigue which Pat Whitney always enjoyed. It brought a touch of drama to a life of incredibly hard work.

Other aspects of the campaign were much more up-front. He put advertisements in the provincial papers, using every ploy he could think of to move the hearts of the Irish people to contribute. In one advertisement which appeared in the *Longford Leader* in May 1924, he pointed out that May was the month of Mary and appealed 'to all the Marys of Ireland' to contribute to a new Irish Congregation dedicated to Mary their heavenly mother. He believed in the personal touch; the advertisements appeared above his own name to which he appended the title 'Missionary Apostolic'. He put advertisements in the *Irish Independent* but after paying out £150 over 6 months he decided that the returns did not merit advertising in a national daily paper.

Before long, Pat Whitney was joined by his cousin Frank and by Tom Ronayne, both of whom were recovering from illness. All three lived in the gate-lodge of the convent when they were not on the road. As Chaplain to the convent, Tom Ronayne was obliged to stay close to base but he contributed to the promotion campaign by working in the office. The fund-raising was conducted independently of the convent. At first, the appeal was couched in general terms. The foundation of the Holy Rosary Sisters was the most pressing need but there were many others. Pat Whitney was keen to appeal for the Vicariate in general in an attempt to leave the project open to include the diocesan priests' movement. Bishop Shanahan agreed with this at the outset but, in November 1924, he changed his mind and instructed Pat to appeal for the sisters only. He had decided that the new congregation would have to be solidly established before anything else could be undertaken.

The appeal was an outstanding success. On 24 February 1925 Pat summarised the financial position in a letter to Bishop Shanahan:

> . . . last January 24th 1924 the individual appeal of the secular priests for S. Nigeria started in an organised way. The result of that appeal deducting all expenses came to about £7,500: £3,000 of which went to the running of the Convent for the year: £3,000 of which went to pay off the debt on the Ulster Bank: £1,000 of which is now in my current account. £400 of which went to pay off your overdrawn account, bills including some of those of the two priests Father Frank and Ronayne while sick.

Apart from the money raised, the contacts with schools and with individuals were laying the foundation of a circle of friends who could be relied on to contribute on a regular basis in the future.

Although the appeal was successful, all was not smooth in the relationship between Mother Xavier, the Superior of the convent, and the diocesan priests. Mother Xavier O'Connor was a strong woman who had come from a prosperous farming background in Co. Tipperary. She had been prioress in Cabra, for a period, and had also served as bursar. Tom Ronayne was the first to cross swords with her when he took it on himself to advise her on the running of the convent. In doing so he was overstepping his role as Chaplain but he was also acting completely in character. In Nigeria he undertook to advise Bishop Shanahan, and in Killeshandra, he advised Bishop Finegan on the latter's rights and obligations with regard to the convent. He was a sincere man, a bit narrow in outlook, but full of enthusiasm for mission work. He saw the defects in every situation and felt duty-bound to draw attention to them. As a result, he alienated many people, especially those in authority, and, afterwards, felt aggrieved that he had been misunderstood. In Killeshandra, he criticised the formation being given by the Dominican Sisters. There was probably some justification for his criticism. The Dominicans had no missionary experience and could not be expected to devise a religious life-style suitable for the tropics. A few years later they were to send out the first Holy Rosary Sisters, dressed in cumbersome habits and with the injunction not to take water between meals. Tom Ronayne could see various shortcomings on the basis of his own experience. It was not in his character to keep his views to himself and before long he had lost the confidence of Mother Xavier. It probably came as no surprise to him. He was keenly aware of his own limitations and was to write two years later to Mrs Martin:

I think it only fair to tell you that most of those who have worked with me consider me a destructive influence. All in Killeshandra except Ursula; Father Leen, the Bishop (Shanahan), all in Cabra and lastly and perhaps most of all Sister Magdalen. They believe I am sincere but destructive.[8]

He was replaced as Chaplain by Edward Leen C.S.Sp. but continued to assist with the appeal until he was recalled to Nigeria in June 1925. There was also some initial conflict between Pat Whitney and Mother Xavier, although it was not of a serious nature. While the postulants were handling the correspondence there was some tension about who should give them instructions. Pat was not one to stand on ceremony and saw them as members of his team. In Mother Xavier's vision of religious life, there should have been more recourse to her as Superior. When the sisters began their novitiate, lay women were employed to do the office work, and so the cause of tension was removed.

Meanwhile, Pat Whitney, Tom Ronayne and Frank Whitney, while devoting all their energies to the appeal for the convent, did not forget the drive for more priests which they considered of greater importance. Pat, in particular, was convinced that an increase in the number of priests was far more important than any number of sisters. This is clear from an entry in his diary, written in 1926 when he had already left the work:

a good community of missionary sisters—and that was the undertaking for which I was working at home—are of course a wonderful blessing in any missionary country. But what I could not for the life of me see was in the present terrible dearth of priests on the mission why divert from the main issue. Or granted readily that we needed sisters and that an appeal for them was necessary, was it not true that the getting of priests was equally necessary, and would it not be only fair to the mission and to the friends of the mission to voice the double appeal for the double need—to give both the same fair chance. I'd have readily given my life at home to work this joint appeal. I tried to do this, but the devil was against it, and as usual he had quite a number of holy people who ably and sanctimoniously helped him out. Or perhaps I'm wrong; perhaps it was me that old Nick had captured to play his game.

Towards the end of 1924, Pat Whitney wrote to Bishop Shanahan with a proposal to step up the recruitment of volunteer priests. He suggested that a mission house be set up in Ireland to accommodate priests on leave and to offer a base from which recruitment could be carried out. He also wanted the bishop to commission a priest whose particular responsibility would be to appeal for men. The Vicar Apostolic was alarmed by these proposals. On his return to Nigeria, he had found a very negative attitude to the volunteer movement among his own Holy Ghost Confrères. They argued that the coming of the volunteers had led to a decrease of Holy Ghost men being sent to the Vicariate. This was an overall loss in terms of missionary effectiveness because the volunteer came as a greenhorn and was likely to stay for only a few years. The Bishop was also afraid that any efforts to develop the volunteer movement at this stage might be detrimental to the convent. In January 1925, he cabled Pat Whitney to return to Nigeria. Bishop Finegan, who was canonically head of the Holy Rosary Congregation, and Mother Xavier, both wrote immediately and asked Bishop Shanahan to reconsider this decision. That Mother Xavier was especially complimentary of Pat is clear from the reply she received from the Vicar Apostolic. He wrote:

> Now as regards Father Pat Whitney I love to read what you write and think of him. It is quite true that Providence has sent him along to take part with heaven and your own good selves and the Sisters, in this great work that is being done at Killeshandra. He wrote to me that he hoped to have all the centres in working order by the end of November. Time and again he both said and wrote that he was ready to do God's holy will regardless of his own feelings, when his will was made known to him through the ordinary channels of Providence. I am writing to him today to keep on at the work until I give him definite orders to return. That will meet your request.[9]

Pat also wrote to Bishop Shanahan expressing a willingness to return but re-stating the case for a mission house and a countrywide appeal for priests. One section of this letter, which is dated 24 February 1925, reassures the Vicar Apostolic that nothing more is envisaged than a mission house and a renewed appeal for volunteers:

> In the first place neither I nor any other priest presently attached to the Nigerian mission contemplate the establishment of a new society. There is no secular priest that I know presently working in Nigeria who does not wish to continue his work for that mission.
> In the second place neither I nor any of the secular priests want a specific field of labour in Nigeria. We do not want seniority on

the Mission or claim equality with the members of the Holy Ghost Order ... Anyone who tries to persuade you, my Dear Lord, that we are out for anything else is the devil's agent.

It is clear that Pat thinks that the Bishop had been approached by some of his Holy Ghost Confrères and warned that the diocesan priests intend to press for independence. His vehement denial is interesting in that it runs counter to his own proposal made in 1921. One cannot but suspect that Pat had made a 'mental reservation' to the effect that the diocesan priests wanted none of these things 'at the present time'. With only three priests on the mission and three at home, they were certainly in no position to pursue their ends just then. They may well have dropped any hopes they had of setting up their own organisation. Nonetheless, the idea was not far from the surface and those who had sounded the warning to the Bishop were well in tune with the situation.

Soon afterwards, Bishop Finegan wrote to Shanahan suggesting that it would be a good idea to appoint someone to conduct a recruiting campaign in the Irish seminaries. On 5 April Bishop Shanahan sent Pat Whitney the following cable:

> Your letter received. Accept congratulations. Gratitude Nigeria. Remain Ireland continue great work. Nigeria sorely needs priests. I appoint you my representative with commission appeal ranks Irish clergy volunteers. God wills it. I approve your action. Draft letter appeal posted. Communicate this Leen.

A letter duly arrived authorising Pat to appeal for volunteer priests and to extend an offer of incardination—the canonical process by which a cleric is attached to a specific diocese—into the Vicariate to priests and students from Second Divinity onwards. Such a move would involve excardination—canonical release—from the cleric's original diocese. For the volunteers who opted for incardination, all claims on the home diocese would cease and they would depend on the Vicariate for everything.

Pat's commission gave new life to the recruitment drive. Three new volunteers were enlisted. They were John Finegan (Raphoe) John Gaffney (Kilmore) and Patrick Kelly (Meath). When they went to Nigeria towards the end of 1925 they brought to eight the number of volunteer priests working in the missionfield. Father Morahan of Achonry had gone out, in 1924, to join Vincent Davey, James McGinley and Tom Mulvaney, while Tom Ronayne was soon to return. Meanwhile, there was a concerted effort to control the growth of the volunteer movement in Ireland. In May 1925, Bishop Shanahan agreed to a request from Bishop Finegan for 'authority over the priests appealing at home in all matters affecting the congregation to the extent of having a controlling influence on the collecting and allocating of funds'. A month later, Tom Ronayne was recalled to Nigeria, ostensibly to help the Bishop with his office work. Frank Whitney, who was unfit to return to Nigeria, was asked by Bishop Shanahan to return to his own diocese. At the time, the volunteer priests saw these moves as attempts by the Vicar Apostolic, prompted by members of the Holy Ghost Order, to prevent any major development within the volunteer movement. A letter from John Gaffney to Pat Whitney, dated March 1926, expresses this view:

> I think it was the crowd at home that got Ronayne pulled out here as he is not secretary at all. The Bishop seems to be under the impression that there was lot of propaganda at home last year, especially by Ronayne, to start a secular movement independent of the C.S.Sp., and he told me he is very displeased with it and distrusts Ronayne as a result . . .
>
> From what I could gather the Bishop is by no means in favour of the secular movement on the lines you have in your head. From what he told me he is by no means pleased with any move to put us on an independent footing here. He wants temporary men all right. But he does not want them to work apart from the C.S.Sp. And his idea is that any of the men here or any that would come, should, if they desire to give their lives in this work, become C.S.Sp. men. But you are not going to get any territory here . . . But you find out where you stand and be sure you see clearly what backing the Bishop will be able to give you. For once he severs his connection with this place, I don't believe he will have any say or any power in anything that concerns this mission.

Bishop Shanahan's opposition to the hopes of the volunteers, as relayed by John Gaffney, was more apparent than real. It must be seen in the context of a personal crisis which he was facing in his own life at the time. He had lost the sight of one eye and was given to understand that the same thing might happen to the other. He raised the matter of a coadjutor bishop with the Holy Ghost Superiors in Paris. They informed him that plans were afoot to divide the Vicariate giving part of it to the American Province of the Order. They accepted the suggestion of a coadjutor but let it be known that they would not be opposed to Bishop Shanahan's resignation. After initially rejecting the suggestion, he changed his mind and submitted his resignation, in February 1926. The removal of Frank Whitney and Tom Ronayne must be seen in this context. The Bishop did not want a campaign for independent status for the volunteers to gain momentum at home because of the uncertainty in the Vicariate. It was for the same reason that he rejected Pat Whitney's suggestion of a mission house, in November 1925. In the letter of rejection, he pointed out to Pat that he was advised by the Holy Ghost Superiors not to go ahead with the house. It was perfectly understandable advice in the circumstances. The volunteer movement was Bishop Shanahan's personal project and there was no guarantee that his successor would share the same enthusiasm for it. Individual volunteers were very welcome and badly needed but something like the mission house would demand a commitment that the Vicar Apostolic, on the eve of retirement, could not give.

In Killeshandra, the fund raising was going so well that Bishop Finegan envisaged that Pat Whitney would be permanently attached to it. To facilitate this, the Bishop offered Pat incardination into the Diocese of Kilmore on condition that the Holy Rosary Sisters would agree to provide him with health and retirement benefits. This offer was made in February 1926.

In January 1925 Mother Xavier had asked Bishop Shanahan not to recall Pat to Nigeria. In spite of this, there was a conflict of interests which would have to come to a head sooner or later. Mother Xavier knew of Pat's preoccupation with the volunteer movement and feared it might pose a threat to the convent. A memorandum entitled *The Incident of Father P. Whitney as recalled by Mother Xavier O.P.* and dated 1954 recalls these fears. It reads in part:

> Father Whitney was a very zealous and apostolic priest; his whole life was consumed with zeal for the missions and the desire to find more priests for the immense needs of pagan Africa. The need for Sisters did not enter his horizon. He had fulfilled the duty given him by Bishop Shanahan; he had raised the money to pay off the purchase debt on the property at Killeshandra. He planned to provide a modest maintenance for a limited number of Sisters, and over and above that, he wished to use his time and his talents to send a steady supply of priests to pagan missions and especially to Nigeria—whose needs were so clear to him. During his time in Killeshandra one group of priests was equipped and sent to Nigeria. With the aid of secular helpers under his direction in the office at Killeshandra, he would be free to work out his ideals.

Mother Xavier decided to establish that the fund-raising effort was for the convent. To do this she had to gain some control over it, thereby depriving Pat of his independence. She was a strong woman who, later on, did not balk at curbing Bishop Shanahan's access to the sisters when she thought the good of the congregation demanded it.[10] In this case, she proposed that the newly professed sisters would resume the duties they had performed in the office prior to entering the novitiate. Sister Ursula would become Pat's Secretary and the lay office staff would be let go. Pat resisted this move because he knew well where it was leading. It was only a matter of time before Mother Xavier would take over the finances and he would no longer be free to devote substantial funds to the recruitment and equipping of the volunteer priests. There was a period of great tension of which Pat wrote in his diary:

> That time of mental wordless conflict and of drawn sad faces was an awful time.

Mother Xavier finally confronted Pat in the presence of Bishop Finegan and her Superior from Cabra. When the Bishop supported her, Pat threatened to move his office elsewhere only to be reminded that the Bishop had been given authority over him. Pat walked out, hurt and angry. In a letter written the next day, 14 March 1926, Bishop Finegan withdrew his permission 'to make any further appeals of any sort to the faithful for the convent, Killeshandra or for the Nigerian Mission'. Pat added a handwritten note to this letter:

> At the visitation March 13th I resigned my whole position because everyone concerned wished me to use novices to do my correspondence and a nun to be my Sec.

A year later he wrote in his diary:

> I remember that evening. I looked back at the place that I had almost thought my home and how the clouds of sunset banked behind it azure, violet and golden and how they mirrored the placid lake beneath, how love, bitterness and disappointment cut my heart and brought forth the scalding tears that remained unshed by a sister's graveside. Inch by inch, bit by bit, with hardship that only God knows I had built up an edifice (an organisation) that I had meant would go far in the saving of Nigeria. It was but a little thing but neat, smoothworking, noiseless—from the human point of view effective. I was proud of it; I knew its silent power. I could

handle it and none other could because it was frail as Dresden china. That day a finger had upset and shattered hopes like a child—two years labours had gone in vain.

No observer could have described Pat's work as labour in vain. The convent was paid for and the machinery was there to facilitate fund-raising on an ongoing basis. But it was fundraising for the sisters only. To Pat everything was in vain because there was no organisation that would ensure a steady flow of priests to Nigeria. Furthermore, the structure he had set up was lost to the volunteer priests. Pat appreciated the contribution which sisters could make to the missions and he was later to be a great help to Marie Martin in the foundation of the Medical Missionaries of Mary. But, he had no doubt that 'the saving of Nigeria' centred on the priest, on the Mass, the sacraments and the parish structures which he had known in Ireland from his earliest days.

Mother Xavier had won the independence of the young congregation. She was fortunate to have Edward Leen to support her and to give spiritual guidance to the sisters. Moreover, the Irish Province of the Holy Ghost Fathers could be relied on for any advice or support that was needed. However, the links between the diocesan volunteers and the convent were effectively cut. The future of the volunteer movement was very uncertain and there was little hope that the dream of an independent society would be realised. There was, however, a bright side for Pat Whitney. He was now free to return to Nigeria and to plunge once again into the work which he loved. At 32 years of age, he was still in his prime and was going back to a situation he knew very well. On Bishop Shanahan's instructions, Mother Xavier gave him £100 to pay his passage to Nigeria.

Pat Whitney sailed on the SS *Aba*, in June 1926. An entry in his diary written during the voyage expresses his disappointment and his determination not to abandon his plan for an organised volunteer movement. He wrote:

> Getting back to Nigeria after miserable failure at home to attain my end which was to send out secular priests sufficient to convert Nigeria. Cause of failure (1) The Holy Ghost Fathers at home were against (2) The bishop of Nigeria did not in his heart want those priests (3) The Holy Rosary convent thought an appeal for priests going out from Killeshandra would injure their appeal for Sisters— Rather they wanted all funds going into Killeshandra to be in aid of them. (4) None of the secular priests in Nigeria were willing to

back me up to the practical extent of coming home to help. (5) Last and chiefest, my own high-strung sense of fair play—which I couldn't get.

The failure is all the more heartbreaking because (1) boys of the proper material are in abundance (2) Mount Melleray Seminary had just opened its doors to students for Nigeria. (3) All Hallows were quite pleased to take such students to finish them. (4) And funds could have been obtained with very little trouble.

In spite of the failure, here and now, I make an act of faith: God will send secular priests to Nigeria, if the Holy Ghost Order does not.

3

St Patrick's Missionary Society is Founded

THE year of Britain's first ever general strike, 1926, saw the inception of the British Commonwealth and the birth of a princess who was to become Queen Elizabeth II. Britain was firmly in control of Nigeria and was pushing ahead with the process of colonisation. Nigeria consisted of two distinct entities which had been two colonies until they were amalgamated in 1914. In the North, a system of indirect rule, whereby the colonial power governed through traditional rulers, operated successfully. In the South, however, attempts to rule in the same way met with only limited success. This was particularly true among the decentralised peoples of the East, where traditional authority was not vested in a particular individual. In this situation, colonial officers governed by means of specially devised courts of law and through warrant chiefs whose authority derived directly from the occupying power. Because this system failed to take cognisance of the traditional unit of authority which was the village council, it met with a lot of opposition. There was sporadic violence from traditional secret societies while the imposition of a poll-tax in the 1920s led to riots and to some bloodshed. Disturbances of this kind did not destroy the overall peace that prevailed in the colony. It has been termed the Pax Brittanica and like the Pax Romana which existed at the foundation of Christianity, it provided an almost ideal climate for missionary work.

In 1926, the Vicariate of Southern Nigeria comprised a rapidly expanding Catholic community. There were 58,428 baptised Catholics and 89,334 catechumens in 1,386 mission stations. These large numbers were the fruits of forty years' missionary work although the greater part of the harvest had taken place in the later years. In 1905 there were only 1,488 Catholics, 1,322 catechumens and 24 stations. The huge increase in mission stations indicates not only more widespread evangelisation but also a greater commitment to education. Every station boasted a school which doubled as a church when the occasion demanded. The only exception to this was the few central stations where proper churches had been built.[1]

There were twenty-eight priests in the Vicariate at the beginning of 1926. Of these, eight were diocesan volunteers. They were Tom Ronayne, Vincent Davey, Fr Morahan, Tom Mulvaney, James McGinley, John Finegan, John Gaffney and Patrick Kelly. By now it had become accepted that the port town of Calabar and the parishes of Eke and Emekuku, in the heart of Iboland, constituted the normal field of operations for the volunteers. There were exceptions to this, however, and the mission records of the time indicate that John Finegan went to Onitsha in 1926 and Patrick Kelly was transferred there in 1927.

In June 1926, Pat Whitney returned to Nigeria and was appointed to Eke to replace Tom Mulvaney who had died earlier in the month. Tom Mulvaney, a priest of Meath diocese, had volunteered for Nigeria in 1923. There was a suspicion that he had tuberculosis but doctors failed to agree on the diagnosis so he went ahead with his plans to travel to the missions. After some time, the symptoms recurred and clear evidence of TB was found. The doctor advised him to remain in Nigeria where the climate was considered more beneficial. He continued to involve himself in all aspects of the mission work and took part in the bush treks up to a few days before his death which occurred on 13 June 1926. Tom Mulvaney was a kindly, cheerful man whose letters convey a great optimism and a genuine love for his parishioners at Eke. Before going to Nigeria, he had worked as a curate in Ireland serving in Taughmon, Oldcastle and Eglish near Birr. On transferring to Nigeria, he learned the Ibo language and after spending six months at Onitsha he was moved to Eke. He became incardinated into the Vicariate of Southern Nigeria, probably in 1925, indicating his desire to stay there for the rest of his life. Some time before his death he wrote a letter to the students of Maynooth which was to be sent in the event of his death. The main point of the letter was that the Nigerian climate was not responsible for his death and that other students and priests should not be afraid to volunteer. The letter reads in part:

> Oh, my God, if only we had sufficient good priests what could not be done with God's help. God enlighten Maynooth men. Maynooth

is generous. Maynooth has sent her most learned, bravest and best and holiest to China. Maynooth is as good today as ever. God grant that she may do for Africa what she has done for China. And you too priests on the mission listen to these words. If you hear God's call to Africa, come. Don't let worldly considerations stop you from winning Africa for God. We all had loving fathers, broken-hearted mothers and sisters and brothers to leave—Ireland too. You will never regret it I assure you.[2]

The letter made a big impression on the students and was used again and again to add weight to appeals for volunteers for Nigeria. Bishop Moynagh recalled the original reading of the letter in his memoirs and wrote:

But the most dramatic impact was by a letter from the late Father Tom Mulvaney (Meath). It was read to us in the College Chapel during one of the evening (weekly) Spiritual talks, I think by Monsignor McCaffrey. Father Mulvaney had written the letter before his death and knowing he was dying. He wanted to assure the students that his death was in no way an effect of life in the dread tropical climate; assured us also that he had already been warned by physicians that he had what was then regarded as an incurable tubercular condition and would have a better chance in a warmer climate.[3]

On arrival, Pat Whitney found his fellow volunteers saddened by the death of their colleague and a little anxious about the proposed changes in the Vicariate. The prospect of a new bishop in place of Shanahan underlined the precariousness of their own position as priests-on-loan. Tom Ronayne, like Tom Mulvaney, was incardinated into the Vicariate. The others were still attached to their home dioceses. In the run-up to the General Chapter of July 1926, the Holy Ghost superiors in Paris had asked the volunteers for their views on the future of the movement. A memorandum was prepared and sent for discussion at the Chapter. In this document, the volunteers asked that the Vicariate would deal with them as a body rather than on an individual basis and that they would be stationed together or with selected Holy Ghost Fathers.

The state of uncertainty continued after Pat's return and so did the discussion among the volunteers. There are five pages in one of Pat's notebooks outlining plans and possibilities. A reference to the appointment of Charles Heerey C.S.Sp. as Coadjutor Bishop, which was announced on 4 February 1927, indicates that the notes were written about that time. It is most likely that they represent the outcome of discussion among all the volunteers. Marginal notes such as 'scarcely possible', 'feasible', 'knocked out' and 'alright' appear alongside various suggestions.

A separate society of priests was envisaged. It would be set up, like the Holy Rosary Sisters, 'for Africa but especially Southern Nigeria'. It was considered to be too soon to go the whole way, just yet. For the present, the volunteers would incardinate into the Vicariate; they would be given scope to 'create and foster a spirit of cohesion among themselves on the mission and be regarded as a body of co-workers distinct from the Order'. The priority was to group them together in one area which would at some future date become a separate territory under the care of the new society. The first steps towards the foundation were to be taken when ten priests were ready to join.

The volunteers paid close attention to the organisation of the proposed society in Ireland. Much would depend on whether the link with Killeshandra was maintained or not. It is extraordinary that such a link was still envisaged in the light of Pat Whitney's experience. The others may have believed that the disagreement was due to a clash of personalities and would not affect the integrated development of priests and sisters which was the original plan. If the partnership with the sisters was to be maintained, three priests would be required in Ireland; one would act as Chaplain to the convent while the other two would raise funds for the sisters and for the new society. The alternative was to leave Killeshandra in the care of the Holy Ghost Fathers and to send one priest home to raise funds and recruit for the new society. Such recruitment would be directed towards priests and students. The students would become priests of the Vicariate of Southern Nigeria 'until the body of seculars on the mission were ripe to form into a Society'. There is a note on the margin of the notebook, dated 2 October 1927, which indicates that the link with Killeshandra was no longer considered feasible. It reads: 'Any connection now between Killeshandra and Maynooth priests is absolutely out.' The plan was well thought out. Careful preparation was envisaged and there was no intention of rushing things.

The notes indicate that Pat Whitney is once more in the thick of things in the Vicariate. In fact he adjusted very well to the change from Ireland and showed little signs of being affected by his traumatic experience in Killeshandra. He resumed his diary on the boat and soon after landing in Nigeria he came to the end of the original notebook. At Christmas, he acquired a school exercise book and continued to record various incidents. This is markedly different from the old diary, which was personal and often intimate in its details. The new diary is written with an eye to publication—not as a personal memoir but as promotional literature for the missions. There are occasional personal glimpses but for the most part Pat talks about the work, the journeys, the crowds of people. Telling people about the missionary task had become a mission in itself. He wrote:

> I would lay down this pen—pencil rather—in two moments, if I could silence an inner voice that keeps telling me that it is my duty to use it as best I can and place the result of its blunted point at God's disposal. Then—let come what will—I will be in no way accountable for the three million people in the Vicariate who have never seen or heard a priest.

He did, in fact, use a large chunk of this diary in a souvenir booklet which he published to mark the foundation of St Patrick's Missionary Society, in 1930. He was full of enthusiasm and full of plans. A letter which he wrote to his cousin, Frank, in March 1928, indicates his inventiveness:

> I wish to the Lord I could manage to have a couple of thousand feet of film scenes from here to bring home with me. I think I could arrange and 'shoot' the thing myself; cash is the trouble. I wonder could you fix up any deal with the manager of the La Scala. If he would—say in the beginning of the next dry season—lend me a first class cinema camera, and let me have films, so many hundred feet each boat for say three months. I'd shoot off the stuff, keeping in my mind what would be suitable to both of us, and let him have the reels back by return of boat for development (for safety the place of development would have to be the quickest place the films could reach from Liverpool). I'd let him have full copyright for all the stuff provided he let me have a free run of copies of the film for lecture purposes. Unless I had rotten luck, it should turn out a profitable investment for him.

Although there is no evidence that this 'deal' ever took place, the plan shows Pat's preoccupation with 'selling' Nigeria and his readiness to try new methods of communication to achieve this end.

Pat felt quite frustrated by lack of encouragement given by the Holy Ghosts to the volunteer movement. He was at pains to point out that 'between the members of the Order on the missions and the few secular priests who are now here (seven in all) there exists nothing but the striving bond of mutual love'. It was members of the Order in Ireland whom Pat held responsible for lack of enthusiasm for the volunteer movement. Bishop Shanahan is not spared his criticism, however, and he writes in a letter to Frank, dated 5 July 1927:

> So far he hasn't shown the slightest sign of giving the seculars a decent show. He has ignored all suggestions. If he fixes up nothing for us within a year five men will have cleared off for good—and that means *finis* for the Maynooth movement. It might be just as well too, because if anything permanent is to come from the Maynooth movement, it must come through working up from a proper missionary foundation in Ireland.

Bishop Shanahan was more interested in the future of the volunteers than Pat realised. He returned to Nigeria in 1927, a much happier and more contented man. Although nothing much could be done for his eyesight he had changed his mind about resigning. Pope Pius XI had personally asked him to continue and invited him to choose a coadjutor. He chose Charles Heerey and ordained him bishop in Killeshandra on 29 May 1927. The proposed division of the Vicariate had been dropped. The American Province of the Holy Ghost Order was offered a Vicariate in East Africa and, in 1932, took over Kilimanjaro in Tanganyika.

In November 1927, Bishop Shanahan called the volunteer priests together and presented them with a set of proposals based on the deliberations of the General Chapter. They were very much different from what the volunteers had in mind and took little account of their memorandum to the Chapter. The Vicar Apostolic proposed to deal with them as individuals, entering a contract with each one for a minimum of three years' service. If any of them wished to be incardinated into the Vicariate, the Bishop would admit them on an individual basis. Those accepted would have to become associate members of the Holy Ghost Congregation. The Bishop agreed to make an effort to station them together.

The volunteers came to the meeting with their own memorandum which was entitled 'The Unanimous View of the Maynooth Nigerian Priests expressed in 1927 at the request of the Vicar Apostolic, Most Rev. Dr Shanahan'. They repeated their conviction that Irish diocesan priests could help solve the staffing problems of the Vicariate and that large numbers could be secured by a proper recruitment campaign. The central point of the memorandum, however, concerned the formation of a new society:

> We have a second conviction that has become more firm each year
> we might say each day that we have worked here. That is: secular
> priests must be safeguarded, helped in many ways in order to
> assure health of soul and body. This can only be done effectively
> by formation of them into a Society. Unless such a Society be
> formed it is our conviction that the taking on of secular priests
> might easily prove dangerous instead of helpful to the missions.

The memorandum went on to reject the proposal that the volunteers
should become associate members of the Holy Ghost Order, on the
grounds that such a move would cut them off from the Irish diocesan
network which was their source of personnel and of financial support.

Bishop Shanahan had great hopes for the Irish diocesan priests'
movement which he had initiated seven years previously. He was also
convinced that the Holy Ghost Fathers were not in a position to
provide the priests needed in his Vicariate. Following his discussions
with the volunteers he accepted that the best way forward lay in the
establishment of a new society which would eventually take on responsibility for the entire Vicariate. He decided to throw in his lot with the
volunteers and to undertake, personally, the task of founding the Society.
A 'Declaration of Intent' was drawn up and signed by Bishop Shanahan
and by Pat Whitney, Vincent Davey and John Finegan on behalf of the
volunteers.

The declaration reads, in part:

> The best means to attain this twofold end (the evangelisation of
> the eight million souls in the Vicariate and the temporal and
> spiritual safeguarding of the Maynooth priests) is the formation of
> a new Society. His Lordship, the Most Rev. Dr Shanahan under-
> takes to form this with the approval of Rome. It is essential that
> the nucleus of it be found among the Maynooth priests now on
> the missions . . . The new Society with the approval of Propaganda
> would undertake full responsibility for the evangelisation of the
> Vicariate. His Lordship would ask for a transition period during
> which the members of the Holy Ghost Order presently on the
> missions would remain on. They would be welcome, if willing, to
> remain on for life.

This was a revolutionary proposal. It is not clear whether Bishop
Shanahan intended to leave his own congregation to be leader of the
new Society. This would not be strictly necessary as he could found it as

he did the Holy Rosary Sisters without actually joining it. Bishop Moynagh, in a handwritten memoir, suggests that when the volunteers failed to agree on a leader, Bishop Shanahan offered to leave the Holy Ghosts and become their leader. This memoir is slender evidence, especially since Bishop Moynagh had no contact with the Vicariate at that time. In any case, the new Society would be linked directly with the Vicariate of Southern Nigeria. The Vicar Apostolic would be the founder and the Vicariate would be the specific missionfield of the Society, at least for the foreseeable future. There is no doubt that if the Holy Ghost Order had supported the project it would have been a great success. Time would prove that there were plenty of prospective members for the Society in Ireland and the support of the Holy Ghosts would have placed a great missionary tradition at the disposal of the early members. However, the Order did not support Bishop Shanahan's proposal but on the contrary was trenchant in its opposition. This is hardly surprising. Students for the proposed Society would have to come from Irish schools where the Holy Ghosts themselves were recruiting. Moreover, Southern Nigeria was among the most successful missions of the congregation. Only a short time previously the Irish Province had resisted a move to give part of it to another branch of the congregation. Now, they were being asked to allow it to pass completely out of Holy Ghost hands. At this time in the Church's history, *territory* was very important to missionary congregations and was rarely given up without a struggle. In the early years of the century, the Holy Ghost Fathers in Kenya had seen a large section of the Vicariate of Zanzibar pass into the hands of the recently founded Consolate Fathers in a move that in modern business circles might be termed a *hostile takeover*. The Irish Province was looking forward to a period of growth and it was not unreasonable to expect that the young men would be given the benefit of reaping a harvest in areas where the back-breaking work of preparation had already been done.

When Bishop Shanahan informed the Superiors in Paris of his intention, he was told that the Order would supply whatever men were needed in the Vicariate and that such a Society was not necessary. He was not convinced, however, that the Holy Ghosts would send enough men and he was conscious of his duty as Vicar Apostolic to do everything possible to evangelise the territory entrusted to him. He thought long and hard before taking any action. The 'Declaration of Intent' had been signed by November 1927; it was late May or early June 1928 before a concrete proposal was sent to Propaganda. In the meantime, the

Bishop had gone through a period of indecision and near depression. He was reluctant to go against his own religious community and yet felt bound to do so. On 21 June, Cardinal Van Rossum put the proposal for a new Society before Pius XI. The Pope gave his unqualified approval and Bishop Shanahan began to think in terms of a house in Ireland and a missionary training centre to prepare the young men for Nigeria.[4] In November 1928, he wrote an optimistic letter to Bishop Finegan which reads in part:

> The Irish Province of the Holy Ghost Fathers is not able to meet the demands of personnel of this vicariate. French Fathers on account of their ignorance of English can be but of little use in a mission where the School holds such a prominent position as a means of evangelisation.
>
> I put the whole matter before the Cardinal Prefect of Propaganda, H.E., Cardinal Van Rossum; proposing as the only way that I could see out of the difficulty, the creation of a new Missionary Society for S. Nigeria. His Eminence, the Cardinal, placed the project before the Holy Father who gave it full approval, with his blessing. This means that I have now to see about getting this new Society on its feet.
>
> If the last few years of my missionary life produce no other fruit than the nucleus of a future Missionary Society that others will organise and perfect, those last years of mine in Africa will not have been lived in vain.
>
> So far nothing has been done. During 1929 we hope to take the initial steps by securing a house somewhere in Ireland with the consent of the Bishop of the diocese. It will be easier to manage than in the case of a Society of Missionary Sisters. Some of the Maynooth Missionary priests here in Nigeria are willing to become the first members of the new Society.[5]

Meanwhile, the volunteers were enthusiastic about the proposal. Pat Whitney was incardinated into the Vicariate, in 1928, with the intention of transferring later to the new Society. A new volunteer, John Browne of Kerry diocese, had arrived in Nigeria at the end of 1927, and was sent to Emekuku. The following year, Joseph McCloskey of Down and Connor came and was appointed to teach at St Charles's Teacher Training College in Onitsha. Vincent Davey went on home leave and James McGinley was recalled to his diocese, in Ireland, after five years of service on the mission. Pat Whitney, Tom Ronayne, Vincent Davey,

John Finegan, John Gaffney, Pat Kelly and Joseph McCloskey were confident that they would be among the first members of the Society, while John Browne was expected to commit himself in due course. This only left them two short of the proposed ten founder-members.

Their confidence was misplaced, however. Strong forces were working against the new Society and within two months of outlining his hopes and plans to Bishop Finegan, the Vicar Apostolic withdrew his support for the project. No proper explanation for this volte-face is given in any of the Bishop's letters. One letter, to Bishop McNamee of Ardagh and Clonmacnois, dated 17 January 1927, states his new position very clearly:

> . . . on the understanding that I would undertake the formation of a Society for secular missionary priests. I placed the matter before his Eminence, the Cardinal Prefect of Propaganda. His Eminence got the sanction of Our Holy Father for the formation of the Society in question. Circumstances have already arisen and are of such a serious nature that I cannot possibly carry out my promise although I have the approval of Rome . . .

Three days before, the Vicar Apostolic had written to the Superior General Archbishop Le Roy, agreeing not to go ahead with the plan. He wrote:

> I think however, that I am well enough known in Rome to pre-clude the possibility of my report being interpreted as hostile to my missionary colleagues or to the Congregation . . . As far as the foundation project is concerned, Your Grace said that Ireland is firmly and definitely committed to the missions and will soon supply all the personnel that we need. Well! In that case I will have to wait. If the Congregation can give me the missionaries without delay, there is no reason for me to begin the Society project. How-ever, if the Congregation cannot for whatever reason give me the personnel which I need, I will be obliged 'sub gravi' to search elsewhere for this personnel.

Clearly, the Vicar Apostolic had bowed to pressure and promises. The big pressure came from the accusation that he was showing his own congregation in a bad light and was therefore, disloyal, while the promise of sufficient men from the Irish Province removed the main reason for going ahead with the new Society.

The presence of opposition within the Holy Ghost Order does not fully explain the Bishop's change of plan. He had gone against the wishes of the Superior General in founding the Holy Rosary Sisters. He could have done so again since he had the Pope's approval for the new Society. It was, however, a much more serious issue this time, affecting the Holy Ghost Order, directly. The Order would lose its most promising mission. There was also an implication that the Holy Ghosts were not capable of looking after the territories given to them, an innuendo which was all the more hurtful because it came from one of their own bishops and one who had repeatedly criticised the number of men tied up in the Order's schools in Ireland. There can be no doubt that the pressure on the Bishop to back down was intense. It was rendered more so by the fact that it came from the Bishop's own confrères, many of whom were close personal friends. It may have been that, at a certain point, the pressure from this quarter became too much to bear and he capitulated.

There was another pressure, however, which might have been the final straw which broke the Bishop's resolve. It was the opposition of those who were collaborating with him on the Holy Rosary Sisters. A document written by one of the first group of Holy Rosary Sisters, Sr Margaret Mary, suggests that the advice of Bishop Finegan and the Dominican Sisters weighed very heavily with the Vicar Apostolic and that it was their opposition which finally persuaded him to abandon the new Society. This document, a memorandum written in 1969, puts the facts of the case as follows:

> When this became known to the authorities of the Holy Ghost Congregation, they considered Dr Shanahan disloyal to his own Missionary Congregation, and made known their disapproval. However, he felt confident of the loyalty and support of Dr Finegan and the Dominican Mothers who knew of his need for priests and had been praying for this intention. With characteristic openness and friendship he wrote to both of his plans. Prejudiced no doubt by their past disagreements with Fathers Ronayne and Whitney, Mother Xavier and Dr Finegan saw in the proposed Society of priests a threat to the Holy Rosary Congregation as they envisaged it. Perhaps they imagined that the Maynooth Fathers would take over the Congregation to work for them. Anyhow they wrote to Dr Shanahan in very strong terms that if he went on with this new Society of Priests he would ruin his own Congregation of the Holy Rosary. These letters caused Dr Shanahan great pain. He took some of the Sisters at Onitsha (Sister M. Joseph was one) for a walk around the grounds and shared his sentiments with them. Before

God he was responsible for the evangelisation of this vast territory. For years he had been begging everywhere for priests to minister to the ever-growing population of baptised Christians as well as to evangelise the areas where Christ was not yet known. The new Society of Irish priests seemed a providential answer to his prayers. He believed that the Superiors of the Holy Ghost Congregation were wrong in opposing the project since they were unable to send sufficient priests to meet the need, and he had gone ahead in spite of their opposition. Now had come this blow from Mother Xavier and Bishop Finegan saying that the new Society would ruin his own Congregation of the Holy Rosary. He had the true mission-ary view—later stated in Papal Encyclicals—that olderestablished missionary orders should welcome new helpers and co-operate with them. However, he said, without Bishop Finegan and Mother Xavier he could not have established the Holy Rosary Congregation. He owed a great deal to them. He would defer to their opinion in this matter, even though it was against his own wishes and views.

Whatever the decisive influence may have been, Bishop Shanahan made his decision, in January 1927, and communicated it to all con-cerned, including the volunteers. They were very disappointed but were encouraged by the fact that the Bishop remained favourable to the project, although no longer as a direct participant. He offered Pat Whitney excardination from the Vicariate and gave him a letter of intro-duction which he could use in Ireland if he wished to pursue further the idea of a new Society. The offer of excardination left Pat free to seek another diocese or to join a Society, although it would not remove him from the Vicariate until he became officially attached to another diocese or Institute.

Pat Whitney left Nigeria in May 1929. Three of his colleagues John Finegan, John Gaffney and Pat Kelly had gone home in March and Pat would have gone with them but had agreed to wait until Vincent Davey returned from home-leave. There were four volunteer priests left in Nigeria. Vincent Davey had replaced Pat Whitney in Eke; Tom Ronayne was in Calabar; John Browne was in Emekuku and Joseph McCloskey was teaching in St Joseph's Teacher Training College in Onitsha. The future of the volunteer movement did not look very bright now that Bishop Shanahan had abandoned the idea of forming them into a Society. The only hope lay in the letter he had given to Pat Whitney recommending, in a general way, the latter's efforts to promote the cause of the volunteers.

A New Beginning

When Pat returned to Ireland, he stayed at his uncle's house in Port which had now passed to his brother James. His cousin Frank, who was now curate in Keadue near Boyle, had been active in promoting the cause of volunteers and had made one very important move. In October 1927 he had been offered an estate at Kiltegan, Co. Wicklow as a possible headquarters for the new Society. The offer came from a businessman named John Hughes whom Frank had met on a visit to the new hydroelectric scheme at Ardnacrusha in Co. Clare. On that occasion, Frank had helped John Hughes and his wife, an elderly couple, to negotiate a slippery bank. The resulting conversation led to the offer of High Park estate for the use of the proposed Missionary Society. Frank Whitney visited the estate accompanied by Canon M.J. Masterson, parish priest of Mohill, and kept in touch with John Hughes although no definite word on the Society was forthcoming. When Pat Whitney arrived from Nigeria he decided to look for permission to establish a mission house at Kiltegan. It would be a base for himself and a facility for the volunteers on home leave. Some day, in the far distant future, it might become the headquarters of a Missionary Society. John Hughes agreed to give the manor house on the High Park estate and twenty acres of land, while Pat applied to Bishop Cullen of Kildare and Leighlin for permission to use it as a rest house for the Nigerian missionaries. Permission was given very quickly but before a final agreement was signed, events had overtaken the plan and the agreement with Bishop Cullen had to be renegotiated. If Pat Whitney had wished for a 'fairy godmother' to make an appearance at this point he could scarcely have dreamt of one so munificent as the English priest who entered his life in 1929. He was Monsignor Arthur Hinsley, the recently appointed Apostolic Visitor to British Africa. Arthur Hinsley, the son of a Yorkshire carpenter, was Rector of the English College, Rome from 1917 to 1928. After a year as an Apostolic Visitor he became Apostolic Delegate and held that post until 1934. He was recalled from retirement a year later to become Archbishop of Westminster at the age of seventy. He became a Cardinal in 1937 and died in 1943.

His appointment as an Apostolic Visitor arose from Rome's desire to exploit to the full Britain's policy of education in the colonies. The Colonial Officer had decided to co-operate with the missionary bodies and to provide considerable finance in return for increasing control of the schools. Arthur Hinsley's task was to ensure that the Catholic missions availed to the full of the opportunities offered. An extract from his own diary outlines his task:

The British Government of today realised that it cannot do without missionary schools if education is to spread among the masses of Africans in its territories. These schools have blazed the trail, so to speak. They have been a great civilising influence and the Government, recognising that education, to be worthwhile, must be based on religion, has been very generous in its offer of monetary assistance to all the mission schools of the various churches, provided a certain standard of efficiency is reached. That desire for efficiency is shared by the Holy See, and it was the Holy Father's anxiety to know how our schools fared in Africa and his desire to see them brought up to such a pitch of excellence that the Government would recognise them all as worthy of the grants offered that was the reason for my visitation. Yet it was not only to make reports to Rome, but the hope of stimulating and encouraging all the workers in our schools with the Pope's own enthusiasm for higher standards in education that inspired me.[7]

Arthur Hinsley fulfilled his task most successfully. His enthusiasm for education and his very personable approach to mission personnel won great support for Vatican policy. His rallying cry, delivered at a conference of missionaries in Dar es Salaam is perhaps his best known statement:

Co-operate with all your power; and where it is impossible for you to carry on both the immediate task of evangelisation and your educational work, neglect your Churches in order to perfect your schools.[8]

Pat Whitney had been home three months when Arthur Hinsley arrived at Calabar. It was 25 August 1929 and he had already visited Basutoland, Tanganyika, Kenya and the Congo. He spent two months in Nigeria and during that time he met the four remaining volunteers and discussed the possibility of a new Society with them. He was particularly impressed by Emekuku where John Browne was Father-in-charge. What he saw there convinced him of the great contribution that could be made by an expanded volunteer movement. He was not unaware of the educational aspect either. He realised how great would be the contribution to education of a team of English-speaking volunteer priests each of whom would come equipped with a University degree. He discussed the matter with Bishop Heerey—Bishop Shanahan was in Ireland—but it was Tom Ronayne and Vincent Davey who really pressed the issue, urging him to use his influence in Rome to promote the idea of a new Society. Tom Ronayne wrote to Pat in Ireland and received a cable in reply which he forwarded to the Apostolic Visitor who had now moved on to Sierra Leone. In an accompanying letter he wrote:

> Father Whitney is ready to go to England or if necessary to Rome to put the full facts before you.

On 28 October 1929 Arthur Hinsley wrote to Pat from State House in Sierra Leone where he was staying. It was the first of fifty letters which Pat Whitney was to receive from Arthur Hinsley, all of which are preserved in the Kiltegan archives. A number of them are written in his own distinguished longhand; all of them manifest continued kindness and interest and also a great forthrightness and honesty which is pre-pared to challenge Pat on certain issues in the interests of the new Society. The first letter reads in part:

> I am heartbroken to find that at Emekuku station two young Irish Fathers—one C.S.Sp. and the other a secular working a district with 61,595 Christians to care for—14,000 baptised and the rest catechumens and of the latter some waiting seven years to be passed for baptism. You know the need for priests of the type of Ronayne and Davey etc. Well it is a joy to me to hear of the atti-tude of Maynooth President, of the gift of Wicklow mansion, and of the readiness of the seculars to listen to the call of the starving souls of Nigeria. Something must be done. I would be inclined to favour a Society under the direct orders of the Holy See. But I know some look on this idea as too ambitious and there is the money question. Could you come to Rome? . . . If you could come we could perhaps get something settled on the spot . . . Anyway please write to me as soon as you get this scrawl and let me know if you can come to Rome.

In a postscript he adds: 'Father Davey is wholeheartedly with any scheme for his own and his brethren's spiritual good and the good of his beloved Nigerians.'

The letter had come in the nick of time. Pat had just received a letter from Bishop Shanahan more or less revoking his earlier letter of intro-duction. Pat writes of this letter:

> . . . he wrote me stating that he had given me an exeat from Nigeria and asked me to get another diocese and to cease all further activity with regard to procuring a Rest House in Ireland.

This change of attitude on the part of the Vicar Apostolic came very suddenly. He may have got cold feet on hearing about the rest house because he would be implicated in it, at least indirectly, as it was to be a service to priests from his Vicariate. The more likely reason for the change was a celebrated gaffe made by Pat Whitney around this time. Accounts of this incident have been handed down in St Patrick's Missionary Society and Sister Margaret Mary has included it in the memorandum already mentioned. Bishop James Moynagh describes it in his memoirs as follows:

> Father P.J.'s rather rambunctious ways led him to making some colossal blunders. For example when he wrote Father Ronayne and Bishop Shanahan and said to Tommy 'We will use the "old boy" [the Bishop] as long as he can help us and ditch him when he becomes an obstacle' (words to that *precise* effect) but put Father Ronayne's letter in Bishop Shanahan's envelope!!! Bishop Shanahan read it, mystified as to who was writing till the horrible truth struck.[9]

Bishop McGettrick, in an interview, gave the opinion that this incident undermined Bishop Shanahan's trust in Pat Whitney. It might well have put an end to Pat's plans for a Missionary Society, but for the timely arrival of Arthur Hinsley's letter from Sierra Leone. Pat was quick to assure the Apostolic Visitor that he was ready to go to Rome. In his reply, Arthur Hinsley named the day. Pat wrote at once to Bishop Cullen, informing him that he had been called to Rome and asking him to postpone all action on the rest house until he returned.

Pat Whitney arrived in Rome on 24 November 1929 and got accommodation at the Irish College. On the following day, he met Arthur Hinsley and the two men discussed the situation of the Irish volunteer priests in Nigeria. Arthur Hinsley urged Pat to seek the immediate establishment of a Society and undertook to show him the way. A memorandum was prepared for presentation to the Prefect of Propaganda, Cardinal Van Rossum and an interview was arranged with the Cardinal. The memorandum requested permission to establish a Society and asked for missions to be assigned to it within the Vicariate of Southern Nigeria. It reads:

> It is proposed that a new Society be formed by the Holy See to aid in the Evangelization of the pagans of Africa.

That the name of the Society be 'The Society of Irish Secular Missionary Priests' under the patronage of Our Lady of Good Counsel.

That the nucleus of the new Society be the Maynooth Missionary Priests who since 1920, have engaged in the work of the missions in the vicariate of Southern Nigeria, and who now wish to become permanently attached to the work.

The document goes on to outline the needs of Southern Nigeria, the work already done by the Maynooth priests, the possibility of getting funds from home, and the offer of the house at Kiltegan, valued at £3,000. It requests that the first mission of the Society '. . . be the stations among the souls of the Ibo tribe of whom Maynooth priests are now in charge, together with the unevangelised tribes to the north of the Ibo tribe, in the present vicariate'.

The interview with Cardinal Van Rossum went very well. The Cardinal expressed his satisfaction with the memorandum but suggested that the Society be named: *St Patrick's Society for Foreign Missionary Priests.* Pat Whitney left the Palace of Propaganda to put the finishing touches to his petition and to await the final decision.

While he was in Rome, Pat set up office in Mater Dei, a convent of the Poor Sisters of the Mother of God which is situated close to Propaganda. His contacts there were Sister Margaret Gertrude Burns and her sister, Sister Francis Borgia Burns who hailed from Killeshandra and had been in Mater Dei since 1915 and 1918, respectively. They had two other sisters in the same congregation and a third who had joined the Holy Rosary Sisters. The nuns gave Pat a great welcome. He said daily Mass there and was given breakfast—two boiled eggs mashed up in a cup with butter and pepper. It was a convenient place in which to prepare for his various meetings in Propaganda and it was to serve the same purpose for Pat on subsequent visits. A strong friendship developed between the convent and the Society. Sister Gertrude was to spend fifty-five years in Rome and Sister Borgia seventy. Both visited Pat in Kiltegan and both were in good spirits, on 17 March 1990, when Sister Gertrude celebrated her 100th birthday in Bath, in England.

Pat Whitney made another significant friendship during this visit to Rome when he met Monsignor Caesar Pecorari who had been Under-Secretary of Propaganda since 1921. Caesar Pecorari was a native of Rome who had already spent thirty years as a Vatican official and was to continue for another eighteen years until he retired at the age of seventy-four. He was to play an important role in helping Pat Whitney to establish the Society and its structures in the early years. The two men corresponded frequently, especially when Pat had difficulty with securing ecclesiastical approval for something. Caesar Pecorari was approached about setting up a chapel in Kiltegan, about founding a branch of the Apostolic Work in Dublin, about establishing a seminary or simply in order to find out 'unofficially' what might be happening in Rome concerning the Society. Often, Pat would choose to consult the Roman secretary rather than an Irish bishop who might also be in a position to clarify matters for him. Communication was hampered by the fact that Caesar Pecorari had very little English. Pat wrote in English; Pecorari's replies were in Latin. Pat's letters to Caesar Pecorari were usually accompanied by a number of Mass offerings which were received with appreciation. Mass offerings also accompanied Pat's letters to Archbishop Hinsley although they were intended for his secretary who acknowledged them, personally, every time. The practice reflects the extremely low salaries of Vatican civil servants at the time and the fact that they were not in a position to augment them by offerings from the faithful. It also says a lot about Pat. While a more circumspect man would avoid a practice that might be construed as a bribe, the thought would not have occurred to Pat. The men appreciated the offerings. Pat was happy to be able to give them, and a little gift was a tried and trusted way of softening up any man.

At Caesar Pecorari's suggestion, Pat cabled Father John Blowick for a copy of the Constitutions of the Society of St Columban. These arrived in Rome on 6 December and were submitted by Arthur Hinsley to the Cardinal Prefect along with a formal petition from Pat asking that these Constitutions might be adopted by the new Society, that permission be given for a central house of the Society, to be known as The House of Our Lady of Africa, Kiltegan, Co. Wicklow and that a territory be designated for the Society. On 10 December Pat got unofficial word from Caesar Pecorari that the petitions had been granted on condition that Bishop Cullen of Kildare and Leighlin would give permission for the central house to be established in his diocese. The question of territory was to be discussed with Bishop Shanahan who was expected in Rome shortly. On 13 December Pat started his journey back to Ireland. In two weeks he had, to his great surprise, succeeded in founding St Patrick's Missionary Society. It was to be a trial foundation —'ad experimentum' was the term used in Rome. There were many hurdles to be crossed yet but to all intents and purposes the Society which the volunteers had hoped for was now a reality.

A Motherhouse

On his way back to Ireland, Pat Whitney called to visit Archbishop Amigo of Southwark and, by complete coincidence, met Bishop Shanahan there.[10] The meeting could not have been very cordial in view of the misplaced letter. Furthermore, Pat did not wish to discuss the question of territory at this stage, because he knew that the Vicar Apostolic would not freely give up the stations which he wanted. Nonetheless, Bishop Shanahan was pleased with what had transpired and agreed to accept Society priests in Southern Nigeria. Pat Whitney reported the meeting to Arthur Hinsley, in a letter written on 27 December. According to this letter the Vicar Apostolic seemed

> quite glad about the formation of the Society without him having to take active part, as he cannot now be blamed for it by the Holy Ghost Order. Also he expressed his willingness to receive any priests I would send to the Vicariate . . . He fairly insisted on his right to send those priests wherever he wished and at the same time stressed his conviction that the Order would immediately insist on a division.

When Pat reached Ireland, however, disappointment struck. Bishop Cullen refused permission for a central house on the grounds that it was a far different request from the one he had acceded to previously. The reasons for his refusal appear in some correspondence of the time. He had got Thomas Keogh, one of his consultors, to make enquiries about the project from Edward Leen who was still Chaplain in Killeshandra. Thomas Keogh's letter, a handwritten note, reads:

> I had a talk with Doctor Leen. He spoke highly of the two priests concerned but both are obstinate and self-opinionated. He thinks Van Rossum's letter doesn't imply more than a temporary sanction to go on with the project until he has got more information from the parties concerned. The whole scheme according to Doctor Leen, is foredoomed to failure and I think he hinted at least, that Doctor Shanahan would oppose it in Rome as being unfair to the Holy Ghost Fathers who did the pioneer work in the Vicariate.

In the light of this opinion from a highly respected Holy Ghost Father who had worked in Nigeria and was closely associated with Bishop Shanahan, it was to be expected that Bishop Cullen would be cautious. He contacted Bishop Shanahan who was now in Ireland only to learn that Pat Whitney was not acting on his behalf, that Pat was no longer a priest of his Vicariate and that Shanahan had himself given up the idea of forming a new Missionary Society. This had to be Bishop Shanahan's approach. He had withdrawn from the foundation as a result of opposition and he had to make it perfectly clear that he was not working, underhand, as it were, for the new Society.

Pat went to see Bishop Cullen and explained his position *vis-à-vis* the Vicariate and showed him the letter Bishop Shanahan had given him when he was leaving Nigeria. Bishop Cullen was mollified but was not prepared to give the requested permission. However, he did issue a letter of recommendation which read:

> I have been much impressed by the scheme which you have explained to me for the evangelisation of Nigeria. It would commend the blessing and support of all who have at heart the spread of the true Religion. Aspirants to the priesthood are numerous in this country, the only drawback being a lack of funds to complete their ecclesiastical training. You however seem confident that the necessary funds will be forthcoming. I hope then and pray that you receive a Mother House for your new Society amid surroundings where it will have a favourable and auspicious start.

Armed with this letter, Pat set out in search of a bishop who would allow him to open a house in his diocese. John Hughes, the donor of Kiltegan, offered him £1,000 to help buy another house if an amenable bishop could be found. Bishop McNamee of Ardagh and Bishop Morrisroe of Achonry showed interest. Then, on 18 January, Pat got an opportunity to present his case before the Standing Committee of the Irish Hierarchy, meeting in the Gresham Hotel, Dublin. On 23 January 1930, Bishop Cullen agreed to allow the central house in his diocese. Whether he was approached by a representative of the Standing Committee, or not, is not documented.

Pat went to London to inform Hinsley that a motherhouse was secured and the latter contacted Propaganda when he went to Rome. On 27 January, Pat wrote to Cardinal van Rossum enclosing letters of sponsorship written by Bishops McNamee and Morrisroe. On 6 February, Propaganda gave its formal approval and a few days later John Hughes made over his house at Kiltegan to four trustees, Bishop Cullen, Monsignor John Delaney V.F., parish priest of nearby Rathvilly, Canon M.J. Masterson, parish priest of Mohill and Patrick F. Whitney, C.C. Keadue. It was discovered later that no proper deed of trust was drawn up and that the four were in fact joint owners of the property.

The erection of the Society was announced in Irish, English and American papers, and on 7 March 1930 formal possession was taken of the house in Kiltegan.

Territory

It was one thing to have a Society; territory was quite a different matter. A Missionary Society could operate successfully in a territory entrusted to another Society. Having its own missionary area, on the other hand, would confirm its identity and would give it the independence to work out its own style and its own missionary methods. Pat wanted territory for the new Society and he wanted a particular strip of territory comprising the missions of Eke and Emekuku and corresponding roughly to the civil district of Owerri. Pat had argued for this area while he was in Rome. He argued that it was particularly suitable for temporary men because English was widely understood there. Furthermore, the volunteers in the field knew the people and Tom Mulvaney had given his life for them. After meeting Bishop Shanahan, Pat realised that his request for this area was unlikely to be granted as it was a central strip of Iboland which would split the Vicariate in two. When division had been talked about, in favour of the American Province, it was the eastern provinces of Calabar and Ogoja which were in mind. Pat wrote to Caesar Pecorari on 20 December, asking him to get the Cardinal Prefect to pressurise Bishop Shanahan to give the requested territory. A week later he wrote to Arthur Hinsley asking him to do whatever he could about the territory. He was under no illusion about the difficulty of getting. Eke and Emekuku. After describing to Hinsley the huge numbers waiting for baptism in these stations he urged him:

> Fight for these souls, my dear Lord, and with God's help we'll not let them or you down. And the fight will be a hard one.

Arthur Hinsley was prepared to fight and would appear to have convinced Propaganda to grant Pat Whitney the area he had requested. Meanwhile, Bishop Shanahan had learned of Pat's request and of the favourable reception it had been given in Rome. Pat had written to Tom Ronayne who passed the word on to Bishop Heerey who, in turn, contacted the Vicar Apostolic in Ireland. As a result of being forewarned, Bishop Shanahan went to Rome armed with a huge map of his Vicariate which the Holy Rosary Sisters had helped him to cut up so that it would fit in his suitcase. He was determined to resist a division along the lines suggested by Pat Whitney. There is a story that Bishop

Shanahan raised the matter with the Pope who took the map he had been given by Propaganda and tore it up—or, in another version, crossed it through with his pen—and told the Vicar Apostolic to divide his Vicariate in whatever way he wished. In any case, Propaganda did not manage to browbeat Bishop Shanahan into surrendering this area as Pat Whitney had suggested and it was now a matter to be settled between the two men.

It was a blessing in disguise for Bishop Shanahan that Pat Whitney had made so bold a request. The Irish Province of the Holy Ghost Congregation was committed to retaining the Vicariate intact. It suited Bishop Shanahan to be able to propose a compromise position by which the less desirable eastern section of the Vicariate would be given to the new Society. It was better to lose an under-developed area than to lose the heart of Iboland where the Church was making wonderful progress. The final agreement was reached in Maynooth and was mediated by the President of the College, Monsignor McCaffrey, who had been kept informed, all along, of developments within the volunteer movement. He had remained friendly with Bishop Shanahan and so was in a good position to bring the discussion on territory to an amicable conclusion. The meeting took place on 8 and 9 March. Pat pressed for Owerri; the Bishop offered Calabar and Uyo. Later the Bishop suggested that Ogoja be included. Pat objected to this and, in the end, settled for Calabar and Uyo. Ogoja was to remain in the Holy Ghost area.

After agreement was reached, Monsignor McCaffrey allowed Pat Whitney to appeal to the student body for volunteers for the new mission. It was a historic appeal which resulted in five newly-ordained priests going to Nigeria later that year. They were James Moynagh, Tom McGettrick, Ciaran Ryan, Patrick J. Costelloe and Cornelius Plunkett. This group was to provide the Society with solid leadership especially in the crucial early years of its existence.

In the end, Propaganda included Ogoja in its commission to the Society. Pat did his best to head off this eventuality and enlisted Arthur Hinsley's aid in doing so. He argued that it was difficult to reach Ogoja from Calabar and that the large number of languages in the area would present too great a challenge for the young Society. Nonetheless, on 24 May 1930, Cardinal van Rossum communicated his decision that the Society would take charge of the provinces of Calabar and Ogoja. For the present, they would be worked under the jurisdiction of Bishop Shanahan. When the Society had sufficient personnel, it would operate the area as a separate jurisdiction.

4

The Society is Established in Kiltegan and Calabar

PAT Whitney took over High Park House, Kiltegan, Co. Wicklow in March 1930. Everything about his new situation was unfamiliar. The house itself, a 'gentleman's residence', contrasted sharply with the thatched cottage in which he was born. The bitter north wind blowing across the snow-covered peaks of Lugnaquilla, Carrig and Keadeen bore no resemblance to the dust-bearing *harmattan* of Nigeria. Moreover, he was on his own—alone as he had never been before. In Maynooth, in Nigeria, in Killeshandra he had been surrounded by people who were pursuing the same general goals. In Kiltegan he depended for company on a few 'handy lads' whom he had brought from his home area to help him get the place in order. He looked forward to the day when his cousin Frank would be released by his bishop and would be free to join him.

The setting was very beautiful and this, at least, was an encouragement to Pat who was very sensitive to the beauty of nature. High Park was a small, richly-wooded estate, five miles from the market town of Baltinglass and forty-five miles from Dublin. Within two miles of the main gate lay the tiny village of Kiltegan which boasted a post office, a hotel and a couple of shops. The main street of the village led up to the grand gate of Humewood which was by far the most stately residence in the district. By comparison, High Park was modest but it did have a compact Georgian residence approached by a tree-lined avenue which wound past an artificial lake through grounds which were designed for enjoyment and gracious living. It was a secluded place with superb views of the Wicklow Mountains but cut off from the road by a generous belt of trees broken by two side-entrances, each with a low gate-lodge. Beside the house a grove of yew trees lent a sombre atmosphere to the simple monument commemorating Nicholas Westby, Member of Parliament and Master of High Park until he died, in 1800.

Any notion that Pat Whitney might have luxuriated in the life of a country squire, even for a day, is dispelled by the following account which appeared in the *Irish Press* on 19 August 1936. The article describes two visits to Kiltegan by columnist Aodh de Blacam, 'Roddy the Rover'. The first of these took place shortly after Pat's arrival:

> Well I remember a week after Easter in 1930, when I moved thither first and found a yellow old country house in a park, looking over a fishpool. Before the door were the bones of an old car, and a priest, his features scorched by the sun of Africa and the marks of olden malaria, was screwing the wheels together.
>
> His Reverence had come from Rome with authority to found a new missionary Society, St Patrick's, and he was fixing up a derelict car to do his errands as he might in the African wilds. In the empty barrack of a house he had built a little chapel, but for household furniture he had packing cases, and at tea we took it in turn with the only knife and the only spoon, and drank out of mugs and jugs and one cracked cup. There was not much but faith to live on at Kiltegan then, and that is hungry fare for a body like Roddy.

High Park, however, had been created by generations of country squires, many of whom served as sheriffs for Co. Wicklow. At the end of the seventeenth century, it had come into the hands of Nicholas Westby who was a descendant of an English family of recusant Catholics whose estates were seized by Parliament and sold in 1653. The Westbys managed to buy back their lands in the name of Protestant friends and in this way to hold their place in society in spite of the laws which discriminated against their beliefs. Thomas Westby settled in Clonmel about 1670 and it was his son, Nicholas, collector of customs at Ennis Co. Clare who acquired High Park by way of dowry, when he married Frances Stepney of Durrow, Co. Laois, in 1698. Their son William made a lot of improvements to the estate and according to the *Ennis Chronicle*, 12 July 1784, he had 'kept constantly above 200 men employed, and expended about £12,000 in building and improving a mountainous tract of land'. Meanwhile, the family had become Protestant and was indistinguishable from the vast majority of Anglo-Irish ascendancy families both in religious practice and in life-style. The Nicholas Westby who is commemorated by the monument was perhaps the most illustrious of the line. He had a large estate in Co. Clare and was a member of the Dublin Parliament. He was held in high esteem by the local population and while this did not save his house which was burned in 1798, it did save his life. An article which appeared in the *Wicklow People*, 16 July 1938 gives the local tradition concerning this episode:

> Before the Battle of Hacketstown, Captain Roche, on the direction of Michael Dwyer, went to Westby of High Park (an M.P. who afterwards voted against the Union) and told him that it would not be safe for him to stay there and that he should go to Dublin without delay. Westby said that he would prefer to die in his own house, as it would not be safe for him to travel to Dublin, whereupon Roche gave him a pass and he finally set out upon the journey in his coach and four, but not before he had ordered his butler to bury the silver. The boys from Imaal, Rathdangan, Kilanout (Killamoate) and all around assembled there at four in the morning and when the butler came in with the spade after burying the silver, they demanded where it was but as he refused to tell them he was piked. A large supply of whiskey, which the rebels sampled freely, was discovered in the cellars. The house was burned to the ground but tradition holds that the occurrence was accidental as Westby was held in fair esteem locally. Hacketstown tradition holds that Westby purchased the whiskey at Tullow on the previous day for the purpose of intoxicating the rebels but this is evidently only a poor justification for the rebels imbibing too freely.

Burke's *Dictionary of Landed Gentry* confirms that the house was burned and that Nicholas Westby voted against the Act of Union although he had been offered a peerage in return for his support. Nicholas Westby did not live long after his defiant stand and died unmarried in 1800 at the age of 49. High Park passed to his brother Edward, a Dublin lawyer, who built a new house on the estate and returned to live there in 1814. The estate at this time consisted of 508 statute acres, as shown on a survey map commissioned by Nicholas Westby in 1784 and preserved at St Patrick's, Kiltegan.[1]

There is little available information on the fortunes of the Westby family after 1800. Local people have many stories which indicate an anti-Catholic bias, hardly surprising following the burning of the house. It is said that the Westbys, as landlords, opposed the building of Killamoate Church soon after Catholic Emancipation and that work on the

Church could commence only after the plot had been, on the advice of Daniel O'Connell, turned into a burial ground. Locals remember an out-house containing a huge boiler which had been used to make porridge for hungry people during the famine. They say the last Westbys in High Park were two old ladies who left about 1920. For a time the house was looked after by a housekeeper called Kate O'Neill who refused to stay following a burglary in which silver and other valuables were taken. Then a Captain Palmer came as caretaker and lived there with his wife and son until the place was sold in 1927.

The Westby family left behind them a solid house, a walled garden with glass-houses, the out-offices usually attached to a country estate, a number of staff dwellings and a selection of fine trees. Apart from this legacy there was no continuity between this Anglo-Irish ascendancy family and the new occupant of High Park. They were rooted in the society from which they sprang, close to the earth, dedicated to pre-serving their heritage and improving it. His horizons, on the contrary, were in eternity; his chief concern was to be faithful to a call summoning him to go beyond security and human esteem in the pursuit of a dream which had its origins in that mysterious world where man and God meet. If he were to search for spiritual antecedents he would not find them within the demesne walls of High Park. He would not have had far to look, however, for close to him in Wicklow were ancient remains which bore eloquent witness to a similar concern. Kiltegan gets its name from St Tegan who established a Church there in the fifth century. The Book of Armagh links Tegan with St Patrick who is said to have given him as a disciple to St Fiacc and later set him up on his own with five disciples.[2] In nearby Baltinglass, on the banks of the river Slaney lie the ruins of a medieval monastery. In 1148, Dermot Mac Murrough brought Cistercian monks from Mellifont and settled them in Baltinglass. For four centuries they continued to give a radical witness to God's pre-eminent claim on the human spirit. From this monastery, referred to as 'The Valley of Salvation', monks went out to establish other centres of spirituality and learning, the most notable being Jerpoint in Co. Kil-kenny. Across the mountains lies the ancient monastic site of Glendalough which was founded by St Kevin in the sixth century. It represents a peculiarly Irish response to the Gospel in a nature-centred life of asceti-cism, prayer and learning. It was a missionary centre from which monks carried the Christian message to mainland Europe. More ancient still are the passage tombs on top of Baltinglass Hill. They date from 2,500 BC and give testimony to religious stirrings in Irish people around the time the first pyramids were being built and long before Abraham left the most ancient city in the world to strike out for the promised land.

Pat Whitney had come to take High Park out of the sedate and relatively peaceful world of self-sufficiency and public service, to cut it adrift from the local community and make it into a base from which to launch a missionary campaign more far-reaching than that of Glendalough. The man who made this possible was a Dublin tea-importer named John Hughes who is a major and colourful character in the story of St Patrick's Missionary Society.

John Hughes

John Hughes was born near Kilkeel in Co. Down, in 1886. He emigrated to Liverpool as a young man and worked in a shop until he had saved enough money to establish his own grocery business. This grew to be a huge enterprise comprising sixty retail grocery stores in and around Liverpool. He maintained strong links with Ireland and things Irish. Seventy-five per cent of his employees were Irish Catholics. They were encouraged to participate in Irish cultural events and to become involved with the firm's Gaelic football team. Whenever possible, Irish produce was sold in the shops, much of it from Ballina, Co. Mayo. John Hughes made Limerick bacon and ham a speciality in his shops and helped to establish a reputation for these products in Britain.

When conscription was introduced in January 1916, John Hughes helped many of the young Irishmen in his employment to return to Ireland. He was brought to court and found guilty of conspiracy to defeat the provisions of the Military Service Act, 'so as to allow persons liable for service to escape liability', was fined £200 and sentenced to twelve months' imprisonment. He served out his entire sentence and on his release he came to live in Ireland although he held on to his business interests in England until 1927, when he sold out to the Liverpool Co-operative Society. In 1923 he set up a tea importing business in Dublin with offices at North Wall which marketed a brand of tea called 'Joy of Home'. The firm also exported tea and had offices in London and Chicago.

John Hughes was a strong supporter of the Nationalist cause. He made large contributions to Sinn Féin and later to Fianna Fáil. He was associated with the foundation of the *Irish Press* and was on the Board of Directors until his death, in 1934. When he died, the *Irish Press* quoted Éamon de Valera as saying of him, 'He was one of the grandest Irishmen I have ever met.' On his return to Ireland, John Hughes purchased a number of farms, among them the Westby estate. He never lived at High Park but put in a manager to run the estate and set about gaining possession of a number of fields which had been alienated in the recent past.

John Hughes was a man who contributed to various worthy causes. In a letter dated 17 October 1927, he offered High Park to Frank Whitney at a bargain price. It was shortly after Frank had met John Hughes and his wife at Ardnacrusha. The letter reads as follows:

> I am of opinion your appeal is the same Missionary Society which I gave £1,000 to in July 1927. See enclosed acknowledgments for same.
>
> If your Society intends purchasing an Irish Property I have a fine property in Co. Wicklow known as The Westby Estate about 450 acres mansion house and farm. House and farm buildings are in perfect repair, a lovely place about 80 acres wood, a small river, a tributary of the Slaney. It would be worth looking at and price about one fourth its value, near Kiltegan and Baltinglass.
>
> P.S. Let me know if your appeal is for same Society as the Father Slattery's.

Frank replied to the letter pointing out that he had no connection with Father Slattery (probably a member of the Society of African Missions) and expressing interest in the property. A letter which Frank wrote to the *Sunday Press*, in February 1972, takes up the story:

> Between 1927 and 1929 there was much correspondence between John Hughes and this writer; there were a few very pleasant visits to Mr. Hughes's home outside Dublin and also visits to High Park, Kiltegan, which Mr. Hughes had purchased prior to my meeting him in 1927. In one of those visits to High Park the then parish priest of Mohill, Canon Masterson, later V.G. of Ardagh and Clonmacnoise, played a prominent part as advisor on the suitability of High Park as a home for the proposed Missionary Society.
>
> After High Park was pronounced suitable Mr. Hughes gave a provisional gift of High Park, the proviso being: (1) that Dr. Cullen gave permission to have the Society established in his diocese. (2) that Rome grant permission to found the new Society. Dr. Cullen gave his permission wholeheartedly subject to approval from Rome for the project.

This letter was written to correct a story told in a previous issue of the *Sunday Press*, that John Hughes had bumped into Pat Whitney and Bishop Cullen in the early twenties while all three were 'taking the air' at Kiltegan. It is the only document I have found which indicates that Bishop Cullen had been approached about the proposed Society before Pat Whitney returned from Nigeria in 1929. The purpose of the letter was to support Frank's own role in founding St Patrick's Missionary Society and it claimed that it was he who first approached Bishop Cullen on the matter. It can be presumed that the approach was made with Pat Whitney's knowledge and also with the blessing of Bishop Shanahan who was actively involved in the plans for the new Society, at that time. When Pat did return, he met John Hughes and later on got the latter to write the following letter to Bishop Cullen:

> I am the present owner of the Westby Estate, High Park, Co. Wicklow near Kiltegan. I am prepared to convey over to Rev. Fr. Whitney in the interest of the Maynooth Nigerian Missionary Priests whom he represents: The Mansion House with the garden and Demesne land, at least twenty Irish acres free of rent adjoining, as a beginning and aid to their work.

John Hughes had given up any idea he had of selling the land, however cheaply. He knew, by now, that the Whitneys had little or no money. He did not offer the entire property, as he had intended earlier, but gave the house, the walled garden and a few fields. It was a measure of John Hughes's sense of responsibility towards his own property. He knew that the two young priests had little interest in farming and that their thoughts were far away in a remote corner of Africa. He decided to hand over the property gradually as the new Society became established, thus enabling the priests to learn how to run it in a viable way. After all the required permissions were received, the first portion was handed to the Society. John Hughes retained the rest of the estate which was managed by a steward named Charles Caffrey. Later, that steward took charge of the Society portion and John Patrick Hughes, a son of John Hughes, took over the main farm. He was in very poor health and it was hoped that the Wicklow air would help him to recover.

From the correspondence of the next few years, John Hughes emerges as a kindly man who liked the young priests and did his best to help them in matters relating to the house and lands. To prepare for their coming he had the house repaired. He had fruit trees and vines planted in the garden and 500 wallflowers in front of the house. He had his men cut timber for the fires and he sent six tons of 'best Wigan coal' and advised: 'a little coal with the firewood will make good fires, and will be less difficult to handle as all the rooms including the basement will require fires for a week or two'. He bought them a milch cow at Baltinglass fair having previously warned by letter: 'the cow must not get into the field where she will get at the yew trees, as they are considered deadly for cattle'. He later bought them two pigs and put more stock on the Society farm. He had an arch made for the gate with the new name of the house, Our Lady of Africa, worked into it. He purchased a sideboard for the dining room which had once been in the mansion which became Kylemore Abbey and sent it to Kiltegan along with a press for vestments.

He was delighted to learn that seven priests had volunteered for Nigeria in 1930 and when he heard that they were coming to Kiltegan for a week he instructed the steward to give 'a couple of best lambs for the dinner'. He also arranged with the Civic Guards to issue Pat with a licence for a .22 rifle which was kept at High Park. He suggested that 'some of the Fathers, before going away to Africa might like to practise with this rifle, as I understand there are numerous wild beasts in the forest, in which they may have to travel through'. One of them did try it out on the wildlife around Kiltegan and according to Pat: 'a rabbit sat up and listened while three shots were fired at him out of it, then in disgust he went away'.

For the next four years John Hughes was friend and father-figure to the priests in Kiltegan. He gave advice freely. He suggested that they mobilise the local residents to apply for electricity from the Shannon Scheme. He advised on insurance, land valuation and other matters. He was slow, however, to hand over the entire estate. The priests were not good managers. On a visit in August 1930, he was displeased by the work of the two men employed in the garden and wondered 'how in the world they have been spending their time'. In 1931, there was no hay saved as Frank had let the cows into the meadow while Pat was in Nigeria. John Hughes concluded that the only hope for the farm was a number of brothers to work it. Pat asked the Abbot of the Cistercian Monastery, Mount Melleray, to loan him a few brothers but he was refused. John Hughes suggested that brothers be recruited for the Society and wrote to Pat Whitney, in January 1931:

> In my opinion the only chance of your raising food, and getting successful financial results from the land is, that you get working

brothers, say three farmers, one gardener and one carpenter to commence with—young men, farmers' sons, between the ages of twenty and thirty, who are prepared to devote their lives and labours to the support of your society . . . I feel sure that unless you can get brothers to work for the Society, any additional land would only be a burden to you and would not cover expenses.

It was probably this advice which caused Pat to assemble a few candidates for brotherhood in Kiltegan in 1932, although he may also have been following the lead of the Society of St Columban which allowed membership to brothers. As a result of his concern for viability, John Hughes handed over the property to the Society in stages. The woods were handed over in December 1930, the farmyard in July 1931 and an additional forty-seven acres in May 1933. The remaining land came into the Society's possession in late 1933 but was not legally transferred until March 1935, one year after John Hughes's death.

John Hughes also purchased an old house at Aghavannagh not far from the Kiltegan property. It was one of a string of army barracks built on the military road between Dublin and Glenmalure after the 1798 rebellion. It was later a hunting lodge owned by Charles Stewart Parnell whose home 'Avondale' was not far away, and later still the country home of John Redmond. John Hughes wished to give it to the Society and pointed out that the hunting rights attached to the property would be a steady source of income. It was not to be. Because Aghavannagh was situated in the Archdiocese of Dublin, Archbishop Byrne had to be approached for permission to acquire the property. He refused on the grounds that there was a waiting list of Orders and Societies seeking admission to Dublin. There was no option but to decline the gift of Aghavannagh which later became a youth hostel run by 'An Oige'.

The priests felt confident in asking John Hughes for help and advice. He was asked for his lorry to carry catering equipment from Lalors in Naas to entertain the Maynooth choir in 1931. Transport was requested for altar stones from the North Wall, pipes for the central heating and a generator. Pat and Frank called on him regularly in Dublin. They invited John Hughes and his wife to attend the ordination of Charles Meehan, the Society's first student, on 21 June 1931. He was also invited to a farewell dinner at the Westbrook Hotel for the 1931 volunteers.

John Hughes died on 12 March 1934 and was survived by his wife and two sons. John Patrick, the son who had lived in Kiltegan, predeceased him by two weeks.

The Early Volunteers

Pat Whitney's appeal in Maynooth, made shortly after the inauguration of the Society in 1930, produced five volunteers who were ordained in June of that year. They were James Moynagh, Ciaran Ryan and Cornelius Plunkett, all from Ardagh, Tom McGettrick from Achonry and Patrick Costelloe from Elphin. Two priests from Meath also volunteered. They were Michael Kilmartin who had been ordained, in Rome, in 1921 and Hugh Conlon, ordained in Maynooth, in 1927. Pat Whitney's personal charisma played no small part in enticing them to volunteer.

Later, most of these men were to be ambivalent in their feelings towards Pat. They liked and respected him but they criticised him and never completely trusted him. On the other hand, many of the lay helpers who were closely associated with Pat, especially in the early years, were unwavering in their loyalty. The same is true of the early students although some of them recount incidents in which students were treated harshly. 'We would all die for him' is the verdict of Joe Kelly, one of the early students. The bishops and priests who dealt with him at close quarters were less unqualified in their praise. Pat's own ambivalence of character and action was responsible for this. Bishop Moynagh, in a memoir written in 1970, gives a description of Pat which seems very accurate. It is helpful towards an understanding of his actions during the early years of the Society's history. He writes:

> Familiar to all who knew him as Father Pat or P.J., he was man of remarkable personality. He had no desire to be the founder of a Society—in fact no ambition to be any sort of leader. His great wish would be, was in fact, to 'bush whack' among his beloved Ibos. He knew and loved them—and was ideally suited to pioneering among them. He was a man of extraordinary faith and unlimited courage—the faith concealed under a rugged, rather rollicking but extremely shrewd personality—what might be described by a literary person as 'subtle peasant cunning'. He had none of the academic polish or indeed aspirations that goes with academic achievements . . . Father P.J. would be typical of that [Maynooth] background 'pucks of brains', happy jolly personality, ever cracking jokes, treating life as great fun, shrewd knowledge of men, deep *unshakeable* faith, but a rather ruthless strain to his character with a touch of craft which prompted him to *enjoy* getting what he wanted, or thought necessary for the work, by rather devious ways rather than by honest straightforward request . . .

Add to all this a towering physical presence (he must have been 6'2" or 3"), massive striking face with alert smiling eyes, a face ever on the verge of breaking up into vast furrows of mirth, a deep bass voice ready to issue in gusts of thunderous jollity, all beneath a shock of beautiful jet black hair, immense physical strength—all add up to a very unusual intriguing personality.

Bishop Moynagh's pen picture gives an idea of Pat Whitney's strengths and weaknesses as he faced, almost single-handed, the task of establishing a missionary society at a time of world-wide economic crisis. His hopes lay with the rural population which he had successfully marshalled in support of the Holy Rosary Sisters, five years previously. In the early 1930s, however, there was less money than ever in rural Ireland due to the fall in world agricultural prices and the tariff dispute or 'economic war' with Britain. Furthermore, the Maynooth Mission to China had stolen all his thunder. Recognised as Ireland's *National* Missionary Organisation, it had been launched in a wave of missionary enthusiasm and it now boasted a network of 'associates' in nearly every parish and National School in Ireland. The Superiors of the Maynooth Mission to China did give Pat their support and advice but, nonetheless, his venture was very much 'bottom drawer', particularly in the eyes of the older Irish clergy whose admiration for the men who surrendered chairs in Maynooth for missionary work in China knew no bounds. Nor was Kiltegan a very desirable location from which to launch a nation-wide appeal. It was far away from any major centre of population and lacked telephone and electricity. Moreover, it was situated in a diocese already supporting a seminary which trained priests for overseas missions in Britain, America and Australia.

Pat Whitney was soon joined by his cousin Frank who had secured a release from his diocese, where he had worked as curate in Keadue, Co. Roscommon. Frank was born in Drumlish, Co. Longford in 1893. He attended St Mel's College, Longford and St Patrick's College, Maynooth and during that long period became very friendly with Pat. Frank was a sincere man who loved to tell stories, to visit his friends and to play cards. He was republican in sympathy and had a great attachment to his native place and to the people he grew up with. Not a natural leader himself, Frank lived in Pat's shadow and was always being egged on to greater things by his more charismatic cousin. His health was never great and his tour in Nigeria was very short. The climate did not suit him but apart from that he was unable to feel at home in a culture which was so totally alien to Ireland and Drumlish. Nor did he get on very well with the Holy Ghost Fathers whom he found much too cosmopolitan for comfort.

After a period of convalescence and a short time on promotion work in Killeshandra, he returned to his own diocese. He was well-liked as a curate in Keadue, where he is remembered as a mentor of the parish football team. Although no longer officially attached to the Nigerian mission, Frank Whitney looked after his cousin's interests in Ireland after the latter returned to Nigeria. He kept contact with benefactors and administered the contributions given for Pat's work. It is clear from his negotiations with John Hughes that he was still deeply committed to the mission in Nigeria. It was to be expected that he would volunteer to join his cousin as soon as the new Society was launched. He came to Kiltegan, in July or August 1930, with the intention of joining the Society although he could not have hoped to return to Nigeria on account of his state of health. He was to serve for six years on the Society administration and to do valuable work in the early years. When that came to an end, Frank was at a loss. As an Irish diocesan priest he would have fitted well into a less demanding parish. As a missionary who could not work on the missions and who could not find a niche for himself in the very limited Society operation in Ireland, he became isolated and disillusioned. He was scrupulously faithful to his priestly duties but found little to challenge him. He tended to blame others for his predicament and to live as independently as possible of the Society, careful not to make demands or to put himself under an obligation to anyone. He never developed close friendships within the Society, and kept people at a distance with an endless string of anecdotes. When he died in 1973, he was buried, according to his wishes, in his native Drumlish, in a cemetery which had once been the property of his own family. His choice was an expression of the alienation he felt from the Society he had helped to found and, at the same time, a tribute to Co. Longford and Drumlish, where he had truly felt at home.

The next priest to come to Kiltegan was Francis Hickey. He was always referred to as Father Hickey or 'the old man', a nickname which he won before the age of fifty. It was easy to be an old man in the early days in Kiltegan and there was a sense in which Father Hickey belonged to the nineteenth century, to a time when every bishop and priest was a 'gentleman and a scholar'. The great Irish churchmen of that century, Bishop Doyle, Archbishop McHale, Cardinal Cullen and Cardinal Moran of Sydney, were his heroes, and he basked vicariously in the glory that was theirs. Father Hickey was born in Ballinastraw near Tullow, Co. Carlow in 1887 into a well-to-do farming family. He was educated at Christian Brothers School, Carlow, at Knockbeg and at St Patrick's College, Carlow, where he was ordained in 1913, for Melbourne Archdiocese. He worked there for twelve years but decided not to return after home-leave in 1925 on account, it is said, of a disagreement with Archbishop Mannix. He was anxious to get into his home diocese of Kildare and Leighlin but Bishop Cullen was not willing to take him. He worked for a while in Birmingham and spent a short period as a novice with the Irish Vincentians but decided against joining the Order. He was still attached to Melbourne until such time as he should find an alternative diocese or institute, when Bishop Cullen recommended him to Pat Whitney. Pat was happy to take him although, at first, there was no question of admitting him to the Society, and his name does not appear, in Pat's letters, among those who were expected to join. He did join, however, on the day the Society was formally established, St Patrick's Day, 1932.

Father Hickey was a man of simple faith and a sincere and honest man. He was regarded as 'a very good priest' although a little eccentric. He found great security in the ritual and law of the Church and was more concerned that things would be done well and according to the book than he was in exploring new ideas or looking for new ways. This frame of mind was shared by Frank Whitney but was foreign to Pat who found it difficult to be patient with the prudence and caution of his two colleagues. However, after five years of wandering, Father Hickey was ready and willing to throw himself wholeheartedly into the new venture. He had his own car, known to the students as 'The Golden Arrow' and he used his personal money to furnish a chapel in one of the reception rooms of High Park House.

With these two companions, Pat set about establishing a promotion network exactly as he had done in Killeshandra five or six years before. He set up an office in the house and employed three secretaries. Maura Young from Dublin had been with him in Killeshandra, and Noreen Rodgers from Keadue and Norah Leydon from Kilmactranny, Co. Sligo were contacted through friends. Norah Leydon later joined Marie Martin to become one of the first group of girls to enter the Medical Missionaries of Mary. She had met Marie Martin at Kiltegan, where the latter was a frequent visitor and was helping to decorate the house. Norah Leydon took the name, Sister Patrick, and, nearly sixty years later, she told the story of how she had come to be in Kiltegan. One

Sunday, after Mass, her father was approached by Pat's sister Mrs Gardiner, who told him that her brother was looking for a girl with secretarial training. Norah had just finished in Maguire's Secretarial College in Dublin and agreed to take the job. Pat met her in the Westbrook Hotel, a popular clerical meeting place, and took her to Kiltegan. He did much of his recruitment in this way. Many of the staff were people from his own home place and a few were relatives. They included a cousin, Maura Whitney, who was housekeeper for a short time.

A secretary's pay was small—£4 a month—and the hours were long, often extending far into the night when there was a lot of mail to be prepared. Pat acquired a few battered typewriters and an old Gestetner. Mailing lists were compiled from various sources. John Hughes was asked for a list of his customers, most of whom were shopkeepers, and he sent on not only the names and addresses but the envelopes already addressed. Letters of appeal were sent out and the resulting contributions, usually sixpence or a shilling, were acknowledged. Frank and Father Hickey travelled to schools and parish halls and gave talks illustrated by a slide show. Miteboxes were distributed to schools and shops while children were given 'prick cards' on which the prick of a pin indicated the payment of one penny. Pat also produced a souvenir booklet to mark the foundation of the Society. It was nicely printed with plenty of photographs and a lot of information about the missions in Nigeria. It carried messages from Archbishop Hinsley, Bishop Cullen and Bishop Shanahan.

In January 1931, the promotion effort got a great boost from the publication of a Society magazine. It was called *St Patrick's Missionary Bulletin* and was printed in Longford by the company which printed the *Longford Leader*.

Hand in hand with this promotion work went the renovation and furnishing of High Park House, now officially called 'The House of Our Lady of Africa', although the name never took on. Within a year, a bath had been installed and also a central heating system. The house was wired for electricity and a second-hand generator was purchased from Count John McCormack.

With all the activity, Pat had little time to concentrate on briefing the seven priests who had volunteered for the missions. They came to Kiltegan for a week in July and Pat gave them a few talks. Bishop Shanahan joined them for two days. Afterwards they went to Dublin where they were supplied with Mass boxes, tropical outfits and white soutanes by the Sisters of the Sodality of St Peter Claver, a sodality that was to become an indispensable part of the support system on which missionaries going out from Kiltegan were to depend. Founded in 1894 by an Austrian noblewoman, Marie Therese Ledochowska, it catered for the needs of missionaries and their converts. By means of a threefold membership of sisters, extern members and promoters, the sodality supplied, and continues to supply, money and equipment for nearly every aspect of missionary work. Kitting out the new missionaries and packing and dispatching their boxes were among the most appreciated services rendered to the 1930 group and to the many groups which followed in their footsteps. Not everything could be got in Dublin, however, and things like sun-helmets and mosquito boots would have to wait for a visit to Horne Brothers and Co. in Liverpool. Meanwhile the volunteers spent August and September with their families and paid a farewell visit to Maynooth before sailing to Liverpool on 28 September. On 1 October 1930, they set out for Nigeria aboard the *Appam*, in the company of Bishop Shanahan and a number of other missionaries. There were five Holy Ghost Fathers apart from the Bishop, one brother and three Holy Child Sisters. The Sisters had been recruited by Archbishop Hinsley to do medical and educational work in the area assigned to the new Society.

The presence of the Holy Child Sisters was very encouraging for Pat Whitney as his new Missionary Society set about its work. The Congregation of the Holy Child Jesus was founded in England in 1846 and had become expert in the education of girls. The story of its foundation is an extraordinary one. The Foundress was Cornelia Connelly, an American wife and mother, who took religious vows simply in order to make it possible for her husband, Pierce Connelly, to become a Catholic priest. Nicholas Wiseman, later Cardinal Archbishop of Westminster, came to know her through English Catholics in Rome and invited her to found an Order of teaching sisters in England, devoted to the higher education of girls. In spite of many difficulties which included harassment by her husband, she succeeded in establishing the Order internationally and in laying the foundations for a tradition of high quality education.

Sister Magdalen Walker had been at school with the Holy Child Sisters from the age of nine and it was she who was responsible for getting them to come to Calabar. On his visit to Calabar, in 1929, Archbishop Hinsley was convinced that an Order of sisters was required to develop Sister Magdalen's work. She suggested the Holy Child Sisters since repeated requests to her own congregation, the Irish Sisters of Charity, had fallen on deaf ears. The Apostolic Delegate approached the Holy

Child Superiors and arranged that Bishop Shanahan should make a formal request. As the sisters were to work in the area assigned to St Patrick's Missionary Society, the Archbishop arranged that Pat Whitney would meet the Mother General and discuss the situation in Calabar with her. The fact that such a distinguished Order of nuns would be co-workers with the Society was a great boost to the founder. It was, however, a cause of great dismay in Killeshandra where Mother Xavier and Bishop Finegan felt annoyed that another group of sisters was being called in to undertake missionary work for which the Holy Rosary Sisters had been founded.

Calabar

The provinces of Calabar and Ogoja had been assigned to the Society but the Bishop agreed that the Holy Ghost Fathers would service Ogoja for the time being. This left Calabar, an area of 6,000 square miles and about a million inhabitants, as the area of operation for the diocesan priests. There were two separate missions or 'parishes', each of them serviced from a residential station. One of these was Calabar, opened in 1903, and the other Anua, opened in 1914, each with a normal complement of three priests. According to the Holy Ghost *Bulletin de la Congregation*, Calabar and Anua had 500 out-stations in 1929. Many of these had started off as schools but following new Government regulations for education in 1926, the vast majority ceased to be maintained as official schools but continued as centres for teaching catechism. For example, there were 411 schools in Anua in 1926 and only 114 in 1930.[3] There had been tremendous expansion over a relatively short period and the mission complexes or 'compounds' were well up to the standards of the time. This description of Anua is taken from Pat Whitney's diary for 1926:

> Anua central mission station is one of the most beautifully laid out and perfectly-built stations in the whole Vicariate. There is a symmetry and completeness about the place, that is difficult even to equal. A beautiful drive, bordered with low evergreens, leads up to the house, which is a two-storied bungalow of modern type. On the left hand side of the entrance is situated the Church, which is a building capacious enough to accommodate about 4,000 people. At right angles at either side of the Church are buildings: boarders' houses, houses for mission boys, and teachers' residences; in the background is an extensive carpenters' shop with buildings

attached to accommodate the workmen. The two full-sized football fields that are passed on the drive, give a sense of ample room, and the neatly laid-out flower beds in front of the Fathers' house give one the feeling that here the Fathers have a home to be desired.

The Holy Ghost Fathers introduced the new priests to the work, giving them a crash course in the local languages to enable them to hear confessions and to master the elaborate greeting rituals which were observed in the area. There was instant rapport between the two groups although it became widely known, before long, that Bishop Shanahan intended to move the Holy Ghosts to other missions which were in great need of priests. When word of this reached Kiltegan, Pat Whitney tried to prevent it and even appealed to the Apostolic Delegate to intervene. He was especially anxious that Phil O'Connor, a man of exceptional personality and talent, would be left to give guidance to the young men. Tom Ronayne was in Calabar but the presence of at least one other experienced missionary was desirable. Pat's intervention was unsuccessful and all the Holy Ghosts were gone from the area within a few months of the arrival of the volunteers. Only Tom Ronayne was left to give guidance to the newcomers. Vincent Davey, Joe McCloskey and John Browne had opted to remain in Eke and Emekuku where they were running busy and successful parishes. Although they were too far away to be of any help to the new arrivals, they had not cut their links with the new Society and were still contemplating whether or not they would join it.

The newcomers faced many difficulties and problems. There was the loneliness, especially acute for the three who were living alone, James Moynagh, Tom McGettrick and Corney Plunkett. Tom McGettrick writes of this loneliness:

> My trouble in Oron was that I had no one to talk to; the teachers in the school could hardly speak English and many an evening my thoughts went back to Maynooth days and the football games and handball alleys. I had more or less made up my mind that when I finished my tour of 3½ years I would stay in Ireland, but that loneliness completely evaporated when a new priest came to live with me in October 1931.[4]

Another element of life on the missions was the hostility of the Protestant missionaries of the United Free Church of Scotland, the Primitive Methodists, the Wesleyans and the interdenominational Qua

Ibo mission. The time was not noted for ecumenical dialogue and, besides, the Catholics had refused to participate in a division of the area among the various missionary groups as the others had done. Tension was further heightened by the fact that many of the mission stations had come over from one or other of the Protestant Churches and many prominent Catholics had been baptised in a Protestant church and some had been Church leaders. The Irish diocesan priests were, from the beginning, drawn into a spirit of mutual suspicion and rivalry. Protestant opposition was a feature of every advance made, especially when it concerned the opening of a new school. James Walsh, writing in *St Patrick's Missionary Bulletin* in 1934, is in no doubt about the negative influence of the Protestant Churches. He writes: 'When the first fathers arrived they found that the struggle was not so much against paganism as against the most powerful forces of heresy.'[5]

Paganism did not pose so great a threat because the fashion of the time dictated a move away from the traditional ways, especially on the part of the young. This is not to say that traditional religion was a spent force. The priests were well aware of its power and the extent to which it permeated people's lives. They recognised its positive effects in creating an atmosphere in which supernatural forces were accepted as an integral part of life. They recognised, too, that traditional religion and its institutions contributed to order and harmony within society and produced local leaders of high calibre. It was the negative effects, however, which made the greatest impression and which found their way more frequently into the promotional missionary literature. There was much emphasis on the influence of evil spirits, superstitious practices and witchcraft. Overt hostility was, however, very rare and the missionaries were largely unopposed in their day-to-day ministry. In times of crisis, however, the old religion tended to experience reawakening. 1930 was such a time. The collapse of the world economy, in 1929, had affected eastern Nigeria very badly. The palm oil trade was severely hit and the resulting hardship, on top of the threat of a poll-tax, caused people to look again to the old ways. Traditional secret societies gained new strength and became more courageous in confronting European influences. Bishop Moynagh writes of his first appointment at Ifuho:

> Also there was an outbreak of the pagan society called 'Eka Ekong'. It was viciously pagan. They went in and made pagan sacrifices on the altars of the weak churches. Loyal church members had to carry machetes to protect themselves and their wives going to Sunday

service. They once interrupted me at Adiasim when I was hearing confession until I was 'saved' by Chief Nyoki, the Okuku of the clan. Eke Ekong were also anti-government because of the economic collapse. Many of the Catechumens were drawn into this and it began to flourish all over Annang country and down to Essene. It was a very pagan play [*sic*] and there were all kinds of sacrifices and the young men joined it because there was no longer work for them selling palm fruits or climbing the palm trees to cut the fruit.[6]

The economic collapse also created personal financial problems for the young priests. They inherited a fairly complex structure with a large number of paid staff. Most of these were teachers and, as there were only a few schools which qualified for any Government grant, the salaries had to come from the local community. As a result of the economic situation, the money was not there and large numbers of teachers were not paid. This put great pressure on the priests. Bishop Moynagh recalls that his predecessor, Father Steigler, advised him to close down his out-stations until the crisis passed—a move which he managed to avoid but only with great difficulty. Mass offerings sent from home enabled the priest to live from day to day although the reduction in the local collections made it difficult to pay those employed around the mission compound.

There was another factor which affected the income of the various missions. It was the contributions of the local Catholics, given as annual dues and on the reception of the sacraments. In the past, it had been an important source of income and the priests were strict in exacting it. A person presenting himself or herself for any sacrament would have to satisfy the priest or the catechist that all dues were paid or that there was a very serious reason for which an exception might be made. The young priests felt that this approach was too severe, especially at a time of economic crisis, and they were much more ready to make exceptions. The result was a big drop in the local contributions. Anua mission, which had been financially healthy, was soon in serious difficulty, and other missions were hit in the same way. It was an issue that was destined to appear again and again in the subsequent history of the Society. Strictness was interpreted as associating the sacraments too closely with money, while leniency was patronisation and failure to encourage the local Church to be self-sufficient.

This was not the only aspect of pastoral policy which was criticised by the young priests. They felt that the instruction given before Baptism had not been adequate and that the people had a very poor knowledge of the faith. This was a result of Bishop Shanahan's policy which concentrated on planting the Church, and was prepared to postpone in-depth instruction until a later stage. The man who had been in charge of Anua for eight years before the changeover had been a firm believer in this policy. He was a celebrated Frenchman called Paul Biechy who later became Bishop of Brazzaville in the Congo. He opened as many schools as possible and was more interested in their evangelising role than in their academic standard. He was much loved by the people and was remembered for his great black beard, his rapport with the chiefs and his gifts of tobacco to help with negotiations. It was of him or of Father Bailey, one of his assistants, that Bishop McGettrick wrote with accustomed humour: 'Between 1926 and 1927 one Holy Ghost Father went around the Oron Parish with a watering can and baptised thousands of people.'[7] The young priests reacted against this and from the beginning they emphasised the teaching of catechism and the training of catechists and they worked towards the establishment of an organised catechumenate.

There was a lot of criticism of the newcomers among the laity, especially in the vicinity of Anua, on the grounds that they lacked maturity and did not display the priestly decorum of their predecessors. It was true that they were very young men compared to Paul Biechy and the other missionaries whom they had replaced. The people were sorry to lose Biechy whose leadership added prestige to the Church in the area and had the spin-off effect of providing more employment around the mission. With his transfer, Anua lost its position as the centre of the Catholic Church in the area and became one of four missions of equal status, each with a resident priest. This was not the doing of the new priests but, nonetheless, they become the focus of criticism and discontent. Many members of their church committees had been Protestant elders before joining the Catholic Church. They were used to running things their own way and were not disposed to accept the decisions of their juniors. This attitude did not have any long-term effects and, in time, the new priests gained the confidence of the people. But it was irritating and distressing for men who had only the very best intentions as they undertook their first priestly assignments. It also served to emphasise their inexperience of priestly ministry either at home or abroad and, especially, their almost total lack of missionary training and orientation.

Sister Magdalen Walker, who had been joined by the Holy Child Sisters in Calabar, made a similar assessment of the young priests. Her school was going ahead successfully but her big preoccupation was the establishment of an African Congregation from the nucleus of a group of girls which she had gathered around her. She did not think that the newcomers would be of any help to her in this work as they were not Religious and were still very young. Having lost confidence in Tom Ronayne, she tried to have Paul Biechy reappointed to the area to act as Spiritual Director to the emerging congregation. The request was refused by the Holy Ghost Superiors in Paris but it did not help relations between the priests and Sister Magdalen whom they found condescending and aloof. It was another small but significant irritant, especially for those who were stationed close to this middle-aged nun whose reputation as an educator was widely acknowledged and who had been for seven years the only nun in the Vicariate of Southern Nigeria.[8]

There were other tribulations too, such as malaria and dysentry, but in spite of everything the newcomers settled down very quickly. They visited the out-stations on a regular basis and managed to keep them going until the economic situation improved. They had motorcycles but the narrow bush paths often prevented their use. On such journeys the priest used a bicycle or went on foot accompanied by porters who carried 'loads', consisting of a camp bed, a mass box, a box of food, a box of clothes and a box of kitchen utensils. They liked the Nigerian people, most of whom were farming folk whose way of life had a lot in common with the background from which they themselves had come. They were forced to lean heavily on the church committees and this, in turn increased their respect for the laity and taught them the importance of lay co-operation. Once a month, or on a Feast Day, like St Patrick's Day, they came together at Anua or Calabar to celebrate and to share their experiences of different areas and different tribes.

It was not until 1936 that the priests in Calabar decided to pay special attention to education. Before that they were concentrating on keeping some 700 stations ticking over by means of two-monthly visits. The pace was very leisurely compared to that of the Holy Ghosts in Iboland. Bishop Moynagh emphasises this in the handwritten memoir already quoted above:

> Where the C.S.Sp. [Holy Ghost] men were dealing in thousands, 5,000, 6,000, 10,000, even 20,000 in a large station and whole clan areas coming *en masse* into the Church, we were dealing in scores or hundreds at most . . .
>
> Where the C.S.Sp. men were building mission houses, churches on a grand scale, we had to be content with simple bungalows, often of mud and wattle.

Apart from occasional visits from Holy Ghost Fathers, the diocesan priests were left to work things out for themselves. Tom Brosnahan and Tom Fox who had travelled out with them on the boat paid a much appreciated visit. Phil O'Connor, whom they liked very much, continued to take an interest even after he had been moved out of the area. Bishop Shanahan they saw little of. He ceased to be Vicar Apostolic in July 1931 but remained on in Nigeria until April 1932 when he went home to Ireland for retirement. Bishop Heerey visited frequently to give confirmation, to inspect the records and to discuss progress. They found him a hard taskmaster. The arrival of reinforcements at the end of 1931 gave a great boost to the work. Those who were living alone had the benefit of help and companionship and everyone felt encouraged that the response from Maynooth was continuing. The newcomers were: Edward Curran from Elphin diocese, Peter Boylan from Kildare and Leighlin, Thomas McDonald from Armagh and Charles Meehan who was officially a priest of the Vicariate of Southern Nigeria. Charles Meehan had been recruited by Pat Whitney while the latter was in Killeshandra. He studied in Mount Melleray seminary for two years and then went to All Hallows where he was ordained in 1931. Frank and Pat Whitney paid his fees in All Hallows out of monies given to help the mission work. They were also involved in the arrangements for his ordination and invited John Hughes to attend. As the Society was not yet established canonically, Charles Meehan was ordained for Southern Nigeria in the understanding that he would join the Society as soon as this became possible.

Relationships

St Patrick's Missionary Society existed on a trial basis through 1930 and 1931. It had no members. It did have a house in Kiltegan, held in trust, and a territory in Nigeria not yet separated from the Vicariate of Southern Nigeria. Pat Whitney had been appointed as Superior of the house by Bishop Cullen and it was accepted that he would handle all matters arising in connection with the Society at home and on the missionfield. This was the normal procedure followed in the foundation of a new Order or Society within the Church. The intention was that those who wished to join would live as a close-knit group and discuss together the many implications of founding a Society. This is what happened with the Columbans, all but two of whom were in Ireland in 1916. They worked out of a base in Dublin before they rented Dalgan in 1917 and had an opportunity to get to know and appreciate one another, to work on the Constitutions and to lay the foundation of a spirit or esprit de corps which would be unique to the group. St Patrick's Missionary Society was denied this normal process of evolution. Permission from Rome had come so quickly and so unexpectedly that only a tiny group of would-be members existed. They were Pat Whitney and his cousin Frank in Ireland, Tom Ronayne in Calabar and Vincent Davey and Joseph McCloskey in Iboland. John Browne, also in Iboland, had not committed himself, and Pat Kelly, who was home on leave, was willing to join or at least to return under Society auspices but was refused permission by the Bishop in Nigeria, pending an investigation into accusations made against him there.[9] The seven volunteers recruited in 1930 were not recruited for membership of the Society; they were to go as temporary volunteers and any decision they might make about joining the Society was a long way down the road.

Pat Whitney had expected that all his colleagues in Nigeria would move to the Calabar area after it had been entrusted to the Society. While they were delighted that Pat got on so well in Rome, they were not prepared to move out of Eke and Emekuku, at least for the present. Pat had no authority to command them to move nor had they any obligation to go as their agreement was with the Vicar Apostolic. It would have been difficult for them to walk away from two huge missions where they had many programmes in hand and where their services were badly needed, in favour of missions which were, by comparison, inactive and undeveloped. Besides, they expected the Holy Ghost Fathers to remain in the Calabar area until the new volunteers had arrived and were well established. Tom Ronayne was in Calabar so, at first, there seemed no great urgency for the others to move.

Then, there were signs that Pat Whitney was making decisions without their consent. The first of these was the decision to bring Frank to Kiltegan with the intention of joining the Society. He asked the advice of the men on the missions; and Tom Ronayne, speaking for everyone in Nigeria, objected on the grounds that Frank was not fit to return to Nigeria. This was the important consideration for them and they did not envisage members who were incapable of active service on the missions. Pat was very upset by their advice on Frank's proposed membership and chose to ignore it. Something similar happened when Pat informed them that Pat Kelly would accompany the first group of volunteers. Again Tom Ronayne objected, on the grounds that there were accusations against Pat Kelly to be cleared up and that this could not be done until Bishop Shanahan returned to Nigeria. Pat decided to send him anyway and it was only when Bishop Heerey contacted Archbishop Hinsley that the decision was rescinded.

The lack of unity between Pat Whitney and Tom Ronayne was a constant feature of the first years and provides a key to understanding some of the early difficulties. Tom Ronayne's tendency to speak his mind had put a strain on his relations with most figures in authority and Pat was to be no exception. On the other hand, there were traits in Pat's personality which provoked Tom Ronayne. Bishop Moynagh sketches these as follows:

> . . . Father Ronayne an over-conscientious and meticulously correct man—a bit legalistic if you wish—a man whom it was thought would be the first Superior General—most correct, gracious in public relations, clearly deeply spiritual. Father Ronayne could not stomach Father Whitney's *drive*, regardless of the lesser illegalities, regardless of whose feet got trodden on, his readiness to *use* people without consulting them and laughing them off when they protested.[10]

Both were sincere and committed men who respected one another but could not work together. This was disastrous for the Society when all authority was vested in Pat, and Tom Ronayne was the only one on the missions who had committed himself.

When the new volunteers went out in 1930, Pat appointed one of them, Michael Kilmartin, as Director. The post did not mean much in terms of authority but the appointment was nonetheless a slight on Tom Ronayne and one which he felt very keenly.[11]

The volunteers of 1930

The seven volunteers were surprised to find on their arrival in Nigeria, in 1930, that of the Maynooth men, only Ronayne was in the Calabar area. Pat had given them to understand that all four would have moved there. He also led them to expect an enthusiasm for the Society among the older volunteers which was not there. Pat was communicating his own enthusiasm and, in fairness to him, he had hoped that the men in Nigeria would move to Calabar. He was at fault in not explaining the latest developments to the new men before they went out. Indeed, he may not have fully realised how much in the dark the men in Nigeria were. They had planned for the Society with the idea that there would be a long period of preparation and that it would be established when the priests on the mission were ready for it. Instead, they got the news that the Society was already in existence and that it had been given territory far away from where most of them worked. They had played no part in negotiations. What news they had was gleaned from occasional letters. The huge territory was out of all proportion to the resources available. Indeed they could hardly believe that the project was viable at all. But Pat's failure to brief the new men on the latest developments was characteristic of him. Why should he sow any doubts in their minds as they would have to adapt to the changed situation when they got out there, in any case. Pat never saw the point of bidding the devil 'Good Morrah' until well after he had met him. The outcome was that the newcomers concluded that Pat had been less than forthright with them.

This opinion was strengthened by the financial difficulties which they experienced from the start. Pat had given them to understand that finance would not be a problem, that school grants and contributions from the faithful would cover all expenses. In giving this assurance, Pat was totally sincere. This had been his experience in Iboland and he did not realise that the same did not apply in the new area, where Catholics were very few and people in general were impoverished by the collapse of the palm-oil trade. When the young priests experienced hardship and worry they concluded that Pat had kept the true situation from them. When they asked for money he had none to send and they felt he was using contributions in order to establish the Society in Ireland to the neglect of the missions. Many years later Bishop McGettrick, who was one of the first group, recalled the resentment they felt but added:

> We were much too hard on Pat. We did not realise that he had nothing to give us.[12]

Pat Whitney was sending Mass offerings, however, and these were a lifeline for the men in Nigeria. The offerings came from priests in Ireland who could not honour all the requests they received to have Masses said. By transferring the obligation to offer Mass and the accompanying stipend, the priests were helping their colleagues on the missions to survive and to further the work. In 1927, Tom Mulvaney wrote in a letter to his brother, Father Patrick Mulvaney:

> There is nothing as valuable as 5/- intentions as I explained before, as it enables a priest here to support his house well.

In 1931, the average stipend was still 5/- but it retained its importance in maintaining the mission house and also financing other projects. Pat Whitney had more than enough Mass offerings to distribute. He was able to supply diocesan volunteers who did not have their own sources and also to send some to the Holy Ghost Fathers in Nigeria. Apart from that, Pat could not afford to send any financial help to those who were working under the banner of St Patrick's Society. He was by nature a generous man but found that the running of the house in Kiltegan and the transport and printing costs involved in launching a promotion campaign consumed the contributions that came in. Besides, he had to refund £600 to Bishop Shanahan for passages and equipment for the 1930 group. Pat saw no difficulty in accepting responsibility for these expenses when he was bargaining for territory with the Vicar Apostolic, in Maynooth. When the bill arrived, early in 1931, he complained bitterly about it to Archbishop Hinsley and to Caesar Pecorari. Pat found that he had nothing left to send to the priests on the field and, moreover, he did not fully appreciate the difficulties involved in working in the Calabar area as against Iboland where he had worked himself.

It fell to Tom Ronayne to communicate to Kiltegan the general dissatisfaction among the priests. This added to the tension between Pat and himself. Before long, the grievances were widely known and had reached the ears of Archbishop Hinsley who was then in Mombasa. In January 1931 he wrote to Pat:

> I do not know all the ins and outs of the misunderstanding but I am informed that the new men out there are discouraged. They thought to find all the Maynooth men working with them, and now it seems there is only Ronayne with whom you the Superior are not on good terms . . . It is worth any sacrifice to change the state of things and prevent a complete collapse. A letter of condescension and of humility from you to Ronayne might do the great deed and produce unanimity.

The priests prevailed on Pat to go to Nigeria on a visit. He was very reluctant 'as that would greatly interfere with development at home' and he attempted to persuade Tom Ronayne to come home. The latter refused and Pat finally agreed to go to Nigeria. He travelled out in April 1931 and returned in June. It was a good visit during which difficulties were ironed out and mutual trust was restored. Tom Ronayne agreed to join the Society as soon as it was formally established. He was appointed to the post of Director to replace Mick Kilmartin who stepped down to facilitate the appointment of the most senior and most experienced man to the post. Vincent Davey decided not to commit himself to joining the Society for the present but promised to reconsider when his three-year tour at Eke came to an end, in July 1932. Joe McCloskey and John Browne made no commitment. Pat Whitney met Bishop Shanahan and Bishop Heerey and reached agreement with them on practical matters relating to the pastoral care of the area.

Towards Official Recognition

On his return to Ireland Pat plunged once again into the promotion effort. He was busy with arrangements for the second group of volunteers who were due to go out in October. Appeals for funds were bearing fruit and contributions were acknowledged in *St Patrick's Missionary Bulletin*. Issues of this magazine in 1931 record a rapid growth of support for the Society. One anonymous donor gave £1,000. There were numerous individual donations, and 'associates', many of them teachers, sent the contents of miteboxes and other collections. Pat's response to this generosity is friendly and direct: ''Tis the prayers and pennies that count,' he writes. Sister Mary Aquin, Convent of Mercy, Longford gets a special mention: 'Imagine, her mite-box collection was £17!' Pat Joe Cole is described as being 'constant as the Northern Star'. As a result of this campaign in the magazine and the funds raised on the lecture tours, Pat was able to send £700 to Tom Ronayne. Following an appeal through Archbishop Hinsley, Propaganda made a special grant of £400 which Pat also forwarded to Nigeria.

John Hughes had transferred to the Society a tract of woodland situated at the edge of the estate, in December 1930. In the following July, he gave the old farm buildings near the house, comprising the stables, a mill, a steward's house and other out-offices. Pat set about turning the buildings that were in poor condition into student accommodation. Already, more than ten students had expressed an interest. Mount Mellaray, All Hallows College and St Patrick's College, Carlow offered to educate students for the Society. In Carlow, a number of burses were set aside to pay the fees of four Kiltegan students.[13]

The Society is formally Established

In spite of a setback in January 1932, when two of the men in Nigeria, Hugh Conlon and Michael Kilmartin, returned to Ireland because of illness, the future looked bright for the Society. It was the year of the Eucharistic Congress in Dublin and the sixteenth centenary of the coming of St Patrick. Pat Whitney saw it as an appropriate time to press for the formal establishment of the Society. He wrote to Bishop Cullen, on 9 February 1932, asking him 'to canonically erect the Society, accept us as its first members and make the first appointments'. On 11 February, the Bishop submitted the Constitutions to Rome and requested permission to go ahead. Permission was granted and on St Patrick's Day, 1932, Patrick Whitney, Francis Hickey and Patrick Francis Whitney took the oath of temporary membership, in the presence of Bishop Cullen. Pat was appointed Superior General and Father Hickey, Bursar. There was no Vicar General although Frank and Father Hickey were to constitute the Superior General's Council.

St Patrick's Missionary Society was now canonically established as a Society of secular priests under the authority of the diocesan bishop. Surprisingly, no publicity was given to this development. There is no reference to the canonical erection of the Society in *St Patrick's Missionary Bulletin*; nor did Pat use his new title of 'Superior General' in the magazine. As far as the readers were concerned, the Society had been established in 1930 and was doing well, with the help of their contributions. Pat Whitney saw no need whatever to confuse them with canonical niceties.

5

Growth in the Midst of Difficulties

THE General Council of St Patrick's Missionary Society met for the first time on 19 March 1932, two days after the Society was officially founded.[1] Present were Pat Whitney, Frank Whitney and Father Hickey. Together, they comprised not only the governing council but also the entire Society. The first formal decision taken was to receive Tom Ronayne and Charles Meehan into the Society. Daniel Walsh C.S.Sp. was to be delegated to administer the oath of temporary membership to the two priests, both of whom were stationed in Calabar town.

In subsequent meetings, the question of admitting students was discussed. There were twenty students loosely attached to the Society who were studying in All Hallows, Mount Mellary, Wexford, Waterford and Carlow seminaries. It was decided that all those who had completed their Philosophy studies would come to Kiltegan for a year of probation, after which they would take the oath of temporary membership and then resume their theology studies in one or other of these seminaries.

It was planned to house the students in the farmyard, which was to be renovated to provide dormitory accommodation and other facilities. Accommodation was also needed for those who wished to become brothers, a number of whom were already resident in Kiltegan. At Pat Whitney's insistence, the steward's house, the best building in the farmyard, was reserved for them. In June, James Holloway, a young priest from Meath diocese who had just completed the postgraduate S.T.L. degree in Maynooth, applied to join. Around the same time, a student in second theology in Carlow named Patrick Kivlehan asked to be admitted. The Council decided to admit James Holloway but postponed Patrick Kivlehan's admission until he was ordained in two years' time.

On 24 September 1932, the first group of students began their year of probation in Kiltegan. It was to be a year devoted to prayer and the study of the Scriptures under the direction of Father Hickey. Eleven were admitted to the probation year. Of these, Jim Holloway was a priest while six of the students had completed two years of Philosophy study and four had just finished secondary school.[2] It was arranged that the group would do a 30-day retreat, following the Spiritual Exercises of St Ignatius Loyola in Dalgan with their counterparts in the Society of St Columban. The rest of the year was spent in Kiltegan in very spartan conditions. On 1 November 1932, two candidates were admitted to a separate probation programme for the brotherhood. They were John Bermingham and Kevin Rooney.

Problems in Nigeria

Not long after the foundation it became necessary for Pat Whitney to travel to Nigeria. The purpose of the journey was much the same as that of his earlier visit in 1931. The goodwill created by this first visit was short-lived. In March 1932, Pat sent copies of the Constitutions to Nigeria so that the priests there could study them. At the same time, he invited Tom Ronayne and Charles Meehan to take the oath of temporary membership. The latter accepted and became a member but Tom Ronayne refused. His objections were based on dissatisfaction with the Constitutions which was shared by the other priests on the mission. They had already received copies of the Columban Constitutions and were given to understand that the Society had adopted these Constitutions as its own.

When the text of the new Constitutions arrived it seemed to differ from its Columban model in certain important aspects. The priests in Nigeria were very much disappointed. They considered that Pat had changed the Constitutions without any reference to them. Tom Ronayne wrote to him:

> Briefly the new Constitutions cut out all dependence on the Sacred Congregation of Propaganda; they deprive everybody on the mission, Vicar Apostolic, Prefect Apostolic and other ecclesiastical Superiors of all voice in shaping the policy of the Society; they compel the mission to support the Society financially . . . and they make the priests religious instead of seculars as you yourself always insisted on.

Most of the discrepancies arose from the different ecclesiastical status of the two Societies. The Society of St Columban was answerable directly to Propaganda while St Patrick's was under the authority of the Bishop of Kildare and Leighlin. The Society of St Columban started out as a diocesan institute and was subject to the Bishop of Galway until it was declared a Society of Pontifical Rite, on 5 June 1925. From then on, it was directly under Propaganda and this fact was reflected in its Constitutions when they were sent to Nigeria for examination by the volunteer priests there. Later, when the St Patrick's Constitutions arrived they showed the Society to be subject to an Irish bishop. No explanation was given as to the fact that this was a necessary interim measure, and the priests whose trust in Pat Whitney was fragile, at the best of times, jumped to the conclusion that they had been misled. Pat's only mistake was his failure to explain the discrepancies. The Constitutions were an exact replica of the most recent Columban Constitutions, amended to allow for the difference in ecclesiastical status.

There was also a disagreement about Mass offerings which were crucial to the priests' survival in Calabar. Pat continued to send Mass requests but had begun to withhold some of the stipends. The priest was expected to offer the Mass for a specific intention while the money given for the Mass was retained in Kiltegan. This caused great resentment among the young priests especially in view of the fact that they were finding it hard to make ends meet. Bishop Moynagh recalls:

> Father P.J. assured us all would be well; we would be kept supplied with Mass stipends and occasional gifts from home. Mass stipends kept coming all right but after maybe six months we were told they were 'dry' intentions—the stipends were needed at home for the essential work of building the Society. There was an almighty outcry, of course![3]

Pat's argument was that the volunteer priests had agreed to forego some of their stipends in order to create a fund out of which end-of-tour allowances would be paid. By agreement, each priest was to receive £30 for every year spent on the missionfield. Pat claimed that he had put this proposal to the volunteers and that they had agreed to it. They all denied this. They accepted that he might have mentioned the matter in passing but denied that any agreement had been reached. It was not a very serious issue but, taken in conjunction with the Constitutions issue, it served to diminish Pat's credibility as a Superior and to increase the discontent among the men in Nigeria. Moreover, the matter was widely known outside the immediate circle of the volunteers and the image of the Society suffered as a result. In a friendly letter, written in April 1932, Daniel Walsh C.S.Sp. advised Pat to visit Nigeria. He wrote:

> Financially, things are as they were but are bound to improve with more people coming in. I heard some whisperings of the money for Mass intentions being retained at home. I would advise you to send on the money at any cost—without my Mass intentions I could never make ends meet and it must be much the same with them. Things are completely different since the price of palm oil went down. To my mind, if you could manage it, the best thing would be that you should come out here for a year or so, get to know the exact state of things, work with your men and win their confidence. If you intend forming a Society and getting the men out here to join up, you will have to come out. It would be a great pity to lose the services of these men, who are doing so well, have got to know the people and won their goodwill. They cannot be forced, they must be won.

At a Council meeting on 12 June 1931, Pat announced that he intended to go to Nigeria. It was decided at the same meeting, since Tom Ronayne had failed to take the oath, 'not to consider any further application from him'. This decision followed a meeting between Bishop Heerey and the General Council of the Society at which they decided that Tom Ronayne would be moved out of Calabar and stationed in the Holy Ghost section of the Vicariate.

Visit to Nigeria

Pat left for Nigeria on Wednesday 29 June. When he reached Calabar, he found Tom Ronayne preparing to go on home-leave. The two men discussed their differences and parted on good terms. It was arranged that Tom Ronayne would visit Kiltegan and discuss the question of joining the Society with the two Councillors. The young priests were very insistent that Tom Ronayne would return to the Calabar area after his leave. Pat Whitney had little choice but to agree, in spite of the previous arrangement with Bishop Heerey. It is a measure of the young men's lack of trust that they insisted that Pat should write a letter inviting Tom Ronayne to return and, in addition, that he should send a cable containing the same message to await Ronayne's arrival in Liverpool. It is clear that Tom Ronayne was held in very high regard by the priests. They resented any suggestion that he was in any way responsible for their disagreement with Pat Whitney. Nearly half a century later, James Moynagh and Tom McGettrick were at pains to restate this position and to emphasise that Tom Ronayne gave nothing but help and encouragement to them in the early years in Nigeria.

Once that matter was settled, Pat and the volunteer priests had some very fruitful discussions. Suspicion melted and agreement was reached. They discussed every aspect of life on the mission and worked out an agreement to be signed by each priest, governing relations with the Society, day-to-day life and home-leave. They agreed to be circumspect about future grievances and to refer them to the Superior in Kiltegan or to the Director in Nigeria. Prior to finalising the agreement, in September, Pat gave a number of spiritual conferences. He insisted that they should not sign the agreement until November, when they would have had ample time to reflect on it.

Bishop Heerey returned from Ireland in August and he and Pat had a number of meetings. In November, three new volunteers arrived. They were Hugh McGrath and Seamus Carraher of Armagh and Matthew Magrath of Dublin. This brought to twelve the number of priests present in Nigeria under Society auspices.

Pat Whitney was satisfied that a good working relationship had been built up with the volunteers. He decided to spend the rest of his visit in Ogoja, which had been without a resident priest for two years. It was typical of him to choose to work in the most remote area—it was then a 250-mile journey from Calabar as there was as yet no direct road. He built a house, later to be known as 'Pat's house'. It was renowned for its lack of amenities as much as for the eminence of the builder. Bishop McGettrick describes it as follows:

> It was a small house built with different materials—bricks, concrete blocks and mud. It was a low uncomfortable house and almost intolerable in the heat of the day. It remained the residence of the Fathers until it was replaced in 1940.[4]

He also visited the various stations and prepared the people for a confirmation tour soon to be undertaken by Bishop Heerey.

When Pat Whitney left Nigeria in May 1933 he was very pleased with what he had achieved. His time with the priests had restored harmony and encouraged them in their enthusiasm for mission work. At home, he found things equally encouraging. The first group of students were about to go home for summer vacation having successfully completed their spiritual programme. Nine were to be admitted to the

Society in September, after which the five who had done Philosophy would return to their respective colleges and the four freshmen would go to Carlow. Jim Holloway was to remain in Kiltegan as Spiritual Director of students while helping out in promotion work. This work had been going very well and the list of contributions, all of which were acknowledged in *St Patrick's Missionary Bulletin*, was growing longer every month. While Pat was away, the magazine was produced by Tom Lynch, a priest of Meath diocese who had worked in Australia and was semi-retired because of deafness. He had recently been involved in producing a diocesan newsletter in Mullingar.

The only big disappointment for Pat concerned Tom Ronayne with whom he had shared so much over the past twelve years. Tom Ronayne had come to Kiltegan in November and the two Councillors agreed to his admission. He wrote to Pat Whitney in Nigeria asking to be received into the Society. The letter failed to reach Pat and at Christmas he wrote to Tom Ronayne saying, 'If you do not intend to join the Society say so.' Ronayne was upset. He felt that Pat was deliberately frustrating his efforts to join without making his position clear. It was another example of the personality conflict that existed between them. He wrote to Pat and said he had finally decided not to join. A few months later he learned that Pat had not received his first letter. Once again he had misunderstood Pat's intentions. However, he decided to stick to his decision. A memoir he wrote in 1957 describes the accident which removed him from the Society and made it impossible for Pat to achieve a reconciliation that might have made the early years of the Society much happier for everyone. Tom Ronayne writes:

> Then came the climax. Soon after this in Spring 1933 Father Costelloe wrote in great distress, to say that a letter which arrived in Calabar addressed to Father Whitney, was blown away in a tornado, and found only then, March 1933, under a press. That Father Whitney was furious and said 'If I had got that letter Father Ronayne would be with us today.' Was the hand of God in that tornado?[5]

Once Tom Ronayne had made his decision, Vincent Davey, who was also home on leave, followed suit. He decided to remain in Ireland in spite of an urgent appeal from Bishop Heerey asking him to return to Southern Nigeria.

The departure of these two men was a great loss to the Society. Tom Ronayne was a missionary *par excellence*. He had worked for the missions long before he reached the missionfield. He had encouraged others to be missionary and had been involved to some extent with the Columbans, the Holy Rosary Sisters and with Marie Martin who was soon to found the Medical Missionaries of Mary. Once he began work in Nigeria, his commitment to that mission was total. His health was precarious due to an irregular heartbeat and, when he was a seminarian, his doctor had advised him to walk only on level ground as rough terrain might be too much for his heart. In spite of this, he struggled on through various illnesses and in spite of the antipathy which his own forthright manner aroused in others. He was to remain in Nigeria, where he joined the Holy Ghost Order in 1938, and died at Onitsha in 1975. Vincent Davey was a much more robust man, a very capable missionary and a good administrator. He was a good footballer and a fine singer. He enjoyed great health and was known to sleep soundly on a table if he had to surrender his bed to someone else. At Eke, he laid the foundations of a local Church which was later to comprise three separate dioceses. A self-sufficient Nigerian Church was his aim and he was rigorous in demanding the few pence of contribution from the local people. He also knew how to win support in Ireland. He was close to the Apostolic Work Society in Belfast, at the time of its foundation, and he established a Mass circle in Ireland by means of which Mass offerings could be directed to Nigeria where the Holy Ghost Fathers— the Frenchmen in particular—had no steady source of such offerings. Vincent Davey could have admirably filled the role of first Prefect Apostolic of Calabar or held some post of authority within St Patrick's Society. He chose, instead, to serve the people of Northern Ireland. He became Parish Priest of Antrim town and died in 1973.

It is difficult to discover Pat Whitney's deepest reaction to the departure of these two men. He certainly wanted them to join and had made overtures to them, time and again. On the other hand, their departure may have brought some relief. Tom Ronayne had been a thorn in his side and he believed him to be a destabilising influence on the young men. Bishop Heerey and Monsignor McCaffrey agreed with him on this although the men themselves denied it. There is little documentary evidence of Pat's relationship with Vincent Davey. Bishop McGettrick claimed that the latter's personal strength and resourcefulness was perceived as a threat by Pat. So, one can speculate that Pat may have had mixed feelings when these men, who had collaborated with him for so long, took their leave. Throughout their lives, they remained friends of St Patrick's Missionary Society. Tom Ronayne gave a students' retreat in Kiltegan in the 1950s and was in contact with Society priests in Nigeria through the years. Vincent Davey was a frequent visitor to Kiltegan and is remembered for his warmth and generosity towards the Society.

The Inquiry

Any feeling of contentment that Pat Whitney may have enjoyed on his return from Nigeria was destined to be short-lived. In July 1933, Bishop Cullen conducted an inquiry into the problems of the Society. He requested written submissions from Pat and his two councillors, from Monsignor McCaffrey, Tom Ronayne, Tom McGettrick and P.J. Costelloe. The last two were selected from among the volunteer priests because they were home on leave at this time. The Bishop enquired specifically about the relationship that existed between the Superior General and the priests. It was a great disappointment for Pat who had worked hard to improve relations.

The initiative for the inquiry came from Archbishop Hinsley, still Apostolic Delegate, and living in Mombasa. The Archbishop, who had kept in close touch with the Society and was in regular correspondence with Pat Whitney and Tom Ronayne, was concerned that none of the priests in Nigeria had entered the Society. He had encouraged Tom Ronayne to join and had urged Pat to accept him, but to no avail. Influenced by Bishop Heerey, who sent regular reports to the Apostolic Delegate on the affairs of his Vicariate, Archbishop Hinsley feared for the continuity of the Society and for the evangelisation of Eastern Nigeria. One of these reports, made in March 1933, stated that the young men on the missions were excellent but that the Society leadership left much to be desired. It continued:

> With regard to the Society at home I think it would be wrong for me to report on it in any official way. The Society in Nigeria I regard as non-existent, for only one man, Father Meehan, has taken the Oath of Membership temporarily and he does not intend to be a life member though he was ordained for Nigeria . . . Father Whitney now in Nigeria, himself is the Society and on the supposition of his withdrawal by death or otherwise there would no longer be a Society of St. Patrick.

Archbishop Hinsley wrote to Bishop Cullen asking his permission to propose to Rome that he (Cullen) be appointed Apostolic Administrator of the Society 'and undertake its reorganisation and control'. It is unlikely that Bishop Cullen, a gentle, paternal figure, who was a friend to everyone in Kiltegan, was anxious for such a radical approach. In any case, Rome did not consider such a step to be appropriate. A letter from the Cardinal Prefect of Propaganda, dated 12 July 1933, reminded Bishop Cullen that the Society, being of diocesan status, was directly under his authority and asked him to investigate its problems and to take whatever steps he considered opportune to remedy them.

The written submissions, which still survive in the Kiltegan archives, outline the events of the previous three years in great detail and with exceptional honesty. It is interesting to note that Tom McGettrick and Paddy Costelloe tried to sidestep the issue. In almost identical words, they argued that as non-members they could not be expected to know about the inner workings of the Society. Bishop Cullen was not satisfied, however, and a second request elicited a very thorough evaluation from Tom McGettrick. There is no evidence that Paddy Costelloe was approached a second time.

The submissions do not contain any serious criticisms of Pat Whitney. The personality clash with Tom Ronayne is considered to be important; there is reference to the financial problems in Nigeria, the lack of experienced missionaries to guide the young priests, the withholding of Mass stipends and the confusion about the Constitutions. There are many examples of Pat's failure to take the views of the priests into account and there is evidence of a lack of confidence among them. Tom McGettrick wrote in his second submission that all was well following the agreements drawn up between the Society and the volunteers but he adds: 'Some of the priests may not have confidence in Father Whitney to make a success of the Society but all are quite satisfied that if these agreements are observed their position on the mission field and the rights of the mission are safeguarded.'

Bishop Cullen sent his report to Rome in January 1934. He suggested that the Bishop's consultors in Kildare and Leighlin would form a combined consultative body with the councillors of the Society. Archbishop Hinsley welcomed this, saying: 'Such a disposition would remove the objection that the Society is a "one man concern".' The second suggestion concerned the organisation of the mission in Nigeria. It was proposed that Philip O'Connor C.S.Sp. would act as provisional Local Superior or, if he were unavailable, that James Moynagh or P.J. Costelloe would fulfil that role. Rome accepted the proposals and in April 1934, Bishop Cullen informed Pat that he was appointing Monsignor John Delaney, Lawrence Brophy P.P. and Thomas Keogh P.P.

as 'consultors' to the Superior General. They were not to be members of the General Council but were to meet with the Council at regular intervals in order to become familiar with what was happening and to proffer their advice.

Pat Whitney was not happy with this development. He realised that the three consultors would cramp his style and, in the years ahead, he was to do his best to keep them out of the affairs of the Society. This was a fatal mistake which was to affect Pat's credibility as a Superior. But he was a man in a hurry and he saw very clearly that these three men, accustomed to a steady ecclesiastical pace, would not be prepared to go along with him. He called the first meeting in June 1934. The next meeting took place in July 1935 and the third was convened in November 1937, at Monsignor Delaney's insistence. Meantime, Pat was to co-opt newly ordained priests onto his Council in an effort to reach the number of councillors specified by the Constitutions and hoping to exclude the consultors entirely.

When Pat Whitney heard that a provisional Local Superior was to be appointed on the missions, he saw it as an opportunity to press for a separate ecclesiastical jurisdiction with its own Prefect Apostolic. He went about this in a manner which typified his approach to getting his own plans accepted by the authorities. Archbishop Hinsley had written: 'On the other side in Nigeria it is proposed that a local Superior be appointed in the person of Rev. Philip O'Connor or failing him in the person of either Rev. James Moynagh or Rev. Patrick Costelloe.' Pat seized on the suggestion but 'misread' the Apostolic Delegate's intention very slightly. He replied: 'By Local Superior I understand you to mean a Local Superior as set out in Article 25 of the Constitution of our Society; one having jurisdiction and subject immediately to the Sacred Congregation of Propaganda.'

This is not what the Archbishop had in mind. He envisaged someone with authority over the men who might be given the powers of a Vicar General by Bishop Heerey. Pat knew this well but he recognised that the reorganisation following the inquiry presented a golden opportunity to press for an independent mission. Characteristically, he presented his request as though it were the Archbishop's own idea. The device was not intended to fool anyone but it served to make the request while putting the onus on the Archbishop to make a case against it, if he did not agree. It represented the strength and weakness of Pat's approach to people. On the one hand it was effective in bringing pressure to bear at exactly the right moment and thereby getting things done; on the other, it smacked slightly of the 'fast move' and did not contribute to his credibility. It was not a calculated approach as much as a way of life. It is a style not much appreciated in modern society with its emphasis on candour but it would have been equally understood and admired in the Areopagus in Athens or at the Fair of Ballinasloe. The aim was to outwit the other, putting him in a position from which he could not withdraw without losing face. While endearing in a philosopher or a small farmer, it is not appreciated in a religious superior and it earned Pat a reputation for craftiness which he scarcely deserved.

In this instance, things went Pat's way. Bishop Heerey refused to release Phil O'Connor for the post as he was his Pro-Vicar, and James Moynagh was appointed acting Local Superior for a time. Archbishop Hinsley agreed to put Pat's request for a separate jurisdiction before the authorities in Rome, and they gave a favourable reply. The Prefecture of Calabar was set up in July 1934 and, on Pat Whitney's recommendation, James Moynagh was appointed Prefect Apostolic four months later.

Progress at Home
The official enquiry did not affect the good relations that existed between Pat Whitney and Bishop Cullen; nor did it halt the growth of the Society. The fund-raising machinery had worked well during Pat's absence. *St Patrick's Missionary Bulletin* continued to place the needs of the Society before its readers and to acknowledge the contributions which arrived in ever increasing numbers. Frank Whitney spent nearly all his time on the road, visiting the primary schools and giving talks and slide shows in various parishes. Everywhere he went he got new promoters for the magazine and new names for the mailing lists. He raised considerable funds as well, particularly in the North of Ireland where he was helped out by Vincent Davey. It was Vincent Davey who put the Society in contact with the Apostolic Work, an organisation of women which gave the tremendous support to the mission effort. This organisation was founded in Belfast by Agnes McAuley as the Irish Catholic Women's Missionary Association, in October 1923. In 1929 the name was changed to Apostolic Work to bring the organisation into line with the Pontifical Apostolic Work, which had been founded in France by Marie Zoe du Chesne in 1838, and had become an official organisation under Propaganda in 1871. In 1935 the Irish organisation became affiliated to the pontifical body. Meanwhile, a branch had been established in Dublin through the efforts of Marie Martin and Pat Whitney who valued its contribution to the missions very highly. The

two branches, in Belfast and Dublin, provided vestments, altar furnishings and Mass boxes for priests on the missions and gave financial help to selected projects. The Apostolic Work was to spread gradually to the whole country and to continue to assist missionaries throughout the world.

The general appeal for 1933–34 raised £4,695, while various special appeals e.g. education fund and specific mission appeals, raised nearly as much again. Donations not intended for a specific purpose went into running costs and improvements at Kiltegan. The *Annual Returns* lists education, renovations and improvements to the farm as the main items of expenditure in Ireland. Nearly £1,000 of mission expenditure was probably spent in equipping priests going to Nigeria and in providing clothing and allowances for those on leave. Mass stipends were received in large numbers and were forwarded to the priests on the missions. Burse money was invested in Dublin Corporation Stock and Dublin Port and Docks Board Stock on the advice of a broker. Students continued to come. Many of them were attracted by the personal appeal of Pat Whitney when he spoke to them in the seminaries they were attending. However, the majority of the early students were put in touch with Kiltegan by priests in the parishes or diocesan colleges. The priests had become interested through classmates and friends who had volunteered for Nigeria. Some would have known Pat Whitney in Maynooth or heard him speak there. Those who returned from Nigeria to take up assignments in Ireland were also important recruiting agents. One priest is worthy of special mention. He is Dom Benignus Hickey, a monk of Mount Melleray and later Abbot of Mellifont, who directed many students to Kiltegan in the first few years. He had been a classmate of Pat Whitney in Maynooth and was now a friend and confidant. Of the students he sent, five were ordained by 1941.

In 1933, seven students were admitted to the probation year and six of them took the temporary oath of membership a year later. Twelve students were admitted as probationers in 1934 and ten of them became temporary members.[6] Patsy Kivlehan was admitted to the Society on probation in 1934, following his ordination in Carlow, as was Tom Lynch, the editor of *St Patrick's Missionary Bulletin*.

Developments in Nigeria

The extension of the Society's work into Ogoja Province was an important development. The province was a vast and inaccessible area to the north of Calabar. It covered 7,529 square miles and had a population of 646,162. The countryside was varied, ranging from the humid low-lands of the Cross River basin to the more pleasant highlands, 3,000 feet above sea-level, to the east and north. Until 1937, there was no motor road in and out of Ogoja. From Calabar, the missionary could trek across the Oban Hills, a route which took from four to six weeks with stopovers at stations along the way. Otherwise he could travel by boat and arrive in six or eight days or he could go by motor-bike, travelling by way of Enugu and Abakaliki, a journey of 250 miles.

The first Catholic missionaries in the area were Fathers Douvry and Mellett who established a mission station at Ogoja, the administrative headquarters of the province. Opened in 1921, it was named after St Benedict and was the only residential station in the area until Okuni was opened in 1934. During the 1920s, Fathers Groetz, Howell and White also ministered there. When Father White left at the end of 1930 there were 19 outstations with catechists in charge, 20 churches, 13 schools, 1,995 christians and 1,262 catechumens.[7] Compared with Calabar it was truly virgin territory and missionary work was further hampered by the presence of twenty-two distinct language groups. From 1930, Patrick O'Connor C.S.Sp., who was attached to Eke parish, also serviced Ogoja. In 1931, Calabar was asked to take it over and Tom Ronayne and Charles Meehan made a number of trips. It was Pat Whitney himself who established the Society presence there. He went to live at Ogoja mission in October 1932 with Thomas McDonald who was a year in the country. They were later joined by a new arrival, Seamus Carraher. These two volunteers from Armagh were to carry on the work in Ogoja Province when Pat returned to Ireland in May of the following year.

In the five missions in Calabar, the priests were fully occupied in the regular visitation of the various out-stations. This was a daunting task. In 1933 there were 27 out-stations in Calabar, 67 in Oron, 95 in Essene, 146 in Anua and 165 in Ifuho.[8] Bishop McGettrick describes the routine in Anua in 1934:

> I tried to get to the bush and do as many stations as possible. I used to do about twenty-five stations every month. I would stay for five of six days at the Centre where we paid all the teachers; and on the first Friday of the month we heard the confessions of as many people as came in. It was a disheartening work as we were unable to give the people the complete attention we would have liked.[9]

Fr Patrick J. Whitney after his ordination in 1920.

Maynooth 1920: (*from left*) Frs Thomas Ronayne, Patrick J. Whitney, Thaddeus O'Connor C.S.Sp. and Bishop Shanahan.

Fr Vincent Davey in 1957.
(He died 28 September 1970.)

Fr Patrick F. (Frank) Whitney
in 1921.

Calabar 1930: (*from left*) seated: Bishop Rogan (Mill Hill, Cameroon), Bishop Shanahan, Archbishop Hinsley, Bishop Heerey. Standing: Fr Thomas Ronayne, the Archbishop's Secretary and a Mill Hill priest.

Bishop Matthew Cullen who established St Patrick's Missionary Society in Kildare and Leighlin diocese.

H.E. William Cardinal Van Rossum C.S.S.R., the Prefect of Propaganda, who approved the foundation of the Society.

High Park House.

Mr John Hughes.

Maynooth 1930: (*from left*) Frs Cornelius Plunkett, Patrick Kelly, Thomas
McGettrick, Patrick J. Whitney, James Moynagh, Patrick J. Costelloe and Ciaran Ryan.

Nigeria 1931: (*from left*) front row: Frs Thomas McGettrick, Patrick J. Costelloe,
Thomas Ronayne, Charles Meehan, James Moynagh. Back row: Cornelius Plunkett,
Thomas McDonald, Peter Boylan, Edward Curran, James Walsh and Ciaran Ryan.

Maynooth 1931: (*from left*) Frs James Walsh, Thomas McDonald, Patrick J. Whitney,
Edward Curran and Peter Boylan.

Fr Francis Hickey with Angelo Cardinal Rossi in Kiltegan in 1967.

A view of the old buildings in Kiltegan showing High Park House and the renovated farmyard with the new three storey building built by Pat Whitney in 1936.

The first Society group to go to Nigeria, 1938: (*from left*) Frs Thomas Loughlin, Daniel Creedon, Thomas Fitzgerald, Joseph B. Houlihan and Matthew Magrath.

The main entrance relocated in Hacketstown parish in 1938–9.

Humewood Castle.

The nissen huts.

There were also the schools to be attended to and an effort was made to build up central schools to the standard required for government aid. This was not easy as there were very few recognised teachers in the area. Teachers in the bush schools were often barely literate, so the emphasis was placed on central schools which drew pupils from a number of stations and educated them to standard IV. Since standard VI level was required in order to be recognised as a teacher, it was decided, in 1934, to provide education to this standard at Anua and Ogoja in schools known as Catechist Training Colleges. In these schools pupils were prepared for the First School Leaving Certificate examination which guaranteed basic recognition as a teacher or entry into Teacher Training College for those who wished to attain a higher grade.

There were also favourable developments in the education of girls. The girls' school in Calabar, run by Sister Magdalen Walker, had received government aid in 1927, and was classified 'A plus' in the inspection. Sister Magdalen's plan was to train a number of girls as teachers and put them in charge of schools in the various missions. The first such school was opened at Anua in 1930. It was run by girls whom Sister Magdalen had trained in Montessori teaching while she herself visited it, for a few days, once a month. The arrival of the first Holy Child Sisters at the end of 1930 gave a great boost to this system. They lived at Calabar and Anua but, following Sister Magdalen's method, they supervised a number of schools which were run by African girls who had been trained in Calabar. Sister Magdalen herself concentrated on those among her teachers who wished to enter the religious life, and she had discussed with the Vicar Apostolic, as early as 1926, the possibility of forming them into a religious congregation. However, Bishop Shanahan was hesitant in giving his support. He may have considered it too risky to entrust the direction of such a venture to a solitary nun who did not have any backup from her own congregation. When the Holy Child Sisters expressed their support for the idea, he allowed the little group to be formed into a pious association or sodality called the Handmaids of the Holy Child. The four girls were admitted to this association at Anua on 15 January, 1931, after Mass celebrated by John Anyogu, the first Nigerian priest of the Vicariate. They continued to be in charge of schools and to live as religious, although it was 1937 before their association became a religious congregation and 1940 before they took final vows.

Magdalen Walker left Nigeria on 1 January 1934 in the knowledge that her work would be carried on and expanded by the Holy Child

Sisters. The rest of her life was to be spent in almost total obscurity and far from Calabar. For over twenty years she lived in England outside the convent, maintained by a small allowance from her congregation and with help from her family. In 1955 she returned to the Irish Sisters of Charity and, the following year, was posted to Northern Rhodesia (Zambia). She was involved, for a short time, in the formation of African sisters and later lived quietly in a convent of her own congregation where she made altar breads until she died in 1962 and was buried at Chikuni. Her remains were later exhumed and returned to Calabar where a street is named in her memory.[10]

Another significant development was the provision of a hospital at Anua. Bishop Heerey had been anxious to launch a medical apostolate and persuaded the Holy Child Sisters to become involved. They secured funding for a medical team which they recruited in Europe. Meanwhile, a small hospital was built at Anua with money given by the Apostolic Work Society of Belfast at the request of Vincent Davey. In 1933, the team of three women, a doctor, a pharmacist and a nurse arrived to staff it. It was the first Catholic hospital in the province and was destined to become a very fine hospital and the focus of an elaborate medical apostolate. Before that was achieved, however, events at Anua were to bring great disappointment to the mission and great suffering to the Holy Child Sisters. Bishop McGettrick who was in Anua at the time tells what happened:

> The hospital opened with a fanfare and it did very well for a year or so. But soon after my arrival, I was told that there was trouble in the hospital—that the pharmacist was making trouble with one Holy Child Nun, who used to assist in the hospital, whom she [the pharmacist] accused of acting immorally with children in the ward and with the Convent driver. People believed this woman. She had a great command of speech and propagated her ideas all over the place. She met one of our fathers stationed in Calabar, and she told him all the story. The father in turn narrated the story to the Bishop. Bishop Heerey, without much thought, believed the priest and wrote to the Mother in Charge of the Holy Child Nuns ordering the accused sister home. When the nun went home, the Society of the Holy Child Nuns took up the case in Rome. And their Cardinal Protector stepped in, and reported the matter to the Propagation of the Faith. The result was that Bishop Heerey got a rather strong letter from the Propagation of Faith informing

him that without a canonical inquiry he should not have sent any sister away, and that they were going to review the entire case. So, Rome reviewed the case and after a month or two, in the beginning of 1935, gave orders that the staff of the hospital was to be removed and another staff recruited. Meanwhile, the hospital should be closed. That ended the first beginning of the hospital.[11]

In his memoirs, Bishop Moynagh confirms the general lines of this account. He says that two sisters were asked to leave the Vicariate as a result of the Anua incident. The medical team moved to Asaba where they entered government service in a leprosy settlement. There was more trouble there and the team broke up. The doctor, Dr Lengauer, who had fled from Russia during the revolution and was a convert from the Orthodox Church, remained in Nigeria for many years, working with leprosy patients. Bishop Moynagh is adamant that there was no truth whatever in the charges made against the sisters.

A few days after the opening of the hospital, Bishop Heerey blessed the foundations of the Sacred Heart Church in Calabar. The building was under the supervision of Charles Meehan with advice from Brother Baldomir C.S.Sp. The people of Calabar paid a monthly subscription towards the building of the church and those who could not pay gave the equivalent in manual labour.

Later in 1933, four more volunteers arrived from Ireland bringing the number of priests in Calabar and Ogoja to eighteen although the actual number in the field at any particular time is difficult to determine due to the fact that some were due for leave in that year. In 1934, seven new priests arrived.[12] This was the largest number, so far, and it augured well for the future. The recruitment of volunteers was the work of Pat Whitney who continued to appeal annually in Maynooth. The Society arranged their passages to Nigeria and provided them with clothing and equipment. Once they left Ireland, however, they had little contact with Kiltegan until they arrived in Ireland again. Then, the Society gave them a small allowance, took care of their medical bills and allowed them to purchase basic clothing on account in Clery's of Dublin. They were welcome in Kiltegan at any time and were pressed into service for promotion work from time to time. Sometimes they were given temporary assignments in their home dioceses.

In Nigeria, the volunteers enjoyed great autonomy. Although officially working within the Vicariate of Southern Nigeria, they were also apart from it. Bishop Heerey had neither the time nor the interest to supervise them very closely. Pat Whitney was worried about this situation. He was conscious of the fact that the priests were very young, the vast majority being no more than four years ordained. They were entrusted with responsibilities far in excess of what they would be given in their own dioceses. They, themselves, were conscious of their lack of experience and felt the need for an experienced man to lead them. Tom McGettrick wrote this to Bishop Cullen in his submission of 1933. He wrote of Tom Ronayne and Vincent Davey:

> The presence of these older men would give the Society an existence and colour which it lacks; at present it seems to me too much an affair of one man. Again it would be very much for the welfare of the Society to have some of the older and more experienced men on the mission field as director. But this should not be stressed too much lest an outsider should be sent to take charge of the mission and then the cure would be worse than the disease. If Father Davey cannot be secured as director on the mission then I do not know who would be suitable unless Father Whitney himself.

Pat Whitney had other thoughts, however. He was prepared to choose one of the young men as Superior. In doing so, he was effectively entrusting the entire apostolic work of the Society to him. His choice was James Moynagh, and it proved to be an inspired choice. As Prefect Apostolic of Calabar he was to give the Society a stability and sense of identity without which it could hardly have survived the turbulent years that lay ahead.

James Moynagh

Although he was only thirty-one years old, James Moynagh's upbringing and priestly experience had prepared him well for the difficult task of governing an emerging missionary diocese. He was the oldest of ten children born, in his own words, 'on a 25-acre stony Cavan farm'. From his earliest years he worked hard on the farm and did not enter St Mel's College, Longford until he was sixteen. After completing his secondary studies there, he went to Maynooth, intent on becoming a priest of the diocese of Ardagh and Clonmacnois. His education was made possible by financial help received from his father's brother who was a priest in Australia. This uncle was the product of a local hedge-school and had been ordained in All Hallows College, in 1882, for the diocese of Sydney. The journey to Australia was so terrible, involving near-shipwreck on the Cape of Good Hope, that he could never bring himself to face the sea again for a visit home. He kept in touch, however, and every year he sent money to his brother to help with the education of his large family. He became a Vicar General in Sydney and died in 1936 at the age of 80.

James Moynagh never felt a desire to join his uncle in Australia and for most of his time in Maynooth he looked forward to priestly work in Ireland. He knew that he would have to go abroad for an initial period, however, as the number of priests exceeded the openings in the diocese, and in 1930 there were twenty-five Ardagh priests on loan to various dioceses throughout the world. At Christmas 1929 James Moynagh signed on for Southwark diocese, in England, where Bishop Peter Amigo was held in high regard by the many Irish priests who served in his diocese. James Moynagh had thought of going to China but when he discovered that the Society of St Columban did not accept men on temporary mission he put the idea out of his head. It was on hearing Pat Whitney's appeal in March 1930 that he decided to volunteer for Nigeria. He recalls in his memoirs the difficulty of the decision:

> I spent a long time at prayer on that day and I said 'if you don't go, who is going to go?' and I realised that this would be extremely hard for my father and especially my mother who wasn't in good health, that I should go to Africa.[13]

An uncle warned him, 'It will kill your mother,' but, nonetheless, he decided to go. The fact that Corney Plunkett and Ciaran Ryan, classmates from his own diocese, were to accompany him was an encouragement.

He did not see enough of Bishop Shanahan to be influenced by him directly; nor was the bishop any longer the dynamic person he had once been, when James Moynagh met him in 1930. He remembers him as 'a vague paternal figure' and, in one of his few recollections of the man, Shanahan is very much the bishop teaching and disciplining his flock. He writes of his first day in Calabar:

> It was Mission Sunday and I know that I said the Community Parish Mass and after the Mass Bishop Shanahan preached to the people and excommunicated a few fellows who had been giving scandal in the Church. One of them was Thomas Asuquo Effiom, a dismissed teacher. He introduced us as the first priests from the new Society and said that Calabar had been neglected and this would no longer be so; that a new group of priests were coming over here now and I think there was some kind of welcome. But I

know that after I went up to have breakfast after Mass there was some kind of storm when Bishop Shanahan dealt with a few fellows who had been giving scandal.[14]

Two Holy Ghost Fathers, Phil O'Connor and Anthony Steigler, took the new arrivals on a tour of the various stations. Afterwards, James Moynagh settled at Ifuho. Anthony Steigler spent his time between Ifuho and Essene and after two months was withdrawn from the area. James Moynagh credits Steigler with giving him a deep respect for the men and women of the church committees and with teaching him how to co-operate with them in the work of the parish. He showed his mettle in keeping all of the 165 stations in Ifuho going throughout the financial crisis of the early thirties, contrary to his predecessor's advice to close most of them. He introduced the Legion of Mary to the parish, at the suggestion of Peter Boylan who joined him in 1931. It was the first Praesidium of the Legion of Mary in the African Continent and was to become an important instrument of evangelisation. He also appointed five travelling catechists who visited the stations where there was no teacher and kept the little communities together by leading the prayers and instructing them in the faith.

When he returned home in May 1934, accompanied by Ciaran Ryan, James Moynagh was a man of considerable experience. He had coped successfully with isolation and loneliness. He had handled his pastoral responsibilities in a creative way and he had weathered a financial crisis and had faced the hostility of the pagan secret societies. His mother had died the previous year and his brothers and sisters were not yet established on their own. He felt a duty of support towards them and towards his father. He had a strong desire to go back but he was undecided. Indecisiveness was always one of his characteristics and even the smallest decisions were made with a certain amount of anguish. This did not deflect him from decision making, however, and once a decision was made there was no lack of determination in following it through. His bishop appointed him as curate in Drumlish, Co. Longford and told him to decide about the future in his own time. He had no idea that Pat Whitney had already singled him out as the first Prefect Apostolic of Calabar. Pat put no pressure on him to return to Nigeria until he had secured Rome's nomination; then he insisted. Bishop Moynagh recalled:

When I was appointed Prefect, first of all he asked me if I would accept this and I didn't want to. I argued with him and told him

I'd leave it over till I had done a retreat. But he was very insistent that I should take it on and he said: 'The lads want you.' I did consider it at the retreat in Longford. I went to Father John Hannon S.J., and I did accept. Father Pat insisted on it, and he was certainly a man who really pressed when he wanted something. I wanted to go back to Nigeria, but not in the position of Prefect Apostolic which I didn't feel capable of attempting.[15]

In December 1934, Pat took Monsignor Moynagh to Rome to introduce him to the office of Propaganda. They stayed with the Columbans and while in Rome Pat looked up his friends in the Convent of the Poor Sisters of the Mother of God and gave them the job of preparing an album of Nigerian photographs for presentation to the Cardinal Prefect. During a two-week stay in Rome Pat visited the convent seven times. Bishop Moynagh remembers one trip to the convent during which Pat had a contretemps with a taxi-man:

> I have a vivid memory of Pat refusing to pay the taxi man! It was a Sunday morning and the taxi men hung around idle and this conflict with a 'black crow' enthralled them! A crowd of idle taxi men joined the argument. Pat would not pay but he argued though he knew not one word of Italian. He was rescued by the Sisters of the Convent.[16]

The issue was that the taxi-man had added unnecessary miles to the journey only to discover that Pat was not a man who liked being taken for a ride.

They stopped in Paris on the way home to get a film on St Thérèse of Lisieux for promotion purposes in Ireland. They also examined a printing press with a view to purchasing one for Calabar. Bishop Moynagh recalls this incident from the stopover:

> We stopped at *La Bonne Presse*—the printers of *La Croix*—to get films of St Thérèse for propaganda, and I went to see a staff member to see a platin press for Calabar. Father Pat said 'Meet me here this evening. Our train is due at 4.00 p.m.' On return the whole place was shut up—it was Saturday. I walked up and down for about half an hour. In despair I went into a Church attached to *La Bonne Presse*. I saw a priest behind a pillar reading his office and I went over. It was Pat! I said: 'Why didn't you wait where I could see you?' He said: 'Did you not see the note I left in the window?' Outside behind one of the iron bars was a scrap of a notebook:

'You'll find me in the Church.' You'd need eagle eyes to see it for the windows of *La Bonne Presse* covered the street.[17]

James Moynagh did not waste any time in getting down to work as head of the Prefecture of Calabar. He immediately turned his attention to the problems at Anua. Word had reached Kiltegan that the Anua chiefs were angry at the closing of the hospital. They said that unless the Catholic mission was to re-open and staff the hospital, the missionaries should withdraw from Anua. It was important to have the chiefs on his side; so, on Pat Whitney's advice, he went to see Marie Martin to ask for help. She was then in St Vincent's Hospital, Dublin recovering from an accident she suffered in Glenstal Abbey, when a radiator fell on her foot. She told him she could find two nurses in St Vincent's and soon afterwards Nurses Powell and D'Arcy agreed to go to Calabar. She also asked his permission to found the Medical Missionaries of Mary in Calabar. In his own words: 'she popped the question to me: would I be willing to accept her if she came out with some Sisters and founded a Congregation in Calabar.'[18]

He was totally against it but capitulated to her charm, confident that in view of her physical condition 'she would never be able to come in any case'. It was a weak moment that he was to regret later although, later still, he was to be very proud of it. Marie Martin could not help with a doctor but he heard of a newly qualified lady doctor in Belfast, Dr Morgan, whom he thought might be interested. He went to Belfast to see her but could not persuade her to come. It was Mick Kilmartin who eventually got a doctor for Anua. He was Dr Dunleavy, a middle-aged widower, a native of Foxford, Co. Mayo. He went to Calabar in November 1936.

Meanwhile, James Moynagh had received a message from Mother Amadeus, Superior General of the Holy Child Sisters asking for an urgent meeting about the future of her sisters in Calabar. Following the incident in Anua, she was not prepared to continue in Calabar unless the Society and the new Prefect wanted the Sisters and agreed to stand by them. He had known one of the Sisters who used to visit a girls' school started at Ifuho and was convinced that the charges were false. He assured Mother Amadeus that:

we wanted them to work and that we had complete confidence in them and said there was no priest in the Society who would accept anything against the sisters like what had happened in Anua . . .

We told her we wanted them and would support them and this is how the Holy Child Sisters continued in Nigeria.[19]

Before he left for Nigeria in April 1935, James Moynagh met the General Council of the Society and an agreement was drawn up governing the relations between the Society and the Prefecture which was to be valid until the end of December 1937. He also pressed the Society for financial help for the Holy Child Sisters who had agreed to increase their personnel in Calabar. And he asked for money for medical work which would now be undertaken without the involvement of the sisters. Pat Whitney's message was clear; there was no money for anything and if he wanted to found the Medical Missionaries he had better make sure there was enough money available. It was agreed, however, that a special appeal for the Holy Child Sisters would be launched in *St Patrick's Missionary Bulletin*.

Pat Whitney and his councillors were happy with the new Prefect. Clearly, he was a man who meant business and someone to whom the Society's work in Nigeria could be safely entrusted. However, in spite of repeated urgings from Pat, he showed little inclination to become a member of the Society. His letters indicate that, at first, he was reluctant to commit himself to a lifetime in Nigeria. In December 1935, he wrote in a letter to Pat Whitney: 'I find it hard to live the sort of life I would like to live, out here.' The following year he applied to join but kept postponing a final decision until 1945, when he took the oath of membership.

All his life he was conscious of belonging to the group of Maynooth volunteers. There is a view within the Society that he, and indeed Bishop McGettrick, never regarded themselves as fully belonging to the Society. He acknowledged the basis for that view when he wrote: 'Perhaps it can be charged to me that I was "shanghaied" into joining St Patrick's Society and that I remained more loyal, in a sense, to Maynooth than to Kiltegan. If so let it stand.'[20] It was not that he lacked respect for the Society but rather that the most creative years of his life, years of the earliest evangelisation of Calabar, were shared for the most part with diocesan volunteers. After the second world war, the number of Society men began to build up in Calabar, but for many years the 'Senior Fathers'—seniority always carried special weight—were Maynooth volunteers. James Moynagh was always conscious of the special contributions of these men to the work of the Society and of the traditions which they handed on to Society members. He always maintained that the Society inherited the spirit embodied in the Maynooth volunteer movement. He said of those volunteers whom he had known:

> They were extraordinary men—their fidelity, the team spirit that was among us, the charity that was remarked upon by outsiders like the Holy Ghost Fathers, the unity and the charity and their total dedication to mission work, even the men who came back for a second or third tour and practically all of them wanted to come back if they were allowed by their bishop, though only two or three joined the Society.[21]

6

Shortcomings of the Founders

WITH the mission in Nigeria in the capable hands of James Moynagh, Pat Whitney could now give his full attention to developing the Society structures in Ireland. There were many encouraging signs. In March 1935 the three Founder Members took the perpetual oath. Brother John Bermingham had become a temporary member and was sent to Calabar on the understanding that he would return in time to take the perpetual oath, on 1 November 1937. In September, Patsy Kivlehan came to the end of his probation period and became a member. A decision on the admission of Tom Lynch was deferred for six months. He was later refused membership but was invited to stay on in Kiltegan for as long as he wished. Charlie Meehan did not renew his oath of membership but agreed to remain on in Calabar as a volunteer. He was later to incardinate into an American diocese.

In September 1935, ten more students were admitted to the probation year. There were now close on forty students. The probationers were in Kiltegan and the others were studying in various seminaries in Ireland and in Rome, where James Lane and Michael O'Reilly studied in the Irish College. This was in line with the original intention. When he was seeking permission to found the Society, Pat Whitney had stressed that no new seminary would be required. This was an important point in selling the idea to the bishops as it would lessen the financial strain on the Irish Church. The application to found the Society which was submitted to Propaganda proposed that 'The Society would recruit its members by educating selected students of sound vocations for the pagan missions in available colleges in Ireland.'

However, as the number of students increased the disadvantages of having them scattered in various colleges became apparent. Carlow was reasonably close and Father Hickey used to visit the students there every week but it was not possible to do the same for students in other colleges. Father John Blowick of St Columban's Missionary Society advised that all the students should be brought together in order to foster unity and the growth of a Society spirit.

In 1935, a possible solution emerged when Clogrennan House, a few miles from Carlow, was offered as a gift to the Society. Bishop Cullen agreed that Society students could attend lectures at St Patrick's College, Carlow and use Clogrennan House as a hall of residence. Father Hickey and Frank Whitney were in favour of this and Pat was prepared to accept it as a temporary arrangement. When he learned that Carlow College would have to be extended to provide the extra lecture facilities, Pat considered that the Society would be committed to the arrangement in the long term, and decided against it. He proposed instead that a full seminary be set up in Kiltegan, and he worked out a plan to renovate the remaining farmyard buildings and to build an additional house adjacent to them. The proposal came to a vote at a meeting of the General Council in November 1935. Father Hickey abstained. Frank Whitney voted against and Pat and James Holloway voted in favour. After the meeting, Pat wrote to the President of Carlow College:

> Dividing our forces at present would mean a double financial strain in the upkeep of two places. I think, also, there would be a grave danger that such a development at the present time would interfere with the uniform spirit which would be necessary to have in the Society, as there could be little contact between the two places.

Immediately, he got down to the formidable task of getting the Seminary ready to admit theology students the following October.

He engaged Desmond Martin, the architect brother of his friend Marie Martin, to design the new building. It was to be erected in such a way as to form a quadrangle with the existing farm buildings, in keeping with college design at the time. Pat himself took charge of the work. He employed local labour and imported a few men from his home area. In all, about fifteen men were engaged in the building work. Pat's day began with meditation and Mass followed by a quick breakfast. By 8 a.m. he was on the site to check in the workers. On summer mornings, he was often on the site as early as 5 a.m. in an effort to meet the October deadline.

The death of Bishop Cullen, on 2 January 1936, proved to be an obstacle. The permission of the local bishop was required to establish the seminary, and until a new bishop was appointed, no permission was possible at diocesan level. Pat enlisted the help of his friend in Rome, Monsignor Caesar Pecorari and special permission was given by Propaganda, in June 1936.

Nine first-year students entered the probation year in September, following the usual pattern. On 8 October, twenty students came from various colleges to enter the theology course. Some were starting the course while others were at various stages along the way. The Rector was Pat Whitney. The Bursar was Father Hickey and the Spiritual Director was James Walsh (Achonry) who was home on leave from Nigeria. The academic staff consisted of Hugh McGrath (Armagh) who was also on leave from Nigeria, and Gerard Montague (Down and Connor) and Thomas Campbell (Clonfert), both of whom had volunteered specifically to work in the College. Those studying philosophy continued to attend other seminaries until 1939 when the first year philosophy course was offered at Kiltegan.

The new College was only part of the overall development which Pat Whitney initiated in Kiltegan at this time. A new office building, erected in 1936, was to serve as the centre of administration and promotion for the Society, until it was replaced in 1975. A telephone was installed in the main house early in 1936. When the office was moved to the new building, shortly afterwards, the telephone remained in the old house, more than 200 yards away. An incoming call during office hours was taken by the kitchen staff who had to shout and gesticulate in order to rouse their counterparts in the office. Then there was the problem of identifying which priest was wanted on the telephone and a mad dash up the hill followed, which left the person in question out of breath for his phone call. Fortunately, calls were few. A water turbine was installed to provide electricity for the various buildings. A sawmill, powered by a very large engine which was usually difficult to start, was set up in the winter of 1936. Raw timber was purchased from local forests at first but, later, trees were felled on the grounds. The timber was processed and sold mostly as building timber and fencing posts. A furniture-making business was also started, producing some good furniture which was sold in Roches Stores and other outlets in Dublin.

The Society headquarters had become a hive of activity. There were the students, a few trainee brothers and a large retinue of workers employed on the farm, in the garden, in the sawmill, in the furniture workshop and on the various building projects. When the building of the College was in progress a total workforce of about thirty was on the payroll. A number lived in while the others, often ten or twelve, were locals who went home every evening. There were usually six girls in the office, and a number of girls working in the kitchen. The workers were 'Pat's people'. He hired them and fired them in summary fashion if they did not measure up to his standards. Such firings were often done in anger and some were let go without pay or travelling allowance. Pat was usually sorry afterwards and, in general, he had good rapport with the employees. He was gruff but kind and, in the words of one man who worked with him at that time, 'he would do anything for anyone'. Jim Holloway had gone back to his diocese in 1936, having decided not to take the permanent oath. The frustration of trying to manage the finances and supervise the workers under Pat's overweening command was too much for him. He was to enjoy a very fruitful priesthood in Meath diocese, becoming a Monsignor, a Vicar General of the diocese and parish priest of Kells. Frank Whitney was usually away on his lecture tours and Father Hickey was strictly of the 'Upstairs Downstairs' school. So, for the workers, Pat Whitney was Kiltegan and Kiltegan with such a large group of lively young people was not such a bad place to be.

Lines of demarcation were strict, of course. No contact was allowed between students and workers. Special precautions were taken with girls. Morning and evening, the office girls followed a route through the woods which was nowhere near the students' quarters. Visitors were discouraged. There is a story told by a cousin of Vin Ambrose about an incident that happened in 1933. She had decided to visit him after he came to Kiltegan. She met Pat Whitney on the avenue and was asked to declare her intentions. When she did, Pat said: ' 'Twas the devil sent you,' and directed her back to 'the world', her mission unaccomplished. From 1934, walking around the grounds was more or less a segregated exercise. The General Council had decided: '. . . that the students' walk during recreation be from the bridge to the main gate and the avenue leading to Mr Hughes's place and that the grounds attached to Mr Hughes's place, exclusive of the groves, be left to the students. This will leave the remaining walks and grounds free for the priests.'

The young people working in the place had great fun. There were dances in Rathdangan and other local centres. The boys were free to go but the girls had to get permission and were never let out without a suitable escort. A number of the lay staff at the time were especially close to Pat. Charles Caffrey was steward on the farm. Pat had presided at his wedding in the Society chapel before going to Nigeria, in 1931. The chapel was not a designated place for marriages so Father Hickey repeated the ceremony in the public chapel in Kiltegan village a week later. Mrs Cafferty worked part-time in the priests' house and both she and her husband were very attached to Pat. Dick Barry was Pat's right-hand man for a number of years. He had been a seminarian in Maynooth but had to leave because of poor health. He got married while he was in Kiltegan. He later became Town Clerk in Mallow and had a large family of whom one became a priest. On the occasion of the Society's Golden Jubilee, he presented a bust of Pope John Paul II to Kiltegan. Jack Farrell was a driver and a trusted assistant to Pat. He later ran a taxi service which grew into a large haulage business. He lived near Baltinglass until his death in 1987. Michael McShera came from Pat's home area. He was a driver in Kiltegan from 1936 to 1938. He turned his hand to everything and from time to time used to run the projection equipment for film shows in various places. He later became a bus driver in Dublin and was happy to be able to visit Africa in later life to see for himself the pattern of missionary life. Marie Deignan was a very efficient housekeeper. She enjoyed Pat's confidence and was well liked by the workers. She drove the car to the shops and got it occasionally to go to a dance. These privileges did not endear her to some of the younger priests and she was cast in the classic role of the priest's housekeeper who is the bane of the curates' lives. Mary B. Campbell came to the office in 1936 and worked there until 1983. She lived at Kiltegan until 1987 when she moved to Dublin. Remarkably, she kept in touch over the years with many of the men and women who worked in Kiltegan in the early days. There were many more than those who have been mentioned here. They were imbued with the missionary spirit of Pat Whitney and his colleagues. Their work was more than just a job and, in later life, they were proud to have been associated with the beginnings of St Patrick's Missionary Society.

Pat started a number of ventures outside Kiltegan, all of them with the aim of raising money for the Society. He leased offices in Trinity Street in Dublin, and used them as a promotion centre. He engaged a number of girls whose chief work was to send out appeals to addresses compiled from voters' lists. They were paid according to the number of envelopes addressed.

He purchased the old barracks in Baltinglass which was in a run-down condition and converted it into a hall. This was a major job as cells and other living accommodation had to be broken down to provide large rooms. There were regular film shows and dances at the weekend. A few of those working in Kiltegan went out to collect the money and to work the projector. Jack Farrell was detailed to collect the musicians, often from around the Wicklow Gap. This provided the people of the area with a level of entertainment which was unique in West Wicklow and was much appreciated. The hall was also rented to local groups, usually on condition that the Society got a percentage of the takings.

A more ambitious project was started in Bundoran, Co. Donegal. It was usual for the Whitney family to spend a week in Bundoran every year. It was probably on one of these breaks that Pat learned that there was a large derelict house for sale on about five acres of land and going cheap. He decided to buy it as an investment but with the intention of using it eventually as a holiday home for Society priests. For the present, money was a priority. His experience with film shows had convinced him that there was a great demand and a high margin of profit. He decided to build a cinema at Bundoran which, like Baltinglass, would double as a dance-hall. He raised the matter of the cinema at a General Council meeting, in March 1937. The cost was estimated at £600; projection equipment had already been purchased at £100.

Frank and Father Hickey were strongly opposed to the idea but it was passed by the Council with the aid of Pat's casting vote. Patsy Kivlehan, who had replaced Jim Holloway on the Council, supported Pat. Timber for the building was transported from Kiltegan on an old Chevrolet lorry which was bought with Bundoran in mind. While working on the cinema, he decided to reconstruct the house, which was only a shell without windows or doors, with the intention of running it as a small hotel. He raised the matter with the Council in September 1937 and got it sanctioned. This time it was easier because Patsy Kivlehan had resigned and Joe Gilmartin and Joe Houlihan had been co-opted on to the Council. Predictably they supported Pat.

The new cinema got under way in the Summer of 1937. Bundoran, a seaside town, attracted a lot of visitors and the cinema had a good season. Meanwhile work on the hotel continued. However, the project attracted a lot of criticism in Church circles. There is no documentary evidence of this but a number of contemporaries remember that the project was regarded at the time as inappropriate and perhaps even scandalous. There was a suggestion that the scheme was in contravention of Canon Law which barred priests from engaging in business. Pat had got the go-ahead from the parish priest of Bundoran. However, the

Bishop, Patrick McKenna of Clogher, was not informed. The matter was brought to his attention by a priest who had previously worked in Bundoran and was unsympathetic to the project. In all probability, he was also unsympathetic to the current parish priest. Bishop McKenna raised the matter at a meeting of the Irish Bishops and called for disciplinary action against Pat Whitney. Bishop James Staunton of Ferns defended Pat on the grounds that what he was doing was intended to raise money for the missions and was no different from what many Irish priests were doing to raise funds for parish projects. Bishop Browne of Galway also spoke up for his former classmate and no disciplinary action was taken.[1]

Pat Whitney had gone ahead with the Bundoran venture without the Bishop's permission. This was hardly an oversight on his part. Indeed, he often neglected to inform the local bishop or the local parish priest of ordinary fund-raising activities. His custom was to weigh up beforehand whether the authority figure involved was likely to refuse and, if he was, to go ahead and try to keep out of his way. It usually worked. Either the person in question took no action or else he confronted Pat, in which case Pat usually won him to his cause. Bishop Moynagh, in a memoir, describes this characteristic of Pat Whitney very well:

> When found 'in fraudem legis' (getting around the law) he looked so innocently guileless, so woebegone and pathetic, so patently sincere, simple and singleminded, so utterly committed to Christ's cause that he often ended by winning a determined and convinced supporter![2]

A number of clergy had no problem with fund-raising methods which were slightly unorthodox. Raising money was the name of the game and a man should be commended for his initiative. A century earlier this would probably have been the general attitude, but the Church had become a very disciplined institution since the first Vatican Council. Since 1875, successive Synods of Maynooth had legislated for uniformity of clerical behaviour in order to tighten the reins on clergy so as to remove even the opportunity for misconduct.

In any case, Pat was beginning to feel the heat by September 1937, and he tried to find a solution which would exonerate the Society. He proposed to the General Council that the Bundoran property be handed over to a lay person by means of a 'confidential deed of trust enabling the Society to take back cinema and hotel any time it wishes'. Meanwhile the income would continue to come to the Society and was to go to the education fund. There were wigs on the green at the Council meeting. Pat was accused of alienating Church property without proper authority, a serious offence against Canon Law. However, the two young priests on the Council supported Pat and the motion was carried. Afterwards, they got cold feet, or more probably, Joe Gilmartin, the more legal-minded of the two, got cold feet. They went to All Hallows, their alma mater, to discuss the matter with some of the Vincentians; the outcome was that at another meeting the two young priests revoked their consent. Bundoran was to remain the property of the Society and a source of embarrassment and strain for everyone.

There was another involvement in cinema at Kilkee, Co. Clare, another seaside town with a great market for entertainment during the holiday season. Pat rented the town hall. He sent down two men and two girls from Kiltegan to run it. The two girls looked after the tickets while the men organised the advertising and showing of the films. A dance was held every weekend. The entertainment was very popular and drew large crowds.

Not all the problems with the cinema-dance halls were canonical. The films advertised did not always arrive on time and Pat would have to get Jack Farrell to go to Dublin for a replacement film and rush it to Bundoran, Baltinglass or Kilkee. The projection equipment was not in the best of condition and there were frequent breakdowns. Kilkee had superior equipment but even in Kilkee there was one celebrated hitch when the reels of *Showboat* were mixed up and the audience demanded their money back. The projectionist got his walking papers as soon as word of the blunder reached Kiltegan. There were also problems with the Performing Rights Society which had more than a little trouble collecting the royalties for music played at the intervals.

Pat Whitney got involved in the entertainment world in an attempt to pay off the debts on the buildings at Kiltegan and to guarantee an income for the Society. Inevitably, he had to go into more debt to launch the project. He had spotted a market that was not being catered for and thought he could capture it. The fact that he chose entertainment as his product was a reflection of his own personality. He was a 'media person' who was fascinated by the power and possibilities of the mass media. His use of newspaper advertisements, slides and films in 'selling' Killeshandra, and later Kiltegan, indicated his flair in this area. It was not at all unusual that he should become involved in introducing Irish rural folk to talking pictures. There was no better time to do it than when these people took their annual break at the sea. Then, they could get their money's worth of Charlie Chaplin, Fred Astaire and Shirley Temple, and at the same time support the missionary work of the Church which was Pat's great preoccupation.

Pat Whitney did not remain long enough in his position as Superior General to put the long-term potential of these schemes to the test; nor was the 1930s a time to be launching such adventurous schemes. The summer of 1937 was to be his last season. The projects served to discredit him in the eyes of many of his peers. They also placed him under great strain and had a detrimental effect on his health. Had he directed his energies into more conventional and more acceptable forms of fund-raising he would have saved himself a lot of suffering. The entertainment ventures were ill-advised but they were nonetheless expressive of Pat's personality and character. They were in keeping with his inventiveness and courage, and they displayed his readiness to do anything and everything to get his missionary project off the ground.

Inter-personal Relationships

Meanwhile, the routine business of Kiltegan continued. Pat Whitney made his annual appeals in Maynooth and helped the volunteers to prepare themselves for Nigeria. Frank was busy promoting the Society in parishes and schools throughout the country. Tom Lynch continued to edit the magazine which appeared monthly from 1935. Jim Walsh, a man who is remembered as being kind and helpful to everyone, was Local Bursar and Spiritual Director of the students. Father Hickey looked after the probationers. The theology students were largely the responsibility of Gerry Montague and Tom Campbell until Joe Gilmartin joined them as Dean in 1937.

Although Pat Whitney held the post of Rector he was not very closely involved with the Seminary. He met students individually from time to time and gave a talk on general topics related to the life of a missionary priest, once a week. He liked to present himself as a strict disciplinarian and there were a number of things, scarcely central to a priest's life, which earned immediate censure and appropriate punishment. One was failure to march to meals in the double line which formed outside the chapel and processed to the dining room which was located in an extension to the main house. It was a very exposed march as the path was overlooked from the priests' dining room. The recalcitrant student was sentenced to breaking stones for a new road during his recreation periods for a specified length of time. This work was all the more humiliating because it was done in full view of the girls in the office who could only guess at the atrocity which earned such a punishment. Tom Mahony is remembered as the one who served the longest period with the stone hammer. Another serious mistake was to be seen by Pat without some implement of labour during the time set aside for manual work. The problem was that there were not enough spades, shovels and brushes to go around so the more enterprising students took to hiding the tools after work in order to ensure that they would not be caught empty-handed the next day.

The students made the most of their limited facilities and restricted freedom. There were no newspapers, radios or gramophones and they depended on their professors to give them sports results and an update of world news. In this way they heard of the abdication of Edward VIII, the bombing of Guernica, the latest on Hitler and Mussolini and the discovery of the Java man. Recreation was football and walking and the ability to find fun in nearly everything. As soon as students became members of the Society they were obliged to make a will. One man left his trousers to one of his colleagues and the buttons of his trousers to another. Tim Carr left all his worldly goods to Frank Allen, a workman whose daily round involved the cleaning out of fireplaces and the distribution of coal and sticks with the aid of a donkey and cart. Frank Allen was a convert from the Church of Ireland and had made Kiltegan his home. More than twenty years later, Tim Carr was to die suddenly in America and the story is that the only will he had ever made was the one in favour of Frank Allen who had died in the meantime. The story goes that Frank had made the Society the sole beneficiary of his will, so all was well. Not every student escapade had a happy ending. Serious breaches of discipline were few but there were isolated incidents. In December 1938, for example, two students who had been in the habit of going to the steward's house for a game of cards were dismissed as soon as they were found out. The minutes of the General Council record that they 'had broken bounds after night prayers and had been in communication with servants'.

Four students, who had been recruited in All Hallows and did most of their studies there, were ordained in March 1937. They were: Daniel Creedon, Joe Houlihan, Joe Gilmartin and Tom Fitzgerald. All four were given appointments in Ireland. Joe Gilmartin was made Dean of the College while the others were appointed to promotion work. Joe Gilmartin and Joe Houlihan were co-opted on to the General Council.

The College staff found it difficult to work under Pat's direction. When the end of the first academic year approached, in May 1937, Pat proposed that he or a member of his Council would sit in at the examinations. The staff objected and said they would not set any examinations if the proposal went ahead. Pat capitulated but the situation did not improve. In September 1937, Joe Gilmartin was promoted to the post of Rector. It was a nominal appointment. Joe was recently ordained and it was taken for granted that Pat would continue to make any decisions that were to be made. In February 1938, an effort was made to establish a disciplinary council and approaches were made to Gerry Montague and Tom Campbell to take the posts of Vice-Rector and Dean respectively. The latter refused and the former, who was to all intents and purposes Rector of the College, agreed, on condition that he would be relieved of his post the following June. It is clear that they considered such appointments a mere matter of form while Pat Whitney was Superior General. Nonetheless, the work of the seminary went ahead and was taken very seriously by the students and by the young men who were their professors. Gerry Montague continued to act as de facto Rector and the students were unaware that Joe Gilmartin had been appointed over him.

There was also quite a lot of tension between Pat and the other priests. Tom Lynch was very annoyed by Pat's constant interference in the publication of the magazine. The greatest tensions were felt among the members of the General Council. The two senior members had great difficulty with Pat's rather unorthodox schemes. They were cautious men by any standard but when faced with Pat's adventuresome approach they became even more conscious of the law and of the possible reaction of Church authorities. Father Hickey was the more conciliatory of the two. He tended to abstain from voting or to go part of the way with most proposals. Frank Whitney took a stronger line and relations between the two cousins became very strained indeed. In June 1937, Pat asked Frank to resign from the Council but the latter refused.

Pat began to show great signs of strain. He tended to shout at people—students, office girls, fellow priests. To those who worked in the office he seemed to be angry much of the time, although he was known to warn people in advance not to take it to heart if he shouted at them. His health, which had always appeared so robust, showed signs of deterioration. From 1936 he had a shake in his hands and his writing began to disimprove. The office staff were very much aware of this and noticed it even in his signature. He also had bladder problems and drank a lot of warm barley water which was a popular home cure for such problems at the time.

He was 42 years old and had never paid any attention to his health. There was a darkness about his complexion which people put down to malaria or blackwater fever, a complication of malaria. There is no evidence that he consulted a doctor at this stage. Nor did he make any attempt to take more relaxation. He even undertook the writing of a novel in his spare time. Nothing survives of this attempt but Mary Campbell remembers him dictating sections of it to her and thinks that some of the other girls may have taken similar dictation. It is not surprising that he should have tried his hand at creative writing. He always liked to write and he had a good descriptive style with a fondness for 'the golden moon', 'the soft hazy heavens' and 'the days when the world was young, when life was a great adventure gilded with wonderful romance'.

James Moynagh in Calabar

Events in Kiltegan had little effect on the mission in Nigeria. The appointment of James Moynagh as Prefect had meant that the priests looked less to Kiltegan. The new Prefect had a businesslike approach and a personal strength which was reassuring. He had his own problems, however. In February 1935, shortly before he left Ireland, he had received a letter from Propaganda telling him that some members of his flock in Anua had sent a complaint about the priests to the Apostolic Delegate. They accused the priests of being overbearing with the people, neglecting their duties, making exorbitant financial demands and being disloyal to the government. When James Moynagh rejected the complaints as false, the malcontents refused to accept him as Prefect Apostolic and demanded that the Apostolic Delegate should visit them. In December 1935, they appealed to Rome once again and Bishop Heerey was asked to send a priest to carry out a formal investigation. Denis Kennedy C.S.Sp. was detailed to come, but by the time he arrived the leaders had apologised to the Prefect Apostolic and peace was restored.

Before long it became clear that James Moynagh proposed to back up the evangelising work of the mission with a competent medical service and a solid network of schools. Nurses Powell and D'Arcy arrived in October to reopen the hospital at Anua. The Prefect Apostolic was also anxious to become involved with leprosy patients, who were particularly numerous in Ogoja. Until he got at least one doctor and some finance, he could do very little. He wrote to Kiltegan in February 1936 requesting £2,000 for various works including the medical apostolate. He had repeatedly asked Pat to look for a doctor but to no avail. Needless to say, the request for £2,000 was not met but Pat did send £200 and Propaganda increased its grant for that year to £755.

The commitment to education had already been made. Central schools had been established in many places. There was a priest in each of the boys' schools in Calabar and Anua. The Catechist Training Schools at Anua and Ogoja were a first attempt to train catechist-teachers. On assuming responsibility for the Prefecture, James Moynagh decided that more priests would have to become involved as full-time teachers. For the present, however, he was hampered by lack of personnel. He decided that he would make a start with the school in Calabar. He put in a second priest with the immediate aim of bringing it up to Form III and hoped to have four priests there eventually. His most courageous decision was to establish a Teacher Training College in Ogoja even though no government grant was available. This College was opened in January 1937, with Paddy Costelloe as Principal and M.E. Archibong, one of the mission's most experienced teachers, as senior tutor. This was a very significant development as the steady supply of trained teachers was to make it possible to upgrade more and more schools and to benefit from government grants. The Holy Child Sisters with their strong commitment to education were making similar progress with the education of girls. They too decided that the presence of qualified women teachers was a priority. In 1937, they opened a Teacher Training College at Ifuho and within five years the Prefecture could boast of a surplus of women teachers.

The routine parish work continued and there was a steady growth in the number of baptised Catholics. For example, from June 1936 to June 1937, 6,013 were added to the number of the baptised.[3] Shortage of priests was the big obstacle to progress and one to which James Moynagh constantly referred in his letters to Kiltegan. In spite of the number of new priests who came, the temporary nature of their commitment made it difficult to build up the number of men in the field at any one time. In 1935, three volunteers arrived. Four came the following year and, although nobody came in 1937, there were sixteen priests in the Prefecture at the end of that year. However, such was the rate of comings and goings that, in the middle of 1938, only nine priests were on the missionfield.[4]

Sickness had always been a factor that depleted numbers without warning. From the end of 1936, death also took its toll. The first priest to die in the Prefecture of Calabar was Larry Leavy. He picked up yellow fever and died on 28 December 1936. In March of the following year, Dr Dunleavy died of malaria. The following July, Fintan Phelan was drowned while going on a sick call. Bishop McGettrick's description of the circumstances of his death is a reminder of the conditions under which the priests worked. It also emphasises the importance they attached to bringing the sacraments to the sick and dying. This was an emphasis deeply rooted in their Irish tradition and one is reminded of W.B. Yeats's 'Ballad of Father Gilligan' where the old priest drops in exhaustion from attending the victims of the famine. There was also the theological consideration that a person baptised or forgiven on his deathbed is a soul who is guaranteed salvation. The Bishop writes of Fintan Phelan's ill-fated sick call:

> He went on a push-bicycle and was accompanied by a man who had a push-bicycle. The man with the push-bicycle had a puncture along the road and stopped to get his bicycle fixed but Father Phelan went on by himself. He had a very bad sense of direction and did not easily locate landmarks. He knew that below the town where he was going there was a river called Qua Ibo River. Apparently he lost his bearing and free wheeled a gentle incline into the river and was drowned.[5]

New Communities of Sisters

There were very promising developments with regard to women religious in the Prefecture. In April 1937, James Moynagh received the first four members into the newly founded Congregation of the Handmaids of the Holy Child Jesus. It marked the fulfilment of Sister Magdalen Walker's dream of a new African Congregation and the end of many years of patient waiting on the part of the four aspirants. They entered the novitiate in 1934, under the direction of the Holy Child Sisters, and three years later took temporary vows. The Congregation was of diocesan status with James Moynagh as ecclesiastical Superior.

Meanwhile Marie Martin had made her first profession in the Government Hospital in Port Harcourt and the Congregation of the Medical Missionaries of Mary was born. She had arrived in Nigeria in January 1937 with two companions, Mary Moynagh and Bridie O'Rourke. The former was a sister of the Prefect Apostolic and had heard about Marie Martin from her brother. Although he had consented to her coming when he had met Marie Martin in St Vincent's Hospital, James Moynagh was soon to have serious doubts. When she wrote to make definite arrangements he tried to put her off.

However, he did talk about the matter to the Holy Child Sisters and they agreed to provide a novice mistress. But he was afraid of the financial implications and he feared for the health of the sisters. He had a number of excuses: the Holy Child Convent being built at Ifuho was not ready; the aspirants should first get a qualification in tropical medicine; the time was not opportune for a European religious community to set up a novitiate in Nigeria.

Then Pat Whitney wrote to say that the group would arrive at the end of the year. The decision had been taken jointly by Pat, Marie Martin and Archbishop Riberi, the newly appointed Apostolic Delegate. Monsignor Riberi had been Secretary in the Papal Nuciature in Dublin and had come to know Marie Martin very well. Now that he was Apostolic Delegate to Africa it seemed an opportune time for her to avail of James Moynagh's long-standing invitation and go to Nigeria. There, she could benefit from the new Delegate's influence and expertise in founding her congregation. Both she and Pat Whitney knew well that James Moynagh had serious reservations but neither of them was adverse to putting on a little pressure. Pat wrote to the Prefect Apostolic arguing that the would-be sisters should go immediately. James Moynagh replied, trying desperately to stall them. In the end, he agreed and the little group set sail from Liverpool just after Christmas, and arrived in Calabar on 19 January 1937.

The unexpectedness of their arrival is captured by Bishop McGettrick in his description of the preparations at Anua:

> Sometime towards the end of 1936, Bishop Moynagh sent me an urgent message that Mother Mary Martin and two companions were coming out early in the new year; he asked me to arrange some accommodation for them in Anua. I went to the telephone and phoned Bishop Moynagh. I said, 'The order will not work; where are they to stay?' He replied, 'What about the old Rest House in the hospital compound?' 'Alright! I'll try to fix it up,' I concluded. I will never forget the next fortnight. I had to get a number of boys; we had to open the place which was full of dust and dead lizards. The walls were dirty and had to be swept, cleaned, washed out and painted . . . It had a good zinc roof and a ceiling but the roof was very low, and there were only half walls separating the different rooms. However, after four weeks of strenuous work, we got the house fairly clean and ready for habitation.[5]

Within a few weeks of her arrival Marie Martin was very sick and was attended by Dr Dunleavy. Then the doctor took ill and died. Dr Noeth, a German doctor from Emekuku, sent Marie Martin to the European hospital in Port Harcourt. It was Holy Thursday, 25 March 1936. During Easter Week, permission to establish the Congregation of the Medical Missionaries of Mary arrived from Rome. James Moynagh dispensed Marie Martin from the three months novitiate which had been planned for her. She made her religious vows in his presence from her hospital bed, taking the name Sister Mary of the Incarnation. The Congregation of the Medical Missionaries of Mary was founded with a single member. In James Moynagh's mind, it was a death-bed profession, a matter of giving her most fervent wish to a dying woman. He wrote of the occasion:

> We received her religious profession in the bed in the hospital and she was carried down to the boat next day and put into one of these 'Mammy chairs', a sort of chair that was winched up on to the deck for any patient who was sick. She was lifted up by crane on to the deck and put into a bed on the boat. Old Doctor Braithwaite, a Scot but a wonderful man, said to me: 'Never let me see that woman in Africa again.' She came back umpteen times but never to work, only on inspection. She went home and I said to myself: 'that will be the end of the Medical Missionaries. Mary Martin is going home and she is finished, and the two girls in Ifuho, how could they get on if Mary Martin dies?'[6]

Marie Martin did not die for another 38 years. She made one of her remarkable recoveries on the boat and went on to bring to fruition what was begun in Port Harcourt hospital. The erection of the Congregation was found to have been invalid on a technicality and it had to be validated by Cardinal McRory who accepted the new Congregation in the diocese of Armagh. Mary Moynagh and Bridie O'Rourke did a six-month novitiate with the Holy Child Sisters in Ifuho and were professed as Sister Joseph and Sister Magdalen on 15 December 1937. Another Missionary Congregation had been launched.

The new Apostolic Delegate was putting pressure on the Irish priests in more ways than one. Antonio Riberi was a native of Monte Carlo but of Italian descent. He had been ordained in 1922 for the diocese of Rome and trained as a diplomat. While entertaining such a man was no problem to the genteel Marie Martin, it was 'heavy weather' for the farmers' sons who staffed the Prefecture of Calabar. The Delegate was interested in every aspect of mission life so his tours of inspection during the day were pleasant enough. It was the evenings at Anua where he had made his headquarters which tended to drag a little. Fortunately, there was a gramophone which gave rise to a nightly ritual, described by Bishop Moynagh as follows:

> We had four or five gramophone records I brought out earlier, Beethoven, and he loved Beethoven, and Pat McDaid used to put on Beethoven and say 'Do you want No. 7 Symphony to-night, Your Excellency, or do you want No. 9?' 'Oh, No. 9, Father McDaid, No. 9.'[7]

Even the irrepressible Tom McGettrick found the going tough and confessed in his book that when the Archbishop left Anua, 'to be honest we were happy to see the last of him'.[8]

The Archbishop had more on his mind than the symphonies of Beethoven. He was worried about the lack of progress in Ogoja and told James Moynagh that he intended to recommend to Rome that Ogoja Province be entrusted to another group of missionaries. James Moynagh did not mind; his only worry was that the Teacher Training College was in Ogoja and that the Prefecture of Calabar might lose access to its facilities. He had also planned a Leper settlement for Ogoja and that would have to be shelved. He wrote to Pat Whitney telling him about the proposal and suggesting that the only thing that could stop it was an increase in the number of priests.

As soon as Pat received the letter he wrote to Moynagh rejecting the idea of division. He also wrote to Archbishop Hinsley asking him to intervene in Rome on the matter. He wrote to Archbishop Riberi pointing out that the Society needed Ogoja as an outlet for students who would be ordained over the next four or five years and assuring him that nothing would be lost by being patient. The last letter was unintentionally patronising. He wrote:

> During the next four or five years a small number of priests would be able to deal with the Catechumenate, and even if there were thousands undergoing instructions with the aid of the native catechists, they could be instructed in such a way that when they did become Christians, they would be all the more fervent because they were kept waiting. In the second place, there is practically no Protestant Mission in any of that area, therefore, there is no fear that souls would be lost.

The argument implied that the Society was doing everything that could be done. The reference to the Protestants was less than helpful. The Archbishop was very conscious of what he called 'the Protestant menace' which struck him so forcibly in Calabar.[9] It was all the more urgent that a largely unevangelised area like Ogoja should be converted before the Protestants got a chance to swing into action. Archbishop Riberi received Pat's letter on his return from a tour of Ogoja during which he had decided that the Province needed four new parishes, immediately, and a staff of twenty-one priests. James Moynagh judged that Pat had put his foot in it and wrote to tell him so.

End of Term

While he was visiting Calabar, the Apostolic Delegate discussed the government of the Society with the priests and, particularly, with James Moynagh. News of Pat Whitney's disagreements with his colleagues in Kiltegan and alarming reports of his entrepeneurial activities had come from priests returning from leave and, particularly, from Matt Magrath who had been in Ireland since late 1936 and had entered the probation year in January 1937. Matt Magrath was a genial, sensible man. He was someone with whom the priests in Kiltegan could share their problems. He was also a man who enjoyed James Moynagh's confidence and who was highly respected by his colleagues in Nigeria, where he had worked since 1932. The men in Nigeria had no serious cause for complaint against Pat Whitney. His appeals in Maynooth had provided thirty-six priests for the mission, since 1930, as well as the five who had volunteered to help in Kiltegan. The Society took responsibility for equipping these men and getting them to the missions. It provided them with Mass offerings on a regular basis and treated them honourably when they returned to Ireland. There was, however, a feeling that Pat could do more and that he was using too much money on developing the Society at home to the detriment of the missions. This is a perennial view held by missionaries in the field who consider the pressing needs of a developing Church to outweigh all administrative and institutional needs at home. It seemed all the more valid to the priests in Nigeria when they heard that Pat Whitney was spending money on refurbishing cinemas and dance halls. Pat and James Moynagh were in regular communication. The letters were friendly and addressed the needs of the mission and the welfare of individual priests. The Prefect Apostolic felt that Pat was too preoccupied with matters in Ireland and that he was not giving enough attention to the missions. When Nurses Powell and D'Arcy arrived, in October 1935, without any supplies '—no instruments, medicines, vaccines—nothing', in spite of repeated requests that they should come with all the basics needed to open a hospital, James Moynagh was flabbergasted. His complaint to Pat was controlled but indicated a long history of frustration, as is reflected in a letter dated 22 October 1935: 'I don't feel angry over all this. We have gone through too much for that. I am merely pleased that you seem to have got two good girls.' He was not so controlled, however, when Pat dragged his heels about getting a doctor, and he wrote to him on 20 April 1936:

> I have again and again said a doctor was necessary for the success of the work. You have—at least twice—told me a doctor was unnecessary. Who is to be judge? Do we conclude that I here on the Mission (with the priests who have some experience of Missionary work) am not capable of forming an opinion on an important matter like that?

The priests in Nigeria felt that the big problem was that Pat Whitney was trying to do everything himself. During 1935, James Moynagh had written several times to Pat suggesting that he delegate some of his authority to another priest. He even went so far as to suggest Father Maxwell of Killaloe as a possible assistant. Pat attempted to get Father Maxwell but without success. James Moynagh then suggested that Jim Holloway should be given the powers of a Vicar General. This was unacceptable to Pat and when Jim Holloway's temporary membership expired, he went back to his diocese. In June 1936, Pat Whitney tried to get Corney Plunkett to come home to become part of the administration. He summoned Corney by cable and wrote to the Prefect Apostolic on 24 June—two weeks after sending the cable:

> I want you to send back Father Cornie Plunkett by the first available boat as his presence and co-operation on the home side is absolutely essential for a couple of years. When I say essential I mean it.

Corney Plunkett was an exceptional man. He was quiet and self-assured and had a great feeling for people. Above all, he trusted others and expected the best of them although he may have been too strong-willed to wield authority which was truly participative. He was deeply religious but in a common-sense way. James Moynagh was slow to part with such a man who had been his close friend since their schooldays. He replied to Pat's request in a letter of 20 June saying, 'If you insist on withdrawing Father Plunkett you will cripple us here.' Moreover,

Corney did not wish to join the Society at the time and yet he felt that in order to be truly effective he would have to be a member. Nobody emerged to share Pat's burdens and he became increasingly isolated. He continued to exchange letters with James Moynagh and, in August 1937, attended the funeral of the Prefect's father and wrote him letters of sympathy. In September 1937 he asked James Moynagh to come home, 'even for a very short time' and hinted that things were not going well in Kiltegan. He made a similar request on 27 October. The Prefect Apostolic was too busy to come. The only letter on file over the next six months is a hurried note from James Moynagh complaining that Calabar would soon be down to seven priests and Ogoja to five. He takes Pat to task for failing to send out the four newly-ordained men.

Meanwhile, in Ireland, complaints about Pat had been made to Bishop Keogh by Frank Whitney and Father Hickey. The Bishop did not think them to be very significant. He knew Pat to be a tough man but was satisfied that the Society was making good progress and that no dramatic intervention was needed. Archbishop Paschal Robinson, the Papal Nuncio in Dublin, also received complaints from some of the priests in Kiltegan. On a visit to Rome in July 1937, he discussed these complaints with the Cardinal Prefect. In August Pat received a letter from Propaganda advising him to live at peace with his confrères and to be guided by Bishop Keogh. Archbishop Robinson corresponded with Pat, in friendly terms, and believed that the Society had a great future.

Pat Whitney and his councillors were coming to the end of their six years in office. The Constitutions laid down that a General Chapter was to be held after six years to elect new Superiors and to review the progress of the Society. In mid 1937, Pat began preparations for the first General Chapter. He wrote to Rome in July 1937, asking for 'the necessary dispensations with regard to age and number of years in the Society, to whoever is appointed Superior General of the Society by the forthcoming Chapter'. The Constitutions demanded that a Superior General be at least forty years of age and a member of ten years' standing. Rome told him to await the outcome of the election and then apply for whatever dispensations were necessary.

Meanwhile, unknown to Pat, the priests in Nigeria had made their approach to the Apostolic Delegate. It is impossible to determine how many of the priests spoke to Archbishop Riberi on the matter. Certainly, James Moynagh and Tom McGettrick were among them. The intervention was not based on vindictiveness of any kind. Their concern was for the future of the Society and at the time there was real concern in

Nigeria that the Society would fold up or, as Bishop Moynagh put it: 'that there would be a collapse of all operations and the bishops of the country wouldn't stand for it'. This was also Matt Magrath's position. The suggestion they made dovetailed very nicely with the Delegate's anxiety to have Ogoja Province developed more quickly. Bishop Moynagh summarises it:

> The view was conveyed to Propaganda that it would be best for the Society and its future if '*P.J.*' was allowed to return to his first love as Prefect Apostolic of a new Prefecture—allowing someone else who had the confidence of the priests to become Superior General.[10]

The Apostolic Delegate conveyed the view of the priests to Rome but he also came to Ireland and carried out his own investigation. There is not a scrap of documentary evidence in the Kiltegan archives which stems from this visit and it is difficult to pinpoint when it took place. The popular memory handed down in the Society is that it was a wrathful visitation, that the Delegate arrived accompanied by the Holy Ghost Provincial with the intention of closing down the Society. Whatever speculations one might have about his mood, he certainly had no intention of suppressing the Society which was playing an increasingly important role in the evangelisation of Nigeria. Mary Campbell remembers the visit and places it at 'the end of 1937 or early 1938'. She knew at the time that the future of the Society depended on it. It can be presumed that the Apostolic Delegate had meetings with Pat and with a number of the other priests and that in the manner of all diplomats he kept his own counsel. There was some straight talking. The Archbishop deplored the facilities in the College and arranged that a committee be led by Dr Lane, Senior Dean of Maynooth, to investigate the situation and see that improvements were made. One suspects that the visit was, on the whole, quite congenial and that neither Pat Whitney nor his Councillors suspected that a change of administration was imminent. Archbishop Riberi had been a friend when he was in the Nuciature in Dublin. The authorities in Kiltegan were still confident of his friendship. When changes were made shortly afterwards they felt he had let them down. There can be no other explanation for the fact that Antonio Riberi, a great churchman who became Internuncio to China, Nuncio to Ireland, Nuncio to Spain, and a Cardinal shortly before his death in 1967, should be remembered in Kiltegan as 'the two-faced Italian' a sobriquet given him by Father Hickey.

Another man who began to take an increasingly active role in the Society towards the end of 1937 was Monsignor John Delaney. He was parish priest of nearby Rathvilly and a Vicar Forane of the diocese. He became one of the trustees who held High Park for the Society in 1930, and in 1934 had been appointed a member of the consultative body. He had celebrated his Golden Jubilee in 1933 and was approaching 80 when he insisted on a meeting with the Society administration, in November 1937. It must be presumed that he was acting on Bishop Keogh's suggestion or at least with his knowledge. Lawrence Brophy P.P. was also in attendance and it was only the third meeting of the consultative body in the three and a half years since it was established. John Delaney was chairman, which is significant in light of the fact that Pat Whitney had been chairman on the two previous occasions. He was a big man with a severe appearance. He had a no-nonsense approach and a turn of phrase reminiscent of Charles Dickens. Pat was asked to account for Society finances, to report on Baltinglass, Bundoran and Trinity Street and to give an undertaking that he would stop the felling of trees on the property. It was a most humiliating experience. The financial situation was not good; there were liabilities of about £8,500, the greater part of which was a loan from the Ulster Bank in Blessington. The accuracy of the accounts was called into question in view of the auditors' comments. The accounts had been audited by O'Loghlen Gillic and Co. since 1934–35 but the most recent report was accompanied by a note which said that because of unsatisfactory records, 'the Accounts are in the nature of reasonable estimates and cannot be regarded as accurate'.

The meeting was followed by letters from John Delaney which indicated that he and Lawrence Brophy had discussed the debt with the bank manager and had made arrangements for the drawing up of a legal deed of trust for the Kiltegan property to replace the original one which was found to be faulty. These letters also refer to the sale of trees to timber merchants which was alleged to have continued in spite of the undertaking given at the meeting; Pat denied this vehemently.

At this time, there would seem to have been some contact between John Delaney and a group of younger priests in Kiltegan. They were Matt Magrath, Gerry Montague, Tom Campbell and Jim Walsh. The impression was given to the office staff that it was this group which had taken over responsibility for the Society under the direction of John Delaney. The recently ordained Society priests did not know where to turn. Joe Houlihan was to recall asking the advice of Bishop Browne of

Galway who was a classmate and life-long friend of Pat Whitney. 'Support your Founder,' was the Bishop's advice.

Prefect Apostolic of Ogoja

Not long afterwards, Rome came up with a solution. In March 1938, Ogoja was separated from Calabar and Pat Whitney was appointed first Prefect Apostolic. On 11 March 1938 Bishop Keogh wrote to him:

> Your *Bull* has arrived. You are to remain in Kiltegan for such length of time as I deem necessary for the initiation of the new Superior into all the workings of the Society.[11]

There was to be no General Chapter. Bishop Keogh would appoint a Superior General in the same way that Pat had been appointed. There would be a new start for the Society and a new direction for Pat Whitney.

Pat Whitney had no doubt that his appointment to Ogoja was a move to get him out of his position in the Society. His feelings were mixed. He was pleased to be returning to Nigeria and welcomed the challenge of new responsibility. He also felt betrayed by those around him, by Archbishop Riberi who had been his friend and by James Moynagh who had not come to his aid when he needed him most. He was convinced that Paddy Costelloe, the man who was to succeed him, did not have the qualities necessary to run a young Society. Because of this conviction, he made one final attempt, shortly before the appointment of the new Superior General was announced, to get Corney Plunkett home so that he would be around to prevent a catastrophe. At this point Corney Plunkett was not among those whom the Bishop intended to serve on the new administration. Pat's letter to James Moynagh making this request was written on 25 May 1938. It is full of bitterness and recrimination and reads, in part:

> Another man, Father Plunkett, was cabled home by me with the authority from his Bishop. You have not shown any desire to facilitate or encourage Father Plunkett's home-coming. Notwithstanding the fact that I who am leaving the place and therefore have no personal interest in the concern, cabled you that his presence here is essential. I am only solemnly warning you now that disastrous results can scarcely be averted from the Society as a result of your failure to do your duty. Your obvious duty was to send Father Plunkett home when a higher authority than you, his

own Bishop to whom he has sworn allegiance [and who] has clearly intimated his wishes both to you and to him. In support of that I am sending you a copy of Doctor McNamee's letter to me and I will ask you at the last moment to reconsider. Again, I repeat that I have no personal interest at stake and I am simply doing what I think will further the salvation of souls.

Father Whitney was a shrewd judge of character and he was correct in his assessment that Paddy Costelloe would have great difficulty in running the Society. He was also correct in his assessment of Corney Plunkett's ability as an administrator. There is no doubt that personal antipathy towards Paddy Costelloe contributed to his judgment. The latter had been closely associated with Tom Ronayne in Calabar and had defended Ronayne's position in the various disagreements with Pat. Pat's letter made an impression on James Moynagh and he wrote to Paddy Costelloe, on 28 June 1938, offering to let Corney Plunkett home if the new Superior General thought it was necessary.

Meanwhile, Pat Whitney did not allow his disappointment and bitterness to prevent him from fulfilling his task as Superior General to the end. He continued to hold routine meetings of the General Council as if nothing had happened. There were students to be called to Holy Orders, oaths of membership to be administered and decisions to be taken on individual students. He was also making plans for his new ministry in Ogoja. Priority would be given to housing for priests and to a leper settlement which had already been mooted by James Moynagh. He launched an appeal for Ogoja which caused much concern at the time as it was feared that Pat would bring a lot of support with him to the detriment of the Society. This type of thinking was completely foreign to Pat who had allowed appeals for various aspects of mission work in the Society magazine. But then, Pat was always totally confident of his ability to win people's support. Those who were to take over the Society had no experience of fund-raising and were very much afraid of the financial burdens they would have to carry. The magazine was not used for this latest appeal. Instead cards were printed carrying a photograph of the new Prefect Apostolic, and requesting contributions for presbyteries and for a leper colony.

New Administration

Patrick J. Costelloe had been a member of the first group of volunteers to go to Nigeria under the aegis of the Society. Born on 15 September

1905, he came from Dysart, Co. Roscommon. His father had been a policeman in pre-independence days and his mother was a teacher. After secondary studies in Summerhill College, Sligo, he went to Maynooth. He was always interested in missionary work and had considered going to China with the Columbans. In the end, he opted for Nigeria, drawn by Pat Whitney's appeal. For a time it seemed that poor health would be an obstacle to ordination but after an appendicitis operation, his health improved and he was declared fit for the rigours of the Nigerian climate. He was a quiet young man. Bishop Moynagh remembered him from Maynooth days as 'the man of contemplation, the man of deep faith and prayer'.[12] His first appointment in Nigeria was to Calabar town where he was assistant to Tom Ronayne, a man he came to admire very much. He became Principal of the Teacher Training College in Ogoja, in 1936, and was still in that post when he was appointed Superior General.

The changeover took place on 16 June 1938, when Bishop Keogh assembled Pat Whitney, the councillors, the diocesan consultors and Paddy Costelloe. The proceedings are recorded as follows in the Minutes of the Meeting:

> The Bishop called on Msgr Whitney to resign formally from his position as Superior General. He did so. The Bishop then declared that St Patrick's Society was deprived of all its governing members and asked Father Costelloe if he were willing to accept the office of Superior General. Father Costelloe replied in the affirmative and was declared by the Bishop appointed Superior General even though he was not a member of the Society and even if he did not intend to become a member. The Bishop said that he made this appointment by virtue of special authority from Rome. The appointment was for a period of six years.
>
> The Bishop appointed as members of the Council with Father Costelloe the following: Father Ryan (if available), Father Kivlehan, Msgr Delaney, Fr L. Brophy, Fr T. Brown. The three members last mentioned, he pointed out, would attend meetings of the Council at certain times to be fixed later.

Monsignor Delaney, Father Brophy and Father Brown were diocesan consultors of Kildare and Leighlin. Patsy Kivlehan was the only Society member on the Council. A month later, Paddy Costelloe told the General Council that Ciaran Ryan was not available but that Corney Plunkett would come in his place. He also announced that the Bishop had appointed Joe Gilmartin as a temporary member of the Council and that he would act as secretary. It was decided at the same meeting that Matt Magrath was to be admitted to temporary membership. His probation period had expired the previous November but it had been extended for a further six months.

A marked feature of the new General Council was the position of the diocesan consultors. In 1934 they were envisaged as forming, with the Society councillors, a consultative body distinct from the Council. Now the distinction had all but disappeared. They became an integral part of the General Council, attending the quarterly meetings and participating fully in the decision-making process, for the next six years. During this period Paddy Costelloe was slow to make any decision without the authorisation of his Council. This amounted to investing his Council with far greater authority than it was given by the Constitutions, according to which the Council is advisory in all but a small number of cases. Paddy's deference to the Council underlines the unusual circumstances in which he was appointed and the extreme caution which he exercised as Superior General. He saw his decisions as provisional on the Bishop's approval and the latter's authority was represented by the three diocesan consultors whom he had nominated to the General Council. This approach also helped to take the heat off the Superior General who found his new job extremely daunting. His own words, expressed on videotape some fifty years later, give an idea of the trepidation he felt on being appointed. 'It was like the end of the world,' he said.

It did not take the new Superior General long to establish priorities. John Delaney made it clear to him at the early meetings and also by letter what was expected. He was to remove any sources of embarrassment that he had inherited from Pat. The properties at Baltinglass and Bundoran would have to go. The sawmill was to be sold. Every effort was to be made to reduce expenditure. A Bursar was to be appointed to keep the accounts, to cut down waste in Kiltegan and to get the farm into profit. The number of employees in Kiltegan was to be reduced. Fund-raising in parishes which had been neglected towards the end of Pat Whitney's term of office was to be revived.

It would take some time to effect all this. Even the disposal of the Bundoran and Baltinglass properties was not simple as there were difficulties with title deeds. It was 1941 before the Society's links with these ventures were finally severed. In the meantime, the ordinary business went ahead. Paddy Costelloe and Corney Plunkett applied immediately for membership of the Society. Corney Plunkett was appointed Rector of the College and Director of Probationers. Jim Walsh was appointed Bursar with responsibility for the general finances. It was decided to send all the recently ordained Society priests to Nigeria with the exception of Joe Gilmartin. In August, Tom Fitzgerald, 'Kerry' Creedon and Joe Houlihan, all members of the first ordination class, arrived in Nigeria. Thomas Loughlin, ordained in 1938, accompanied them as did Matt Magrath who had finally become a member. John Lavin, the only other member of the 1938 class, went out the following October.

A relatively minor decision, taken in October 1938, conveys something of the style of the new administration. This was the decision to dismantle the main gate and to erect it at one of the side entrances to the property. Although the Society house and the College were situated in Hacketstown parish, a sizeable portion of the property was in Rathvilly. At the time of the foundation, it was agreed with Bishop Cullen that the Society would pay its church dues to Hacketstown. No objection had been raised to this but the situation might arise in the future that Rathvilly would make a claim. To obviate this, the main gate was moved into Hacketstown Parish because Canon Law laid down that in the case of a dispute as to which parish a religious institute belonged, the location of the main gate was to be the deciding factor. The granite stones were numbered, loaded on a donkey cart and erected at another entrance on the Hacketstown side of the boundary stream. It can be presumed that the octogenarian John Delaney was the one chiefly responsible for this change. Nonetheless, 'Our Lady of Africa' gate, which still stands at a little used entrance, is a fitting symbol of a new direction adopted by the Society as it emerged from the turbulent days of Pat Whitney's administration. The high-profile years were over and, for a long time, the Superiors were at pains to avoid anything but the most discreet publicity. From now on, the Society was to go quietly about its affairs in Ireland, careful to avoid anything that might raise eyebrows among the Irish clergy.

Bishop Keogh expected Pat Whitney to spend time with his successor and had suggested the middle of the following year as a suitable time to leave for Ogoja. Pat was not keen to stay that long in Ireland. He was anxious to get started on his new work and he was also uneasy with the idea of having to watch many of the things he had struggled for being changed. Besides, Paddy Costelloe's style was too different from his own to make a meaningful exchange possible. He envied him his ease with prayer and the care and devotion with which he celebrated the liturgy, but he did not expect him to achieve much as Superior General. In Pat's view, he lacked the courage and the ruggedness demanded for such a role. Bishop Keogh agreed to an earlier departure and, in October, Pat left for Nigeria accompanied by seven diocesan priests, five of whom were newcomers. Patsy Kivlehan and Jack Lavin, both members of the Society, also accompanied him. On 9 November 1938, James Moynagh handed over Ogoja to the new Prefect who was given a staff of nine priests.[13] There were now seventeen diocesan volunteer priests on the missions and nine Society priests. In Ogoja, only Pat Whitney, the Prefect Apostolic, was a member of the Society. Brother John Bermingham, the only brother who was a member of the Society, was coming to the end of his third year in Calabar. He had not returned to Ireland to take the perpetual oath in 1937 but had renewed his commitment for one year. He was now due to come home on leave. There were also eight sisters, all of them in Calabar.

New Superiors
and New Problems

FROM October 1938, there was a great air of optimism and enthusiasm in Kiltegan. Corney Plunkett had arrived from Nigeria while five young priests had come from Maynooth, to teach in the College and to help with the promotion effort. It was a new beginning. Nowhere was this more apparent than during meals in the priests' dining room. This fine room overlooking the College and the little lake was a centre of lively conversation and superb clerical wit. There was friendly banter and spontaneous laughter punctuated by the clatter of dishes and the shrieks of the kitchen staff as the dumbwaiter, laden with empty plates, descended too quickly to the basement below. Not everyone shared in the jollity. At the head of the table sat Paddy Costelloe, a slightly built, intense man, and on his right and left sat Frank Whitney and Father Hickey. The three seemed cut off from the general jollity, intent on silently and politely acting out the disharmony that existed between them.

Frank and Father Hickey were co-founders of the Society. For six years they had been at the helm, not exactly steering but at least keeping an eye on the compass. The changeover had been devastating for them because not only did they lose their influential positions but they were also removed from the works in which they had been engaged on a daily basis. Father Hickey ceased to be Director of Probationers and Frank was not confirmed in promotion work. The good of the Society demanded these changes but it was a problem to find suitable work for the two men. Paddy Costelloe wrote to James Moynagh for advice. The latter had little to offer; he pointed out that Frank had proved unable for the rigours of Nigeria and that, at fifty-one, Father Hickey was too old to adapt to life on the missions. Frank was appointed to the office and Father Hickey was given a minor teaching post in the College. It was a great humiliation for both of them and neither could hide the disappointment and bitterness they felt. While Pat Whitney had been honoured with a post of responsibility, they were effectively removed from responsibility. The situation was very difficult for Paddy Costelloe. The decision had been taken by the Bishop but it was Paddy who had to live with the knowledge that the two founding members had been side-lined. It was he who had to sit beside them at every meal and watch them walk together afterwards, presumably discussing their grievances and finding some fault or other with the new dispensation.

Paddy Costelloe accepted that his new position as Superior General expressed God's will for him. At the level of faith he had no problem but at other levels the strain soon became apparent. He became withdrawn and isolated from his fellow priests. His health took a turn for the worse and he spent a lot of time in bed. Over the next twelve years he was to suffer a lot, and those associated with him in administration were to suffer with him. Some of them found it difficult to approach him. Others, for whom communication was less of a problem, were slow to burden him with new problems and tended to keep them from him in so far as they could.

In spite of these drawbacks, Paddy Costelloe was an effective Superior General. He was totally committed to getting the Society established and was determined that it would find a respectable and trustworthy place among missionary bodies in Ireland. He was a modest and unassuming man who preferred a simple, even ascetical, life-style. He was meticulous in matters of protocol. He was courteous in his dealings with bishops and parish priests. He dressed carefully, opting to wear the knee-length tonsure jacket on all but the most informal occasions. Although he did not possess his predecessor's easy style of letter writing, he was painstaking about correspondence. Nothing was more likely to provoke a crisis in the typing pool than the unintentional substitution of 'Dear Mr So and So' for 'Dear Father So and So' or 'Reverend' for 'Very Reverend', so determined was he that no offence would be given.

On 20 February 1939, the new Superior General got an opportunity to speak on Radio Éireann. He confined himself to a simple description of the good effects of Christianity in an African home and expressed the hope that Kiltegan continue to send out missionaries:

There is every reason to believe that this wish will be realised, that our missionaries will continue to go forth, year after year, to labour in pagan lands for the formation and preservation of happy Catholic homes like those we have in our own little island.[1]

There was no over-statement, no heart-rending appeal. He confined himself to a simple statement of the facts which made the needs of the Society obvious without labouring them. It was a measure of his approach to promotion work, an approach which was to be very fruitful in terms of vocations and financial support.

Monsignor Whitney is taken ill

Even as Paddy Costelloe made his radio appeal, there was a letter on the way from James Moynagh with news of an event which was to bring him great trouble and put to the test his powers of leadership. It was the final breakdown in health of Monsignor Pat Whitney. Pat's illness came as a great shock, although not without some warning signs. In July 1938 Pat had written to his successor to say that he was not feeling well. He was indisposed for a while during the voyage to Nigeria, causing some concern to the Holy Rosary Sisters who were on board. He was well enough to go for a swim when the boat called at Takoradi in Ghana, where his companions noticed that he had very bad varicose veins. At Calabar, James Moynagh was surprised at how much Pat had deteriorated over the past four years. He found him a little unfriendly but he attributed this to Pat's bitterness over recent events in Kiltegan. Looking back on the occasion he said, 'It was obvious that the man at that time was very depressed.'[2]

Pat Whitney arrived in his new Prefecture with great plans for the future. He came laden with supplies much of which remained in packing cases on the verandah of the mission house in Ogoja for a long time. He had brought with him a Ford Prefect car, several motorcycles and an outboard motor for use on the Cross River. He was not long in going about the work of getting the Prefecture of Ogoja on its feet. Up to now there were priests living at Ogoja, Okuni and the Teacher Training College. Now, Abakaliki and Kakwagom also became residential stations. Pat himself lived at Okpoma near Ogoja where he built himself a mud house and started work on a church made of cement blocks. He initiated a building programme in each of the missions, the extent of which can be gauged from a letter of Manus McClafferty, written on 6 March 1939, who wrote:

At Ogoja there is nothing but building: a new Oratory, 100 ft by 24 ft which will cost about £400, a new teacher's house, a new dormitory for the College and the ceiling on the entire college. No mission could possibly stand it.

Pat hoped to get the Medical Missionaries of Mary to open a hospital at Ikom and was negotiating with the Holy Child Sisters for a convent and school at Okuni. He was in touch with Paddy Costelloe about developments. Their letters were friendly and, for Christmas, Paddy sent him a cheque as a gift. Pat mislaid the cheque and had to write for a replacement.

Life seemed as it should be for Pat. There was plenty of activity, lots of hard work and everything was geared towards the spread of the Gospel. But Pat was failing. He was losing control of his body and he could not face up to it. There was no one with whom he might discuss his predicament and his fears. In front of the young priests he was determined to be the rugged missionary he had always been, inspiring them to work ever harder for the cause to which he had invited them. He needed to get away from their good humour and their inquisitiveness. That was why, in Bishop Moynagh's words he 'went out and got a mud house built for himself seven or eight miles out and lived a kind of lonely life out there.'[3] The depression increased but he was determined to keep going. While cycling at Obudu, on Christmas Eve 1938, he fell off the push bicycle and broke his collar bone. He made light of it but agreed to go to Enugu hospital for treatment. The priests had no idea how he was really feeling. They thought he was foolish to be working so hard but reported to Kiltegan that he was in 'great form'.

Then one morning in early February, Pat arrived at Ogoja mission in a distraught condition. Fathers Duffy, Leavy and Sandvoss who were present could make no sense of him. He wandered from room to room, partly dressed. He lay on the beds in turn and eventually fell asleep on the floor. The Holy Child Sisters arrived to discuss their plans to come to Ogoja but the Prefect Apostolic was incapable of discussing anything with them. Word reached the mission that Pat had been seen in this condition around Ogoja town and that the white people, in particular, were talking about it. They concluded that he was under the influence of alcohol, although they had never seen him drinking to excess. They got in touch with James Moynagh who reported the matter to Kiltegan. He too was puzzled by Pat's condition and wrote in a letter to the Superior General, dated 12 March 1939: 'It is very difficult to prove that it is drink but if it is not drink it is mental and anyhow it is probably both.'

Two weeks in hospital restored Pat's health to the extent that he was in control once again. He appointed Manus McClafferty as Pro-Prefect and formally handed over to him. Then he left for Ireland. He was accompanied by Charlie Smith, a Kilmore priest, who had only come out with Pat Whitney a few months previously. Charlie too was having health problems which were to prevent him from living in Africa in the future.

Pat had every intention of coming back and was convinced that a few months' rest in Ireland would restore him to health. The priests had other ideas, however, and were of the opinion that Pat would never be fit to resume his responsibilities as Prefect. James Moynagh wrote to Paddy Costelloe that a new Prefect should be appointed as soon as possible. In subsequent letters he made suggestions as to who this might be and considered Corney Plunkett or Tom McGettrick to be the only suitable candidates. Manus McClafferty wrote on 14 February 1939:

> I hope that Rome will see their way to appointing a new Prefect soon. If they allow Monsignor Whitney to return there will be a general exodus of us to Calabar or somewhere else.

Meanwhile Paddy Costelloe had met Pat at the boat in Dunlaoghaire and took him to the Mater Hospital in Dublin where he was to spend six weeks. Paddy visited him once during this time and was under no illusion as to the delicacy of the situation. James Moynagh had warned him:

> God help you all at home when Monsignor arrives. I don't know what you shall do. He informed Manus he would be back in July but that is quite impossible and he can hardly mean it. If he has not sent in his resignation to Rome you must ask for his removal.[4]

Nobody else from Kiltegan visited Pat in hospital and he felt bitter about that. He was under the care of a Dr Noone, who advised him to have all his teeth removed, a fairly common remedy, at the time, in a whole range of illnesses. There appears to have been no firm diagnosis of his condition.

Pat was discharged from the Mater Hospital at the end of March but did not return to Kiltegan. He had written to ask Paddy Costelloe to meet him in Wynne's Hotel, at very short notice. When the latter failed to turn up, Pat remonstrated with him, wondering why he didn't telephone if he was unable to come. In his reply, Paddy pointed out that he did not consider the expense of a telephone call justifiable in such circumstances. It was an effort at self-justification rather than an intended slight but it infuriated Pat. That his successor did not consider him worth the price of a phone call was grist to the mill of his anger. There was always a lot of anger in Pat. It is a constant theme in the diaries of his early years in Africa. Angry outbursts against his parishioners caused him great regret and evoked the resolution to control his temper in the future. In his final years as Superior General the anger increased and became even more aggravated during his illness. Paddy Costelloe became the principal object of this anger. The new Superior General could scarcely do or say anything which his predecessor did not interpret as a slight or insult and the latter's reaction was out of all proportion to the offence given. Nowadays, such anger would be expected in the case of debilitating illness and efforts would be made to lead the person concerned to readjustment and acceptance. In Kiltegan, at the time, there was little understanding of such matters. The young men had little experience of sickness and death. They tended to oversimplify life in terms of obedience to the will of the Superior without due regard for the real problems of the subject. In the case of Pat Whitney, they were confronted by a particularly challenging situation, a Founder who demanded that they exercise authority over him and then refused to abide by their decisions.

Pat went to Sligo and stayed with his sister, Mrs Gardiner. His mind and heart were in Ogoja and he immediately launched an appeal for funds. The open letter of appeal which he sent to his various supporters read in part: 'It is all very well for the doctor to order one a rest but when I think of ten priests out there in my Prefecture, who are depending principally on what I can send them for their support, I must put the appeal of those priests to you before I can even think of resting.' At the same time, he began to make demands on the Society for medical and other personal expenses. These were relatively modest demands but they raised the issue of the obligations of the Society to a member before the implications of the Constitutions had been worked out. It was a delicate situation for the new Superior General who wanted to avoid any precedent that might lead to excessive claims in the future. Pat demanded a holiday allowance of £3 a week which was refused. He then submitted a bill for personal clothing which he had purchased at Clery's. At the time, this was common practice and it was understood that priests could purchase certain basic items of clothing at Clery's and put them on account. In Pat's case, the bill was referred back to him. There followed a dentist's bill arising from the removal of his teeth.

Payment was refused on all counts on the grounds that the Prefecture Apostolic of Ogoja was responsible for debts of this nature incurred by the Prefect. The Society referred the matter to Propaganda which confirmed that Ogoja was responsible. It was believed in Kiltegan that Pat had considerable funds at his disposal. It is impossible to verify this but for Pat the central question was not the money but the recognition and *pietas* that payment of the bills would demonstrate. Pat then sent a document to Bishop Keogh and to the other trustees of the property, criticising certain changes made in Kiltegan. These included: sending priests to Nigeria who should have been kept at home for promotion work, dispensing with the services of a number of the lay staff in Kiltegan, moving the main entrance and changing the name of the Society magazine to *Africa*. He also alleged that money from the Ogoja appeal was being lodged in the name of the Society, something which was not in fact happening. It was an angry letter in which the feeling of being rejected by the Society predominated. He wrote:

> Since I returned to Ireland I have been in hospital pretty seriously ill; I have had visits from the African Missionaries and the Holy Ghost Fathers, but with the exception of a visit from Father Costelloe I have not received a line from any priest in Kiltegan.

This letter was the first of many acrimonious exchanges between Pat Whitney and the administration of St Patrick's Missionary Society.

Paddy Costelloe reacted calmly to the crisis in Ogoja caused by Pat's sudden departure. He suggested to the priests that they explain the position to the Apostolic Delegate and in due course he made contact with Propaganda. In May, the Cardinal Prefect instructed him to request Pat 'to resign freely from your position as Prefect Apostolic of Ogoja because of ill health'. It was August before Pat could bring himself to accept the inevitability of resignation. He wrote directly to the Cardinal offering his resignation and asking to be allowed to return to Nigeria 'as a simple priest'. The reply, sent through the Superior General, suggested that work in an Irish diocese would be more suitable for him than a return to the missions. Paddy Costelloe relayed this and added: 'I assure you that if you wish to remain in the Society, I will do everything possible to make life pleasant for you.' Again he had struck the wrong chord, as Pat's reply makes clear:

> I'm convinced that during the next few years I would not be happy in Kiltegan and that I would not be able to do anything

that would help. That is the reason why I asked permission from the Cardinal Prefect to seek missionary work elsewhere.

I would ask you to let me know what you and the Council of the Society would allow me to do. I can easily get work in such a diocese as San Diego where I would have a very much better chance of fully recuperating my health, but I do not want to apply to any Bishop until I know what is permissible.

I do not want anyone to go out of his way to make life pleasant for me.

Paddy Costelloe's reply underlines his inability to comprehend Pat's real needs, much less try to provide for them. His lack of sympathy can only be accounted for by the great pressure he experienced under the burden of office. His letter, dated 29 September 1939, reads in full:

I am very grateful for your letter of the 25th September. It is our wish that you spend your holiday in Kiltegan; it is a very healthy place. Moreover, this arrangement would save money for the Society. I shall be grateful if you will let me have, as soon as possible, the names and addresses of benefactors which you have. Now that you no longer hold a position of responsibility I expect that you no longer need them.

The Council has no objection to your incardination into San Diego or other Diocese.

Apart from the difficulty of dealing with his predecessor, Paddy Costelloe's first year in office was very satisfactory. The College was going very well. Six students entered the probation year in 1938 and seven in 1939. Twelve students became priests in 1939, the largest number to be ordained until 1948. In fact there were two classes in 1939. One was ordained in June and the other in October. This was the result of a decision, taken with Rome's approval, to ordain students at the end of the first term of Fourth Divinity. This reduced the entire course to slightly over six years. Paddy Costelloe made the customary appeal to Maynooth students and secured four volunteers for Nigeria and three for the College in Kiltegan.[5]

The outbreak of war, in September 1939, was to create special problems for the Society. The most serious of these was the difficulty and danger involved in travelling to Nigeria. Getting a ship was difficult. Word was usually received at very short notice and the journey was hazardous. No one was left in any doubt of the danger involved when on 18 September, the aircraft carrier H.M.S. *Courageous* was sunk in the Atlantic with a loss of 500 men. Three days later a group of missionaries left for Nigeria as part of a military convoy. John F. Sheehan, who was one of the group, remembers a close call when the ship had left the convoy and was sailing out of Dakar in Senegal. At ten o'clock at night, Ned McElligott noticed, from the position of the moon, that the ship had made an about turn. Apparently an enemy submarine had been detected and the Captain had decided on evasive action and followed a zig-zag course back to Dakar. The priests had their life-jackets ready but did not need them. The ship arrived safely in Dakar and, after a twenty-four hour stay, proceeded without incident to Lagos. The priests got a smaller boat to Calabar and thus completed their journey in seventeen days as compared with eleven days in peacetime.

Developments in Calabar

From 1938, a recurring complaint in James Moynagh's letters to the new Superior General was shortage of money. In November 1938 he wrote:

> . . . the people have hardly any money and all the schools we had built are beginning to scatter. Some of the missions are in debt and passages homeward and the medical mission have eaten up my reserves.

However, this did not prevent him from pushing ahead with education. Not only was he convinced of the intrinsic value of education and its potential for evangelisation but he was also conscious of its prestige value. So great was this element that many of the missionaries were convinced that without a respectable achievement in education the Catholic Church would cease to exist in large areas of Calabar and Ogoja. In his memoirs, Bishop Moynagh reflects on the fine educational facilities run by the Presbyterians and Methodists:

> . . . the prestige thing, the thing that had an influence with the people, was education and we were regarded as nowhere in education because we didn't have one Secondary School in Calabar or anywhere else at the time, and if we hadn't moved during the war years we were finished. I think that the great advantage we had, and it was providential to my thinking, that we were able to get priests who were graduates straight away from Maynooth, who

were accepted by the Government Department as graduates and were able to come out during the war years when other institutions were at a standstill and were even stuck for any kind of staff. But we were getting these men from Maynooth who were able to staff St Patrick's, Ogoja, and Holy Family, and of course we were able to get lay graduates as well as priests.[6]

One way to ease the money difficulty was to set up a minor seminary in Calabar. Up to now, boys considered suitable to be priests were sent to Onitsha for secondary studies at St Paul's seminary. By establishing a seminary attached to the Sacred Heart School in Calabar, it was possible to save the cost of transporting students to Onitsha and also to avail of the grant which Propaganda gives to seminaries. This was a way of strengthening the secondary section of the school while providing appropriate education for boys interested in becoming priests. In 1939, it was decided to build a separate secondary school in Calabar, to include the minor seminary. Called St Patrick's College, it was to become the pride of the Prefecture. Before long, inter-Church rivalry was to be translated on to the playing-field, as St Patrick's challenged the prestigious Hope Waddell Institute and eventually managed to subdue it. The outbreak of war made building work expensive. James Moynagh bought cement for £250 and corrugated iron for £100 at the end of 1939. A year later, he asked Kiltegan for another £300 or £400 to buy more materials. Paddy Costelloe sent him £500 and published his letter in *Africa*. The name 'St Patrick's' had special significance for the people of Calabar. This was the name of the first secondary school, opened in Calabar in 1911 by pioneer missionary, Father Lena, but closed down on his departure three years later. By giving the same name to the new college, James Moynagh was making a gesture for conciliation to the Efik people who still revered the memory of Father Lena and were often less than positive about those who succeeded him.

In May 1938, a number of Catholic Efiks had made complaints to Rome about the missionaries. It was the latest episode in a long-running feud which went back to 1924, when there was a crackdown on prominent parishioners who had deviated from the Church's discipline on marriage. James Moynagh referred to it in a letter to the Superior General, written on 8 July 1938. He wrote:

> The Calabar crowd have written Rome in May. The same kind of complaints you would expect . . . our arrogance, harshness, carelessness about liturgy, burials, etc., scandalous treatment of the

people charging money for sacraments, etc. etc.—*signed by about seven polygamists*. Otherwise things are very quiet.

Much of the discontent centred on marriage. Observing the discipline of Christian marriage has always been a problem for communities in Africa. It was very important for the early missionaries to stress the full demands of the Church in order to establish Christian marriage as something more than a theoretical ideal. This called for a strict enforcement of the Church's discipline, which led to excommunication and the imposition of public penances. It was an unpleasant side of the missionary's task, unpleasant for the people but no less unpleasant for the priest who had to take a hard and unpopular line on issues which were an integral part of traditional life.

One of the most basic challenges was to ensure that members of the Church would marry in accordance with Canon Law. This meant that both partners would have to be Catholics. The local bishop could dispense from this requirement but the Prefect Apostolic of Calabar was very slow to do so. There was a serious problem as the vast majority of those baptised were boys from the mission schools. Inevitably, most of them would choose non-Catholic partners. However, if a young man wished to marry in church he had to see that his partner was baptised. It was in order to facilitate this that the mission set up Marriage Training Centres, or 'marriage quarters' at the central mission stations. Girls were expected to spend two or three months in these centres being prepared to receive the sacraments and being instructed in housekeeping and childcare. The practice had a parallel in traditional society where girls spent a period in seclusion before circumcision and marriage. The priests did not draw attention to the similarities between the two practices, probably because they regarded the traditional institutions, known as 'fattening houses', as grossly pagan.

The young missionaries were often less than gentle in persuading young people to participate in these pre-marriage courses. The girls were usually positive in their attitude as it offered them a chance to learn something new—even the rudiments of reading and writing were taught. But to the families at home it was an inconvenience as the girl's food had to be sent to the mission and the household was deprived of her services while she was away. In many cases, the couple would already have entered a traditional marriage so it was the husband and his family who were discommoded. There was some dissatisfaction and the attitude of the priest did not always help. This was particularly true of Tom McGettrick, in Anua, who tended to dragoon people into participating. He admits:

> On the first Sunday of every month, after Mass, I used a kit-car, the only one in the diocese, to go out to some of the stations and bring in the women. I instructed or rather ordered their husbands to come in that evening with their wives' belongings and some food.[7]

The matter was taken up by the Ibibio Union, an association to which all adults of the Ibibio tribe paid an annual subscription. One of its main social contributions was the provision of overseas scholarships for selected students. The officials of this association complained to the District Officer, in July 1939, that Tom McGettrick was arresting women and holding them against their will in Anua. Reports appeared in the press, where the Catholic mission was accused of operating 'prisons and penance houses'. This was a reference to a practice which was distinct from the pre-marriage courses. It referred to a group of people doing a kind of public penance in the central mission prior to being reconciled to the Church following some flagrant breach of discipline. The *penance* consisted of manual work around the mission compound and attendance at Mass and prayers. James Moynagh became alarmed when he heard a rumour that the matter was to be brought up at a debate in the Legislative Council. He contacted the Lieutenant Governor in Enugu and arranged for an official inspection of the marriage quarters at Anua.

The inspection took place in the presence of a large crowd which included representatives from all the other missions. Even those among the Catholic community who had been critical of the marriage courses were prepared to rally to the defence of the Church. The matter was debated publicly and, in the end, the Lieutenant Governor and his officials could find no fault with the practice. Tom McGettrick was unrepentant and continued to advocate these pre-marriage courses in Anua and later in Ogoja. James Moynagh was less enthusiastic and never promoted the idea in the Prefecture of Calabar. The incident also led to a rethinking about the practice of public penance. The practice of relegating those seeking readmission to the sacraments to a special place in church during services was to replace the period of work and prayer at the central mission. Before long, this practice too fell into disuse.

As a result of this incident, the Catholics withdrew from the Ibibio Union and formed their own association which they called *St Joseph's Catholic League*. They were determined to imitate the Ibibio Union by sending Catholic students overseas. However, James Moynagh convinced them that the priority was secondary education and reminded them that there were few, if any, Catholics with sufficient basic education to gain entrance to university overseas. They agreed to devote their resources to secondary education, on condition that the Prefect Apostolic would secure funding for overseas scholarships when Catholic students had reached the required standard. It was a promise which James Moynagh was to honour and one which brought students from Calabar to University College Cork and the Royal College of Surgeons, among other third level institutes. The League promised that they would build a secondary school at Abak, by August 1942. Its resolve was considerably strengthened when the Ibibio Union made fun of the proposal and regarded it as the Ibibio equivalent of a castle in Spain. A permanent organiser, Joseph Udo Adadiaha, was appointed by the League and money was collected. Catholics came from far and wide to help with the building. The project became a rallying point for the entire Catholic community and in January 1942, well before the projected date, the school was ready. It was called Holy Family College, to emphasise that it had its origins in an attack on the Catholic ideal of family life. Like St Patrick's in Calabar town, Holy Family College, Abak, became an excellent secondary school. It was situated in a predominantly Protestant area and, at James Moynagh's insistence, it accepted Protestant boys and guaranteed them complete freedom in the matter of attendance at Church services. This kind of tolerance was rare in the 1940s but was typical of Moynagh who always had the ability to transcend accepted attitudes and the courage to try new ways.

Another worry frequently expressed by James Moynagh was the youth and inexperience of the priests in Calabar. This resulted from the quick turnover of volunteer priests. Many were recalled by their bishops while others were dispirited by illness and by the isolation of life in a strange culture. There was a cinema in Calabar and, even during the war, recently made films were imported from Europe. It offered occasional entertainment especially to those within easy reach of Calabar. There was a golf course in Calabar and others in Ogoja and Enugu. The priests went on occasional shopping trips to Enugu where the Holy Ghost priests always extended a warm welcome. School football matches were another outlet and at one time four priests played on a second team in the school in Calabar. The houses were hot and uncomfortable. There was little to nourish the spirit except the daily spiritual exercises. Most priests had only a very rudimentary grasp of the language, and working through an interpreter was an obstacle to satisfactory communication. There was a lot of work for which the priests were ill-equipped. Men with a strictly academic training were expected to be architects and builders. Even those who had a natural flair ran into difficulty. There was a problem about the pillars in Calabar Cathedral and work had to be suspended for a time until Brother John Bermingham, who had built a fine church in Ifuho, was called in to rectify the situation. But there were those who had no talent for building, like Jimmy Lane, who was to build a two-storey house without making any provision for a stairs. It was small wonder that a number of the men were in bad shape after a tour of duty. In letters to Kiltegan, James Moynagh described various individuals who were doing exceptional work as being 'a bit run down' or 'all nerves'. In these circumstances, Irish bishops often advised their priests not to return nor was James Moynagh anxious to take them if there was a likelihood of serious health problems. He remarked in one letter: 'you could hardly guarantee anybody's health out here (barring Fr McGettrick's . . .)' referring to his colleague's exceptional constitution.[8] In November 1939, Calabar had only one man, Tom Reynolds, who, apart from the Prefect Apostolic, had been more than two years in Nigeria. The war made matters worse as it caused many volunteers to decide against returning to the missions because of the dangers involved in travelling.

There was a strong emphasis on prayer. James Moynagh reported that priests were very conscientious in the matter of the daily discipline of mental prayer and office; rosary was often recited in common after the evening meal and the practice of spending a day every month in prayer together was generally observed. In May 1939, James Moynagh proposed that one of the Society members be appointed to act as spiritual adviser to his fellows. Out of this proposal grew the appointment of a 'Holy Man' who kept a fatherly eye on the priests and protected their interests in the case of conflict with the Prefect or bishop in whom all authority was vested. Gradually this priest was given funds for emergency situations and, after the 1962 Chapter, he was replaced by a Regional Superior who was given authority over the members of the Society.

Among the other works undertaken in the Prefecture of Calabar, the hospital at Anua made favourable progress. Sisters Joseph and Magdalen, the two Medical Missionaries who were professed in Nigeria had gone there in January 1938. They were joined, soon afterwards, by Maeve Keane (Sister St John) who hoped to do her postulancy in Nigeria and then return to Ireland for novitiate. Later in the year, Norah Leydon

(Sister Patrick) and Honora Murphy (Sister Oliver), both qualified in midwifery, arrived. It was intended that they would do the noviceship in Nigeria. Sister Magdalen had to go home for health reasons so the number of Medical Missionary personnel in Anua, at the beginning of 1939, was four, of whom only Sister Joseph, the Prefect's sister, was professed. The late Dr Dunleavy had been replaced by Dr Dufey and his wife, who were sent out from Germany by the Wurzburg Institute. They did great work in Anua but left hurriedly on 2 April 1939, having been summoned to defend the fatherland. They were expecting their first child and were heartbroken to have to leave. The hospital was closed for a short time but soon afterwards Joe Barnes, a young Irish doctor working in Emekuku, came as *locum*. He stayed in Anua for four months until Dr Streyrath, another German, came to replace him. Bishop McGettrick said that this man was 'a real Nazi who knew *Mein Kampf* by heart'. Bishop Moynagh remembers him as 'a simplistic kind of chap' who believed the Germans would win the war in a matter of three months, but a good doctor. He was interned in 1941 as an enemy alien, and the hospital was closed again until the arrival of Dr Gerry Connolly, a young doctor from Cavan, in March 1942.[9] In the meantime, the Sisters continued to hold an out-patient, ante-natal clinic and began to visit the women in their homes, travelling in pairs, on the carriers of two bicycles piloted by trustworthy men!

Another development was the publication of a magazine entitled *Catholic Life*. It was printed on the diocesan printing press which also undertook the printing of a hymn-book in Efik. The printers found themselves running short of the letter 'k' and James Moynagh instructed Matt Magrath to bring back a supply when he was returning in 1938. He was also to bring: '*Two* wings i.e. shafts i.e. sidebars for my glasses. I can't get proper ones here.'[10] Only a few issues of the magazine had been printed when work had to be abandoned due to war-time shortages. It was revived later and was to enjoy great prestige and achieve nationwide circulation until civil war in Nigeria closed it down once again. It was revived, once more, in the seventies and has continued to appear since then.

New Prefect in Ogoja

The Superior General had gone through the usual procedure of having a Prefect appointed to Ogoja. In May 1938, he submitted the names of possible candidates to Rome, although he had made it known that his choice was Tom McGettrick. Then Pat Whitney's resignation had to be secured, and it was November before Tom McGettrick got word of his appointment. He was in Arochukwu, the holy place of the Ibos, having a blister on his heel dressed by his houseboy. It was a strangely appropriate setting in which to hear the news of his elevation. He was, in many ways, an unlikely prelate. He was renowned as a 'bushwhacker' and there was a boisterousness about him which was never quite at ease in the 'sacred purple'.

Thomas McGettrick was born at Killavil, Co. Sligo, on 22 December 1905, the third child in a family of five. He attended Killavil National School and later Cloneen National School. He got a partial scholarship to St Nathy's College, Ballaghaderreen, the diocesan college of Achonry diocese. He entered Maynooth in 1923, and his seven years there passed quietly. He did a pass B.A. and did not do any theological degree, thus following the common practice for all but the very academically inclined. Although he never distinguished himself as a sportsman, he loved sport and particularly enjoyed handball and swimming. As ordination approached he calculated that he could be fifteen years ordained before a vacancy arose in his own diocese and was faced with the prospect of finding somewhere to work in the meantime. He did not feel attracted to England for the dubious reason that he did not think 'he would be good explaining Christian Doctrine to people who did not believe in God'.[11] The real reason was probably an anti-British bias which he had been given by his grandfather, James McGettrick, a Fenian who left his children and grandchildren in no doubt about Ireland's wrongs and England's wrongdoing. He applied for a diocese in Oklahoma but was told that he would not be accepted on a temporary basis. It was Pat Whitney's appeal, in March 1930, which persuaded him to opt for Nigeria. He spent his first tour in Oron, coming home on leave in 1933 in the company of Pat Whitney who had been on an extended visit to Nigeria. His father died a few months later. During his leave, which lasted almost a year, he visited the schools in Achonry diocese on behalf of the Society and did six weeks of parish work in Kildare and Leighlin. In May 1934 he returned to Anua where he was noted for hard work, inexhaustible energy and remarkably good health.

Anua mission prospered under Tom McGettrick. Catholics increased from 10,000 in 1936, to 20,000 in 1939. The mission was divided into seven zones each of which was to become a separate parish, later on. However, Tom McGettrick was a harsh pastor. He was rough with the people, failing to listen to their views and dealing out severe punishments to those who deviated from the straight path. It was a great temptation for a priest to adopt this line and such conduct was not uncommon.

The privileged position of a white man in a colonial set-up allowed great latitude in dealing with the local population. More to the point, where priests were concerned, the tradition of the people condoned great harshness in the exercise of authority. The lay committees were themselves very harsh, even going so far as to inflict physical punishments on people for breaches of Church discipline. Missionaries found themselves in the position of having to modify the decisions of these committees in order to bring them into line with Christ's teaching on mercy and forgiveness. In his zeal and enthusiasm, Tom McGettrick failed to do this and adopted a severity which was against his own nature. He was, at heart, a kind and benevolent man and came to look back on this period of his life with regret. In an interview given in October 1988, two months before his death, he said that his only real regret was his harshness towards people in the early years.

On receiving the news of his appointment as Prefect Apostolic of Ogoja, Tom McGettrick accompanied James Moynagh to Enugu to meet Archbishop Riberi who had come to Nigeria on a surprise visit. The Apostolic Delegate confirmed the appointment although it was to remain unofficial until the formal decree or papal bull arrived from Rome. Tom McGettrick travelled on to Ogoja while James Moynagh and the Archbishop travelled to Calabar in a Ford V8. The Delegate wished to investigate the complaints which had been made to Rome in the previous May. It was an ill-fated journey. The car was involved in a collision and turned over. The two prelates had to climb out through an open window. The Prefect Apostolic was unhurt but the Archbishop suffered a fractured collar bone. Clerical commentators were to put it down to an accidental kick from James Moynagh, known to have a mean left foot, during the scramble for safety! After a visit to Port Harcourt for an X-ray and treatment it was a somewhat disgruntled Apostolic Delegate who met the dissidents and a number of other lay leaders in the old convent in Calabar. The meeting was short. Their main complaint, at this stage, was that work on the Cathedral had been suspended. Archbishop Riberi urged them to work in peace with the missionaries and left for Lagos.

In Ogoja, Tom McGettrick did a quick visit of the out-stations and returned to Anua to await his documents of appointment which arrived on 9 January 1940. On 2 February, he left Anua and formally accepted the Prefecture of Ogoja from the Pro-Prefect, Manus McClafferty. There were eight priests in four residential missions and two in the Teacher Training College, all of whom were diocesan volunteers. The building programme had done little for the living accommodation of the priests. There was a small but well-constructed house in Abakaliki which had been built in 1938. There was Pat's house in Ogoja. Kakwagom had a small hut on top of a hill, called 'the Crow's Nest' and Okuni had a small rest house, originally intended for short stays. Okpoma, where Pat Whitney had lived in a makeshift house, was no longer to be a residential station. There was £60 in the bank in Enugu.

The new Prefect needed a holiday. He had been in Africa since the middle of 1934 and admitted to being tired. In a short time he had laid his plans for the future. He would concentrate on education as a first step towards evangelisation. He would also seek to establish a medical service, starting with a leper settlement which he hoped would gain support from the British Imperial Leprosy Relief Association and would be staffed by the Medical Missionaries of Mary. In May 1940, the first of a series of appeals for help with leprosy work appeared in *Africa*. The anonymous writer of the appeal describes the priorities of the new Prefect in language which shows little concern for inter-Church dialogue:

> The Province of Ogoja, because of its remoteness from the coast and the absence of passable roads, has not received the same attention from the Civil Administration as Calabar, with the result that statistics of the province are largely tentative. Catholic missionaries have been the first to penetrate this area and until now the monopoly of missionary endeavour has been in Catholic hands. The Protestant sects, which infest Calabar, have never been anxious to anticipate the Governmental advance so that up to the present, Ogoja has been largely free from the devastating activity of the proselytizer with his accompanying creeds, and the tempting material advantages which his apparently inexhaustible resources of wealth can offer. It is Msgr McGettrick's ambition to secure his Prefecture from the encroachment of sectaries by an immediate push in two directions: he must build hospitals and schools.[12]

Shortly after arriving, Tom McGettrick discussed the funding of the Leper Settlement with local Government Officials and received a definite promise of support. He finalised arrangements with the Holy Child Sisters, who agreed to establish a girls' school at Ogoja, under Sister Osmund de Maille. A grant of £1,000 from Propaganda helped to overcome the financial difficulty. He would finish the mission houses begun in Kakwagom and Ogoja and after that there would be no building 'until the Germans are beaten'.

Going on leave posed a problem for Tom McGettrick. It was difficult to find anyone to run the Prefecture while he was away. He did not want to appoint Manus McClafferty, the former Pro-Prefect nor did he wish to offend him by appointing a junior man. Manus McClafferty was a fine missionary but Tom McGettrick felt he did not have the tact required to run the Prefecture well. A strike in the Teacher Training College, the previous year, had considerably damaged the Pro-Prefect's reputation for diplomacy. Noel Sandvoss had been Principal and, following the introduction of new bucket-type latrines, he had, at the Pro-Prefect's suggestion, decided that the students would empty the buckets themselves, thus cutting down on hired labour. The students refused and stopped using the toilets. A number were threatened with expulsion and all the students walked out. It was a major crisis especially in the light of the great need for teachers. In a letter to Paddy Costelloe, James Moynagh wondered, rather appropriately, whether the priests had 'gone potty' up in Ogoja. In the end, the authorities had to back down to the great embarrassment of Noel Sandvoss. However, it was Manus McClafferty who was held primarily responsible, especially by the priests in Calabar, for allowing the situation to get out of hand. Tom McGettrick asked James Moynagh to send Matt Magrath to Ogoja as Pro-Prefect. Kiltegan was consulted but already Paddy Costelloe had decided that Peter Joe Duffy, who was on his way back from leave in Ireland, would take the position. When the latter arrived in Calabar, Matt Magrath had already gone to Ogoja and Tom McGettrick had left for Ireland. James Moynagh apologised to the Superior General and appointed Peter Joe Duffy Father-in-charge in Anua. It was June 1940. British troops were surrounded on the French coast and over 300,000 of them had to be evacuated from Dunkirk. As he boarded a British passenger boat in Lagos, Tom McGettrick, accompanied by J.B. McCartan and Michael McHugh, wondered what lay in store in England. The ship was part of a convoy of twelve ships guarded by two armed sloops. On the voyage, the Captain told them 'that there might not be an England when we got there'.[13]

Illness and death of Monsignor Whitney

As Ogoja geared itself for new development, Pat Whitney was involved in a struggle to cope with the daily tasks of dressing himself, saying Mass and communicating with those around him. He had not given up hope of a cure. Soon after leaving the Mater hospital he consulted a 'Natural Therapy Practitioner' in Farnworth, Lancashire. Whether or not he travelled to see this man is not clear. It is possible that he only sent a blood sample which was how the therapist monitored his progress throughout the period that followed. Natural medicines were sent regularly from England and Pat was put on a high fibre diet. Paddy Costelloe and the Council were not happy that Pat was staying with his sister and continued to urge him to come to Kiltegan. Whenever Pat asked for a living allowance he was told that the Council would not approve of an allowance unless he came to Kiltegan.

Meanwhile, his health showed no sign of improvement and Dr T.J. Kilgallen, a general practitioner of Boyle, Co. Roscommon referred him to a Dublin specialist, Mr Parker. The specialist diagnosed degeneration of the cerebellum, the lower back part of the brain, and 'a degenerative lesion of his central nervous system'. There is no mention of a specific disease and the general nature of the diagnosis indicates some uncertainty on the part of the specialist. He was referred to Professor Leonard Abrahamson who recommended that he go into a Nursing Home. Instead, he returned to Sligo but agreed, with very bad grace, to go to Kiltegan. He asked for travelling expenses and £2 was sent by return. Immediately, he got a bad attack which Dr Kilgallen described as 'an acute exacerbation of his symptoms—sleeplessness, tremor, anorexia'. He had advised that Pat would need the services of a night nurse. A letter from Paddy Costelloe was less than sympathetic and unintentionally derogatory towards the nursing care given by his mother and sisters. He wrote:

> I am indeed sorry to learn that you are so ill. Everything seems to point to the folly of your not having carried out the instructions of the Council to come here where you would have been properly cared for.

He repeated the official position taken by the Society administration that it 'does not accept responsibility for any expenses other than those incurred with its express approval'. Pat went into a Nursing Home at 37 Lower Leeson St and was attended by Dr Abrahamson, who gave him a daily injection of some substance designed to stimulate the production of natural cortisone.

While in the Nursing Home, he was visited by Tom McGettrick who had arrived safely in Ireland and had spent some time at home, in Killavil. Paddy Costelloe had asked Tom McGettrick and Corney Plunkett to visit Pat and to ask him to abide by the Constitutions which he himself had drawn up. They found Pat in bad shape. They helped him to say

Mass and Tom McGettrick held the chalice for him at the consecration and communion. Later, they discussed his differences with the Superior General. Pat agreed that he had helped draw up the Constitutions but said that he never understood them to mean what his successor thought they meant. The visit helped towards reconciliation. As he began to feel better, Pat moved to a guest house called Haddington House in Dun Laoghaire so that he could keep up twice-weekly visits to the doctor. On Christmas Eve 1940, he returned to Kiltegan. Outstanding bills were paid and there followed a period of relative harmony.

Pat was withdrawn and made no contact with those whom he knew in the office. He did visit the neighbours and, from time to time, he borrowed a pony and trap from the Pierces, a Protestant family in Rathdangan. He is remembered driving out in this pony and trap; his clothes seemed to sit badly on him and sometimes he was unable to close the door of the trap. Students of the time remember him reading his breviary on the walks and exchanging a few words about tree-planting or whatever work they were engaged in. A letter which Pat wrote to his classmate James Fergus, later Bishop of Kilalla, on 4 February 1941, gives a rare and humorous insight into his anguish, his pride in the Society and the alienation he felt from the new Superiors. It was written in a shaky, though much improved, hand and reads in part:

> My bust-up in health nearly broke me in every way. It seemed that all zest for life was gone with Africa. You know the young men and how wide is the gap between them and us—men of great devotion and prayer, very careful in the carrying out of the liturgy and ceremonial of the Church, easily scandalised by the like of me. Now there are forty men in Africa, and over twenty here—all first class, a reproduction of the Maynooth Mission of John Blowick's time. My job was done—if I could only die decent. And it was only after a Dublin specialist working on me with a Jewman called Abrahamson that I got a few holy people to pray for my recovery. The specialist pronounced me incurable that the spinal fluid was at an advanced state of decay, and I would soon be unable to talk or walk though I would retain my intelligence perfectly. I asked him could he do nothing. He said he would try the induction of a gland but could promise nothing till he saw results. The prayers worked thank God. On Mission Sunday I said Mass and have done so since. On Xmas Eve he allowed me back to the care of the local Dr. here, the injection to be continued a couple of times a week.

The local Dr. is a brother of Ned Maguire. Says he to me the first day I went in:

'Is this thing doing you any good?'

'Don't know,' I told him.

'Well,' says he, 'it didn't do much for a patient I had on it for six months—a young nervous wreck who never had any hair—but it did one thing to him that lost him to me. It gave him a beautiful head of hair and he promptly went and got married.'

Well he likes how I'm doing, and I'm quite happy as long as I can say Mass.

Pat was dissatisfied with the care in Kiltegan. Dr Abrahamson had advised: 'I think it would be as well to let him live the life for which he feels able. I know how difficult this may be in an institution like yours, but in a case of this kind, it is wise to give every latitude, however unreasonable the patient seems to be at times.' He complained of the diet, the draughts and the lack of nursing care. At the beginning of April 1941, he was moved to Beaumont Convalescent Home. In June he had become more incapacitated and the Mercy Sisters who ran the Home asked Paddy Costelloe to move him to a Nursing Home or to Kiltegan, as Beaumont did not provide nursing care. While in Beaumont he made contact with Mr Unsworth, the natural practitioner in England whom he had given up for some time. He also changed his doctor and attended Dr Colm A. McDonnell who was in practice at 3 Upper Ely Place and would seem to have followed a course of therapy similar to that of Mr Unsworth. Dr McDonnell sent several reports to Kiltegan, one of which reads: 'I think it will be the best part of twelve months before he will be back to normal health.' Pat remained in Beaumont until July, when he moved to Miss Phillip's Nursing Home in Upper Mount Street, an institution which catered particularly for clergy.

By the end of September, he was anxious to go home to his family again. The Superior General tried to dissuade him in a friendly letter, suggesting a brief visit home, and then a period in Kiltegan or Drogheda where Mother Mary Martin had offered him a room. It was a fitting offer. When Marie Martin was looking for a place to go with her first aspirants, Pat had offered her accommodation in Kiltegan. Although she opted for Glenstal, she did not forget Pat's kindness and the two remained good friends. However Pat was not open to either offer. His doctor had advised convalescence at home—no doubt at Pat's own insistence—and home it would be. From Sligo, the cat and mouse game started all over again with Pat requesting a living allowance and Paddy Costelloe refusing in the name of the Council and demanding that he return to Kiltegan.

In December, Pat brought the matter to the attention of the Papal Nuncio, describing how unsuitable Kiltegan was for a sick person:

> In Kiltegan there are drafts in every room; logs are only burned in the furnace and elsewhere and the necessary consequence to me would be deadly chills. There is no nurse, housekeeper or servant within call if one requires anything at night as I do. To prepare meals there is one harassed cook to cater for 100 people on a very indifferent range. She would not get from the Bursar what she would require. Last year I handed my menu to Father Costelloe. He handed it to the cook and there was no further remarks passed on it.

The Papal Nuncio passed the letters on to Paddy Costelloe who explained:

> Our Council disapproves of Msgr Whitney's remaining away with his relatives, believing that he should have the spiritual advantages available here. I have no authority to act contrary to this decision.

Through January, February, March and April 1942, Pat continued to live with his sister and correspondence with Kiltegan continued in the same vein. Paddy Costelloe's letters upset Pat so much that his sister, on the advice of the doctor, stopped giving them to him entirely. When she explained this in a letter to Paddy Costelloe he expressed indignation that a lay person should open the letters of one priest to another.

At the end of April, Pat went to Miss Phillip's Nursing Home again and stayed five weeks. He had asked the Superior General's permission to go home and was again refused. This was the usual procedure when he was at odds with Kiltegan. He asked permission, even though he had already decided what he would do. Occasionally he sent a telegram with the message: 'Please give me immediate instructions' or words to that effect. Paddy Costelloe tried to get him into Linden Convalescent Home but there was no vacancy. Meanwhile, Pat had gone home again, this time to his brother's house in Port where he had spent so many happy days and where he had written the early letters to Archbishop Hinsley and to Propaganda about the formation of the Society.

He was very ill when he arrived and he needed constant nursing care. He was attended by his mother and sisters and other friends. His mother had been with him in Sligo and now she was with him in Port. He managed to sat Mass in his room a few times but it soon became obvious that death was not far away. He was anointed on 14 June. He agreed to go to a Nursing Home in Dublin soon afterwards and asked for a Society priest to accompany him. Paddy Costelloe wrote to John McGuinness, a young priest who had been ordained for the Society in 1940, and who was staying with his family in nearby Mohill, to make himself available. When John McGuinness arrived on 27 June, Pat was too weak to travel. John McGuinness wrote to Kiltegan saying: 'I could only make out a few shreds of what he was trying to say.'

On Friday 17 July 1942, Monsignor Pat Whitney died. The news reached Kiltegan by way of the death columns in Saturday morning's papers. Arrangements had been made to remove the remains to St Mary's Church, Carrick-on-Shannon on Sunday evening and to have the burial in the family plot in Kilronan cemetery, on Monday. Because of wartime restrictions, no unapproved cars were allowed on the roads. Paddy Costelloe cycled to Baltinglass, or perhaps Blessington, to catch a bus for Dublin. He got the only evening bus travelling from Dublin to Longford and from there he cycled to Port House. He asked that Pat Whitney's remains be buried in Kiltegan. The Whitney family had already discussed this. Pat had left no will nor had he left any instructions as to where he should be buried. Some members of his family felt that his mortal remains belonged in Kiltegan but his sister, Mrs Gardiner, was not too sure that this would be his own wish. She argued that as he had chosen to stay with his family during his last illness, he would also have preferred to be buried with them. Besides, Pat's antipathy towards Paddy Costelloe had been communicated to the family and it influenced their decision on the burial. The fact that arrangements had already been published in the paper, before Paddy Costelloe's arrival, was a strong argument for leaving things as they were. The Superior General had to resign himself to officiating at the Founder's burial away from Kiltegan in spite of the fact that it raised eyebrows among some of the clergy.

Paddy Costelloe celebrated the Requiem Mass on Monday, in the presence of Bishop McNamee of Ardagh and Clonmacnois. There were over 100 priests present and a large number of religious and lay people. A number of Society members were in attendance. John McGuinness was deacon at the Mass, and Cornie Plunkett was sub-deacon. Frank Whitney had come from Drumlish where he was on holidays and Maurice Hayes had come from his home in Limerick. Among the students present was Joe Dollard, who, like Maurice Hayes had come to Longford by bus and cycled the rest of the way. Father Hickey, who was away from Kiltegan at the time, missed the funeral because a telegram he had received from Frank misled him as to the day. The burial took place in the little cemetery of Kilronan where the piper Carolan is buried. Pat's name was later inscribed on a side panel of the large limestone celtic cross which marked the family grave. A year later, almost to the day, his mother Mary Anne Whitney was laid to rest beside him.

The exact nature of Pat Whitney's final illness is not known. His death certificate gives the cause of death as 'arterio-sclerosis, cerebellar degeneration and cardiac failure—four years certified'. Arteriosclerosis, which is a hardening of the arteries, could have affected the cerebellum by reducing the blood supply to that part of the brain. Atheroma, a build-up of fat in the arteries, which is usually associated with the former condition, could also account for the heart failure. However, there was no mention of arteriosclerosis or heart failure or the high blood pressure associated with them in the few letters from Pat's doctors which have found their way into the archives. The tradition in the Whitney family is that Pat suffered from Parkinson's disease and sources within the Medical Missionaries of Mary quote their Foundress as saying that he had Parkinson's. There is a problem with this diagnosis in that Parkinson's does not manifest the pattern of recovery and relapse which can be deduced from accounts of Pat's illness. He manifested a few symptoms of Multiple Sclerosis but not enough to in-dicate the presence of that disease. He could possibly have had a tumour in the brain or suffered from a rare specific disorder of the cerebellum. In the end, no definite conclusion can be reached except to say that he suffered from a neurological disorder which got progressively worse over the last six years of his life.

There is an impression among many members of St Patrick's Society that Pat Whitney's illness and death was related to the abuse of alcohol. There is, however, no evidence for this. There was a very vague rumour in the mid thirties that Pat was drinking too much. This rumour may have arisen from observation of the shake in his hand and as a footnote to the bad press he was getting for the Bundoran venture. Lay people who worked in Kiltegan at the time never heard anything like that and they never noticed any sign of alcohol abuse. Quaintly enough, they put Pat's tremor down to old age and the effects of a lifetime in the tropics. Pat was forty at the time, and he had spent no more than six years on the missions. Those who accompanied him to Nigeria in 1938 did not notice any particular partiality towards drink. He was much more interested in the mechanical racing dogs on the ship and managed to pick a few winners. The next time drink was mentioned was in connection with Pat's breakdown in Ogoja. At first, the priests suspected that drink must have been the cause although, in Manus McClafferty's words, 'no one appears to have seen him take more than was good for him'.[14] Later, they were convinced that he had been drinking and referred to the fact that members of the European colonial community thought so, and a doctor is quoted as saying 'Monsignor Whitney is too fond of the bottle'. The young priests presumably thought that Pat did his drinking with the colonial officials. As relative newcomers, they may not have known that rumours such as these were the stuff of European clubs throughout the colonies. It may well be that Pat Whitney took alcohol when he felt the attack coming on but there can be no doubt that alcohol did not cause the breakdown. A Medical Missionary Sister quotes Mother Mary Martin as saying that Pat Whitney had suffered a lot from the false accusation of alcoholism due to a mistaken interpretation of his symptoms. The story of alcoholism, which has persisted within the Society, is based on these rumours and on the presupposition that because he ran dance-halls and cinemas and put letters into wrong envelopes that he was a 'wild man' and inevitably a hard-drinking man. Without any risk of compromising the truth this image of the Society's Founder can be laid to rest.

A sort of reinstatement of Pat Whitney took place in July 1963, when his remains were transferred from Kilronan to the Society cemetery in Kiltegan. The cemetery had been newly designed by Pearse McKenna to give pride of place to the Founder's grave, for which a massive tombstone of Wicklow granite had been prepared. A Latin inscription on the stone commemorates Pat Whitney as the Founder of St Patrick's Missionary Society. The event was made possible by a reconciliation with the Whitney family which has since given three of Pat's nephews to the missions. Seamus Whitney is a priest of St Patrick's Society. Ciaran Whitney, a priest of Elphin, has worked in Ogoja and in Kitui, in Kenya, and Padraig Whitney has worked as a lay-teacher in Ogoja. Sadly, the two co-founders of the Society chose not to be buried in Kiltegan although Pat's remains were there before they died. In July 1973, Frank Whitney was buried in his native Drumlish, where he now shares a plot with Bernard Hughes, another Society priest from the parish, who died in 1982. Father Hickey, who died in 1972, chose to be buried in his native Ballon. In spite of a lifetime of service to the Society and a reasonably contented retirement in Kiltegan, he never recovered from his estrangement. He willed his modest collection of books and his chalices to the Jesuits.[15]

8

The War Years

FROM the beginning, the new administration in Kiltegan had an excellent relationship with the two Prefects Apostolic in Nigeria. Paddy Costelloe asked James Moynagh and Tom McGettrick for advice. He enquired after the needs of the missions and went to great lengths to honour any requests that were made. These requests were many and various, especially during the war when supplies were hard to come by in Nigeria. They included tinned butter, 260 bolts with nuts (15" x ⅝"), a loan of £2,000 and a doctor for leprosy work. The main request, however, was for more priests and especially priests with university degrees who would staff the secondary schools and Teacher Training Colleges. The two Prefects had no doubt whatever that priests should be directly involved in education. When Paddy Costelloe proposed that an order of teaching brothers might replace the priests in the schools he got little support. Tom McGettrick avoided the issue by pointing out that he did not have accommodation for brothers. James Moynagh accepted that brothers might have a role in technical education and perhaps in Teacher Training but he would not accept the idea of handing over the secondary schools to them. He wrote on 23 April 1943, in a letter to Paddy Costelloe:

> Education is our primary contact with the people and will be so increasingly. The majority of our catechumens come from our schools. In fact, the evangelization of Africa depends on what kind education is to be. Therefore, if some of the finest religious orders devote themselves to it even in countries where Christian education

is the rule how much more should our priests consider the chance to teach as a golden opportunity not something to pass on to Brothers. *Your first concern* will be to see that Kiltegan men are specialists in education.

The school was to be the point of contact where the lay leaders of the future would come to know the priests and build up a relationship of trust with them.

All the Maynooth volunteers were university graduates and their degrees were acceptable to the Government in Nigeria, in the assessment of schools for grants. Of the early Society priests, only a few had degrees so the missions had to rely on the volunteers to provide staff for the schools. A small number of men taught without degrees but when it came to eligibility for Government grants a certain number of teachers with recognised qualifications were required. Lack of men with science degrees was a particularly pressing problem and James Moynagh states repeatedly that without a good science department a school could not hope to compete for students with the Protestant schools and would be forced to close down.

Soon after the outbreak of war it became apparent that Maynooth could no longer be relied on to answer the needs of the schools. The response was good in 1940 and seven priests went out but after that there was a sharp decline. No volunteer went out in 1941, only two in 1942, one in 1943, none in 1944 and one in 1945. From 1946 there was a slight improvement but it was never to reach the numbers of the 1930s. In the ten years from 1930, 58 priests volunteered while in the ten years from 1940, only 25 volunteered and of these 3 remained in Kiltegan.[1]

Meanwhile, the number of Society priests was steadily increasing. There were 25 priest-members in 1940. By 1945, the number had risen to 58. In 1941, there was a dramatic increase in student-numbers with a probation class of 27. All the students were now together in Kiltegan. First-year philosophers had been taught there in 1939, while second philosophers finished their course in Carlow. In the autumn of 1940, everyone came to Kiltegan. The large intake, in 1941, put a great strain on student accommodation. Paddy Costelloe appealed in *Africa* for contributions for a new college and mentioned the undesirable alternative of turning away students, 'telling them there was no room'.

The financial position of the Society was steadily improving also. By mid-1939 the bank deficit had been reduced by over £1,200. A year later, another £3,000 had been paid off and, by 1942, there was a credit balance. The auditors were satisfied with the records and wrote, with regard to the 1939 audit: 'There was a marked improvement in the books and records and the system has now been put on a proper basis.' In 1940, Jim Walsh was recalled to his diocese and posted, in Tom McGettrick's words, 'to the Cul-de-sac of Achonry'. He was replaced as bursar by the newly ordained Vincent Kiernan. Much of the income came from the postal appeals and from visitation of parishes and schools. The magazine *Africa*, now edited by Vincent Chambers, continued to play its part, describing the needs and acknowledging the donations received. An appeal for the Holy Child Sisters and an account of their work in Nigeria became a regular feature of the magazine. Money was still in short supply; 500 trees were sold off and student fees or 'pensions', fixed at £35 in 1939, were essential to the economy. There was an insistence on the payment of pensions and reductions or remissions were made only after a close scrutiny of an individual student's circumstances. The St Joseph's Young Priests Society helped in a number of cases.

With the prospect of another big class in 1942—twenty-five eventually came—something had to be done about accommodation. At a meeting of the General Council, in November 1941, it was decided to make enquiries about the possibility of renting Humewood Castle, a nearby manor, the owners of which were living in France. If Humewood was not available, a temporary extension would be made to the existing College. After enquiries and negotiations with the representatives of the owners, a rental agreement was drawn up and Humewood became home to the Probationers for four years.

Humewood

Humewood Castle, the ancestral home of the Hume family, belonged to Catherine Hume-Weygand who had married a French colonel a few years previously. Her father-in-law was General Maxime Wegand the Supreme Allied Commander at Dunkirk and defender of the Weygand-line up to the fall of France. The Humes had come to Kiltegan in 1704, and were prominent among the Wicklow gentry. During the 1798 rebellion, William Hume MP set up the Humewood Cavalry to fight the insurrection, by arming 200 of his tenants and neighbours. Humewood became a garrison and a refuge for local Protestant families. In October 1798, William Hume was shot and killed when he rode over to a party of rebels disguised in red coats which they had captured from the military. The insurrection was soon crushed in most places but, in the Wicklow mountains, a party under the command of the legendary Michael Dwyer continued to harass the establishment and to evade capture. William Hoare Hume succeeded his father as commander of the Humewood Cavalry and for four years he pursued Dwyer and his men. The two protagonists came to respect one another and in the end Dwyer surrendered to Hume after the latter had persuaded the Government to offer him safe-passage to America. When the government reneged on its promise and transported Dwyer to Australia, Hume was so furious that he rode to Dublin and slapped the Chief Secretary in the face on the steps of the Viceregal Lodge.

The present house is considered to be 'one of the most remarkable of Victorian houses'.[2] It was built in 1870 to the design of William White for a grandson of William Hume named William Hume Dick. He had taken the name *Dick* to honour his late uncle, a Dublin merchant who had left him a lot of money. From now on Humewood was to become a holiday home as Hume Dick and his descendants spent most of the year in their homes in England, France and Scotland. Hume Dick's granddaughter, Catherine Marie, inherited Humewood on the death of her father, in 1939. Recently married and living in France, she was prevented by the war from travelling to Ireland for the customary summer visit to her ancestral home. Her husband, Lt Colonel J.S.A. Weygand had never visited Humewood.

In October 1942, an agreement was drawn up between Madame Hume-Weygand and Fathers Costelloe and Plunkett, giving the Society the use of Humewood as a place of education for students at an annual rent of £130 and subject to termination on three months' notice by either party. The agreement was signed on behalf of Madame Hume-Weygand by her attorney Madam Grace O'Mahony of Grangecon. The solicitors were Brown and McCann of Naas. Even before the agreement was signed, the probationers had taken up residence in Humewood with Corney Plunkett, their director, and Jimmy Lane his assistant. Hugh Markey, a Dalgan priest, who was teaching the theologians and living in High Park, served part-time as Spiritual Director. A number of priests awaiting a sailing to Nigeria also moved to Humewood. Sean Meehan remembers an occasion on which Paddy Costelloe arrived on horseback to announce that there was a boat going out at the end of Easter week 1943. Paddy Reilly, Jack Lee, John Moynihan and Dominic Conway were waiting to travel. They went home to say goodbye to their families. Transport was precarious and Jack Lee missed the boat.

The other three made the sailing. It had been arranged that a firm called Horne Bros would deliver their sun helmets to the boat, at Liverpool. The representative failed to make contact with the priests and Paddy Costelloe expressed the hope, in a letter to James Moynagh, that the lack of helmets would not affect their health. Jack Lee sailed in July. The boat was torpedoed and Jack found himself in the water, 'having lost everything but the faith', as Mick Reilly told the students in Kiltegan. Three Holy Rosary Sisters found themselves in the same predicament. They were rescued and the American Red Cross were able to supply Jack with a new set of breviaries and other essentials which enabled him to continue on to Nigeria.

Corney Plunkett continued as Rector of the College although he lived in Humewood. As he was also Vicar-General of the Society he had a very heavy work-load and James Moynagh advised Paddy Costelloe to relieve him of some of the responsibility. However, this was not possible until 1944. Priests and students enjoyed a friendly and informal relationship which was exceptional at the time. Students were addressed by their Christian names and were joined by a number of priests for football, gardening, tree-planting and other outdoor activities. The professors were for the most part young Maynooth volunteers who had recently completed post-graduate studies. Some, like Gerry Montague, completed their doctoral theses while in Kiltegan. There was nothing soft about the life and to keep warm some of them would go to a nearby bog and buy their own turf. All were capable men who would soon be required by their bishops for special assignments. As a result, there was a quick turn-over of staff and two or three years was the general length of time spent in Kiltegan. Gradually, young Kiltegan priests like Jimmy Lane and John McGuinness took over the teaching posts although Kiltegan was to continue to avail of the services of diocesan priests right up to the 1980s.[3]

The volunteers who served in Kiltegan were to remain on friendly terms with the Society. Many of them achieved positions of prominence in the Irish Church. Gerry Montague was Dean in Maynooth and later parish priest of the Falls Road in Belfast and an Archdeacon. Tom Campbell became a Monsignor and Vicar General of Clonfert. Jim Kavanagh went to the army and later became an auxiliary bishop of Dublin. Denis Meehan became Professor of Classics in Maynooth. He resigned because of ill-health and worked as a diocesan priest in California. Later he joined the Benedictine Monastery of Vallyermo, lectured in the University of California and wrote a number of books. Mick Leahy became professor of Scripture in Maynooth. Dominic Conway became

Rector of the Irish College in Rome, and later Bishop of Elphin. While in Rome he acted for a time as Society representative there. Others to serve in Kiltegan were Vincent Chambers (Raphoe), Joe Abbott (Meath), Seamus McLoughlin and Tom Lavin (Elphin), Dan Duffy (Clogher) and Joe Moran (Tuam).

The war disrupted the meetings of the General Council as the three diocesan consultors were frequently unable to travel due to the shortage of petrol. This was an additional burden on Paddy Costelloe who had been asked by the Bishop to seek the opinions of the consultors by letter before each council meeting. He did it faithfully whether on formal matters such as the promotion of students to the priesthood or more domestic matters such as the purchase of a new cooker.

In September 1942, Charlie Smith entered the probation year and, a year later, became a member of the Society. He was to be a key figure in establishing the Society in such a way as to ensure its financial viability in the future. Charles Smith, the youngest of six children, was born in Cavan in 1909. His parents were small farmers whose thrift and industry set them apart from their neighbours. Charlie attended St Patrick's College, Cavan, the diocesan college of Kilmore diocese. He went on to Maynooth and was ordained in 1934. He wanted to go to Nigeria but Bishop Finegan refused him permission. The bishop's disagreement with Pat Whitney, in the days when the latter was fund-raising for Kille-shandra, had effectively closed the Society mission to Kilmore priests. Pat Whitney had assured the Bishop that he would keep Charlie in Ireland until he made a decision about joining the Society, but to no avail. Charlie went to Brentwood diocese in England and remained there until Bishop Finegan's successor allowed him to go to Nigeria. He went to Ogoja with Pat Whitney, in November 1938, and returned to Ireland with him four months later, partly to accompany the ailing Prefect Apostolic but also because his own health had not been good. He spent a period in hospital and then did odd jobs around Kiltegan such as trimming the avenue and clearing the rhubarb garden. Soon afterwards he was appointed manager of the office with responsibility for the pro-motion and distribution of *Africa*. He soon proved himself to be an exceptionally keen manager. Under his direction, the circulation of *Africa* increased from 10,000, in 1940, to 199,000, in the 1960s. In 1945, he started the Mission League. This later became the Mission Circle, which comprised thousands of members who donated regularly to the Society. Many members became life-time supporters and in many cases the support was maintained by their children.

Charlie Smith's business sense was a family affair. One of his brothers was a successful builder and the other two founded a chain of garages. Charlie combined this natural aptitude with a simple spirituality. He trusted in God and was singleminded in his devotion to spreading God's Word through missionary work. He was Spiritual Director to the students in the early 1940s and many remember the warmth and simplicity of his message. Kindness to people, faithfulness to prayer, devotion to Our Lady, was his formula for successful missionary work. He became Bursar General in 1944 and Vicar General in 1950. He held the latter post until 1972. However, his principal charism did not lie in leadership but in the ability to organise and communicate to people the urgency of missionary work. He was very personal in his approach and was able to give comfort to people in trouble. His memory was never as good as he would have liked and he often made major blunders as to people's names and family circumstances. It made no difference to their response to him. He was ably assisted in his work by Mary Campbell whose extraordinary memory made up for Charlie's more than occasional lapses. Between them, they built up an outstanding promotion network which Charlie managed until 1973. Central to it was a loyal and committed office staff which included Molly Byrne, Maisie Dowling, Kitty Bookle and many others.

Wartime on the Missions

At the beginning of the war, the colonial authorities declared Calabar a danger area and the schools in the town were closed down for a short period. When it became apparent that the Germans had no immediate designs on Nigeria, life returned to normal.

The big headache was getting missionaries out and getting them home for a holiday or for medical treatment. A number, including James Moynagh, extended their tours. This left them in urgent need of a holiday and as there was no congenial place in Eastern Nigeria, James Moynagh rented a house in Buea in Cameroon as a holiday home. Here, priests and sisters were able to enjoy a break in a favourable climate. This move was an example of Moynagh's enlightened leadership. He was prepared to go ahead although he felt sure he would be criticised for wasting money. He wrote to Paddy Costelloe in February 1943: 'It costs a bit but when travel home is so uncertain I consider it wise to keep people well.' The Superior General was not at all critical and gave his unqualified approval to the project.

In spite of the difficulties and dangers involved, there was a lot of travelling during the war. All the newly ordained except those given appointments at home succeeded in making the journey to the mission-field. No one was lost. In fact, not a single Catholic missionary among the hundreds who travelled to and from West Africa during the war was lost. Tom McGettrick came across a soldier who felt that there was more to this than chance. He wrote in *Africa*:

> One officer on board who never went to Church himself naively confessed that they always liked to bring a few Catholic 'Padres' as they remarked that during the course of the war they always got through safely when a priest was on board. How useful, one might say, to be regarded even as a mascot.[4]

Lack of motorised transport on the missions was another problem. The motor cycles which had become indispensable to the missionary work of the priests could no longer be kept on the road. Tom McGettrick describes the situation:

> One by one the motor cycles developed incurable complaints; one by one they were consigned honourably and not without regret, to blocks in the mission garages where, covered with dust and rust, they await the time when spare parts are available. Our Ogoja fleet of six are all invalided some of them permanently. This imposed, to my mind, the greatest hardship on the Fathers here in this Province of 7,200 square miles. Out-stations 30 to 50 miles had to be visited on push-cycles and even these were not easy to secure. It meant slow motion, long, arduous journeys in tropical heat; it slowed down our striking power immensely as schools, stations and the sick could not be visited as often as formerly.[5]

The war led to food shortages in Nigeria and to a big increase in food-prices. The missionaries were never hungry but the Irish staples—bread, butter and milk—which had to be imported, were often in short supply. Building materials, too, were scarce, and very expensive. There were few permanent buildings erected during the war. Because he had some supplies in hand, James Moynagh was able to go ahead with plans for St Patrick's College, Calabar. Brother John Bermingham finished it, in 1942, and reactivated the building of the Cathedral which had been interrupted due to structural errors. Holy Family College, Abak was opened in January 1942 but consisted of temporary buildings. The first Teacher Training College in the Prefecture of Calabar was opened at Urua Inyang, in 1944. The story was much the same in Ogoja. A good mission house was built in Ogoja town and nearby a permanent school which was used as a church on Sundays. A priests' house was built at Afikpo and also a convent which was described as 'semi-permanent'. Another convent was built at Abakaliki. Shortage of school supplies also posed a problem and every available scrap of paper was put to use in lieu of exercise books.

Early on in the war, John Sheehan, Carthage Cantwell and Enda Davis were sent to the British Army as chaplains. Towards the end, Jim Byrne became a chaplain and John Sheehan left to join the General Council in Kiltegan.

Tom McGettrick had great difficulty in getting back to his diocese. Matt Magrath was in charge of the Prefecture of Ogoja in his absence and was anxious to be relieved. James Moynagh had made several approaches to the government authorities to ask for preferential treatment for Tom McGettrick on the grounds that his presence in Nigeria was important for the development of the colony. Finally, in February 1942, he got a passage with a military convoy sailing to Madagascar. He had been a year and nine months at home. There were thirty-one other missionaries with him including Society members, Christy Donlon, Joe Gilmartin, Con Murphy and Paddy Doyle and volunteer priests, Joseph Scott and Patrick Meenan.

Bishop McGettrick gives an entertaining description of the journey in his *Memoirs*. The boat was a North Atlantic liner which was intended for 850 passengers. There were 3,000 aboard on this journey to Africa. The experienced missionaries avoided the drinking water which tasted bad, and slaked their thirst with the meagre rations from the bar. In the tropics, the boat became 'a frying pan made warmer by the foul language of the occupants'. The missionaries slept during the day and stayed on deck all night playing musical instruments and singing Irish songs. They left the convoy at Freetown and took a smaller passenger steamer to Lagos and went from there to Onitsha by lorry. This group brought to forty-four the number of priests in Calabar and Ogoja. Four of the priests went to Ogoja with Tom McGettrick while two went to Calabar. Dr Connolly who accompanied them went to Emekuku to stay with Joe Barnes and to prepare himself to take up duty at Anua hospital.

On his arrival in Ogoja, Tom McGettrick was pleased with the comfortable house which had been completed since he left. Tom Leavy had begun the work with the intention of building a small church. Later, it was decided that priests' accommodation was a priority. Manus McClafferty made the necessary adjustments and the building became a fine house which was to be Tom McGettrick's residence, as Prefect

Apostolic and later as Bishop, for 34 years. A slight problem arose when it was discovered that the original monies used were from a donation of £100 given to Pat Whitney by Kathleen and Mary Duignan for the building of a church. Tom McGettrick undertook to 'try and explain to them'.

The Prefect Apostolic had returned to Ogoja with £12,000 which he had collected for leprosy work. £8,000 of this was raised by the sale of raffle tickets which were distributed throughout Ireland by the priests, students and office girls in Kiltegan and by the students of Maynooth College. To start the leprosy work, however, he would need a doctor and a number of nurses. He had no immediate prospect of getting these. So, while Paddy Costelloe looked for a doctor in Ireland, Tom McGettrick turned his attention to evangelisation and the opening of schools. In 1943, he reported to Kiltegan that 100 schools had been opened. Two years later, there were 200 'mud-walled, mat-roofed buildings' throughout the diocese which served as churches and schools. The Prefect Apostolic was particularly encouraged by government plans to pay teachers' salaries in the near future. This measure was to make a huge difference to Ogoja and Calabar. It would be possible to employ sufficient qualified teachers and to develop an excellent network of schools. Moreover, the salaries earned by priest-teachers would contribute significantly to the overall development of the missions.

The Holy Child Sisters had opened three girls' schools in Ogoja in 1940, but supervised them from Ikot Ekpene which was 140 miles away from the nearest one. This situation continued until February 1945, when the Holy Child Convent at Afikpo was opened. Three sisters, Mothers Bernard, Cecilia and Helen took up residence there and ran the Primary school and a Domestic Training College for girls.

In January 1944, the death of Martin Hannon, a volunteer priest from Tuam was a big blow to Ogoja. Although he was an exceptionally strong man, he developed blackwater fever and died six days later. The cablegram from Ogoja, dated 13 January, stated the sad facts:

> Father Hannon developed black water fever six days ago. Died this morning. Everything possible was done. Two Medical Missionaries here on holiday nursed him night and day. Two doctors in attendance continuously. Break sad news to father, mother and Archbishop.

In July 1945, Con Murphy, a Society priest from Bere Island, Co. Cork, died of malaria in Enugu hospital. He had come to Ogoja in February 1942.

The return of Matt Magrath to Calabar, in 1942, following his period as pro-Prefect of Ogoja, was welcomed by James Moynagh. The two were good friends and together they formed a creative partnership. Both were men of ideas. Matt, in particular, loved to find new ways of doing things without always considering the practicalities involved. In James Moynagh, he found a ready listener who took his ideas seriously and often acted on them. A holiday they spent together in 1941 gave them an opportunity to lay typical plans. They went to Gboko to stay with the Holy Ghost Fathers there. One night James Moynagh got a seizure which appeared to be a heart attack but which, on medical examination, turned out to be an allergic reaction to Ovaltine. They continued their holiday in Jos and the following request from Matt Magrath to Kiltegan resulted from their discussions:

> Another thing is this; Government is very anxious to get down to the question of making Nigeria self–supporting and all kinds of schemes are being put up for the producing of stuffs on the spot that used to be imported and they ask our cooperation; I think we could do a lot. Could you help in the following: Get a man who is interested and get him to visit various factories and find out in detail the method of making, say the following: soap from palm oil (formula wanted and detailed method); tallow candles, and wax do., pottery (how to make a potter's wheel); glazing; spinning and weaving of cotton; if possible the plans in detail of a fast working spinning wheel and loom; if possible a loom and spinning wheel to be sent out . . .[6]

Matt Magrath was always involved in schemes. He set up a cold store in Calabar which supplied fresh meat to the various missions. It worked well except that Matt neglected to exact payment from many of his customers and, in the end, the project proved not to be viable. James Moynagh was not blind to the disadvantages of Matt's exuberance. When the Cathedral in Calabar was being finished he transferred Matt out of Calabar because he knew that the latter would spend too much on it. There was no other way out of it because, try as he might, the Prefect Apostolic could never resist Matt Magrath's enthusiasm.

Lay Missionaries

The 1940s brought expansion and development to lay-missionary involvement in the Society's missions. The first lay missionaries in the area were the women who took over the girls' school in Calabar, in

1921. Then, in 1933, the controversial medical team, consisting of Dr Lengauer and Misses Shallow and Daunt, opened Anua hospital. Next to come to Anua were Nurses D'Arcy and Powell—followed shortly afterwards by Dr Patrick Dunleavy. The German couple, Dr Dufey and his wife, came in 1937. After they were recalled to Germany Dr Joe Barnes did locum for four months until Dr Steyrath arrived in 1939. When he was interned in 1941, Anua hospital was closed down until Dr Gerry Connolly arrived in March 1942.

There was a new departure, in December 1942, when Pearse McKenna, a young Dublin architect and John Turner, a 55 year old laboratory technician, also from Dublin, offered to serve on the missions. Paddy Costelloe offered the laboratory technician to Calabar and the architect to Ogoja. James Moynagh, conscious as ever of the difficulties of life in Nigeria, was reluctant to accept a man of John Turner's years. Both men were offered to Tom McGettrick. He welcomed them wholeheartedly although he was not sure what he could do with an architect as he had no money to build anything at the time. John Turner went to Nigeria in 1944. He went first to Ogoja but was reassigned to Anua where there was greater need for his skills. He spent twelve years in Anua and during that time trained many locals in laboratory work. He retired in 1956 but decided, a year later, to go to Kenya where he worked for three years in the Franciscan Sisters' hospital at Muthale in Kitui diocese. In 1960, John Turner retired to St Patrick's, Douglas, and died on 17 March 1971. He is buried in Kiltegan. Pearse McKenna arrived in Ogoja in 1946, and was seconded to Onitsha for a while where he designed a number of churches. Then he returned to Ogoja and surveyed and mapped the sites which had been set aside for churches, mission houses, schools and hospitals. Over many years, while working in Dublin, he designed buildings for Ogoja and made frequent visits during his vacation to monitor progress. He also did work in Calabar and, at home, he designed the extension to St Patrick's, Douglas, and was the architect of the new college in Kiltegan.

A third man to extend the concept of lay involvement on the missions was Mr Eddie Ryan. He was a foreman with T. &. C. Martin and Co., Mother Mary's family firm. Leaving his wife in Ireland he went to Calabar, at the end of 1945, to finish the Sacred Heart church under the direction of Society priest, Austin Gogarty. Brother John Bermingham, who had supervised all but the final stages of the work, had come to Ireland earlier in the year and had decided to leave the Society. Born in Garbally, Co. Offaly, Brother John was the only one of the small group of brothers to survive Pat Whitney's administration. Although the 1944 Chapter retained the provision for brothers in the Constitution, it decided not to recruit them for the present. Brother John remained the sole survivor. He had gone to Calabar in 1935, and had supervised many of the early buildings. He was highly thought of by James Moynagh and the priests but found life in the tropics very difficult. He was exhausted after his first tour but, nevertheless, decided to return. He was touchy about anyone interfering in his work, which made his position as the only lay-brother among a group of Irish priests very precarious. When he decided to leave the Society, the Superiors seemed to be genuinely sorry. He asked for a loan of £20 and was given a gift of £50. He is said to have got a job in England, working on the buses. Eddie Ryan stayed fifteen months in Nigeria. He finished the church in Calabar, built the priests' house nearby and the priests' house at St Patrick's College. While he was away, the Society paid his wife £6 per week out of Calabar funds. Meanwhile, on the mission, Eddie Ryan was supplied with food and cigarettes and when he returned home he was given a gratuity of £200 on James Moynagh's instructions. He later moved to the USA.

The first lay graduates went out at that time. They were Patrick McLoughlin from Sligo and James Burke from Limerick. They served in Calabar from 1946 to 1949. Advertisements were placed on student notice boards in the universities. No other teachers were attracted in the forties because the salaries offered were far lower than those offered by the Nigerian Government for similar work. In 1947, one of the Nigerian students in UCD drew attention to the fact that two advertisements placed side by side on the college notice board spelled out the discrepancy. A Kiltegan advertisement offered £200 per year to Science-graduates while a Nigerian Government advertisement offered £750. In September 1947, the first Legion of Mary envoy, Maurice O'Connor, left for Nigeria. He was going out to promote the Legion in various parts of West Africa beginning in Calabar where the organisation had made its first appearance on the African continent, in 1933.

Lay missionaries have continued to work alongside Society priests and to form an important part of the Society's extended family. Apart from their contribution to mission work, they have added a new dimension of spontaneity and youthful vitality which has become more important with the passing years.[7]

The 1944 Chapter

The first General Chapter of the Society took place, at Kiltegan, from 14 to 23 June 1944.[8] The members of the Chapter were the office-holders of the Society viz. Fathers Costelloe, Plunkett, Brophy, Browne and Monsignor Delaney and four elected representatives. Those elected were Father Hickey, representing the priests in Ireland; Matt Magrath and Joe Houlihan, representing Calabar; and Bernard McGuirk, representing Ogoja.

The main business of the Chapter was the election of Superiors. Paddy Costelloe and Corney Plunkett were re-elected to the posts of Superior General and Vicar-General. Joe Houlihan, John Sheehan and John McGuinness were elected to the council and Charlie Smith was elected as Bursar. This marked a new stage in the Society's growth. For the first time, there was a full complement of Superiors elected in accordance with the Constitutions. The Bishop of Kildare and Leighlin retained his role as overseer but the diocesan consultors were no longer involved in the affairs of the Society.

Among the matters discussed was the appointment of newly ordained priests. It was decided that priests would go to the missions immediately after ordination. This was a significant decision in that it ruled out the emergence of a group within the Society which had no missionary experience and it helped to safeguard the exclusively missionary character of the Society. Length of tours was laid down at four years for a first tour and five years for subsequent tours. The Chapter felt it necessary to legislate against the arbitrary extension of tours. This was aimed at the ecclesiastical Superiors. Up to now, the last word lay with the Prefect Apostolic who might decide that a man's tour would be extended for the sake of the work. In future, he would need the consent of the Superior General and his Council before he could keep a man longer than the specified time. It was the first example of Society Superiors legislating for the protection of members against the ecclesiastical authority. The length of a priest's home leave was set at 'about ten months'. During this period a man was expected to do a retreat other than the annual retreat prescribed by the Constitutions. A refresher course, consisting of a series of lectures was to be arranged for those on leave although there was no obligation on priests to attend.

The Chapter decided to appoint a 'Mission Spiritual Director' in each area. This was in response to suggestions made earlier by James Moynagh who felt the need for some Society figure distinct from the Prefect Apostolic. This official, referred to as *the Holy Man*, was to have a low-key mediating role which was to be extended in subsequent Chapters until he became a fully-fledged Superior. The 1944 Chapter specified his duties as follows:

> . . . 1. to represent the views of Missionaries in his area to the Society Authorities at home; 2. to sometimes conduct the monthly day of recollection in so far as prudence and circumstances permit; 3. to make every endeavour to provide spiritual books where needed; 4. to promote temperance in matters of drink and encourage members to take the pledge recommended by the Chapter. He should have for his chief care the spiritual welfare of his brother-missionaries and should endeavour to promote a spirit of charity and good-fellowship among them.

Another office which was created was that of Mission-Representative. The holder of this office was to deal with specific requests from the missions, send out Mass-offerings, take care of travel arrangements and look after the shipping out of equipment and supplies.

Perhaps the most unusual decision of the Chapter was the recommendation that all priests of the Society should take a temperance pledge. This recommendation is presented as follows:

> The Chapter, realizing the dangers arising from intemperance in the matter of drink recommend that all priests of the Society should take the following pledge;
> 1. Not to take an intoxicating drink while home on holidays.
> 2. Not to take spirits at all.
> 3. To practice great moderation in the consumption of non-spirits.
> 4. Not to force or entice anyone who has the Total Abstinence Pledge, to drink.

This recommendation might seem to indicate a serious problem of alcohol-abuse on the missions. In fact, there was not a serious problem. A few priests were drinking too much and the spectre of the Founder's supposed drinking habits still hung over the Society. There was more than a little puritanism among many members. A luxury such as a radio was frowned on by many. Duty was paramount and a few days' break with the Holy Ghosts in Enugu might earn a man a reputation for self-indulgence. Paddy Costelloe did nothing to add balance to the situation and may have influenced the Chapter's recommendation on drink. He, himself, was a non-drinker and was rather narrow in his ideas about priestly decorum. He was also afraid that any hint of scandal might damage the good name of the Society and thereby impede its work. Furthermore, at this period of his life, he believed that problems could be best avoided by exercising tight control.

Nowhere was this more apparent than in Paddy Costelloe's management of the men around Kiltegan who had returned from the missions and, for one reason or another, were not going back. Although there were only a few of them, they posed a big problem for the Superior General in his first and second terms of office. Their situation exposed the weakness of his leadership as did Pat Whitney's illness. Paddy Costelloe was excellent in his dealings with those who seemed to be trying their best. With those who refused to toe the line or were in any sense wayward he was less able to cope. He adopted a very disciplinarian attitude to those who were staying in Kiltegan because they had a problem with drink or with cultural adaptation to Africa or some other behavioural problem. He tried to keep them under tight surveillance and confined to Kiltegan as much as possible. His approach, which was regarded as over-severe by his contemporaries, had the opposite effect to what he had intended. Those he was trying to control enjoyed the game of outwitting him, giving him the slip and getting away without his knowledge. One priest had a car which he parked in a neighbouring farmyard to facilitate a getaway. He chose a Protestant family, possibly to spare the conscience of a Catholic neighbour! Jimmy Lane, who was in Kiltegan at the time, thinks that Paddy never knew about the car, although nearly everyone else did. It was Paddy Costelloe's great burden that every time he took disciplinary action against someone he immediately began to feel remorse. The result was great personal anguish which adversely affected his health and served to isolate him from his fellow priests.

In April 1945, living-conditions in Kiltegan took a turn for the better with the arrival of three Medical Missionary Sisters to take charge of the housekeeping. A section of High Park House was set aside as a temporary convent. This required the permission of Bishop Keogh who delegated Father Doyle of Baltinglass to inspect the house and to judge whether the sisters' quarters were suitable. With his approval the sisters took up residence in mid-April. Mother Mary had declined any remuneration apart from bed and board. The presence of sisters made a great difference, particularly to the students. They did the best they could with the very simple food and succeeded in producing a more attractive diet. They also took care of those who were sick. The General Council discussed alternative sisters' quarters and thought of renovating a house in the garden which was used by workmen. The sisters left Kiltegan in 1950, because of a change of policy in Drogheda; it was decided that work of that kind was not compatible with the aim of the congregation. In Joe Gilmartin's time as Superior General, efforts were made to revive the arrangement but nothing came of it.

Meanwhile, on the missions, strong bonds of friendship were being established between the Society and the Medical Missionaries of Mary. Priests and sisters came from the same social background, were close to one another in age and depended on one another for many things. Their mutual co-operation and genuine friendship gave great strength to both groups. For priests in remote missions there was a danger of losing touch with many of the refinements of life—'going bush' was the colonial term for it. However, their association with the Sisters restored to the priests a measure of gentleness and forced them to face a side of their lives that they might have preferred to ignore.

The Holy Child Sisters also fulfilled this role but to a lesser extent, in the early days. The priests had a great working relationship with them and appreciated their extraordinary contribution to education. At an informal level, however, they found 'the mothers', as they called them, a bit grand and they were a little discomfited by their formality and their genteel ways.

9

Post-war Initiatives

THE war ended in Europe in May 1945. In August Japan surrendered following the bombing of Hiroshima and Nagasaki. As the world began to recover from the destruction of the previous six years, St Patrick's Society began to make new plans and to push ahead with projects which had lain dormant during the war.

Some kind of response to the problem of leprosy in Ogoja had been in the pipeline for over ten years. James Moynagh and Pat Whitney had planned to do something about it along the lines followed in various leper colonies throughout Nigeria and other parts of Africa. However, neither had got round to it and when Tom McGetttrick was appointed Prefect Apostolic of Ogoja in 1939, nothing had been done. From the beginning, the new Prefect was drawn to the lepers and was deeply moved by their suffering. This was a mark of his deep humanity which was to mellow further over the years, influenced, no doubt, by regular contact with leprosy patients. The lepers seemed to speak to the 'soft centre' of Tom McGettrick. This was an aspect of his personality which he tried to disguise by wearing the mask of a hard-boiled, impassive missionary. The need to do this characterised his leadership and communicated itself to his priests and the sisters until it became an ethos of Ogoja. Tom McGettrick was 'the boss'. He expected those around him to go to the limits of self-sacrifice. In turn, he could be relied on to support them and to speak highly of them, behind their backs. With the lepers however, his true warmth and human sympathy appeared. He recalled his first impressions as follows:

On my first visit to the stations in Ogoja I saw outside every church five or ten lepers, some of whom with their nodular faces resembled animals more than human beings; some were without fingers and toes; all had pinched stomachs and furrowed face lines. They held out their hands and beat their bellies hoping for a dash [of money] to buy food. Their misery could pierce the heart of any miser and make him open his purse; their hunger could penetrate a stone wall . . .[1]

The fact that Tom McGettrick was delayed in Ireland by the war was providential as far as leprosy work was concerned. He raised £12,000 and went back with enough money to get a leprosy project under way. He cajoled a site for a leprosy treatment centre out of the Ogoja chiefs whom he entertained with 'a large calabash of palm wine, a dozen bottles of gin and a few bottles of whiskey'. As he enjoyed a drink himself, he had no hang-up about alcohol and understood its capacity to induce good humour.

It did not prove easy to get medical staff. While in Ireland, Tom McGettrick had appealed to medical students in the universities. In 1943 Paddy Costelloe appealed to medical students in Cork and Belfast, on his behalf. In the end it was Dr Joe Barnes who had left Emekuku and come to Ireland to do his M.A.O. examination who came to the rescue. He agreed to take on the leprosy work and arrived in Ogoja in September 1944.

It was Joe Barnes who designed the project. He first visited established leper settlements in other parts of Nigeria. Then he travelled the Prefecture on a war-time Raleigh bicycle to establish the extent of the leprosy problem and to consult with priests and local authorities. He decided against the idea of a large segregation camp, like the world-famous Molokai, although he regarded segregation as essential. Instead, leper villages were set up within the confines of each clan area, each with its own law court, church, school, bathing-pool and water supply. Each resident was given the use of a plot of land which gave a measure of self-sufficiency to those who could work it. These villages were to be serviced from a medical centre in Ogoja and another in Abakaliki. Each centre would have a hospital for those in need of operations, with in-patient care and living quarters for patients who were so incapacitated that they could no longer take care of themselves. The project was to be called the Ogoja Leprosy Relief Scheme.

The Prefect Apostolic 'wrote letters to every convent in Ireland, England and America that had a medical wing', in search of nurses.[2] In the end, it was Mother Mary Martin who agreed to send sisters and in April 1946, three Medical Missionaries arrived. They were Sister de Lourdes Gogan, Sister Teresa Connolly and Sister Philomena Doyle. On 1 May, the very first injection was given in an open shed on the side of the proposed leprosy centre in Ogoja. It was an injection of chaulmoogra oil, involving a large syringe and a broad needle. Each patient was to receive an average of 110 injections per year, while undergoing treatment. A hospital was built as planned and later an occupational therapy workshop in which shoe-making, tailoring, basket-making, carpentry and printing were undertaken. A number of young men were given training which enabled them to treat leprosy sufferers in the villages. A similar centre was opened at Mile Four near Abakaliki, in 1947. By 1950, there were nine villages with 3,023 patients, attended by two doctors and 8 nursing sisters.

By agreement with the Church of Scotland, the Catholics confined their leprosy work to three districts and left the remaining three to the Protestants. This avoided wasteful duplication of services and helped to promote understanding between the Churches. In 1952 the Church of Scotland asked the Catholic diocese to take over its leprosy unit at Ikom, and this became a large treatment centre under Catholic auspices.

Dr Joe Barnes spent seven years at the leprosy work. During this time he married his wife Betty whom he met in England. She was a doctor also and the two worked in Ogoja for a further two years. Joe Barnes became a renowned skin specialist in Dublin. He remained a close friend and confidant of many St Patrick's Missionaries and shares with Bishop McGettrick the credit for establishing the Ogoja Leprosy Relief Scheme. He was highly regarded by the latter who wrote of him:

> How I admired that man! I remember giving him Communion at the 6 a.m. Mass. He had a light breakfast before he mounted his faithful steel horse; cycled to Obudu, 30 miles; worked at the leprosy site and returned in the evening through a road that was hilly and dusty in the hot season. I saw him often with his singlet off in the tropical sun working with lepers clearing scrub for a house or a farm. I learnt more about charity from him than from all the theological books I ever read in my Maynooth days.[3]

Another pioneer leprosy doctor was Sister Mairead Chambers who arrived in 1947. She spent two years with Joe Barnes in Ogoja before going on to develop the Abakaliki centre. Dr Sean Flannery came from Anua to relieve Joe Barnes for a brief period in 1947. Then, when Joe Barnes and his wife left, finally, in 1952, they were replaced by Dr Denis Freeman who worked in Ogoja until 1956. He married in 1954, and was joined by his wife, Dr Rita Freeman. Lilian Murphy, a retired schoolteacher from Liverpool gave seventeen years of her life to the education of lepers and their children. She left Ogoja in 1967 and in June 1990 was approaching her 98th birthday.

Tom McGettrick was to remain the friend and patron of leprosy sufferers throughout his long life. Something of their appreciation was expressed by the head man of a leper village in a video recording made on the occasion of Bishop McGettrick's funeral in 1989. 'For us,' he said, 'McGettrick is next only to God.'

Leprosy work was not the only medical initiative taken by Ogoja diocese at the end of the war. In 1946 a general hospital was begun at Afikpo to Pearse McKenna's design. It was opened under the care of Dr Sean Flannery and three Medical Missionary Sisters. Dr Godfrey Hinds began more than twenty years of service there, in 1949.[4]

Student Training

The advent of peace in Europe led to the loss of Humewood and to a new accommodation crisis for the students. In June 1946 Madame Hume-Weygand wrote to the Superior General announcing that she would be returning to Ireland in August and asking to be allowed to spend ten days at Humewood. She had not visited her ancestral home for more than six years and her husband had never been in Ireland. She had never met Paddy Costelloe but had heard about his ill-health and wished him well. In fact, Paddy was visiting Nigeria at the time, so Corney Plunkett replied to the letter, offering to facilitate the Weygands. When they arrived in August they were a little taken aback by the damage which four groups of students had caused to the house and furniture. A list was made of the breakages and the damage caused. This included torn blinds, broken chairs and chipped fireplaces. A red felt door had been 'cut with a knife'; the carpet in the library had been 'stained heavily with ink'; the billiard table was in a mess with 'all cues destroyed at the top, repaired with odd nails—some of them broken entirely'. Madame Weygand decided to take back Humewood. She gave the Society a year in which to make alternative arrangements. It was agreed that she would have vacant possession at the end of June 1947 and that repairs would have been carried out by then. In the short term, she offered the billiard table for sale through her solicitor in Naas. One more group did the probation year in Humewood and after that the beautiful Victorian house became once more a family retreat. Madame Hume-Weygand remained on friendly terms with the Society and visits were exchanged during her annual visits to Humewood. From 1947 the probationers were housed in Nissen huts, tunnel-like structures covered in corrugated iron sheeting. Three of them were used as dormitories and the fourth contained a chapel, a classhall and a recreation room. Heat was provided by pot-bellied stoves fuelled by laurel wood which was in plentiful supply. A shelf at the end of each dormitory held the enamel basins which were filled each night in preparation for the morning ablutions. It was not uncommon to find that a layer of ice crystals had formed on the water before morning. To the enthusiastic young men, most of whom were 17 or 18 years of age, it was only a slight inconvenience, which would prepare them for the hardships of missionary life.

John Sheehan, who was a member of the General Council, was appointed Rector of St Patrick's College, Kiltegan, in 1944. He held this post until 1947, when Jimmy Lane took over. John McGuinness, also a Councillor, was Dean and a third Councillor, Joe Houlihan, was local bursar, a post which was later held by Joe Kelly. Michael O'Reilly, who had been ordained in Rome in 1939, also taught in the College. Bill Dunne, who was ordained in 1944, joined the College Staff in 1946, having received a licentiate in theology in Maynooth. Bill Mullally, home from Calabar, also taught in the College for a short time and Catch Cantwell taught the Probationers. It was decided to send more young priests for theological training and in 1946, Matt Grehan and Kevin Longworth were sent to Maynooth. In 1948, Ciaran Needham and John Mahon were sent to do theology and Canon Law respectively. In 1949, Denis Newman was sent to Maynooth for Canon Law.

In September 1947, the first group of Society students began to study for degrees in University College Cork. This marked the end of a long search for hostel accommodation close to a University, a search which began soon after the 1944 Chapter. Before that, the necessity for Society men to get degrees had been a recurring theme in James Moynagh's letters, especially since 1941, when the number of Maynooth men began to fall. The Chapter recommended that a House of Studies be established close to a University but left the establishment of such a house to the General Council.

Paddy Costelloe set about fulfilling the wish of the Chapter without any delay. The matter was discussed in the Council, and in October 1944 the Vicar-General, Corney Plunkett, wrote to the Bishops of Cork, Dublin and Galway to seek permission to open a house of studies for university students. Bishop Cohalan of Cork gave permission readily. Bishop Browne of Galway wanted a letter from the Superior General, on receipt of which he would place the request before the diocesan Chapter. Archbishop McQuaid acknowledged the letter but deferred a decision until the following March, when he sent for Corney Plunkett and approved a house of studies in Dublin. However, he recommended that it would be on the north side of the city, presumably because of the large concentration of religious houses on the south side. Meanwhile, the General Council had agreed that 'University College Cork would be most suitable for students' and at Bishop Cohalan's suggestion, Father Bastible, Dean of UCC was asked to look out for a house. Before he had found anything, Charlie Smith had called into estate agents in Dublin and located two properties, one at Castleknock on twenty-six acres and the other at Raheny on sixteen acres. There followed a lot of indecision on the part of the Council. Finally, they agreed on Raheny, the property of Mrs McCarville, which was on sale for £8,500. An offer of £6,000 was made and matters dragged on until August when Corney Plunkett and Joe Houlihan were authorised to purchase it. Jimmy Lane was appointed Rector of the new house and Ned McElligott, who had been recalled from Nigeria to do a degree, was to accompany him. Nobody in Kiltegan knew much about buying property and there is no indication that they had engaged a solicitor. They thought the deal was going through but when the university opened, matters were not yet finalised. Jimmy and Ned moved into a hotel and the latter enrolled for First Arts in UCD. Then, Dublin County Council made a higher bid for the property. Since the Society had not entered into a binding agreement, the house went to the County Council. Jimmy Lane wrote to Archbishop McQuaid asking permission to stay in temporary accommodation until another house was found. The Archbishop was displeased by the letter. He had no intention of approving such a haphazard arrangement. He suspended his permission and, in effect, Dublin was closed to the Society. Jimmy and Ned returned to Kiltegan and the joke among the priests was that Ned, a highly sensitive man, had been 'sent down'. He was never to get an opportunity to do a degree.

In the summer of 1946, Corney Plunkett went to Cork to search for a suitable house. He stayed with the Society of African Missions in Blackrock. While he was there Father Coakley, the parish priest of Douglas, told John Sheehan that they should look at Windsor, a large house owned by the Sutton family and situated on the estuary of the River Lee. It was a beautiful house which had been named Windsor to commemorate a visit of King Edward VII to Cork in 1903, when Abraham Sutton, as Lord Mayor, received a knighthood. There were about six acres of lawns and gardens and a farm of fourteen acres. Corney Plunkett thought the house too pretentious but the Council did not wish to miss another opportunity. They asked the Sheehan family solicitor, Donal McCleland to bid at the auction, which took place later in the year. Corney and Bill Dunne travelled to Cork for the auction. The car skidded on the icy road and Corney hurt his finger. At the auction, they found themselves bidding against a woman called Julia Scraggs and went as far as £9,000, at which stage the property was withdrawn. Later the Society agreed to add another £500 which, with £500 fees, brought the price to £10,000. The Suttons had a private chapel in the house and they donated the altar and furnishings to the Society.

The first group of students took up residence in Douglas in September 1947. The house was renamed St Patrick's although the name Windsor was still used by the local people. The first Superior was Joe Kelly. Joe had been in Ogoja and had spent a short period on the staff in Humewood. He enrolled for a degree and, like the students, he cycled the three miles to the university. He remembers those years as the happiest of his life. About half the students were sent to university while the other half followed the ordinary seminary course in philosophy. At first the philosophers were taught in Kiltegan, but in 1955 they moved to Cork. This relieved the monotony of spending seven years in one place and opened up new opportunities for valuable extra-curricular activity in the city. Those in university did degrees in Arts and Science, for the most part, and a handful did the Bachelor of Music degree. Later, as priests, they were to teach in schools and colleges on the missions. After some time, the vast majority gave up teaching for full-time parish work.

Guidance and Growth

Through the forties the same four men continued to set the policy of the Society. They were Paddy Costelloe and Corney Plunkett, at home, and James Moynagh and Tom McGettrick, on the missions. All had been members of the same class in Maynooth. They were good friends and were very loyal to one another. Corney Plunkett was the unifier. The two Prefects could write to him 'off the record' and he knew well how to humour them and how to humour Paddy Costelloe through his personal difficulties. Paddy Costelloe was resolute in his dedication to the missions. His mind was always on Nigeria and what was needed there. He spared no effort in accommodating the two Prefects Apostolic and frequently asked them for advice. However, it was James Moynagh who exerted the greatest influence on the future shape of St Patrick's Society. This was a measure of his own leadership but no less a measure of the trust his colleagues were prepared to place in him.

James Moynagh's letters to Kiltegan were full of suggestions on almost every aspect of the life and work of the Society. He emphasised the importance of priests in the schools and was the first to promote the idea of a university hostel. When priest-graduates were not available he encouraged Kiltegan to recruit lay graduates. He wanted unmarried men as he considered Nigeria unsuitable for lay-women. He was always conscious of the difficulties involved in missionary life and believed that only a strong person who was used to hardship would be successful. He thought that priests who had been reared in a town were at a disadvantage from the start. He wrote to the Superior General on 7 April 1940:

> Another tip: It was given me by Fr. Slattery of the African Missions 5 years ago. If you can avoid it don't have *townies* in St. Patrick's Society and if you are doubtful about any Maynooth man ask him is he from the town or from the country. I'm not going on Fr. Slattery's word now but on my own experience. Not one man in twenty from the town is suited to foreign missions. As American slang says 'they can't take it'.

He suggested that efforts should be made to broaden the mental horizons of Kiltegan students and that magazines such as *The Tablet* might help to do this. When asked by Paddy Costelloe for suggestions on stocking the library, he sent a long list of books which included titles by Aldous Huxley, Graham Greene and Evelyn Waugh. The list was compiled with help from John Corkery, an Ardagh priest who went to Calabar in 1945 and later became Librarian in Maynooth College. The benefits of typing was a constant theme. He wanted every priest who arrived in Nigeria to be able to type. He saw education as an ongoing process and believed that priests should be always learning. He wrote to Paddy Costelloe on 10 August 1949:

> The thought occurred to me that every man going home should do a few months' Refresher Course in which he would get a few talks from theologians or attend a few lectures e.g. in Cork. I am

very strongly convinced that every man going home should spend
some time . . . doing something useful for his work e.g. some
course of lectures in the University or Technical School, Cork and
at the same time go through some definite Revision of Theology.

James Moynagh was also enlightened in his attitude to the capabilities
of Africans. At a time when many Europeans considered the African to
be intellectually inferior and limited in qualities of leadership, James
Moynagh had every confidence in the Christians of Calabar. He took it
for granted that they could run their own local Church or their own
country just as the Irish people could. He himself was to attribute his
empathy for the local people to the fact that their social and economic
backgrounds were very similar to his own. Just as he could assume
authority in the Church, so could a local man with a similar vocation.
In 1946 he sent the first Nigerian laymen to University College, Dublin.
He was reluctant to send them to England as he was afraid they would
be influenced by Communism, which he believed to be infiltrating
Nigerian society. The Superiors in Kiltegan co-operated fully with his
plan to educate as many Nigerians as possible in Ireland. The expenses
were met by Kiltegan, on the understanding that they would be repaid
out of Calabar funds at some future time. In subsequent years many
students attended University College Cork, and in 1950 James Moynagh
acknowledged his indebtedness to the Society for 'the score of African
students in Ireland', and promised to pay back the money borrowed
out of school grants.

James Moynagh was also deeply committed to an African diocesan
priesthood. There was nothing unique about this. Bishop Shanahan
had shown a similar commitment although, subsequently, there was some
tension in Holy Ghost territory between recruitment for the diocesan
priesthood and recruitment for the Order. There was no question of
admitting Africans to St Patrick's Missionary Society in the early days.
The Society perceived itself as a missionary wing of the Irish diocesan
priesthood. To set up a priesthood like their own, Society members had
to recruit priests for the local diocese. As diocesan priests, they would
be identical with Society priests except for canonical membership which
was seen as little more than a prerequisite for missionary work. The
establishment of a diocesan priesthood was to be a priority in every diocese to which the Society supplied priests. It was James Moynagh who
first promoted the idea. It received strong support in the 1950 Chapter
and it was James Moynagh who pushed it to its logical conclusion when,

in 1953, he accepted the appointment of an African Auxiliary bishop, the first African Catholic bishop in West Africa.

James Moynagh was a man who did not interfere with the work of his priests. He trusted them to carry out their responsibilities. He expected them to survive and run their missions on the contributions of the local people and whatever support they could get from home. He lacked the ability to convey his personal appreciation to his co-workers. He was a bit fussy and anxious in his manner. The early Society priests felt that he favoured the Maynooth volunteers. In fact, he thought very highly of the Society priests. He wrote to Paddy Costelloe in 1940:

> Now as to your young St. Patrick's priests I have nothing but praise to offer. They are superior to the most of the men though I'm proud of Maynooth, more steady, more humble, less wilful. They don't come out with the idea that they know everything.

He never departed from this view but he was not good at communicating how he felt to those around him. In his anxiety for the work, he bemoaned the lack of experienced men, the lack of graduates, the lack of training in this or that field, and he neglected to show his appreciation for those who were doing the work. At one level, he was 'one of the boys'. He liked to play cards and could write to Paddy Costelloe, in 1946: 'If Cavan win the All Ireland spend 5/- on a cable. Spend it anyway if they are even in it.' At the same time, he was remote and distant and too pernickety to make people feel at ease in his presence. At this personal level, he was no match for Tom McGettrick who was warm and friendly in manner and was able to inspire great affection and loyalty in those who worked with him.

James Moynagh and Tom McGettrick were good friends. There was the occasional tense moment when one diocese got more young priests than the other. After the allocations of 1946, the Prefect of Ogoja wrote bitterly to Kiltegan on 26 August:

> To say I was disappointed when I got your letter re. the appointment of new Fathers is to put it mildly. I have come to the conclusion that a man in my position needs to be a cadger, a crank, a fellow that inspires fear, a sort of sparring cock who for the sake of the missions is ready to fight with everyone around him. In other words had I complained more and demanded more I do not think you would make a five-to-one division.

This criticism which was communicated to all and sundry, in Tom McGettrick's usual fashion, caused some irritation to his counterpart in

Calabar, who wrote to Corney Plunkett on 24 March 1947: 'I was also a bit annoyed when I heard complaints from the Northern territory about the undue share we were getting of the men coming out when actually in proportion to the number of souls . . .' It became a kind of seasonal chant which was surpassed only by the rumpus caused by the withdrawal of a man for Society work in Ireland.

A letter written by Tom McGettrick on 8 October 1946, asking the Superior General to petition Rome to have Moynagh made a bishop, is indicative of the rapport that existed between the two men. It reads:

> In a letter recently received from the Apostolic Delegate, Mombasa, I was given to understand that Calabar would be raised to a Vicariate and Monsignor Moynagh a Bishop, if you took up the matter with Propaganda. You know as well as I do that Calabar deserves that honour long ago, and no one has ever deserved the consolation of the Consecrating Oils more than Msgr. Moynagh. It will also be a great help to the Society at home. Monsignor Mathew seems anxious that he be consecrated in Ireland but these details can be arranged afterwards.
>
> Please take up the matter with Propaganda and Monsignor Mathew will throw in his weight (which is considerable) when he visits Calabar after Christmas.

In 1947 Calabar became a Vicariate and James Moynagh was appointed its first bishop. Technically, it could not be made a diocese until the Nigerian Hierarchy was established. This did not happen until 1950. Meanwhile, a Vicariate was the highest possible status attainable by a jurisdiction in Nigeria. Calabar, like other Vicariates, was to be governed by a bishop who was regarded, for the time being, as a Vicar of the Pope. The event was a milestone in the history of the Society and a vote of confidence from Rome. Ten years before, the Society's survival was in doubt. Now, it had joined the mainstream of missionary life with one of its territories being advanced in the order of approval and one of its members being made a bishop.

James Moynagh was ordained bishop in Maynooth College on 7 September 1947 in the presence of many of the volunteers who had helped to build up the Catholic community in Calabar. The consecrator was Archbishop D'Alton of Armagh. He was assisted by Bishop Keogh of Kildare and Leighlin and Bishop McNamee of Ardagh and Clonmacnois. Among those present was a younger brother of the new bishop who was a diocesan priest in England. Bishop Moynagh became Titular-Bishop of Lambesis, following the custom of giving missionary bishops, and others who had no actual diocese, title to ancient dioceses which were no longer residential Sees. Lambesis was once a flourishing diocese in that part of North Africa which is now Algeria. It disappeared in the Muslim advance of the seventh century and now existed only in name. It was chosen for the Vicar Apostolic of Calabar to link Nigeria to the early Christianity of Roman Africa which, in its time, was a light to the Christian world. The title preserved the memory of an ancient faith and stressed that it was the same faith which was now being handed on in Nigeria.

In December 1947, the first African priest for the Vicariate of Calabar was ordained at Ifuho. He was Dominic Ekandem who, like so many of his peers, had been baptised as a schoolboy and had influenced his parents to follow him into the Church. Before going to the senior seminary, he had spent three years in teaching and catechetical work in Calabar. As Bishop Moynagh was still abroad, the ceremony was performed by Bishop Heerey. The new priest said his first Mass at Anua before an estimated 4,000 people who gave full vent to their joy when the Mass was over. *Africa* described it as follows:

> Then the celebration of the great event began in earnest. Rockets soaring into the air; blunderbusses were fired—old muzzle-loaders which made one wonder if it would be safer to stand in front of them or behind. Then the band played. One band had only an eight-bar repertoire, but it made up for it in volume and indescribable endurance.[5]

For Dominic Ekandem it was the beginning of a long and illustrious ministry as priest, bishop and Cardinal.

The long-awaited opening of the Cathedral in Calabar took place on 6 June 1948. It was attended by Bishop Rogan from Cameroon and Bishop Heerey, who preached the sermon. The latter recalled how he had laid the foundation stone in 1933, 30 years after the appointment of Patrick McDonnell as first resident-priest in Calabar, and added:

> . . . the people of Calabar have passed through many storms. They have ignored the false shibboleths of those who would say that Christianity is a foreign import and not for the Africans. They have remained loyal and have given substance to their faith in the beautiful cathedral which they have built.[6]

Phil O'Connor, who had initiated the 1930 volunteers, was there, as was Tom Ronayne who was now a member of the Holy Ghost congregation. The ceremony was also attended by senior government officials including a representative of the Governor. There was a lunch in the convent for 109—'men only'.

That evening the guests were entertained to a production of *H.M.S. Pinafore* by the students of St Patrick's College. The show was produced by Noel Sandvoss who had volunteered for a second time in 1947, having done a tour of Ogoja from 1938. There was a cast of thirty-five chosen from among the 340 boys in the school. Mother Lucy provided the piano accompaniment while Austin Gogarty and Kevin Longworth looked after the stage. The show was performed in the public library in Calabar. At the last minute, the curtain rope broke and when the pieces were tied together, the knot would not pass easily through the rings. John Corkery watched the show, perched on a beam above the stage and pushed the knot through the rings every time the curtain was pulled. It worked perfectly.

The following table indicates the extent to which the Church had taken root in Calabar and Ogoja in mid 1949. The figures represent the fruit of thirty years' involvement by Irish secular priests and twenty years' by St Patrick's Society.[7]

	Calabar	Ogoja
Population	899,503	726,233
Baptised Catholics	64,568	11,436
Catechumens	28,500	13,500
Nigerian Priests	1	0
Irish Priests	34	20
Holy Child Sisters	14	6
Handmaids of the Holy Child	20	0
Medical Missionaries of Mary	9	8
Primary Schools	248	233
Secondary Schools	3	0
Teachers and Catechists	1,262	590
General Hospitals	1	1
Lay Doctors	2	2
Major Seminarians	3	0

The Maynooth volunteers were now greatly outnumbered by Society priests and there were fewer than ten diocesan priests on the missions at any particular time. Following the lean years of the war, during which few had volunteered, James Moynagh wrote: 'I'm beginning to fear that we can reconcile ourselves to the fact that the Maynooth effort for

Nigeria will probably dry up as it did in the case of China.'[8] There was however, a slight recovery from 1946 onwards. Over the next three years 9 Maynooth priests volunteered, providing badly needed graduates at a time when Society priests with degrees had not yet come on stream.[9]

A remarkable feature of the decade was the advances made in the education of girls. This was the work of the Holy Child Sisters who supervised a network of girls' schools especially from their headquarters at Ifuho, where they ran a Teacher Training College for girls. In 1946 they opened Cornelia Connolly College at Uyo, the first girls' secondary school in Calabar. In that year, there were twenty-five girls' primary schools with 3,695 pupils, and there were 1,182 girls in boys' schools. The ratio of school-girls to school-boys in Calabar had increased dramatically in recent years. In 1936 there were 1,643 girls to 11,284 boys; in 1946 there were 4,877 girls to 14,809 boys.[10] Meanwhile, in Ogoja the education of girls was only beginning. The Holy Child Sisters found great opposition to it among the pagan chiefs. Nevertheless, they turned out about ten women vocational teachers a year from Afikpo and placed them in schools in Ogoja and Calabar. In 1950 Tom McGettrick wrote of 'a growing demand for education for women' in Ogoja, although progress was much slower than in Calabar.[11]

In Calabar, there were two incidents of groups breaking away from the Catholic Church. One group took the name Udo (Second) Catholics and the other became known as the Holy Face Church. The Udo Catholic group emerged in Ikot Ekpene. It started with a dispute between the head catechist, Dominic Inyang, and several stations within Ifuho parish. Trouble began in 1939, when an effort was made to remove Dominic Inyang. There was personal hostility to him and general opposition to the mission policy of employing outsiders as catechists and teachers. A number of the dissidents were aggrieved because they were removed from their teaching posts on account of polygamous marriages. The stations were interdicted by Matt Magrath who was the father-in-charge, and James Moynagh was called in to mediate. Dissatisfaction continued and, in the end, about 400 people left the Church.

They did not seek to establish an independent Church but thought of joining some existing body. In mid 1941 they associated themselves with Rev. Bressi Ando who had come from the Gold Coast as a missionary of an independent church called the African Orthodox Church. They were attracted to him because his Church was close to the Catholic Church in ritual and it tolerated polygamy. Under Rev. Ando, a number of small churches and schools were established and at least one Catholic church was taken over by the dissidents.

James Moynagh was very worried by the breakaway. He was afraid that many of those catechumens who were a long time waiting for baptism would join the Udo Catholics. To counteract this, he instructed the priests at Ifuho to be more lenient in their examination of candidates. The new Church failed to get government recognition for its schools and broke up within a couple of years. A few of its members returned to the Catholic Church but the majority became affiliated with the Methodists.

The Church of the Holy Face had its origins in a legitimate Catholic devotion which had found its way from Ireland to Anua in the 1920s. It came from the Archdiocese of Cashel where a branch of the Arch-confraternity of the Holy Face had been established in 1889. Catholics in Anua got their hands on some leaflets and became correspondents of the Cashel branch of the confraternity. Images of the Holy Face appeared in the homes of devout men, many of whom had a special room for prayer in their houses. Some of these rooms had altars, many with a kind of tabernacle holding an image of the Holy Face. Veneration of the Holy Face came to be linked with healing, and healing properties were attributed to the image. The devotees were exemplary Christians and many attended daily Mass and Communion. The devotion was well established by the mid forties when Tom McGettrick was father-in-charge in Anua. James Moynagh had reservations about certain aspects of the devotion but Tom McGettrick was more indulgent. Bishop Moynagh wrote in his memoirs:

> They began to appear in frocks somewhat like loose soutanes with a cross stitched on in front and the words 'pious man' stitched underneath. I became dubious about this group when I saw this display of symbols. It was a matter in which I disagreed with Father McGettrick then Father in charge at Anua. He regarded the soutanes as a mere funny display of faith, and since they were 'sound Christians, why worry'.[12]

Joe Houlihan, who worked with Tom McGettrick and later took over from him, gave further encouragement to the devotion. Later a prayer house was set up which became a focus for healing. A sign outside the door proclaimed it 'Holy Face Church'. In 1944 James Moynagh ex-communicated the organisers and declared that a visit to the prayer house for purposes of healing was 'a sin against the Faith which is reserved to the Bishop'. The movement spread to four or five nearby stations but did not expand beyond Anua parish. It became associated with the American Mennonites in the fifties and was later admitted to membership of the United Independent Churches fellowship as the Holy Face Catholic Church.

These breakaway groups are but two examples of the thousands of independent groups which have grown up in Africa both inside and outside the historical Churches. Some experts, such as Dr David Barrett, see in this movement towards independence, the emergence of a genuine renewal of Christianity in terms that can be understood by African people. Others consider it to be, in many cases, no more than a revival of traditional religion in neo-pagan guise. Many missionaries today see this tendency as a challenge to the Church to be more adaptable and to take greater account of African cultural factors without diluting the message of Christ. The Holy Face devotion with its healing overtones may have spoken to a deeply felt need of African people which was not answered by traditional 'Irish-style' Catholicism. However, it did not give rise to any soul-searching among the priests in Calabar in the 1940s. The only reaction to it would appear to have been a refusal by the Church authorities in Calabar to sanction any sodalities or confraternities outside Calabar town until well into the fifties.[13]

The missionaries were preoccupied with establishing the Church with all its essential elements of faith and practice. The multiplicity of Christian Churches in Calabar and the facility with which new Churches or sects were founded did not make their work any easier. An African pilgrimage to Rome, organised in May 1950 to mark the Holy Year, was an opportunity to emphasise universality and papal supremacy. It was decided that a delegation would go from Calabar and Ogoja, led by Tom McGettrick. The missionaries who went were either coming on home-leave or had travelled to Rome from Ireland. There was also a small number of Nigerians, including Dominic Ekandem. The delegation joined fellow-pilgrims from all over Africa at an audience with Pope Pius XII and, afterwards, celebrated Mass in the Catacombs of St Agnes. Matt Magrath, who was among them, was struck by the parallel between the Church in ancient Rome and the Church in Nigeria. He wrote of the event:

> There is a sense of intimate union with the early Church which these young African Catholics feel very strongly: the tombs of the martyrs in Rome, the Mass box in Nigeria; the Catacombs—the mud and thatch of the bush Church. The parallel is so striking

that it cannot be missed. Beginning must be in poverty and perse-cution. The Cross is part of our life. We pray then for this young Church whose representatives are here. Persecution is bound to come in one form or another and only prayer can guarantee the faith and courage that will be needed.[14]

10

The Society Spreads to Eastern Africa

THE General Chapter, held in Kiltegan from 17 June to 1 July 1950, was a milestone in the Society's history. For the first time, the Chapter consisted entirely of Society members. The status of the Society had not changed. It was still a diocesan institution but was now virtually independent of the Bishop. Since the Chapter of 1944, Bishop Keogh had not considered it necessary to play an active role in the affairs of the Society and had no representative on the governing council. In accordance with the Constitutions, the Chapter was composed of the outgoing Superior General, the five general councillors, the Bursar General and eight delegates elected by the priests. Representation was on the basis of one delegate for every twelve priest-members. At the time the delegates were elected, there were ninety-two priests in the Society.[1]

The first item of the agenda was the election of the Superior General, the councillors and the Bursar General. This was by far the most crucial business facing the Chapter and, in the minds of many Society members, it was the only significant business. The choosing of a Superior General was considered to be of primary importance. It would have to be a new man, as Paddy Costelloe had already served the statutory two terms.

The rest of the agenda reflected the problems of the Society at the time. The most pressing problem was the inadequacy of the accommodation in Kiltegan. The Chapter's primary concern was for the students who had very little living space. The students, themselves, took this deprivation in good part and, with characteristic humour, they nicknamed one of their dormitories after the infamous concentration camp at Belsen. The college staff, however, was concerned that open dormitory accommodation tended to encourage a boarding-school mentality at the expense of maturity and personal responsibility. Furthermore, the Society had to face up to the prospect of having to turn away suitable candidates in the not too distant future, for lack of housing. Accommodation for priests was a problem, too, especially while the college was in session. It was not uncommon for one of the residents to hurriedly evacuate his room for a colleague who arrived unexpectedly from the missions or elsewhere.

A second problem was posed by Society priests who had proved unequal to the Nigerian climate. A high fall-out rate had always been a feature of the Nigerian mission. At first, it did not create a problem of placement as diocesan volunteers could return to their dioceses and there was enough work around Kiltegan to absorb early Society members who were unfit to return to the missions. However, as membership increased, so did the number of priests who were invalided from the mission. A number of these returned after a period of convalescence but, for others, Nigeria with its oppressive climate and multiplicity of diseases was no longer an option. The Society was faced with the task of placing these men. All that was available was temporary parish work in Ireland and England and even this was hard enough to secure at a time when vocations to the priesthood were on the increase. Moreover, such work was most unsatisfying for young men who had hoped to spend a lifetime on the missions. The possibility of securing a mission territory with a more favourable climate had been mooted and was to be considered by the Chapter.

In a dramatic new departure, the Chapter elected Joe Gilmartin as Superior General. Pat Whitney and Paddy Costelloe had been Maynooth volunteers. In passing over the other Maynooth men and electing Joe Gilmartin, the Chapter was opting for someone who had joined the Society as a student and was a member of the first group to be ordained in Kiltegan. Then, as if to retreat from so bold a step, the Chapter chose all four councillors from among the former volunteers. Charlie Smith became Vicar-General; Paddy Costelloe was returned as second councillor; Corney Plunkett and Matt Magrath took the remaining two places. Vin Kiernan who had come to Kiltegan immediately after his secondary schooling in St Finian's, Mullingar, and had been ordained in 1940, became Bursar General.

The Chapter was very cautious in its approach to the other problems before it. It was accepted that additional accommodation, including a new college, would have to be provided. There was no agreement on the best course of action, however. A number of delegates supported the idea of buying a new farm which would be more viable than High Park and might be a more suitable location for the new college. Others were slow to commit the Society to such a major step and while various interim solutions were proposed, no decision was taken on the new college. The Chapter document states:

> As regards site, the general opinion of the Chapter was not opposed to building at Kiltegan, but it was not considered wise to take a final decision at the moment. The Superior General and his Council were left free to do what they considered best in the circumstances, bearing in mind the options voiced by the delegates.

The Chapter was no more adventuresome in its decision with regard to new mission territory. This is not surprising as the delegates were keenly aware of the need for personnel in Nigeria and had no wish to jeopardise the work there in any way. The decision was given as follows:

> After considerable discussion the Chapter decided that the time was not yet opportune to undertake a new mission territory. It was felt that for the present, sufficient temporary appointments can be procured elsewhere for priests unable to work in Nigeria. The question of a new territory should however be kept in mind.

Father Joseph Gilmartin

Joe Gilmartin was born in Claremorris, Co. Mayo, in 1912. His father, John Gilmartin, was a Sergeant with the RIC until he retired in 1911, at the age of 50, and settled in Claremorris. He had attended Queen Victoria's Golden Jubilee celebrations in London in 1887, as a delegate of the RIC. In 1914 he moved to Sligo with his wife and five children and, two years later, purchased Knocknarea Hotel at Strandhill. In 1922 he built a new hotel called 'St Patrick's'. Meanwhile, Joe, the youngest child, attended Strandhill National School and then went on to Summerhill College. On matriculating he decided to become a priest and went to All Hallows College where he heard about St Patrick's Missionary Society from Pat Whitney. With three classmates, he opted for the Society in the year of its foundation. Pat Whitney's personal magnetism was a big factor in his decision, and, throughout his life, Joe Gilmartin remained a great admirer of Pat's faith and courage and achievement. Ordained in 1937, he was retained in Ireland to serve on the College staff, on the General Council and in the office until 1942, when he went to Calabar. He did two tours in Calabar, during which time he served as Principal of St Patrick's College, Calabar and later as General Supervisor of Education for the Vicariate. It was in this post that he gained the reputation for administrative ability, firmness and understanding which made him a strong favourite to be the next Superior General.

Joe Gilmartin was a very shy and private man. It took great effort on his part to make any approach to those he did not know well. As a result, he appeared to be cold and rigid and, as often as not, displeased with the world. Close friends and family knew a different Joe Gilmartin. With them, he was warm and friendly. He liked to give little gifts and enjoyed the occasional game of bridge or poker. Whatever his mood, he was meticulous. Minutes of a meeting were fine-combed for any trace of ambiguity or possibility of misrepresentation. If he gave a dinner party for his friends, he spared neither effort nor expense to make it a memorable occasion. He appreciated the good things of life but made use of them very sparingly and always discreetly. He had a clear mind and was decisive when the need arose. Honour was a very important virtue for him and one could easily imagine him, in other circumstances, falling on his sword because honour demanded it. He would feel pretty miserable about it but he would do it all the same. The job of Superior General weighed heavily. There were long silent spells during which he said little to anyone and nothing at all by way of small talk. Breakfast-time was never a good time but, once it had passed, Joe Gilmartin got down to running the Society decisively and with great integrity.

He was ideally suited to the task of building on what Paddy Costelloe had achieved. His innate cautiousness and attention to detail ensured that the Society would continue to be thought well of in Ireland. His decisiveness was important at a time when the Society was ready to develop its own structures and to take on new missions. The priests found him more approachable than Paddy Costelloe. Although, by nature, he was more reserved than Paddy, he was not submerged by the job as Paddy had been and could be more natural with people. The fact that he was 'a Society man' from the beginning helped to boost the confidence of the priests.

New Moves

There was a number of significant changes around Kiltegan. Jimmy Lane and John McGuinness, who had been associated with College and administration since ordination, were appointed to Nigeria. Paddy Costelloe became Rector of the College and won the respect and confidence of the students whom he treated with great kindness and consideration. Now that he was relieved of the burden of being Superior General, he entered a new phase of his life where his simplicity, friendliness and interest in people could reassert itself and blossom. Slowly, his health improved and he was to have close on another forty years in which to put behind him the pain of the early days. Frank Whitney, to his great delight, was made bursar of St Patrick's in Cork. This appointment was seen at the time as an example of the new Superior's powers of diplomacy. The previous administration had made a number of efforts to place Frank in a chaplaincy but no suitable opening had been found. Meanwhile, Frank and Father Hickey formed a kind of Greek chorus commenting on all that was happening around Kiltegan and unnerving the younger men who were trying to keep the show going. In appointing Frank to Cork, Joe Gilmartin was giving him a post within the Society while at the same time separating the two founder-members and so helping them to come to terms with the past. Peter O'Reilly, who was spiritual director in Cork, became Frank's assistant and took on the bulk of the work. Frank was to spend more than twenty years in Cork, where he enjoyed a good relationship with the young priests who had charge of the students. Joe Gilmartin did his best for others who had personal problems and tried to get them whatever help was available. He was not afraid to put pressure on those who were reluctant to seek help. On one occasion, he arranged for a man with an alcohol problem to go to a treatment centre in England. To make sure that nothing went wrong, he accompanied him to Dublin airport. Unknown to Joe, the priest in question had booked a flight to New York. He gave Joe the slip at the airport and made it to the United States where he served as a priest until his death, twenty years later.

The early fifties saw the spread of the Society's operations to the USA. Twenty years before, it was Pat Whitney's intention to appeal for support to the Irish in America. Nothing had been done about it, apart from occasional visits by individual priests to their relatives in the States. Joe Houlihan had made such a visit in 1949 and, the following year, on completing his term as councillor, he returned with the specific intention of raising money for the Society. However, an organised promotion drive was not envisaged at this stage. Joe Houlihan arrived in July 1953, and during the following months he wrote to Kiltegan from New York, Boston, Washington and other places. He visited the Columbans in New York and the Medical Missionaries of Mary in Boston. He made contacts with various priests and diocesan officials and became convinced that the Society needed a base in the United States. He had little difficulty in convincing the Superiors of the wisdom of this suggestion, especially since the various Society bank accounts were operating in the red at the time. Meanwhile, he was tireless in his efforts to raise money and make contacts. He arranged for parish supplies and appeals and had a number of priests sent out from Kiltegan to honour these commitments. He was given the freedom of presbyteries and used the postal addresses of Irish-American friends. Secretarial services were provided by Joe Houlihan's cousins who typed and duplicated letters and promotion material in the offices in which they worked. With considerable difficulty, an appointment was arranged with Bishop Fulton Sheen, the National Director of the Propagation of the Faith. Like so many others, Bishop Sheen was charmed by Joe Houlihan and the two became firm friends. Bishop Sheen was to be chosen to ordain Joe Houlihan a bishop in 1960. In 1953, Joe Houlihan purchased a house in Camden, New Jersey, for the Society, with the approval of the diocesan authorities. A contract with the diocese was signed in May of that year. The Society had now an official standing in the United States and was in a position to launch a systematic promotion drive.

The Chapter had recommended that the building of a new college should be postponed for some time. However, some short-term solution had to be found to relieve the pressure on student accommodation. It was decided to extend the university hostel in Cork and to establish it as a College offering the two-year course in philosophy which had up to now been given in Kiltegan. Plans were drawn by Pearse McKenna and a two-storey building comprising kitchen, dining rooms and sleeping quarters was added to 'Windsor'. In 1955, the philosophers joined the university students in Cork and until 1986, when the college was closed down, all the students, with a few rare exceptions, spent at least two years of their training there. Joe Gilmartin made no serious effort to acquire a new premises as a minority group within the Chapter had suggested. An auctioneer who had been approached earlier about a property in Dublin wrote, in 1952, to say that a Mrs Ryan in Waterford was anxious to sell her house and 350-acre farm to a religious congregation. Joe Gilmartin and Paddy Costelloe went to see it. The asking price was £25,000, one third of which could be paid in instalments. A 1703 chalice and a relic of the True Cross, which were kept in the private oratory of the house, were to be given as gifts to the purchaser. It was decided not to buy the property and the matter of finding an alternative site for the proposed new college was shelved until the next Chapter.

'Windsor', St Patrick's, Douglas, Cork which was purchased in 1947. The new wing (*right*) was built in 1955 and a third storey was added in 1963.

A group of students returning from University College Cork in the 1950s.

Episcopal ordination of Bishop Ekandem in Calabar 1954: (*from left*) front row: Bishops Kelly S.M.A., Biechy C.S.Sp., Ekandem, Moynagh, Finn S.M.A. Back row: Monsignor Anyogu, Bishop McCoy W.F., Bishop Hagan C.S.Sp., Archbishop Heerey, Monsignor McGettrick.

Missionaries on motorbikes.

Dr Joseph Barnes.

Mr John Turner.

Dr Godfrey Hinds with his wife, Nancy, on their wedding day.

The new College, Kiltegan, built in the late 1950s and early 1960s.

Mr Pearse McKenna, architect of many Society buildings in Ireland and on the missions.

Fr Liam Doyle (*left*) and Fr Thaddeus Smythe in familiar difficulties in the Kerio Valley, Kenya.

Sr Sean Underwood M.M.M. fuels the Turkana mission aircraft with the help of
Fr Gerard O'Carroll and parishioners.

Episcopal ordination of Bishop Joseph B. Houlihan, Loreto Convent, Eldoret, 1960:
(*from left*) sitting: Bishop Dominic Ekandem, Bishop Houlihan and
Bishop Maurice Otunga. Standing: Frs James P. Bohan, John Maher of Kerry
diocese (hidden), Morgan O'Brien, Francis McNabb and Liam deVeale.

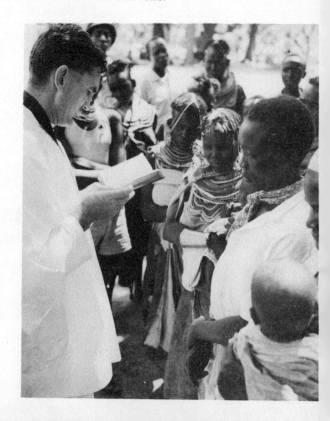

Fr Leo Staples, pioneer missionary
among the Pokot people of Kenya,
conducts a Baptism ceremony.

Bishop Joseph B. Houlihan with Kenyan politician, Raymond Wood.

Bishop William Dunne with Kitui pioneer Paul White C.S.Sp.

Kiltegan June 1962: (*from left*) Kevin Longworth, Joseph Gilmartin, Ciaran Needham,
Archbishop Sergio Pignedoli, Charles Smith, John McGuinness,
Carthage Cantwell and Edward Fitzgibbon.

The four Superiors who headed St Patrick's Missionary Society from 1938–90:
(*from left*) Joseph Gilmartin, Peter O'Reilly, Peter Finegan and Patrick J. Costelloe.
The photograph was taken in 1984.

Kenya

The Society undertook a mission in Kenya in 1951. It was a surprise move in view of the Chapter's decision to postpone any move on a new mission. For the second time in the history of the Society, it was a gifted Apostolic Delegate who intervened to push the Society forward. This time, it was Archbishop David Mathew, a man vividly remembered by Society priests for his problems with flatulence. That difficulty aside, Archbishop Mathew was an extremely intelligent man with a superb grasp of the political situation in Africa and he could see the implications for the Church. Bishop Moynagh was to say of him:

> The most efficient and most effective delegate that I met was Archbishop Mathew. His was the finest intellect. While some of these conferences of ours used to drag on for three days, this man would go through more work in a single day and showed extra-ordinary perception as to what was at the heart of the matter.[2]

The Archbishop, in turn, appreciated the Society. He visited Kiltegan in 1947, and addressed the students. In a letter to Joe Gilmartin, written in July 1950 to congratulate him on his election as Superior General, Archbishop Mathew wrote 'What I as an outsider (if I may so express it) find so encouraging is the homely friendly spirit of the Society.' It was in this letter that the Apostolic Delegate asked whether the Society intended to look for a new mission. It was an exercise in diplomatic fishing. For some time, Rome had been planning the establishment of a new Prefecture in the Kenya highlands. It was hoped to hand it over to English-speaking priests as it was an area of predominantly British settlement. Moreover, the Archbishop knew that the Society had already considered sending men to Kenya.

This had come about as a result of a chance meeting between Paddy Costelloe and Bishop Cavallera of the Vicariate of Nyeri, in Kenya. The meeting took place in the summer of 1949 in Our Lady of Lourdes Hospital, Drogheda, where the bishop was a patient. Bishop Cavallera was an Italian Consolata missionary whose diocese was in the heartland of the Kikuyu tribe. He wanted English-speaking priests and sisters to work alongside the Italians who staffed his Vicariate, and asked for two priests to teach English in his minor seminary for a period of three or four years. English was a problem for the Italian missionaries. They spoke Kikuyu fluently but had little opportunity to learn English. Only a few years before, they had been interned by the British as enemy aliens. They had little rapport with the English officials who ran the colony and had great difficulty in giving the pupils in their schools the command of English required for advancement in Kenya. Paddy Costelloe considered the offer and was particularly impressed by the fact that Nyeri enjoyed a pleasant climate. He wrote to Archbishop Mathew for advice but before receiving a reply he decided to accept the offer. Ned McElligott and Peter O'Reilly, two men who had been invalided home from Nigeria, were assigned to Nyeri. They were to travel out in February 1950. Early in the New Year they were told that the project was 'off'. No explanation was given nor was any explanation expected at that time. It is impossible, now, to determine the reasons for the sudden change of plan.[3] It is probable, however, that the proposed Kiltegan involvement in Nyeri gave the Delegate the idea that the Society might be used in Kenya to staff the proposed new Prefecture.

In any case, there were no further developments until Archbishop Mathew's letter of congratulations arrived in July 1950. Joe Gilmartin realised that the Society would be looking for a new mission in a couple of years. New missions were not easy to come by and to ignore an overture from someone who knew the Society and its needs would be to miss a golden opportunity. He replied in September 1950:

> Calabar/Ogoja would have no difficulty in absorbing all our priests for the next two or three years; however, we would gladly undertake any foreign mission which you would suggest. It would be desirable that a mission with a climate less difficult than that of Calabar and Ogoja be obtained so that suitable missionary work be obtained for priests who were unable, for reasons of health, to work in these territories. It is the wish of the Council, however, that while reference be made to the desirability of such a mission, it was to be emphasised that any mission, no matter how difficult, would be gladly accepted.

Archbishop Mathew recommended to Propaganda that the proposed new Vicariate be offered to St Patrick's Missionary Society. Propaganda made the formal offer of the territory in March 1952, and it was accepted immediately by the Superior General and his council. The announcement was not made public by Propaganda until the end of April. Meanwhile, Archbishop Mathew mentioned the possibility of the new mission in Lagos much to the chagrin of the Prefect Apostolic of Ogoja whose letter to Joe Gilmartin, dated 21 March 1951, bears witness to the secrecy which surrounded such decisions at the time. He writes:

You ask for co-operation. I promise it whole-heartedly. But there cannot be co-operation without trust. We have to trust and respect the rights and the manliness of those under and over us. For God's sake do not be making secrets out of the time the cows are milked at Kiltegan, and let the men there know what is going on. That smoke screen of silence about quite normal matters: the secret air which surrounded even the normal movements of the people in authority bred feelings of distrust and certainly shattered co-operation. You feel terribly foolish in a situation where you are supposed to know about something and you are told by an outsider. An example of that was the meeting in Lagos. Archbishop Mathew talked publicly about the possibility of Kiltegan getting another mission in East Africa. He spoke about it to all the Archbishops and Bishops. I knew nothing about it. Bishop Moynagh did. But isn't it as good to tell all than have outsiders giving you the first edition. It is only one case in point. What I said about the men at home is also true of the men here. A line now and again to us giving us general news and how you are getting on at home would help to unite us all and bond us together for the common work. I know you have done much since you came into office to dispel the clouds of distrust but I ask you to continue until not a shadow of them remains.

News of Propaganda's plan was not well received by the Mill Hill Fathers, out of whose diocese the new Prefecture was to be carved. They were no more enthusiastic about losing a portion of their territory than the Holy Ghost Fathers had been, twenty years before, in Nigeria. The Mill Hill Superiors had hoped to retain the area and develop it as a Mill Hill Prefecture. The men in the field were also anxious to stay on. Their disappointment on losing the Prefecture to Kiltegan was publicly and humorously expressed by one of their number, Bill Powdrill, in a parody of 'Hail Glorious St Patrick'. Bishop Frederick Hall, the Mill Hill bishop whose Vicariate spanned the whole of Western Kenya, had no such reservation. He was keenly aware of the potential for development in all parts of his Vicariate and was happy to be able to surrender some of it to another missionary group. He wrote to Kiltegan in May 1951 and asked for four priests to be sent out by the end of the year. The first group of Kiltegan priests left Ireland for Kenya on 5 December 1951. The following day they boarded the *Durban Castle* in London, and sailed through the Mediterranean, the Suez Canal, the Red Sea and round the Horn of Africa to Mombasa. It was a journey of twenty-four days. The priests were Bill Dunne who had been teaching in Kiltegan and had edited *Africa* for a time, Joe Murray who had done a tour in Nigeria, Denis Newman who had just completed the L.C.L. course in Maynooth, Liam Doyle who had done a philosophy course in Louvain and Mick Brennan who had been assigned to Calabar. Mick was awaiting an opportunity to study tropical agriculture in the West Indies in preparation for development work in Calabar when he was deflected to Kenya.

Kenya, in 1951, was very different from Nigeria. British interests had come in much the same way to both places. Kenya took a different turn with the building of the Uganda railway which reached a papyrus swamp called Nairobi, in 1899. From there the railway slowly wound its way up and down the escarpments of the Rift Valley to reach Port Florence, now Kisumu, on the shores of Lake Victoria, in 1902. British administrators had identified Kenya as 'Whiteman's Country' and soon the railway was to carry an influx of settlers to the fertile and healthy highlands.[4] In 1902, in order to encourage settlement, the colonial authorities gave 100,000 acres of land to the wealthy and adventurous Lord Delamere who proceeded to risk his family fortune in the development of agriculture in Kenya. The land occupied by the settlers was regarded by the British as vacant land because the African tribes had not yet established rights of ownership to it. The decision on what constituted ownership rested with the colonists and, as more and more settlers arrived, the native peoples were constricted in diminishing tribal areas.

Kenya became a prosperous colony although the prosperity was for whites only. Africans in Kenya were denied the social and political development enjoyed by their counterparts in Nigeria. The settlers were hostile to attempts by the British colonial administration to better the lot of the African population. Schools for Africans were few and the only concession to African participation in government was the appointment of Eliud Mathu, a member of the predominant Kikuyu tribe, to the Legislative Council of the colony in 1944. A loosely organised political party known as the Kenya African Union (KAU) formed itself in support of Mathu. It grew into an organised party under the gifted leadership of Jomo Kenyatta, recently returned from a 15-year stay in England. In 1948 the shadowy Mau Mau movement was born. Drawing its adherents principally from the Kikuyu tribe, this movement was purportedly committed to the same political ideals as KAU but was pledged to terrorist methods. There was intimidation, murder, secret oathing and widespread fear. In October 1952 a state of emergency was declared. KAU was banned. Kenyatta was arrested to begin a period of seven years in detention. Mau Mau fighters disappeared into the forest, whence they emerged to harass government sympathisers among their own people and, to a lesser extent, the white settlers. Suspects were rounded up and vetted or detained in camps situated away from the Kikuyu homeland. Up to 80,000 people passed through these camps during the emergency, which continued until 1961.

This was the political scene that greeted the five Kiltegan men who were met at Mombasa docks by Jim Barrett, a Holy Ghost Father who was Principal of St Mary's School, Nairobi. The ecclesiastical scene was far more tranquil. The country was divided among three missionary congregations. The Holy Ghosts had come in 1889. They started at the coast and later went to Nairobi with the railway and fanned out from there. Their territory in Kenya belonged to the Vicariate of Zanzibar until Nairobi diocese was set up in 1953 and Mombasa in 1957. In 1902, the newly founded Consolata Fathers came from Turin to work with the Holy Ghosts. Three years later they established a separate Vicariate in the Mount Kenya area, following a coup de grace delivered in Rome. The Mill Hill Society entered Kenya from Uganda and established a mission at Port Florence, on Lake Victoria, in 1904. The area was part of the Vicariate of the Upper Nile with headquarters in Uganda. In 1925 it was broken off from Uganda to become the Prefecture Apostolic of Kavirondo and, in 1932, the Vicariate of Kisumu. Much of the highland area of this Vicariate with large areas of adjacent lowland was to be handed over to the Kiltegan priests. For a time, however, they were to work alongside the Mill Hill priests and under the authority of Bishop Hall.

The overnight journey from Mombasa to Kisumu was made by train in the company of Jim Barrett. It was a journey through the empty plains of Tsavo which were home to elephants and wild cats and wandering Masai herdsmen. In Nairobi the newcomers saw the well-developed mission of the Holy Ghost Fathers, the fashionable St Mary's and Loreto schools and the diocesan farm at Limuru. Towards evening they boarded the train again for the 250-mile journey to Kisumu. Before long they had reached the area that would soon be theirs. They passed by extinct volcanoes and lakes, through ranchland and farmland, up and down with the extraordinary terrain until they reached Kisumu. It was a 14-hour journey. From Kisumu they went to join the Mill Hill priests each of whom was manning one of six parishes in the area to be staffed by St Patrick's Society.[5]

Compared with Calabar and Ogoja, this part of Kenya seemed empty of people and lacking in life. The European settlers lived in isolated farmhouses. They frequented their modest though exclusive clubs, and visited the towns of Nakuru, Eldoret and Kitale for shopping, to go to the cinema or to attend the occasional amateur drama production or sporting event. The decadent set associated with 'The Happy Valley' and immortalised on celluloid was confined to the very rich and their camp followers. Although some of them lived in the area around Naivasha and Nakuru, they were not really part of it. They belonged to Nairobi and to the Empire, and with India gone, since 1947, the Empire was no longer the bulwark that it once had been. There were Asians in the towns, in trade and services and in the offices. Among them, the Goans were Catholic and strong supporters of the Church. They brought a touch of home to the town churches: flowers, candles, pretty cloths and wax polish. The Africans were migrant labourers on the farms or manual workers in the towns. Home was in the tribal area or 'reserve'. In the highlands the African was an outsider. He had no land and no security except a menial job which was held at the whim of a foreigner. To move around, he needed a 'kipande' or identity card. Adjoining the white settlement were tribal reserves where people lived at subsistence level on small farms in the uplands or as pastoralists on the semi-arid and arid plains of Baringo and Turkana.

Schools in the area were few. There were good schools for Europeans and Asians. The Loreto Sisters ran one such school for girls in Eldoret. The African population depended on scattered primary schools, all but a few of which taught pupils only to Standard Four. In 1949, the Beecher report had recommended the expansion of primary education. The government was trying its best to implement these recommendations but the majority of settlers were opposed to it. In the highlands, the settlers owned the land and had the power to frustrate government plans for education at local level.

The Mill Hill missionaries had established catechumenates through-out the area. These were akin to the bush schools of Nigeria. A catechist taught religion, a little reading and writing and arithmetic, if he knew it. When the Kiltegan men arrived, there were hundreds of these primitive schools. Twelve of them had been registered with the government and developed as far as Standard Four. They were good schools by the standards of the time. A thirteenth, at Three Rivers, was registered but only went as far as Standard Two because the farmer would not allow further development. There was a Catholic Teacher Training

College at Kiminini with a small Intermediate School attached. The College was relocated nearer Kitale in mid 1952, and the Intermediate School continued at Kiminini in the charge of Mrs Fairbanks. The Franciscan Sisters took this school over in 1954, and developed it as a girls' secondary school which was to achieve a national reputation for excellence in the years ahead.

The tiny Catholic communities were centred on these schools or would-be schools. Many had become Catholics in their home areas and continued to be influenced by the Christian community of their home village as contact with home was nearly always maintained. In the towns, Goans and Seychelles formed the backbone of the communities. There was also a floating population of Africans and a small number of Europeans whose doughtiness amazed and amused the young Irishmen. There was Mrs Newall, a retired interior decorator, who had come to farm in the Subukia Valley and who lived alone throughout the emergency. She came to Nakuru for shopping every Friday, went to the 6.30 a.m. Mass and joined the Fathers for breakfast, her revolver at the ready beside her saucer. In general, the newly arrived priests kept their distance from the Europeans. Advice to that effect had filtered down from the Apostolic Delegate and, besides, there was a good measure of mutual distrust based on ethnic origins and conflicting designs for the African population. It was a nerve-racking situation for the missionaries. They needed the good-will of the settlers for without it they could not visit their little communities on the farms or develop their schools. They could not be seen to support the aspiration of the African for independence and had to be careful to avoid a confrontation with individual settlers on the potentialities of the black race in general. All contacts with colonials were sensitive. A visit to an out-station required permission from the farmer or estate manager. The priest was precluded from staying overnight in the school because it would be offensive to the white man and his family. An invitation to the farmhouse had to be declined as it would involve an association with the colonials that the priests themselves considered undesirable. Some situations were exceptionally sensitive. For example, the District Commissioner in Kapenguria invited Dinny Newman to sit in briefly at the trial of Jomo Kenyatta in January 1953. To the colonist, Kenyatta was an 'African leader to darkness and death'.[6] To the missionary he was an ambiguous figure, a violent man, maybe, but also a symbol of hope for his people. The situation demanded artfulness, as did the public prayers on Empire Day or the prayers for the Queen on the occasion of her coronation, in June 1953.

As in Nigeria, education gave the missionaries access to the people. In Kenya, it had a further implication, bound up as it was with the nationalist aspirations which preoccupied people at the time, especially the Kikuyu. Kenyatta advocated education for Africans; the settlers were against it. In pushing education, the missionaries were demonstrating, in the only manner open to them, that they were for the African struggle and against the settlers. The establishment and supervision of schools was a suitable challenge for energetic young men whose numbers increased rapidly in the years immediately following.[7]

Communication with the people was facilitated by the existence of Swahili, a lingua franca that was easy to learn. Bishop Hall was impressed by the enthusiasm of the Kiltegan priests for the language. He wrote of Joe Murray, less than six weeks after the latter's appointment to Nakuru town: 'He has done remarkably well at Swahili.'[8] Within six months, most of the priests were preaching in Swahili, which gave them an accessibility to the people denied to their counterparts in Nigeria where no common African language existed.

The work of the Society in Kenya received a great boost with the establishment of the Prefecture of Eldoret on 29 June 1953. This was followed in July 1954 by the arrival of the first Prefect Apostolic. He was Joseph B. Houlihan, a man of enormous energy who had missionary experience in Nigeria and who had built up many useful contacts during his time on the General Council in Kiltegan and while fund-raising in the United States.

Nigeria and the race for the schools
In the 1950s the Church in Nigeria was preoccupied with what a headline in *Africa* magazine described as 'The race for the schools'.[9] The race was against time and against Nigerian nationalism which was now in its final burst towards self-determination and independence. As an interim measure, a new constitution, drawn up in 1951, provided for regional houses of assembly. In the East, the National Council of Nigeria and the Cameroons, Azikiwe's party, was in control. This party had socialist leanings and advocated a welfare state with state control of education. The missionaries saw this as a great danger. In Eastern Nigeria, in particular, the school had been the mainstay of the Church. The prospect of losing the schools was a great cause for alarm.

The new Apostolic Delegate, Archbishop Mathew, had warned of this danger on his first visit to Nigeria in 1947, and had stressed the urgency of developing an African leadership among the clergy and laity.

It was in response to this that laymen were sent abroad to get university degrees. In Ogoja and Calabar, the threat to the schools was met on two fronts. A herculean effort was made to consolidate existing schools and to build many more while there was still time. An effort was also made to develop religious instruction and other pastoral initiatives outside the school so that dependence on the schools would be lessened and any damage caused by the eclipse of the Catholic school would be limited.

In 1953, the Minister of Education in the Eastern Region outlined Government plans to introduce a phased programme of universal primary education. The Church welcomed the proposal but saw it as the first step in government control of education. The Churches had not been consulted and were kept in the dark as to the full extent of the Government's plans. However, there was no doubt in Church circles that its influence in education would be curbed and certainly that further expansion would be severely restricted. It was decided to make an all-out effort to increase the number of Catholic schools before the advent of full self-government within the regions, which was due in 1956. The article in *Africa,* mentioned above, describes the position as follows:

> This year (1956) Nigeria hopes to attain to complete independence. It is unquestionable that one of the first enactments of a native government will be to prescribe universal compulsory education. It is practically certain that in 1957 this law will be passed. As soon as this happens, there will be an unprecedented rush on the schools. In any place where there is no school to take the rush, the State will provide one . . . and it will be a State School. New schools after the Compulsory Education Act will, it seems very probable, be allocated on a 60/40 basis, i.e. out of every 100 new schools, 60 per cent will be State Schools and the remaining 40 per cent will be divided among the missions of various denominations, the proportion being decided by the number of their existing schools. Where there are no training centres, again the State will provide them.
>
> It is therefore a race against time. Wherever the Church loses ground now, it loses it for good. Wherever the Church puts a school now it eliminates the need for a State School.[10]

This 'race for the schools' began in earnest in 1953. Between 1952 and 1957 Teacher Training Colleges in Calabar increased in number from 3 to 13; Junior Primary Schools from 221 to 335 and Senior Primary

Schools from 82 to 135. Similar figures for Ogoja are not to hand but there is every indication that the pace of growth there was at least as fast. The annual report prepared for Rome in 1955 puts the number of schools in Ogoja at 461 and points to an increase of 41 on the previous year.[11] This expansion was made possible by an enormous investment of time and energy in education on the part of the priests, the Holy Child Sisters and the Handmaids of the Holy Child. Both these congregations of Sisters were engaged in the education of girls. In addition to a network of primary schools, the Holy Child Sisters had established Cornelia College, Uyo and Marianhill College, Calabar, by 1956. Among the priests, every available graduate was put into full-time teaching or educational administration, while most of the others were school managers. The pressure of getting close on 1,000 schools 'opened, staffed, settled down, and running smoothly' is captured in this extract from *Africa:*

> In Calabar and Ogoja, two supervisors, two education secretaries and thirty school managers will be working day and night all through this month to sort out the tangles in the placing (to the best advantage) of 3,758 teachers and in the accommodation of something between 120,000 and 150,000 pupils.[12]

Universal primary education was introduced in 1957 and the Government backed down on many of its measures to exercise greater control and to curb expansion. Parents were allowed to choose the agency which would educate their children. In the Eastern Region, 60 per cent of the parents of registered schoolchildren opted for the Catholic agency. In Calabar, where only about 6 per cent of the population was Catholic, a massive 33 per cent opted for Catholic education. In Ogoja, the Catholic Church was the only agency, voluntary or governmental, which was involved to any great extent in education. In these circumstances, universal primary education offered the missions a great opportunity of expanding its influence through education with the sanction and backing of the Government.[13] Schools built without permission, after 1953, were registered, and the fevered expansion of the previous four years ceased. There was an actual decrease in the number of schools as some existing schools were closed in order to consolidate with a view to better overall standards.

The contribution of St Patrick's Society to education was considerable. It got involved in education primarily to further its evangelising goals, but it was, nonetheless, committed to providing first-class educational facilities. Although this aim was achieved, the contribution to education was limited. In Calabar and Ogoja, the Society established and supervised an efficient school system and provided excellent teachers. However, little was done to develop the school curriculum to meet the needs of an emerging African nation. Bishop Moynagh attempted to introduce agricultural science in the secondary schools run by the Vicariate and he recruited a number of Irish Agriculture graduates to teach in the schools. Four technical schools were opened in the 1952–57 period and other efforts were made to promote technical education in the years that followed. These moves met with only limited success, chiefly because they aroused hostility in the government officials concerned and did nothing to correct the academic bias of education to which the Government was irrevocably committed. The education offered by the Holy Child Sisters was innovative and was widely praised in official circles. Nevertheless, it was considered too expensive as a general approach to the education of girls.

One negative element in the rapid expansion of mission schools in the 1950s was the lack of gentleness with which it was put into effect by many of the missionaries. A number used high-handed methods and bullying tactics in acquiring sites, exacting local contributions and dealing with teachers. This can be explained by the pressure under which the missionaries worked, by the tendency to justify the means by the very laudable end, and by the subconscious assumption that Africans were less sensitive to abuse than Europeans. This less than gentle approach was not confined to educational matters or indeed to this period. However, it was exacerbated by the emergence of a more sophisticated and more politicised African with whom the missionary no longer enjoyed the rapport which had been there when the former was a schoolboy. Faced with this new sophistication, which was often overtly European, the missionary was not unknown to respond with sarcasm and cynicism.

The Africans would appear to have accepted any such gracelessness with great tolerance. Looking back from the more tranquil vantage point of later life, many of the missionaries regret their behaviour and wish that they had tempered their zeal with greater respect.

The Apostolate outside the school

Educational matters tended to absorb the missionary at the expense of other aspects of the apostolate. This was widely recognised at the time and, from 1948 onwards, attempts were made to renew the catechumenate and to seek new ways of deepening the faith. An important initiative was the introduction of the Confraternity of Christian Doctrine. This was an official association of lay people who dedicated themselves to the work of religious instruction on a voluntary basis and without any pay. It had worked well in the United States and was introduced to Calabar, in 1951, on an experimental basis. It was extended to the whole Vicariate of Calabar in 1953 and also introduced in Ogoja. Within a few years, this movement resulted in a dramatic increase in adult baptisms and prepared for a time when the school could no longer be relied upon for religious instruction.

Lack of contact between the priest and the ordinary people was seen as a drawback, especially in Calabar, where there was concern to deepen the faith. Ogoja was, by contrast, in the period of first evangelisation. In Calabar it was decided to subdivide the five huge parishes and, between 1948 and 1950, ten new parishes were created. In 1951 the celebration of Mass in family compounds was allowed for the first time and, in 1953, Bishop Moynagh urged his priests to spend more time in the out-stations. The Bishop was especially concerned with the 18–25 year age-group, many of whom had fallen away from the Church. He blamed this situation on their difficulty with Catholic marriage law, the failure of Church committees to give them any say in community affairs and the lack of an organised youth ministry. Ned Fitzgibbon's efforts to mobilise the youth of Calabar town were exceptional. He ran a Catholic youth club and coached the town football team to become All-Nigeria Champions, winning the Governor's Cup in 1953. So great was his renown that his next return from leave was greeted by a front page headline in the *Nigerian Daily Standard:* 'Father Fitzgibbon has arrived'. The monthly magazine *Catholic Life* was revived in an effort to cater for the younger and more literate Catholics. It grew from a circulation of 4,000 in the early fifties to 15,000 in 1957. Four American lay-missionaries, with training in printing and journalism, arrived that year to staff the diocesan press. With their efforts and those of Frank Morris and Alfie Rushe, the magazine reached a nationwide circulation of 70,000 in the sixties. The Legion of Mary was active in the campaign to reconcile those who had lapsed. There were sixty-eight praesidia in Calabar in 1952 and 148 in 1957. Ogoja had twenty-two praesidia in 1952. Associated with the Legion of Mary was a 'Rosary Crusade' established by Pat Laffey and promoted by Patsy Kivlehan. It encouraged prayer and devotion in the villages and aroused interest in the Church among non-Christians.[14]

The Church in Ogoja was still only preparing for a direct onslaught on evangelisation. Priests were fewer in Ogoja—twenty in 1950 as compared with fifty in Calabar. This was a perennial sore point with Tom McGettrick who wrote to Kiltegan in 1953: 'Ogoja has become the Cinderella of St Patrick's Society'. Leprosy work and the provision of general medical care was a priority matched only by the drive for primary schools. The first secondary school, which was built by Tim Carr to the design of Pearse McKenna, was opened in 1953. The Prefect Apostolic wished to name it in honour of the Assumption of Mary which had been declared a dogma of the Church in 1950. He compiled a list of thirteen titles and called in five teachers to make the selection. They narrowed it down to Maryknoll and Mount Assumption, and the Prefect himself made a final decision for Maryknoll. In 1950, the number of baptised persons was only 11,500 or 1½ per cent of the total population.[15] By 1955 there were 24,037 baptised Catholics in thirteen residential missions, now referred to as parishes. The Prefecture had two general hospitals, two leper hospitals, sixteen leper villages and four teacher training institutions. There were eight convents with twenty-six sisters. The number of priests had increased to thirty-two and, by 1957, had reached forty-two, as compared with seventy in Calabar.[16] The death of Enda Davis in 1955 at the age of 45 deprived Ogoja of an experienced missionary who had served as Supervisor of Schools for the diocese. He had come home terminally ill some weeks previously.

Nigerian Hierarchy

In 1950, the Nigerian hierarchy was established. Bishop Heerey of Onitsha became Metropolitan Archbishop of Eastern Nigeria and all existing territories became dioceses. Archbishop Mathew was pressing the bishops to agree to admit Africans to the hierarchy. It was taken for granted that the first Nigerian bishop would be from the predominantly Catholic Ibo tribe. The Holy Ghost bishops were slow to move. The Superiors in Paris wanted the Archbishop to be succeeded by a European and wanted to retain a number of bishoprics within the Congregation. This would involve the appointment of African members of the Congregation as bishops, which posed a problem, as a number of diocesan priests were senior to them. A solution was sought in the establishment of an independent diocese in favour of a Nigerian diocesan priest. As the debate continued, the Apostolic Delegate raised the question with Bishop Moynagh. The latter welcomed the suggestion and agreed that the only priest in his diocese could become an auxiliary bishop. The announcement was made in September 1953, the Golden Jubilee of the establishment of the mission in Calabar. It was not a diplomatic move and it put a temporary strain on Bishop Moynagh's long-standing friendship with Archbishop Heerey. Dominic Ekandem was made a bishop in Calabar on 7 February 1954. Bishop Moynagh was principal consecrator, Paul Biechy, now Bishop of Brazzaville, was co-consecrator with Bishop Rogan of the Cameroons. Other pioneers such as O'Donnell, Ronayne, Mellett and Howell were also present. Archbishop Heerey, himself a pioneer in the Calabar area, preached the sermon. Corney Plunkett represented the Superior General. Less than three months previously the second Calabar priest, Isidore Peter Umana, had been ordained at Ifuho. He was to be followed by Emmanual Afang Ide, in 1954, and Brian Davis Usanga, in 1956.

The next episcopal appointment came as no surprise and caused no ill-feeling. It was the nomination of Tom McGettrick as Bishop of Ogoja. It was announced in January 1955, fifteen years after he had first taken over Ogoja. He wanted the ordination to take place in Ireland and resisted Joe Gilmartin's suggestion that he might be ordained in Ogoja. He needed a rest and felt that the ceremony would not make much sense to the people of Ogoja. He explained in a letter to Joe Gilmartin written on 11 February 1955:

> Further it would have little meaning here as I have dressed like a Bishop and did a Bishop's work since 1939. The night it was announced here I overheard a conversation in the kitchen between the boys. The cook said: sure he was a Bishop before now they make him a Bishop again. The driver who was listening answered: he be Junior Bishop before; now they make him Senior Bishop. It about sums up the situation as the people here see it.

The ceremony took place on Sunday 22 May in the College Chapel in Maynooth. Cardinal D'Alton was consecrator assisted by Bishop Keogh of Kildare and Leighlin and Bishop Fergus of Achonry. Bishop Philbin of Clonfert preached the sermon. It was the third and, almost certainly, the last time that the Bishop of a Nigerian diocese would be consecrated at St Patrick's College, Maynooth.

Expansion in Kenya

The appointment of Joe Houlihan as Prefect Apostolic of Eldoret took the priests in Kenya by surprise. They had expected that the post would be given to Bill Dunne, a man who seemed eminently suitable for it. The story goes, however, that Bishop Hall was opposed to Bill Dunne's appointment because he considered him too young and too urbane to run a rugged missionary diocese. Agreement was reached on Joe Houlihan. He was seven years older than Bill Dunne and was not a man of whom urbanity, in any form, could be predicated.

Joseph Brendan Houlihan was born in Ballyferriter, Co. Kerry in 1911 and educated at St Brendan's College, Killarney. He joined All Hallows College and with three members of his class signed on for St Patrick's Missionary Society in 1932 and was ordained five years later. He went to Nigeria in 1938 where he was renowned for his enthusiasm, hard work and more than a little derring-do. Bishop McGettrick bears testimony to his hard work in Anua and recalls, as an example of his zeal, an occasion when Joe Houlihan was rushing to a sick-call with an African youth riding pillion on the motorcycle. Some fancy driving caused the boy to be hurtled into the bushes without the knowledge of the young priest who only missed him a mile further on. Fortunately, the boy was not seriously hurt. The story presents a fitting image of Joe Houlihan's life. It was a life full of zeal and haste but deficient in care and attention to consequences. Joe Houlihan spent six years on the General Council, from 1944, and was engaged in promotion work in the United States when offered the post of Prefect Apostolic. He had reservations about accepting it himself and many who knew him wondered about his suitability.

Joe Houlihan was gifted with deep faith which was to see him through a life of exceptional tribulation. He was totally committed to missionary work, was generous to a fault and possessed a beguiling charm which drew people to him wherever he went. He was not a good listener, however, and kept people at a distance with humorous banter which enabled him to evade confronting the person or the issue before him. While acting as local bursar in Kiltegan, the Medical Missionaries, who were then house-keeping, asked him to buy some rice. As rice was new around Kiltegan, he responded with a joke. A few hours later the Sisters got a phonecall from the local grocery shop. It was Joe Houlihan asking what kind of rice did they want. It was always like this. A request might be a trap; it might catch him wrong-footed; it was best to play for time with a joke. He was also a careless builder. In Kiltegan he had built a hen-run which could never contain the hens. Later, he would build houses with second-hand doors or windows of differing size and design. People saw in him a great likeness to the Founder of the Society. Bishop Moynagh said of him:

He was as near as he could be to a replica of Pat Whitney and I have a notion that Joe Houlihan took his standards from Pat Whitney, his drive, his methods of bulldozing any opposition that stood in the way of his objectives, except that Joe Houlihan more or less adapted it to his way of life. That was my impression and also that of other people.[17]

Joe Houlihan would have been pleased to be compared to Pat Whitney, whose ruggedness and zeal he admired. However, Pat had a more complex personality than Joe Houlihan. He had an appreciation for beauty and language which the younger man lacked and he was by far the more confident and more reflective in his judgments.

Joe Houlihan arrived in Eldoret in July 1954, ready to give himself completely to his new work. Calabar was to be his model and he was determined to reproduce in Eldoret everything he had found in Calabar. Even the controversial marriage training centres were to be replicated.[18] He brought with him a printing press and was accompanied by two lay graduates whom he had recruited in Ireland to staff the Teacher Training College. He persuaded Mother Kevin, whose Franciscan Missionary Sisters for Africa had made a great impact in Uganda over the previous fifty years, to set up two convents in Eldoret, one at Kiminini in 1954, and a second at Nakuru in 1955. In 1956, he got the Holy Rosary Sisters to staff a hospital which was newly built in a very remote area of the diocese called Ortum. He also wanted very much to start immediately on the establishment of a local clergy. He initiated a junior seminary-cum-Intermediate school, which was opened by Brian Cunningham at Matunda in January 1955. Only a man of faith and vision would have started a seminary at that stage. There were not enough baptised boys available within the Prefecture to fill the first class and a number had to be imported from Kisumu. New missions were opened very quickly. Leo Staples went deep into the Suk Valley where he pioneered missionary work among the Pokot and built Ortum hospital. Mick Brennan moved into Baringo which was a sparsely populated and semi-arid area of about 7,000 square miles. With Donal Walsh, he built a house at Kituro. Shortage of priests forced the closure of this mission in August 1956, but it was reopened at the end of 1958. Bill Tuohy became first resident priest in Molo, in 1956.

Joe Houlihan undertook a 2,000-mile tour of his vast Prefecture in 1955. This tour included a reconnaissance of the 23,000 square miles of desert which lay to the north. Called Turkana, it was a restricted area which could be visited by outsiders only by government permit. The Kenya police provided him with an aeroplane to survey the area and the Prefect Apostolic left with a plan to train catechists from among the nineteen members of the nomadic Turkana tribe who were Catholics. He wrote to Kiltegan: 'We have also a caravan under construction, which we will rig on to a jeep. The cost will be colossal, but somehow we've got to make it possible for a Father to go along with them.'[19] On this tour, the Prefect visited some of the detention camps for Mau Mau suspects which had been built in the area. There were transit camps in which suspects were screened, and detention camps proper for long-term detainees. These camps became an important point of contact with Kikuyu people. Mass was celebrated in the camps and the story is told that a supposed Mau Mau warrior, acting as sacristan, asked Mick Brennan if he should mark the 'oratio imperata', a special prayer ordered by the Bishop, in the Missal. He had obviously been well instructed by the Consolata Fathers or the Holy Ghosts in his home area. It was the transit camps which proved most important. A word from the priest could clear a man held in one of these camps. So it became important for Catholics to identify themselves to the priest and to be seen to be upright men. It was the beginning of a huge influx of Kikuyu into the Church.

It was a wonderful beginning for the Society in a new territory. Joe Houlihan seemed set to be a great missionary bishop. However, some of his shortcomings were soon becoming obvious. Among these was a preference for poor mission buildings. The Prefect Apostolic thought that good buildings were an extravagance and a waste of money which, spread more thinly, might achieve greater results in terms of evangelisation. He was displeased, for example with the mission house completed in Nakuru by Bill Dunne in 1955. The house was well built although small by comparison with the fine house built at Ugep in Nigeria about the same time. To Joe Houlihan it was much too grand and he made his views known with characteristic irony. 'How is the little stable of Bethlehem coming along, Bill?' he would ask. The father's house-cum-chapel-cum-printing press at St Joseph's, Kitale was another early example. It was designed by the Prefect on the back of an envelope, on the site, and built to his specifications by J.P. Bohan. It was a dingy brick structure without indoor plumbing and with a round room at one end which had been built around the printing press. When the Prefect decided, some weeks later, to move the press to Eldoret, the room had to be knocked down to get it out. Shortage of money was a contributory factor, but poor planning and failure to seek the views of the priests and to note what was happening in other dioceses were more significant. At the back of it was Joe Houlihan's almost total disregard for the intrinsic value of something beautiful or proportionate or tastefully done.

St Patrick's Missionary Society took over another territory in Kenya in 1956. It was the Prefecture Apostolic of Kitui, situated in a low-lying area of marginal land East of Nairobi. It was part of Nairobi Archdiocese until it was declared an independent Prefecture in February 1956. The area had been evangelised by the Holy Ghost Fathers, notably by Paul White and his brother Jim. The Northern part of the Prefecture had been part of the Consolata diocese of Meru. The area was not considered 'Whiteman's country' and so had never been settled by Europeans. The first Kiltegan man to go to Kitui was Bill Tuohy who had recently opened the mission at Molo. He was so put off by the lack of response to the Church and by the poverty of the area that he tried to get the Superiors in Kiltegan to change their minds. He returned to Eldoret but as he was regarded as having refused an appointment he was given no work there. This was with Joe Gilmartin's backing and Bill Tuohy had no alternative but to return to Ireland. Donald McDonagh went to Kitui from Eldoret on 1 October 1956. In early November he was joined by Celsus Heenan, a volunteer from Clonfert, and Pat Magee, a newly-ordained Society man. On 19 October 1956 Bill Dunne was appointed Prefect Apostolic. A native of Delvin, Co. Westmeath and a past pupil of St Finian's College, Mullingar, the new Prefect Apostolic was thirty-six years old. He held a degree in theology from Maynooth, had experience of teaching and had been a successful Supervisor of Schools in Eldoret. Bill Dunne had been a delegate to the 1956 Chapter and afterwards had remained in Ireland for his regular leave. He returned to Kenya in early 1957, and before taking possession of his Prefecture he attended the consecration of Maurice Otunga, the first Kenyan to become a bishop and a man destined to be Kenya'a first Cardinal.[20]

The 1956 Chapter

The third Chapter of the Society was convened on 18 June 1956. Present were the six ex-officio members and thirteen delegates.[21] Joe Gilmartin was re-elected to the post of Superior General and Charlie Smith was returned as his Vicar. Kevin Longworth, John McGuinness and Carthage Cantwell were elected councillors while the post of Bursar General was to be filled in future by appointment. The Chapter decided to apply to

Rome for pontifical status for the Society, whereby it would come directly under Propaganda. This would entail a revision of the Constitutions and the appointment of a representative in Rome called a Procurator. It was also decided, by a vote of 12 to 7, to build the theological college at Kiltegan and to begin work on it as soon as possible. The other business of the Chapter was routine and indicated a high level of satisfaction with the way things were going on the missions and at home. The only hint of difficulty is found in a recommendation to Society members not to drink spirits, to practise moderation in the use of other alcoholic beverages and not to entice teetotallers to drink.

St Patrick's Missionary Society was running very smoothly as it approached the Silver Jubilee of its foundation which was quietly celebrated on St Patrick's Day 1957. There were 299 members, 158 priests and 141 students. Of these 131 were in active service in Africa, and were divided among the various jurisdictions as follows: Calabar 62; Ogoja 38; Eldoret 28; Kitui 3. Since 1950, thirteen diocesan priests had volunteered for Nigeria and, in 1957, there were eight of them on the missionfield. The total number of diocesan volunteer priests who had gone to Nigeria had now reached 103.[22]

11

Postscript
1957 – 1990

JOE Gilmartin's second term as Superior General, from 1956 to 1962, was a time of great optimism for St Patrick's Missionary Society. This was typified by the erection of a modern theological college in Kiltegan, built in an open plan and with great emphasis on space and light. A simple functional design was in keeping with the Society's tradition of economy, while the use of first-class materials and the incorporation of a granite-cladded tower represented stability and self-assurance. Joe Gilmartin had got Pearse McKenna to prepare sketch plans for presentation to the 1956 Chapter. The Chapter approved of them and Pearse McKenna was asked to go ahead with the final plans. Building work began in August 1958 and the students took up residence at the end of 1961, although the kitchen and diningroom were not ready until 1963. The building of a chapel and a priests' residence, which were part of the original design, was postponed until the debt on the initial phase of the building was cleared. A large assembly hall became a temporary chapel and a makeshift walkway was erected to link the main building and the diningroom. It was destined to be a permanent structure, as the next phase of the building was never undertaken. By the end of the sixties, a decline in student numbers had set in and, before long, it was evident that a large chapel would not be required and that accommodation for priests could be provided within the college.

In 1961 Ireland celebrated the fifteen hundredth anniversary of the death of St Patrick by observing a Patrician Year. During the year, the missionary work of the Irish Church was very much to the fore. The Papal Legate to the Patrician Congress in Dublin was the Prefect of

Propaganda, the exotic Cardinal Agagianian. The distinguished figure of Cardinal Rugambwa, the first African Cardinal, electrified the crowd assembled for the commemorative Mass at Croke Park and reminded them of the advances which had been made in the African Church. There was also a big missionary exhibition in Dublin's Mansion House.

On the closing day of the Patrician Year, 17 March 1962, a baptistry to the memory of Pat Whitney was formally opened in Drumboylan Church where Pat had been baptised. This memorial includes a beautiful mosaic which links the missionary work of St Patrick to that of Pat Whitney and other modern missionaries. Inset in the mosaic are stones from Croagh Patrick and Lough Derg and from two holy wells associated with the saint. There are also three stepping stones taken from the Shannon at Drumboylan where, according to tradition, the local people made a fording place to allow St Patrick to cross the river. Boylan, who was St Patrick's driver, is said to have died there and given the place its name. The memorial was erected by the parish although the Society was closely associated with it. There was a strong Society presence at the opening ceremony and *Africa* recorded it with five pages of photographs and a summary of the sermon preached by Edward Curran, a former volunteer.

Mission in Brazil

The question of the Society becoming involved in South America was raised in December 1960, in response to a letter of Pope John XXIII to the bishops of Ireland. In this letter, the Pope called for Irish priests to work in Brazil following similar initiatives from countries such as Spain, Belgium, Canada and the USA. He went on to single out St Columban's Society and proposed that it would act as a kind of promotion agency for diocesan priests volunteering for South America. The Pope wrote:

> In this connection we like to think of the zealous Society of St Columban which, established with the encouragement and active co-operation of the Irish Bishops, blossomed forth like a fragrant flower, from the National Seminary of Maynooth and its devoted charity. For it extends its spiritual solicitude also to various Latin American countries such as the Argentine, Peru and Chile. There its members lend aid to local Bishops and Priests, to the great benefit of souls.
>
> We so highly esteem and praise the work of this Society that it is our earnest desire that its activities may continue to increase and

be enriched by the accession of new strength. This may be achieved by Irish diocesan priests volunteering to work in those countries for a fixed period of time or for life, under its direction.

We think, therefore, that it would be of great benefit if necessary powers and faculties be given to this Society to recruit, to send to Latin America and help in every way those priests who have duly secured permission both from their own Bishop and from the Bishop of the diocese to which they are going.

St Patrick's Missionary Society was not mentioned and it became clear that it would have to get involved in this new missionary venture if it wished to remain in the forefront of the Irish missionary movement. The Society's request to Propaganda for approval for a mission in South America, which was made with the blessing of the Irish bishops and of St Columban's Society, spells this out:

With the growing interest among the Irish laity and the turning of young priests' thoughts and aspirations more and more towards South America, the Society senses that public opinion expects such a move from its ranks and that, therefore, its failure in the matter would cost it much in prestige in Ireland whence it largely depends for vocations and finances. On the other hand, the undertaking of such a mission would most probably enhance its appeal to youth and people, as well as the esteem of the Hierarchy which it enjoys, and, in general, benefit all its work.[1]

The Cardinal Prefect of Propaganda gave the Society the go-ahead although, as Brazil was not strictly speaking a 'mission-country' and therefore not under the care of Propaganda, the matter was referred to the Pontifical Commission for Latin America. On advice from that quarter, the Society sent Ciaran Needham to Brazil early in 1962 to examine the possibilities. Although the Society had asked for a single parish, the Apostolic Nuncio in Brazil proposed two sparsely populated areas in North Brazil called Maraba and Uruchi, which were to become independent dioceses. The Society favoured a commitment in the city of Sao Paulo, where Ciaran Needham had been shown three available parishes at the periphery of the city. The necessary approvals were received and the first three priests took charge of the parish of Cotia in 1963. They were Ciaran Needham, Tony Terry and Enda Burke, a volunteer from Killaloe diocese.

The Society never envisaged sending a large number of its own priests to Brazil. Facilitating diocesan volunteers was to be a major part of its contribution and, by 1970, ten priests had volunteered. In the next ten years, nine priests volunteered, and in the following decade, a further twelve. As in Africa, the number on the mission has fluctuated because of the temporary nature of the commitment. The Society gradually built up its own number to twenty and has maintained it around that figure.

Cotia, the original parish, was then an old-fashioned town with a rural hinterland. The parishes taken on subsequently were in the rapidly developing suburbs, occupied by migrants who had come to look for work in the city. Portuguese was the language of the people and the priests had no option but to master it. The work was mainstream parish work—Mass, sacraments, funerals. Because the people had lost contact with the Church and were poorly instructed in the faith, Bible groups were organised in the houses and an effort was made to relate the Gospel to the precarious situation of the people who were struggling to survive and to establish themselves in the city. There was also, from 1964, the harshness of a military dictatorship with strict surveillance and a climate of fear and mistrust.

Priests belonging to the Society in Brazil were influenced by the concern for the poor that surfaced in the South American Church following the meeting of the Latin American Bishops at Medellín, in 1968. Out of a decision to be concerned primarily for the poor and an application of the Gospels to the huge problem of poverty, there grew a theology of liberation which challenged ordinary people to take responsibility for their own deliverance from poverty and oppression of every kind. Many Brazilian bishops, including Cardinal Arns of Sao Paulo, Cardinal Lorscheider of Fortaleza and Archbishop Helder Camara of Olinda-Recife, were to the fore in confronting social evil and were prepared to stand up to the dictatorship. The result was a new hopefulness among priests and lay people: they were not powerless; they could do something about the social structures which fostered injustice. This concern for justice has characterised Society priests in Brazil and has been communicated to their colleagues in the less radical African Churches.

In 1979, the Society took on a commitment in the Archdiocese of Olinda-Recife. It was the first engagement outside Sao Paulo apart from a sojourn in the Amazon forest undertaken by Jock Thorlby and Tony Terry as part of a missionary commitment by Sao Paulo diocese. Later, a number of temporary commitments were made to other dioceses.

Ciaran Needham broke new ground in 1975, with a new-style seminary in his parish in Sao Paulo. Inspired by the example of the many working-class Brazilians who were doing University courses by night, he provided similar facilities for those wishing to become priests. The seminarians were drawn from young men in full-time employment who were already involved with the ministry of the church in some capacity. Teachers were drawn from conventional seminaries and other institutes. Five or six men were ordained in the following fifteen years.

Two Desert Missions

In 1961 the Society began mission work in the Turkana desert in Northern Kenya. It was not a new mission, in the strict sense, as it had come to the Society with the Prefecture of Eldoret in 1953. However, it bore little resemblance to the rest of Eldoret or to any of the Society's other missions. It was a vast expanse of sand and rock, baked and broken by the sun. The Turkana people were nomads whose livelihood came from camels and goats. They lived on the blood and milk of those animals, and they garnished this diet with the scanty herbs of the desert. Their clothing was made from animal skins and their myths and wars and honorific titles had all to do with flocks and herds. It was a harsh place which pushed the endurance and resourcefulness of its native inhabitants to the limit. It proved no less challenging for the missionaries, who were to play a major role in keeping the tribe alive through two devastating famines and an equally significant role in providing it with a secure bridgehead in the modern world.

On 8 December 1961, the first priests took up residence in Turkana. The residence was a tent in the middle of a famine camp near Lodwar and the immediate task was to dole out food to the starving people who had lost their animals in a catastrophic drought. The first to arrive were Joe Murray and Ray Murtagh, although the latter was replaced within weeks by Mick Brennan. In March 1962 the first Medical Missionaries of Mary arrived and a permanent base was set up at a second famine camp at Lorugumu. The sisters—Andrea Kelly, Bernadette Gilsenan and Campion Campbell—set up clinics in the camps and, in January 1963, opened a primary school for famine children at Lorugumu. Other schools followed and, in 1966, a hospital was opened in Kakuma. From there the sisters serviced various other centres all over the region by means of a light plane piloted by one of their number. A close association with Kenya's famous 'Flying Doctors' made it possible to provide exceptional medical services to the people of Turkana. On

11 January 1968 the Prefecture Apostolic of Lodwar was set up with John Mahon coming from Nigeria to take up the post of Prefect Apostolic. There were five priests in the New Prefecture although the number was doubled later in the year with the appointment of five of the newly ordained.[2] In January 1969, a boys' secondary school was opened in Lodwar. It started with forty pupils, the vast majority of whom were brought in from outside the Prefecture and only two of whom belonged to the Turkana tribe.

The next twenty years saw the extension of medical and educational services and the gradual establishment of parishes. Each parish was associated with some humanitarian service, such as the provision of food and medicine, irrigation, fishing and education. The mission was assisted by various aid agencies, including the German agency *Misereor* and the Irish agency *Gorta*. The development of girls' education, pioneered by Sister Clothilde of the Ursuline Sisters from Sligo, forms a major part of a very creditable achievement in education. Alongside the development work, there was a sustained effort to build a Christian community. The priests learned the Turkana language and produced a Turkana catechism and prayerbook as well as translating the texts required for the liturgy. Lay catechists were sent for training to inter-diocesan centres and occasional courses were provided locally. A development-education programme introduced in 1979 did much to involve the laity in the running of the Church.

Turkana became a diocese in 1978 and John Mahon was ordained Bishop in a colourful open-air ceremony. The first two African priests were ordained in 1982, with two more in 1985. The first member of the Turkana tribe to become a priest was ordained in 1988. The following year, Tony Barrett received a Doctorate in Philosophy at the University of Chicago for an anthropological thesis entitled 'Sacrifice and Prophecy in Turkana Cosmology'. It was a unique achievement as no other priest of the Society had produced a comparable work on the customs and traditions of a tribal society. It is one service among many that members of the Society and their associates have rendered to the Turkana people. The Turkana mission is very special for the Society because it represents missionary life at the limits—the limit of all that is socially familiar, the limit of endurance, patience and perspective.

In 1962, the Society took on a new mission in Northern Nigeria which was to become the Prefecture Apostolic and, later, the Diocese of Minna. This territory was co-extensive with Niger Province and had been part of the vast Archdiocese of Kaduna which was in the care of the Society of African Missions. Minna was very different from the other Nigerian missions of the Society. Situated in the Muslim north of the country, it was a semi-desert area of low population-density. In size, it was larger than Ogoja and Calabar put together and only slightly smaller than Ireland. There were five residential missions, thirty-seven primary schools and a Catholic Teacher Training College. Irish Sisters of St Louis ran a primary school and a clinic in Minna. Out of a population of 715,728, there were only 4,500 baptised Catholics and 2,000 catechumens. The principal tribes, the Hausa and Fulani, were Muslims but there were a number of smaller tribes, like the Gwari, who practised traditional African religion. It was from these so-called pagan tribes that the missionaries hoped to gain adherents for the Church. Very few of them had been baptised and the existing Catholic community was made up mostly of people from other parts of Nigeria. Of these, the Ibo were by far the most prominent.

The first Society priests, Charlie Napier, Jim Noonan and Jerry Kiely, arrived in Minna in September 1962. They were joined by Tom Lucey who was on the General Council in Kiltegan but was sent out to fill the post of Supervisor of Schools, for a time. At the end of 1963 Ned Fitzgibbon, who had been in the Catholic Secretariat in Lagos, was made Prefect Apostolic of Minna. A steady stream of young priests came to Minna in subsequent years which made possible the expansion of education and the establishment of new missions. In a solidly Muslim area, it involved an unobtrusive approach which respected the predominant culture.

The high level of illiteracy and lack of educational facilities gave a great opening to the Church. Schools were developed with the help of funds from various Aid Agencies and expertly managed by the priests, the Sisters of St Louis and the Alexian brothers. The Medical Missionaries of Mary sent a team which included Sister Dr Margaret Mary Nolan—the legendary 'Maggie May'—whose work in developing Anua hospital had earned her an OBE, several medical fellowships and the Nigerian Order of the Niger. The medical work which had been started in Minna town by the St Louis Sisters was extended, by the Medical Missionaries, to include rural health centres in outlying areas.

These various services to human development gained acceptance for the Church among the Muslims and gave access to the non-Muslim. It was only when the Ibos were driven out of the area in the pogroms that preceded the civil war that the locals were attracted to the Church and were converted in large numbers. Ned Fitzgibbon was moved to Port

Harcourt in 1973 and was replaced by Bishop Christopher Abba, formerly a diocesan priest of the Archdiocese of Kaduna. The first Irish diocesan volunteer to work in Minna was Tom Crawford from Limerick diocese, who came in 1977. Later, Limerick made a commitment of two priests to the diocese and Kilmore diocese did likewise in 1983.

Crises of the Sixties

Peter O'Reilly succeeded Joe Gilmartin as Superior General in June 1962. His Council consisted of Charles Smith V.G., Denis Newman, Sean Meehan and Thomas Lucey. They were to hold office for ten years, four years longer than was the earlier practice. This change was suggested by Propaganda Fide, in the interest of cutting down the expense of frequent General Chapters.

Peter O'Reilly had proved himself a very able administrator as a local bursar and later as Bursar General. He was now to show great strength and resolve as Superior General. The mission to Minna, which had been decided upon by the previous administration, went ahead immediately. Then attention was given to the many student applicants who did not have the Leaving Certificate and had to be refused admission. To cater for this group, Auchentroig House in Buchlyvie, Scotland was purchased from Brigadier and Mrs A.W. Crawford and opened in July 1965. It was to serve as a school for mature students intending to go to the seminary, preparing them for O-level examinations and as a centre for promotion work. It was to be the Society's only base in Britain, until 1971, when a presbytery in Slough, near London, was offered as a promotion centre in exchange for the services of one priest in St Ethelbert's parish. This was to become a Society parish in 1980 and a second parish, Datchet, was added in 1987. As an educational facility Buchlyvie was used by other dioceses and societies and by 1990 had been involved in the education of 23 Society priests, 24 other priests and 7 professed brothers.

Such peaceful expansion was not to continue for long into the sixties. The Society became preoccupied with two very traumatic events. One was a crisis of authority in the diocese of Eldoret and the other, the civil war in Nigeria, which was to involve the majority of Society personnel. These two events dominated the life of the Society in the 1960s and had a big influence on its subsequent history. The great flowering of political, civil and personal freedom which characterised the decade and found expression in the Second Vatican Council had a profound influence on Society personnel and their work. For a long time, however, this spirit of the age was but a backdrop against which the Society struggled to hold on to its missions and to honour its commitments to the people entrusted to it.

Problems in Eldoret

The Eldoret problem went back almost to Joe Houlihan's arrival as Prefect Apostolic in 1954. Some of the priests who were in Eldoret at the time remember 1956 as the year in which working as a team under the new Prefect seemed doomed to failure. For all his personal charm and undisputed apostolic zeal, Joe Houlihan was not a good leader. His personality lacked the solid centre which enabled men like James Moynagh and Tom McGettrick to plan with others how new challenges should be tackled and then to trust others to execute the plan. Because of the situation in Eldoret, where there was little or no income forthcoming from the local people, the priests were almost totally dependent on Joe Houlihan for financial support. This meant that his personal limitations affected everyone. Priests were forced to go into debt with local traders and then to come to the Prefect Apostolic to settle the account. The latter's custom was to pay off a portion of the debt, maybe two thirds, and to leave the remainder in abeyance. It was his way of keeping a priest in check and limiting his capacity to spend. For young priests with no experience of money matters, this continuing debt was an albatross which could never be shaken off. No amount of economising would help matters and there was no possibility of unburdening themselves to the Prefect Apostolic in a constructive manner. The more submissive had to be satisfied with a witticism—often worth quoting—while the more spirited found themselves in open conflict which could end up in transfer to another parish. There was no attempt to solve the problem by reducing the rate of development. Joe Houlihan wanted maximum development in the shortest time and was happy to pay for it in an unending hassle with his priests.

Up to 1964, the discontent was contained within the diocese. The Superiors in Kiltegan were aware of it but saw it as part of the normal give-and-take involved in the exercise of authority in a missionary setting. By July 1964 the situation had become more tense and the Bishop's consultative council which consisted of five Society priests began to talk in terms of raising the matter with Rome through the Papal pro-Nuncio in Nairobi. The increase in tension may well have been occasioned by the granting of large sums of money by the German relief organisation *Misereor* for the building of three hospitals in Eldoret diocese. The priests were unhappy with the standard of building and with the giving of account. The Bishop would cut corners in building or buy a second-hand appliance out of the grant for a new one. There is the story of a second-hand lighting plant purchased for Kakuma at £35 when a grant of £600 had been received. The Bishop saw nothing wrong with this as the money saved would go to another urgent and equally deserving aspect of mission work. It was the priests and sisters on the spot who were left with the inconvenience of a broken-down generator or an unsatisfactory building. When Peter O'Reilly heard of the suggestion of bringing the matter to the Nuncio, he intervened with characteristic decisiveness. He arranged a meeting to take place in Rome, attended by himself, Bishop Houlihan and two of the Eldoret diocesan consultors. The priests asked that Liam Doyle, who was Regional Superior in Kenya and who was due home on leave, would also attend. There was to be the utmost secrecy about the whole affair. Rome had been chosen because Bishop Houlihan was there at the time attending the Vatican Council. The meeting took place in the autumn of 1964 and an agreement was worked out to surmount the twin bugbears of poor financial management and inferior building methods. A diocesan procurator was to be appointed to manage the finances. Another priest was to administer the grant-money which came from *Misereor* and a group was to take charge of all building work. The appointments were made and matters improved for a while. When Bishop Houlihan returned from Rome he played golf with the priests, wielding the golf club like a hurley but, nonetheless, putting in a creditable performance. There was an air of great optimism and a feeling that Eldoret was on a new and steady course. The feeling was shortlived, however, and by July of the following year the Rome agreement, which had never been signed, was abandoned. Peter O'Reilly continued to press for an amicable solution based on tolerance and mutual understanding. In a visit made in 1965, he urged the priests to practise fraternal charity, to be obedient to the Church and loyal to the Bishop and the Society. As a practical measure, he agreed to grant a special living allowance of £180 per annum to each priest, with an additional £20 to any priest who was living alone. This was one of the many visits to Eldoret made by Peter O'Reilly and his councillors in an effort to restore harmony.

In spite of the difficulties, there was a lot happening in the diocese which had a staff of forty Kiltegan men and two volunteer priests from Goa. In 1967, there were two congregations of religious brothers, the

Patricians from Ireland who staffed St Patrick's, the first diocesan secondary school, and the Xaverians who staffed the Teacher Training College. There were various congregations of sisters including the Franciscans, Holy Rosary, Medical Missionaries, Mercy (Cork) and the diocesan Assumption Sisters which Bishop Houlihan had founded. There were mission-hospitals at Ortum, Kakuma and Eldama Ravine and an aeroplane which serviced clinics throughout the vast Turkana region. There was a mobile cinema for use in catechetical work. There were eighty junior seminarians in an attractive new college in Eldoret and four senior seminarians in Nairobi. The phenomenal development seemed only to add to the strain which, since the breakdown of the Rome agreement, had taken on a measure of bitterness and vindictiveness. The priests were divided on the issue. The majority favoured confrontation while a small group were opposed to it. By mid 1967, Peter O'Reilly was convinced that there could be no solution short of the resignation of the Bishop. He was under no illusion however on the difficulty of getting Rome to remove a Bishop who was not guilty of any flagrant misconduct. The fact that the Society had proposed Joe Houlihan for Bishop seven years before, after a seven year trial-period, left the case for his removal very weak indeed.

These considerations counted little with the priests whose frustration was mounting throughout 1967. A council of priests had been set up in February of that year, in accordance with a recommendation of the recent Vatican Council. In October, the council of priests asked Bishop Houlihan to resign and wrote to the Apostolic Nuncio, Archbishop Guido del Mestri to ask for an official inquiry into the whole affair. The Nuncio met the priests and, later in the month, sent a confidential letter to each priest asking his opinion on the proposal of the priests' council. The Nuncio was very well briefed on the situation and had been in touch with Peter O'Reilly on the matter for some time. He was in the process of implementing Rome's own plan to solve the situation which was far more long-term than the solution demanded by the priests. The plan was to divide the diocese so that those who had special problems with the Bishop could work in a separate jurisdiction, while the area left to the diocese of Eldoret would be more manageable. This plan went ahead and early in 1968 the Prefecture Apostolic of Lodwar and the diocese of Nakuru were established. The former consisted of the vast Turkana desert while the latter comprised Nakuru district which had belonged to Eldoret, and Kericho district which had belonged to Kisumu. Later, Baringo district was also attached to Nakuru. John Mahon, a Society priest working in Ogoja, was appointed Prefect Apostolic of Lodwar. Nakuru was made a diocese, immediately, because of its importance as the provincial capital. It was to receive an African bishop in the near future but in order to prepare for this, Denis Newman, a member of the General Council in Kiltegan, was appointed Apostolic Administrator. He was to hand over the diocese, in 1971, to the dynamic Bishop Raphael Ndingi who had been Bishop of Machakos since 1969. The new diocese also included an area around Kericho which had been part of Kisumu diocese. The Mill Hill priests were to stay in this area but were to receive reinforcements from the Society. The first Kiltegan men to join them were Gerry Roche and Paddy Gallagher who went to Kaplong in 1968.

Before these changes were announced, the morale of the priests disimproved further. In early January 1968 the priests sent a petition to the Nuncio asking for a solution to the problem and threatening to ask the Society to withdraw them if no solution was found. The petition was signed by thirty-eight priests, who also signed a letter to the Bishop asking, once more, for his resignation. This move was an act of desperation. It was also undiplomatic and naïve. Rome was not likely to take favourably to a threat of any kind and, besides, could not be expected to find an instant solution. The Society leadership was dismayed at the suggestion. The priests were left in no doubt that withdrawal as a group would amount to betraying a sacred trust and that it was out of the question. Peter O'Reilly put it to the priests that it was now a matter of loyalty to Rome, to the Society and to the people of Eldoret. The separation of Nakuru and Lodwar did little to improve matters in the mother-diocese. In April 1968, twenty-two priests signed a petition to the Nuncio asking him to continue to work for the removal of Bishop Houlihan. The authorities in Kiltegan decided not to send any more newly-ordained priests to Eldoret and allowed those who came home on leave the freedom to return or to take temporary appointments elsewhere. By August 1968, there were only twenty-one priests in the diocese of Eldoret and this number was to be further whittled down until it dropped to fifteen the following year. The situation took on many of the elements of farce. Long letters of accusation and counter-accusation passed between the Bishop and individual priests. Often, copies were sent to the Regional Superior and to the Apostolic Nuncio. Pastoral work in the diocese was at a low ebb. The priests felt beleaguered and abandoned. The Bishop found himself with no place to turn. He got some encouragement from fellow-bishops who were dismayed at the prospect of the priests of a diocese forcing a bishop out and advised him not to resign. He hung on in desperation believing himself to have been the victim of a new and dangerous spirit of rebellion entering the Church. In May 1969, Kiltegan priests were sent to Nandi district, a part of Kisumu diocese adjoining Eldoret. The first to go were Frank McNabb and Tom Laffan. They were joined by Seamus Deignan, Joe O'Driscoll, Martin Boyle and Bernie Corrigan in the following months and by Len Cummins and Noel McHenry some time later. Nandi district became part of Eldoret diocese in 1975.

A General Chapter had been scheduled for June 1968 but had to be postponed for a year because it was impossible to hold elections in Nigeria owing to the civil war. This was not an ordinary Chapter at which new Superiors were elected. It was part of the renewal process which took place in all Religious Orders and Societies in the aftermath of the Vatican Council and was convened on instructions from Rome. When the delegates assembled in Kiltegan, in June 1969, the Superior General read a letter from the priests in Eldoret asking for a solution to their problem or, failing that, to be withdrawn from the diocese. In this letter they referred to a rumour that an African auxiliary bishop was about to be appointed and went on to state that thirteen of the fifteen priests who were in Eldoret at the time, did not think that this appointment would solve the problem. In the opinion of a number of those who were present at the 1969 Chapter, the matter might not have gone any further but for the determination of Joe Gilmartin to have something done about it. Many delegates from Nigeria were not very sympathetic with the priests in Eldoret. They found it hard to imagine how priests could feel so sorely put upon by any bishop. The priests in Nigeria were caught up in a civil war. The problems of the priests in Eldoret seemed minor, by comparison.

However, Joe Gilmartin, who was then doing parish work in Kitui and was an ex-officio member of the Chapter because he was a former Superior General, was determined to find a solution to the Eldoret crisis. It was he who had nominated Joe Houlihan for Eldoret, in the first place. He was his classmate and friend and, in spite of the debacle in Eldoret, Joe Gilmartin continued to admire Bishop Houlihan for all his great positive qualities. But, at this stage, the good of the Church and the good of the Society demanded drastic action and there was none better than the former Superior General to face such a challenge. His considerable moral authority influenced the Chapter and a delegate was sent to Rome with a memorandum asking Propaganda Fide to remove

Bishop Houlihan or otherwise to relieve the Society of its responsibility for Eldoret. Once again, a former Apostolic Delegate was strategically placed and very willing to help the Society. He was Archbishop Sergio Pignedoli who had been Nuncio in Nigeria and was now Secretary of Propaganda. The Archbishop was a good friend of the Society. He is quoted as saying that he would not let the Society be crucified over the Eldoret problem. He presented the memorandum to Cardinal Agagianian, the Prefect of Propaganda, and a favourable solution was worked out. Rome was to announce the appointment of an African auxiliary Bishop within a month and he was to be ordained Bishop by Pope Paul VI in Uganda on the first day of September. Then, Bishop Houlihan would have an opportunity to resign honourably and, if nothing happened within two months, he would be pressed to do so.

Everything went according to plan although when two months passed and there was no sign of the Bishop's resignation the priests became uneasy again. The Society administration kept in touch with Rome on the issue and, in December, Bishop Houlihan was summoned to Rome to meet Cardinal Agagianian. It was arranged that he would take leave of absence from his diocese for one year, leaving Bishop Emilio Njeru, his auxiliary, in full charge. Bishop Houlihan proceeded to America where he undertook a fund-raising drive for the diocese. The Society increased the number of priests in Eldoret, and when Rome was satisfied that the priests were working well with the new bishop, Bishop Houlihan was asked for his resignation.

Shortly after he had submitted his resignation, fate was to strike the diocese of Eldoret another cruel blow. On 12 September 1970, Bishop Emilio Njeru was killed in a car accident on his way to visit his native diocese, Meru. In normal circumstances, an Apostolic Administrator would have been appointed. However, Rome took account of Bishop Houlihan's desire that an African should take over and, instead of making an interim appointment, a new bishop was hurriedly appointed. He was John Njenga, a priest of Nairobi Archdiocese who was Secretary General of the Kenya Catholic Secretariat. (He was to govern Eldoret diocese until 1989, when he was transferred to Mombasa. His successor was Cornelius Korir, who became Bishop of Eldoret in June 1990 when he took over the diocese from Kiltegan priest, Tom Smith, who had governed it in the interregnum.) Bishop Houlihan was offered a teaching post in the National Seminary in Nairobi. He served there until the end of 1974, after which he took up a pastoral appointment in Kisumu diocese. In February 1975, he was appointed first National Director of the Propagation of the Faith in Kenya, a position which allowed him to remain in his parish. On Thursday 4 December 1975, Bishop Houlihan was taken ill on his way to celebrate an out-station Mass and was dead on admission to Kaimosi hospital. He is buried in Turbo, in Eldoret diocese, close to the headquarters of the Assumption Sisters. Nearby is the grave of Morgan O'Brien, an equally apostolic Kerryman with whom he had argued many times about matters of architecture and finance.[3]

War in Nigeria

In the midst of the Eldoret affair, another crisis befell the Society on its West African front. There was a military coup in Nigeria in January 1966, followed by a backlash against the Ibo tribe. On 30 May 1967, the eastern region, which contained the heartland of the Ibo people, seceded from the four-region federation and proclaimed its independence as the Republic of Biafra. A last-minute decision by the Federal leader Lieutenant-Colonel Yukubu Gowon to divide the country into twelve States—to accommodate the major tribal groups—had failed to avert the catastrophe. Calabar and Ogoja were within the boundaries of the new secessionist state, although only on the borders of Iboland. Parts of Ogoja and Calabar were Ibo country. The rest of Society territory was occupied by tribes who did not favour the secession but were, nevertheless, part of it. As Nigeria prepared itself to regain control, the Federal leader warned foreigners to leave the area for their own safety. Neither the authorities in Kiltegan nor the priests in the field had much difficulty in deciding that the proper course of action was to stay with the people in their time of trial. This was also the position of the other missionaries, including the Holy Ghosts whose missions were at the heart of Iboland. There was little hope that Biafra would be allowed its independence for long. It was only a question of waiting for the blow to fall. The schools were closed and those involved in school work attached themselves to nearby parishes. While it was Society policy to stay, the decision in particular circumstances was left to the men on the spot. It became established practice that where men had to leave their mission or were impeded from functioning in a constructive way, they returned to Ireland. Before long, it became clear that the presence of school men was not helpful in parishes. It was no time to be expanding pastoral work and the extra men were a strain on supplies. Moreover, no one knew what to expect. Many of the Federal troops were Muslims from the north and there was no reason to expect them to be friendly. Even if the missionary was accepted as apolitical, there was danger of being mistaken for a white mercenary, a number of whom were engaged in training Biafran soldiers. In these circumstances, many priests left for home. The majority of these left from inside Biafra using dangerous night-time flights through the island on San Tomé and on to Lisbon. A few left through Cameroon.

Meanwhile, hostilities began on 6 July 1967. Federal troops, for some time massing on the borders of Ogoja, attacked Obudu. The Biafran soldiers repulsed the attack but were then withdrawn from the area to defend Abakaliki. As a result, the Federal troops, having occupied Obudu, entered Ogoja, on 12 July, without meeting any resistance. However, the peaceful arrival of the Federals coincided with the 11 o'clock chimes of the Cathedral clock. The soldiers thought that the church bell was being rung as a signal to the Biafran troops and they became decidedly unfriendly. (Another version of the incident was to surface behind the Biafran lines where it was rumoured that Bishop McGettrick had rung the Cathedral bell to welcome the Federal army.) Shooting broke out and the Cathedral and the Bishop's house were fired on. John Mahon, who was celebrating Mass at the time, had a narrow escape as did lay volunteer, Vincent Kearney, who was grazed by a bullet. Another bullet, apparently intended for Bishop McGettrick, missed him by inches. Three hours later, when it was finally established that there were no Biafran soldiers in the area, things quietened down. The Colonel-in-charge apologised to the Bishop and arranged with him to supply food to the Ibo refugees who were quartered in the Training College.

Ogoja diocese was now cut off from its normal supply bases and had to rely on Jos, 314 miles away, for essential provisions. It was to have a very strong army presence, especially for the next eight months while it remained an important route for supplies and reinforcements from the north. Moreover, the diocese was divided. The Abakaliki/Afikpo area was in Biafran hands while the rest of the diocese was under Federal control. All communication links between the Bishop and his missionaries in the rebel area were cut off. It was left to Des O'Connor, the Vicar General, who was living at Abakaliki, to provide the leadership necessary for the difficult time ahead. Moreover, the people on the Biafran side became very hostile to the missionaries, who included Medical Missionary Sisters and Dr Godfrey Hinds. Reports of the bell-ringing incident were taken as evidence that Bishop McGettrick was anti-Biafran. Verbal abuse at roadblocks was common. Even the Catholics joined in with such taunts as: 'you are a pikin [child] of that Bishop who helped the Nigerian vandals to take Ogoja'.[4]

Calabar had been under fire from Federal gunboats for some time. Then on 18 October 1967 the Federal soldiers landed and took the town in a week of fierce fighting. For the priests at the Cathedral it was a week of danger and uncertainty. There was the risk of being shot accidentally or by design. There was the sight and smell of death and also the mental suffering of being powerless to help the many Ibos trapped in the town. Frank Morris, in a diary written during that terrible week, captures the anguish of one particular incident:

> I looked around the door and there was this man, thin and gaunt, with hair on his face as he had not shaved for a week. He had a rosary in his hand and he began 'I beg. I beg.' This was too much for me. We went back to the house and I said there was no possibility of keeping him on the premises, that searches were too frequent and that in fact he had been there during the corporal's search. So we got the houseboys to take him out and put him on the road. We were upstairs and of course he didn't want to go. He begged and shouted and made a burst to go up the stairs. It was desperate. Anyway they took him off. I presume he did not last too long. Although it was sending a man to certain death to put him out of the compound, yet there were in all sixteen of us counting the cook's family to be thought of, for anyone sheltering men was shot out of hand.[5]

Fortunately, the commanding officer Colonel Benjamin Adekunle, who was known as the 'Black Scorpion', was well disposed towards the missionaries. While this was a help, it was no guarantee in a war situation characterised by heavy gunfire, frequent searches and an abiding suspicion of the Europeans who had chosen to remain in rebel Biafra. Food was scarce and the priests survived by drinking holy water which was in plentiful supply. The town was devastated and remained a very uneasy place for some time. By 12 November, it was possible to have the first Sunday Mass in the Cathedral. There were forty in the church where, on a normal Sunday, there would have been more than 4,000.

Not many missions suffered as much as Calabar did. In many outlying places it was a question of letting the war pass by. There was the occasional bomb to remind them of the deadly times. Some priests were confined to their compounds by the advancing troops. A small number spent a few days in military custody. A few were ordered out of the area by the military command. For others, it was a question of seeking out the new military commander in order to report to him. In general, the senior officers treated the missionaries well. The greatest danger was from soldiers who were not always sure of the distinction between the missionaries and the hated mercenaries.

The war was to affect Bishop Moynagh's life in a dramatic and unexpected way. He was on a Confirmation tour around Anua and Essene when the Federal army arrived in Calabar town. As Archbishop Heerey had died the previous year, Bishop Moynagh was now the senior Bishop in Biafra. He began to consider the possibility of getting outside agencies to intervene in order to bring about a settlement. Having had no contact with the outside world he didn't know how much Rome knew of the situation. He knew Archbishop Pignedoli very well. He had also met Ted Kennedy during a visit to America and he hoped that the American senator might be able to help. Having discussed the matter with a number of bishops within Biafra, he arranged to meet the Biafran leader, Colonel Ojukwu. He was impressed by the Colonel's sincerity and formed the opinion that the Biafrans would accept practically any terms which the Federals might offer. The Federals were not open to any compromise but Ojukwu felt that a joint appeal from the Vatican and the World Council of Churches might persuade them to negotiate. Bishop Moynagh decided that the scheme was worth a try. Bishop Godfrey Okoye, the Ibo bishop of Port Harcourt, was to accompany him. They had to take the perilous Lisbon route, flying at night, in a DC8. There were a dozen French mercenaries on board and rumours of a dead colleague. There was no food on the plane and no seats. After stops at San Tomé and another Portuguese airport in Africa, they headed away from the African coast and then travelled north to Lisbon. There they met Monsignor Dominic Conway—later Bishop of Elphin—who was on his way into Biafra as a papal envoy, to scout out the possibilities of peace. The Bishops went on to Rome and afterwards, Bishop Moynagh went to London and Bishop Okoye to Germany. They secured promises of a joint appeal for a settlement from the Holy See and the World Council of Churches. This was to have no effect and the war raged on to the bitter end.

Missionaries in Ibo areas found themselves in a different situation from those living among tribes which did not favour secession. Among the Ibos, the war was seen as a life or death struggle and the people moved before the Federal advance. In the tense situation which prevailed just behind the Biafran front lines, the loyalty of all non-Ibos was in doubt. The commitment of the foreign missionaries to the cause was also called into question. In Afikpo suspicion and hostility continued to mount. The arrival of Dominic Conway in Afikpo on 16 February 1968, accompanied by Archbishop Arinze of Onitsha helped to ease the situation. Dominic Conway had visited Ogoja a short time previously after which he had returned to Europe and then flew in to Biafra by the San Tomé route. At Afikpo, he preached at a special Mass attended by military and civil authorities. He assured the people that Bishop McGettrick was concerned for them and that there was no truth in the rumour that he had betrayed them. The presence of Archbishop Arinze who was chief-celebrant at the Mass, and who enjoyed immense prestige among his own people, lent authority to the claim. It was a turning-point in the relationship between the people and the missionaries. As their hour of greatest trial approached, they enjoyed a unity and mutual respect which had been missing for the previous eight months.

In late February, Ugep, on the other side of the Cross River from Afikpo, was taken by Colonel Adekunle and his marines who had pushed on from Calabar. The two priests in Ugep were safe. To the North, two Federal contingents closed in on Abakaliki from different directions. Troops and inhabitants fled before them towards Afikpo which was 50 miles away. The priests and sisters had gathered to await the arrival of the Federals in Sharon Secondary School, five miles from the town of Abakaliki. The commanding officer was very courteous to them. Ogoja diocesan priest Joseph Ukpo, who had made his way from Afikpo against the stream of refugees, joined the missionaries at the school. From there he made his way to Ogoja to become the first priest from that side of the diocese to meet Bishop McGettrick in nine months.

Afikpo was thronged with refugees from Abakaliki. Mayfield, the compound of the Holy Child Sisters, had been commandeered as a commando training camp. The British mercenary in charge had mounted an emblem of a skull and cross-bones on the entrance gate. There was a pogrom directed against spies and other enemies of Biafra. Easter passed quietly with large crowds of people at Mass. Then on the Friday of Easter week, 18 April 1968, Federal jets bombed Afikpo at dawn and at the same time Colonel Adekunle's marines landed at the river bank. The Biafran troops on the river put up little resistance and fled before the enemy. The people in the town began to flee in panic and many died. The priests in the mission house, the Medical Missionaries and Dr Hinds in the hospital, and the Handmaids of the Holy Child in their convent, spent the next two days sheltering from bullets and shells. The two priests put cotton wool in their ears and kept the oil stock open beside them so that they could administer the sacrament to one another in the final moments, if the need arose. They saw a band of Federals passing by. Then twenty Biafran soldiers arrived in a burst of gunfire. They asked the priests to hear their confessions. Arrest by Federal troops, which happened on Sunday, was a relief but nonetheless terrifying. Rory O'Brien describes the forced march of sisters and priests with Doctor Hinds and a number of Nigerian lay helpers as follows:

> One sister whispered for absolution. We had no inhibition now as we prayed aloud 'Jesus, Mary and Joseph save us. Into your hands, O Lord, I commend my spirit.' The soldiers continued to threaten us with death—'You Godly people, we will see if your God will now come down and save you. What can He do for you now, you are wicked people.' 'Hands up' they repeated as we began to tire and droop. Sister Deirdre whispered to me—we were forbidden to speak—'Will we all be shot?' 'No,' I replied, 'we will work our way out of this somehow.' It seemed a vain hope as I could not see anything but the worst happening.

Later, they were to be taken across the river to be interrogated by the Brigade Commander. The situation was still volatile as Rory O'Brien's account shows:

> A soldier asked, 'How will we get these Godly people across the river?' 'Make them swim across,' another replied. 'No,' said the first soldier. 'I do not want trouble with their Jesus and their Peter.'[6]

The Brigade Commander gave them a warm welcome and offered them whiskey or soft drinks. They were taken to Ugep mission where the weary band, numbering about thirty in all, received a warm welcome from the resident priests, Cahal McBride and Ned Grace.

Afikpo was to be recaptured by the Biafrans and later liberated once more by the Federals. Afterwards, there was much unrest and a lot of hunger which was alleviated by the Red Cross. The priests in Ikot Ekpene also experienced great hardship as the area was taken and retaken by the opposing forces almost until the end of the war. The other missions of the Society escaped the worst excesses of the war. The priests and sisters played a big part in the distribution of relief supplies and in the provision of medical care. Later, there was a big push to rebuild the economy and a number of successful development programmes were launched with the aid of overseas funding organisations.

Finally on 12 January 1970, General Ojukwu surrendered to the Federal government. The war ended with less vindictiveness than had been expected. However, all but a few of the Holy Ghost Fathers were expelled from Eastern Nigeria. The solidarity they had shown with the Ibo people was not appreciated by the Government. In particular, their involvement in the provision of relief supplies to beleaguered Biafra was seen as a major factor in prolonging the war. The Catholic Church, in general, was criticised by the Nigerian media and the future of missionary work in Eastern Nigeria looked very insecure. The Nigerian Government was very slow to give entry permits to missionaries. There was no policy of exclusion. Applications were accepted but in a large number of cases no visa was issued. Already in January 1968, four priests and seven sisters, recently returned from Europe, using the proper channels, had been ordered out of Ogoja diocese by the Civil Administrator because they had not received his permission to return. Bishop Murray of the English Province of the Holy Ghost Fathers gave them work in Makurdi diocese and after about two years they returned to Ogoja. The few who had been expelled during the war were obviously unwelcome. The many who had gone out by the San Tomé route were also suspect. Each case was considered individually and very few visas were given. The Society had the problem of a large number of priests unable to return to their missions. Some were fixed up in temporary appointments in Ireland, England and America. Others were sent to missions in Kenya where, with newly ordained priests many of whom would have gone to Nigeria but for the war, they made possible a great expansion of the Society's work. The 1969 Chapter decided that new possibilities for mission work would be investigated and, in the following year, a number of those displaced from Nigeria went to Central Africa and the West Indies.

Bishop Moynagh was one of those who failed to get back to Nigeria after the war. After completing his unsuccessful peace-mission he spent a while in hospital and then, in August 1968, applied for the necessary papers to return to Nigeria. At this time the entire diocese of Calabar was in Federal hands and the battlefield had moved to the Ikot Ekpene area. No visa was forthcoming. Repeated applications met with no success, and, in 1969, he resigned his post as Bishop of Calabar. After thirty-eight years in Calabar he was now a displaced person. The Society offered him an appointment in Central Africa but he felt too old to attempt the necessary adaptation. In 1970, he was made parish priest of Annaduff in his native diocese of Ardagh and Clonmacnois. It was a difficult assignment for a man who was used to being at the centre of things. In 1975, he returned to Kiltegan and spent his remaining years there or with the Medical Missionaries of Mary in Drogheda. In 1980, he attempted once more to go to Nigeria. It was the Golden Jubliee of his ordination. Everything seemed fine as he left Dublin Airport but before he had reached Amsterdam word had come to Kiltegan that he was not cleared to enter Nigeria. Officialdom there had not forgiven him for his peace mission which it interpreted as an act of collusion with the rebels. Bishop Moynagh accepted that he would never see his beloved Nigeria again. He died in 1985, and is buried in Kiltegan.

The Church flourished in Nigeria after the war. Gradually, it became easier for missionaries to get visas and the Society was able to maintain a strong presence there. There was a great emphasis on parish work as the control of mission schools had passed to the state following a government edict, issued in 1971. An upsurge of indigenous vocations lessened the pressure on foreign missionaries. Church leadership was gradually transferred to Africans and the missionary assumed a more ancillary role. Bishop Brian Davis Usanga replaced Bishop Moynagh in Calabar in October 1970. That year marked a new Society commitment in the Archdiocese of Lagos. It started with the appointment of Julian Connolly and Pat Laffey to the parish of Ajegunle but later more men were sent in to staff four other parishes. Bishop Joseph Ukpo became Auxiliary Bishop in Ogoja, in 1971, and, in the same year, Bishop Ephraim Obot became Auxiliary in Ikot Ekpene. In 1973 Bishop Ukpo was installed as Bishop of Ogoja and the Abakaliki area became a diocese under Bishop McGettrick. In the same year, Ned Fitzgibbon was put in charge of Port Harcourt diocese which was vacant due to the death of Bishop Okoye. He was replaced in Minna by Bishop Christopher Abba. Society priests were already working in Port Harcourt alongside indigenous diocesan priests and members of other Societies. In January 1976, Ned Fitzgibbon was consecrated in Rome and became Bishop of Port Harcourt. In May 1983, Bishop Ekandem became the first Nigerian Cardinal while remaining Bishop of Ikot Ekpene.[7]

One initiative which illustrates that the missionary wheel has come full circle in Nigeria is the Missionary Society of St Paul. This Society of secular priests was founded by the Nigerian bishops in 1977, with special encouragement from Cardinal Ekandem. It could be described as the Nigerian version of St Patrick's Missionary Society although it has no juridical links with the Society. The two Societies have similar constitutions and both have their origin in a diocesan priesthood. Moreover, Kiltegan was invited to get the Nigerian Society off the ground by giving priests to staff the seminaries and to serve on the General Council. The first eleven priests of the new Society were ordained in 1986.[8]

Another indication of Nigeria's passing to a new stage of Church development was the withdrawal of Society priests from Ikot Ekpene diocese in 1987. This happened fifty-seven years after James Moynagh arrived in the area as the first resident priest. In 1963, Ikot Ekpene became an independent diocese under Bishop Ekandem, although still dependent on missionary priests. As diocesan priests increased, the number of Society priests was reduced. Finally, in 1987, when there were forty-four diocesan priests, it was possible to withdraw the remaining Society men and assign them elsewhere.

New Missions Following Nigerian War

Central Africa

In December 1969, Dinny Newman, then Apostolic Administrator of Nakuru and Alfie Byrne, formerly of Nigeria, were sent to visit a number of dioceses in Tanzania, Malawi and Zambia which had made requests for Society priests. Mzuzu diocese in Malawi was chosen for the inauguration of a Society Mission to Central Africa and the first priests arrived there on 16 March 1970. They were: Alfie Byrne, Frank Morris, Padraig O'Maille and Pat McGivern. They found a diocese which had been well developed by the White Fathers who had established the first Catholic mission there in 1938. Although situated on a healthy plateau along the Western shore of Lake Malawi, the area was rugged, with bad roads and a scattered population, very different from the experience of these priests in Nigeria. After orientation, they continued to live with the White Fathers and did not set up Kiltegan parishes. This was a new departure and it remained the norm until the 1980s when the half dozen Society priests took a decision to work as assistants in parishes run by diocesan clergy.

When Bishop Jobidon, the Canadian White Father who was the first Bishop in Mzuzu, retired he was replaced by Kiltegan man, John Roche, who was appointed Apostolic Administrator in 1987. He had been Superior of the Society's Central African Region since it was established in 1979.

In 1973, the first Society men moved into the south of Malawi, to Chikwawa diocese, a hot and backward area in the lower valley of the Shire which is a tributary of the Zambezi. The great ancestor of modern

African missionaries, David Livingstone, had passed this way in 1859, on an expedition which cost the lives of his wife Mary and of many of his colleagues from the Universities Mission to Central Africa. Life had not changed much in the Shire Valley in the intervening years. The Church had been established by Dutch de Montfort Fathers who had nineteen priests in as many parishes under the leadership of Bishop Vroemen. There were two diocesan priests. Catechists were well trained and even at that early stage were taking care of the Blessed Sacrament reserved in out-stations and were performing baptisms. The first Kiltegan priests in Chikwawa were Patsy Foley, Donal Keane and David Walsh. They started work at the end of 1973 after completing a language course and were joined soon afterwards by Peter Gillooly. Society personnel was built up to ten over the years with responsibility for six parishes and a commitment in the minor seminary. Galway diocese pledged two priests to Chikwawa in 1981 and Jack O'Connor and Aodan Glynn were the pioneers. Later, Kiltegan priest, Oliver McHugh became Vicar General under Bishop Mkhori.

In September 1973, the Society sent four priests to the Archdiocese of Lusaka in Zambia, which had been evangelised by the Jesuits. Peter Finegan, Frank Taylor and Brendan McCarron took charge of two parishes in the city—one of them the Cathedral parish—while Michael Murphy was seconded to a secondary school at Isoka, 600 miles away. The Society later took on another city parish and two rural parishes, supplying about ten priests. Peter Finegan and Frank Taylor successively held the post of Vicar General to Archbishop Emmanuel Milingo, whose healing ministry attracted the attention of the world press and earned the disapproval of Rome. Later, Eamon Hayden and John McLoughlin worked in diocesan administration under Archbishop Mungandu.

The Society began its association with a second Zambian diocese, in 1975, when Ned Ryan and Billy Feerick started work in Chipata. This had been a White Father diocese but was now in the charge of Bishop Mazombwe, a Zambian who had gained an international reputation as Chairman of AMECEA, a body comprising the bishops of Eastern Africa. At first the newcomers lived with the White Fathers but from 1978 they staffed separate missions along with volunteer priests from Ardagh and Clonmacnois, which had made a commitment to supply four priests to Chikwawa. One of the volunteers taught in the Junior Seminary. Billy Feerick held the post of Diocesan Procurator from 1981 to 1989 when he was recalled for administration work in Kiltegan.

In 1980 the newly-established Region of Central Africa procured a house in Lilongwe with some parish responsibility attached. The Regional Superior and his assistant reside there. A number of priests became involved in third-level education—Padraig O'Maille in the University of Malawi and Pat Kelly, Frank McAuliffe, Benny Bohan, Paddy Hagan, Tony Sheerin and Pat O'Sullivan in various senior seminaries in Malawi and Zambia. The Society has directed many lay missionaries to Malawi and Zambia, in recent years, and has facilitated the diocese of Galway in sending a team of lay volunteers to Chikwawa.

Grenada

In October 1969, Patrick Webster, the Bishop of St Georges, Grenada, requested the Society to send 'two or maybe three good priests' to work in his diocese. A year later the first three Society priests arrived in Grenada. Paddy Hannelly and Padraig MacCormac arrived on 4 October 1970 by air while John F. Sheehan arrived by boat four days later. They found themselves in a miniature country—a British colony—consisting of a group of islands of which the largest, Grenada, was only twenty-six miles long and thirteen miles wide. The majority of the population, which numbered about 120,000, was Catholic. However, the level of religious practice was low, church marriages were few and there was only one native-born priest in the diocese. By coincidence, he was the Dominican, Iraneus Alexander, who had studied for a time in Kiltegan in the 1960s. The English province of the Dominican Order had staffed the diocese for many years with the aid of individuals from other dioceses and congregations. The climate was good because of the windward position and the mountainous terrain. The scenery was magnificent.

Starting with a parish on the island of Carriacou, the Society built up its presence over the years to take charge of seven parishes and to supply a priest-teacher in St David's Secondary School. Society priests organised vocations exhibitions in the early years and aroused new interest among the youth in the priesthood and religious life. Life in an island paradise was marred only by a sense of isolation and claustrophobia and a Church lacking the dynamism found in many of the African missions. There has been a lot of political tension, going back to pre-independence unrest in 1973. In 1979, a coup d'état brought a left-wing government to power, led by Maurice Bishop. He was, in turn, overthrown by the army in 1983 and, days later, US marines invaded Grenada. The Society experienced personal tragedy in 1973, when Pat

Walsh died in a fall from a church tower which was under repair. In 1979 Michael Burns, a lay volunteer and a graduate in Agriculture from Ballymacward, Co. Galway, was drowned in a swimming accident in Grenada.

In the 1980s, Oliver Leavy, a Society priest, forged links between the Church in Grenada and Catholics in Ireland and the United States when he took a parish musical group, 'Youthquake', on successive tours. The group gave many public performances and, on its last visit, sang at Sunday Mass on Irish television.

Society Renewal

After the second Vatican Council, St Patrick's Missionary Society embarked on a programme for the inservicing and renewal of its members which was to become an important feature of Society life and a prime responsibility of successive administrations.

The special Chapter held in 1969 was the first major step towards updating the Society in line with Vatican II. In preparation for this Chapter a series of major position papers was prepared and distributed, in book form, as source material for pre-Chapter meetings. The Chapter document *Missionary Service* dealt in a comprehensive way with the challenges facing the Society in the wake of the Council but did not propose a specific renewal programme. In December 1969 the Superior General, Peter O'Reilly introduced the idea that contemplation was a serious lack in the Society. In a series of articles in the newsletter *Ad Invicem*, under the general title of 'The Missing Dimension', he stressed the need for prayerful sabbaticals and suggested that some priests might take time out from regular pastoral ministry in order to devote themselves to a more contemplative life.

The 1972 Chapter returned Peter O'Reilly as Superior General with Stan Connolly as Vicar General and Liam deVeale, Tom Lucey and Eugene O'Reilly on the Council. Eugene O'Reilly took a special interest in renewal and organised a 'think-tank' at which various recognised thinkers discussed the needs of priests at a time of crisis for the priesthood. The need for personal renewal emerged as a top priority and was actively encouraged by the Superiors. Existing courses such as the Irish Missionary Union (IMU) courses at Glenart, of which there had been three in 1971 and five in 1972, received new emphasis and many Society priests attended them in subsequent years.

In 1974, a number of Society priests in Kenya were exposed to a new approach to adult education known as the psycho-social method. This was based on the teachings of the Brazilian educationalist, Paulo Freire, and was introduced to Kenya by Anne Hope and Sally Timmel with encouragement from Irish layman Enda Byrne of the Kenya Catholic Secretariat. It had come by way of South Africa, where Anne Hope had worked with Steve Biko. The method starts from the premise that ordinary people can transform society and emphasises that education for transformation consists in discovering truth together rather than in receiving it from someone who already possesses it. Various workshops were held throughout Kenya and a national programme of leadership training emerged. It was known as DELTA (Development Education Leadership Teams in Action). Participation in DELTA and associated workshops gave priests a new approach to the formation and govern-ment of their parishes that was in line with Vatican II. It helped to integrate human development with spirituality and catechesis and taught skills for working with groups. The result, in many cases, was a greater involvement by lay people in the parish and the diocese.

The psycho-social method found particularly fertile soil in Kitui where Bishop Dunne, who had been made a Bishop in 1964, had, on his return from the Council, set up all the participative structures recom-mended by the Church—council of priests, parish council, diocesan pastoral council. Through DELTA, priests and laity learned to value these structures and to use them to good advantage. Later, when the need for a more integrated programme was recognised, the diocese set up its own programme which concentrated on the faith dimension. This was called PILT (Parish Integrated Leadership Training).

In October 1974, Donal Dorr, who had been involved in student formation and who had recently returned from a tour in Nigeria, was appointed to the newly created post of Pastoral Mission Theologian. His brief was to help Society priests to explore ways of solving pastoral problems. It soon became apparent that there could be no genuine pastoral renewal which was not integrated with personal renewal. In looking for a way to effect this integration, Donal Dorr came across the psycho-social method during a visit to Kenya. He organised a workshop for priests, in Kiltegan in September 1976, using basic principles of the method and learning as he went along from those who had been involved with it in Kenya. The workshop was attended by forty priests who were home on leave from the different Regions and was the first of five such workshops to be held in Kiltegan. As well as addressing the priests' own problems, these annual events helped to familiarise the participants with the psycho-social method which was later introduced to many of the Society's missions. The method was also to have a great influence on meetings held within the Society and made for greater participation among the rank and file membership.

Alongside the workshops, there were other opportunities for renewal. Retreats were encouraged and Peter O'Reilly asked the Jesuits in Manresa Retreat Centre to design a course for spiritual directors which could be availed of by Kiltegan priests and other interested missionary groups. A programme centred on the Spiritual Exercises of St Ignatius was offered, first at Kiltegan in 1976, and afterwards, on a regular basis, at Manresa. These courses provided an opportunity for individual renewal while making available more than twenty priests with skills in spiritual direction. In 1976, with a view to promoting and integrating spiritual and pastoral renewal, a series of booklets, *Food for Renewal*, was distributed to those who were interested. Sabbaticals were encouraged and a number did year-long courses in various universities and other institutes.

The 1978 Chapter elected Peter Finegan as Superior General with Paddy Hagan as Vicar General, and Vin MacNamara, Seamus Farrell and John Keenan on the council. This Chapter made the startling statement: 'All members of the Society are students', and proceeded to call for the setting up of 'an integrated missionary formation programme, at home and in the areas where we work'. Padraig O Maille was appointed Programme Director with a role in both student training and ongoing formation. Workshops continued for a while but were replaced in 1981 by more traditional seminars with some influences from the workshop. Every encouragement was given to individuals to take time off for renewal, and suitable courses were found. When Padraig O Maille returned to the missions, Mick Browne provided advice on these matters and made the necessary arrangements.

In 1984, Peter Finegan was returned as Superior General with Vin MacNamara as Vicar General, and Mick Rodgers, Tommy Greenan and George Corr on the council. The Superior General's interest in personal development was a factor in the decision of the Chapter to adopt the Ministry to Priests Programme, for the Society. This programme, designed by the American-based Center for Human Development, had already been set up in various dioceses in America and England. It was followed by 276 Society members. Alongside this, a steady stream of priests took part in renewal programmes such as the three-month course at Marianella, the ten-week course organised by the National Conference of Priests of Ireland and the 16-week Faith and Mission

Course in Dalgan organised by the IMU. Other courses were more specifically and intensively geared towards personal awareness and development. These included Clinical Pastoral Education and the Personality and Human Relations Programme (PRH), which was first followed by Society priests in Zambia in the early seventies and was later to be taken by the students and many priests. Society renewal was the special responsibility of Vin MacNamara.

New Missions after the Golden Jubilee

As the Society approached its Golden Jubilee, to be celebrated in 1982, the idea of a new mission was in the air. Such an undertaking was seen as a suitable memorial for the jubilee year. It also corresponded to the fact that many of the dioceses in which the Society were involved were becoming more self-reliant in priests and could afford to spare Society men for new missions. Various invitations had been received and were explored. In the end, the Society chose the Sudan because of the desperate situation of the Church there.

Sudan

In August 1983 the first Kiltegan group, led by Leo Traynor, went to the diocese of Torit, an area of Southern Sudan adjoining the Kenyan diocese of Lodwar. It had been excised from the Archdiocese of Juba, a month before, and had been made a separate diocese under Bishop Paride Taban, whose staff was to consist of five Sudanese priests, the six Kiltegan men and three other missionaries. They were to minister to an area more than one and a half times the size of Ireland. With Leo Traynor were John Garry, Tom McDonnell, Niall Geaney, Tim Galvin and Jim Kennedy.[9] As all Catholic missionaries had been expelled from Southern Sudan in 1964, the Church was very dispirited. Many people had abandoned the faith for lack of leadership and instruction and most of the mission buildings had fallen into disrepair. Under the leadership of Bishop Taban, the new arrivals planned to restore the church buildings, and to revitalise the Catholic community as well as attempting to evangelise those who had not yet heard the Gospel. It was a daunting task.

Some advances were made but the onset of war and famine shortly after the diocese was established brought them to a standstill. The Kiltegan men were divided between Torit, Kapoeta and Chukudum, situated in three different language areas. They were involved in parish-work, junior-seminary teaching, famine-relief and leadership training.

John Garry launched an ambitious project on a Church-owned farm at Palotaka, by which he hoped to train local farmers in food production with the assistance of *Gorta* and other agencies. Hopes were high but were destined to be shortlived. In early 1983, an insurgent group, *Anyanya 2*, became active in resisting government forces. This group was later overshadowed by the Sudanese People's Liberation Army (SPLA) which had its origin in a mutiny within the Sudanese army led by Colonel John Garang de Mabior.

The SPLA gradually took control of large areas of Southern Sudan. Travel became dangerous and the work of the priests was severely restricted. The first serious incident, involving Society priests, took place in November 1985, when Tim Galvin and Jimmy Farrell were withdrawing from Chukudum because of increased guerilla activity in the area. The SPLA was not friendly to the Church and a number of priests and sisters had been kidnapped. In order to avoid this, the priests left Chukudum for Torit, intending to pass through part of Uganda. On the way, they were attacked by bandits. Jimmy Farrell was shot in the ankle. While searching for water and possible assistance, Tim Galvin lost his way and wandered for a night and a day in the trackless bush before being discovered by local hunters. Jimmy Farrell made his way to Uganda and was successfully treated in Kaabong hospital. A Sudanese seminarian, also wounded in the attack, had to have his leg amputated. On Easter Sunday 1986, Palotaka was looted by the SPLA and John Garry, whose farming project was beginning to thrive, was forced to withdraw after a close brush with death.

Meanwhile, Torit had come under heavy attack and the minor seminarians and their teachers moved to Juba. Kapoeta was under siege for a time but the priests had withdrawn before it was captured. Leo Traynor was still in Torit when the SPLA took the town in February 1989, after a 12-month siege which reduced the inhabitants to starvation. With Bishop Taban and two other priests, he was taken to an army post in the bush where all four were held prisoner for three and a half months. Finally, Juba was surrounded and was pounded by heavy artillery on two occasions in January 1990. An air-corridor remained open and it was by this route that the last four Society priests left Juba in March 1990 on instruction from Bishop Taban who wanted them to join him in Torit where the Church was being allowed to function in the breakaway region. At the time of writing, two of the priests are back in Torit diocese while five of the others hope to return in the near future. Two have been reassigned to Kenya, at least for the present. All nine feel a deep bond with their mission in the Sudan, whose people have suffered more grievously than any other people among whom the Society has worked.

Southern Africa and Cameroon

As the number of indigenous priests grew in its traditional missions, the Society began to look to areas of greater need. New missions were considered on the understanding that each new venture would involve a small group of Society men who would work in a needy diocese until enough local priests were available. As far as possible, the Society would undertake to promote the diocesan clergy and to work towards a self-reliant local Church. By the middle of 1988, various places had been visited and a decision had been taken to send priests to four dioceses in three different African countries. The priests arrived in all four missions in January 1989.

Joe O'Connor, Fintan Byrne, Noel McHenry and Mick Morris went to Mutare diocese in Zimbabwe. This area had been evangelised by the Jesuits who handed it over to the Irish Carmelites in 1953. It was formerly known as Umthali and had come to world attention during the Rhodesian war when Bishop Donal Lamont supported the freedom-struggle. His stand earned him deportation in 1978, and a hero's welcome when the war ended in victory and independence for the indigenous Africans, in 1980. Bishop Lamont retired in 1982 and was succeeded by Bishop Alexio Muchabaiwa. It was felt that the Society's experience in newly independent African countries would fit it for the challenge of a mission in Zimbabwe. Many who had experienced the dynamism of the Church after national independence in Nigeria and Kenya were very interested in this new mission. Although there were nine indigenous priests in the diocese, the overall number of priests had dropped over the years from 52 to 35. The other priests consisted of 19 Carmelites, 3 volunteers from Killaloe and 4 Nigerian Holy Ghost Fathers. The Society agreed to take on one town parish and one rural parish with two priests in each.

Priests were sent to two separate dioceses in South Africa which are situated in the north-east Transvaal, a stronghold of the supremacist Conservative Party. The area is chiefly made up of tribal homelands which enjoy a certain political autonomy. However, these homelands are not single geographical units but are intersected by white areas and by other homelands. The Society felt drawn to the area because of the social and racial injustice which singles it out as especially in need of the Gospel.

Furthermore, it was hoped that the Society's experience of establishing the diocesan priesthood would be of benefit, where local priests are very few.

Seamus Farrell, Sean Smith and Sean MacSuibhne went to Lyndenburg-Witbank, one of the South African dioceses. Although the diocese had an African bishop, Paul Nkumishi, it had only one local diocesan priest. This is a pattern in South Africa where racial distinctions have been an obstacle to the recruitment of Africans. The diocese depended largely on the twenty-five Comboni missionaries whose Italian-based congregation had been responsible for its development. As with other missionary societies, their numbers had been declining and in the absence of a growing diocesan priesthood there was a great need for reinforcements from other quarters. Since his appointment as bishop in 1984, Bishop Nkumishi, who came from the neighbouring diocese of Pietersburge, had re-opened the junior seminary and had emphasised the need for local vocations. After language study, the Kiltegan priests were given charge of this seminary and have been encouraged to pay special attention to vocations for the diocesan priesthood. They have also taken charge of a parish and of a Pastoral Centre with facilities for leadership training and communications.

Tom Devoy, P.J. Fitzgerald and Pat Deegan went to the diocese of Tzaneen, also in South Africa, where the Missionaries of the Sacred Heart were hard pressed to service a diocese the size of the Irish Republic. Before the arrival of the three Kiltegan men, the staff consisted of fourteen Sacred Heart priests, two diocesan priests and four married deacons, under the leadership of Bishop Hugh Slattery. The newcomers were assigned to parish work.

The fourth mission was to the Archdiocese of Bamenda in Cameroon, one of the three dioceses in English-speaking Cameroon. Formerly a Mill Hill diocese, it had twenty-five indigenous priests and an African Archbishop, Paul Verdzekov. The thirty missionary priests were drawn from the Mill Hill Society and six other groups. Rory O'Brien, Dermot Nolan, Mick Bennett and Victor Dunne went to join this sizeable team of priests. Two of them lived together in a rural parish while the other two became assistants to African parish priests in town parishes.

The Society in the 1990s

The 1970s and 1980s, two decades which saw the spread of St Patrick's Society to six new countries, were years of crisis for missionary work in general. The number of missionaries declined worldwide and the continuing need for missionary institutes was questioned. A discussion, initiated in mission countries, centred on the need for a moratorium on missions which would involve the withdrawal of missionaries for a period in order to give local Churches an opportunity to become self-determining. Although no moratorium took place the discussion served to undermine the confidence of missionaries and caused them to question the necessity and usefulness of their work. Meanwhile, the missionary institutes—religious orders and societies—became less prominent in the Church as the initiative for pastoral planning passed from their hands into the hands of local bishops. Reports from missionary conferences pointed to an identity crisis which was leading missionary institutes to search out a new identity for themselves, appropriate to the late twentieth century.

St Patrick's Missionary Society was, to a large extent, untouched by the crisis and did not experience the need to change its direction in any significant way. The origins of the Society in the diocesan priesthood may well have contributed to this. Kiltegan priests tend to identify with the missionary diocese to which they are assigned and do not experience the need for a Society identity to the same extent that other institutes do. The Society never enjoyed a high profile in the Church and scarcely noticed the decline in influence experienced by older and larger institutes of its kind. Moreover, the relative youth of the Society had made it possible for a large number of the members to continue in the active apostolate on the missions into the 1990s. These factors, alongside the continuing support of its benefactors, have enabled the Society to keep on doing what it has been doing from the beginning without feeling any great need for major change. Meanwhile, the Church has pursued the discussion of the missionary question and has come to the conclusion that specialised missionary institutes are indispensable to its work of preaching the Gospel.

At the time of writing this book, August 1990, St Patrick's Missionary Society has 391 priest members, whose average age is 50.8 years. The total membership including those who have died and those who have left the Society is 506. Of these, 62 have died, 20 have been incardinated into other dioceses or joined religious orders and 33 have definitively left the ministry. Of the 391 remaining priest members 10 are on extended leave of absence; there are 244 attached to the various missions mentioned in this book; 72 are engaged in pastoral work in Ireland, England, Scotland and the USA (one of these, John Magee, is a diocesan bishop in Ireland, having been made Bishop of Cloyne following years of service in the Papal household); 11 are in retirement or on sick-leave while 3 are engaged in special works in Rome and the USA; the remaining 51 are involved in Society administration student formation or attached to one of the Society's promotion houses. The Society has been careful to retain its exclusively missionary orientation and has not taken on parishes or other works outside of the mission countries. There are a few exceptions to this: responsibility for an inner city parish in Chicago was undertaken for a few years in the eighties and the Society runs two parishes in England which are associated with the promotion effort.

The vast majority of Society members have spent most of their lives engaged in routine missionary work in schools or parishes. There has been little or no specialisation apart from those who have been trained to provide Seminary education for students of the Society and, in more recent years, for diocesan students in African seminaries. Sixteen members have received doctoral degrees, most of them in Theology and Canon Law. Of these, Vincent MacNamara and Donal Dorr have written books on theological topics.

There are 36 seminaries attached to the Society. The probation period or Spiritual Year in Kiltegan is followed by an undergraduate course in Maynooth leading to theological studies in Dublin where the Society acquired a student hostel in 1990 in order to avail of the facilities of a joint missionary institute. In recent years a number of students have gone to the missions for pastoral training and experience before completing their studies, and this is to become the norm. The annual average number ordained to the priesthood for the past five years has been 3.4, whereas around 9 or 10 ordinations per year would be required to keep Society membership relatively stable in the future. A change in policy with regard to the admission of students from the mission countries, where vocations to the priesthood are on the increase, could quickly reverse this trend. The possibility has been under discussion for some years but the Society is slow to depart from its roots in the Irish Church and to become an international body. There are a number of non-Irish members in the Society already, most of them from Scotland, but they are not numerous enough to affect significantly the Irishness of the Society. Many of those who oppose internationalisation argue that the primary task of the Society is to promote the diocesan priesthood on the missions or to facilitate African Societies as it has done in the case of St Paul's Missionary Society, in Nigeria.

Throughout the sixty years of its existence, St Patrick's Society has continued to recruit diocesan priests for temporary missionary service.

In the first thirty years, 103 were recruited and in the next thirty years 101 volunteered. Not all were from Irish dioceses and not all were Irish. Of the early volunteers, Father Hickey was a priest of Melbourne and William Brodie a priest of Menevia. From 1957, an increasing number of Scottish and English priests volunteered and, to date, 12 priests from Scotland and 6 priests from England and Wales have worked with the Society. Of the diocesan priests who volunteered in the 1930s, 6 became permanent members of the Society. Of those who volunteered in the following 50 years, only one became a permanent member. He is Paddy O'Reilly of the Archdiocese of Dublin who volunteered in 1966 and has since made an outstanding contribution to the Church in Kitui, especially in the areas of development education and the training of local leaders. One member of a Religious Order has spent many years as a volunteer with the Society in Turkana. He is a Carmelite priest, Robert McCabe. Since 1978, nine Irish dioceses have committed themselves to providing a number of priests for particular missions on an ongoing basis.[10] On the missionfield, the volunteer priests participate fully in the life and work of the Society and, when they return to their home dioceses they, almost invariably, continue to maintain close links with the Society. Lay missionaries, too, have continued to work with the Society and are engaged in increasingly varied and specialised works on the missionfield.

Towards the New Century

It is unlikely that St Patrick's Missionary Society will experience any major change of direction in the last decade of the twentieth century. The eighth General Chapter which was held in Kiltegan from 18 June to 20 July 1990 expressed satisfaction with the existing missionary policy of the Society which is summarised as follows:

(a) planting the Church among those people and groups among whom it is not established;

(b) staying on with the young churches until they become an effective presence in that area, and in certain circumstances staying even longer at the invitation of the young churches in order to promote fellowship between the young churches and the older ones;

(c) renewing the church among peoples or groups where it is in such a state of regression or weakness that it is clearly in need of outside assistance to provide the minimum effective Christian witness.[11]

This amounts to a ratification of the traditional ministry of the Society which is, in the main, pastoral work in mission parishes. This parish ministry has occupied the vast majority of Society members, especially since the mission schools passed out of the hands of the Church. It is likely to be the chief apostolate of the Society in the future.

A decision on the internationalisation of St Patrick's Society will probably be taken before the end of the century. It will be a difficult decision. The Society must ask itself whether it has the charism and resources necessary to facilitate priests of different cultural backgrounds to engage in missionary work. The presence of such priests would undoubtedly enrich the Society. To recruit and train them, however, would make great demands on the Society's limited resources. More-over, the whole idea would be at variance with what has been, up to now, one of the primary aims of the Society: to concentrate on building up local diocesan structures and the diocesan priesthood. International-isation would also put a strain on the social coherence of the Society which has stemmed to a great extent from the Irishness of the members and their friendship and fellowship with the Irish diocesan clergy.

It is probable that new missions will be undertaken within the next ten years and that personnel will be withdrawn from existing missions to staff them. This is almost inevitable in view of the increasing number of vocations to the diocesan priesthood in the older missions of the Society. Such new missions present many difficulties. The social and cultural uprooting involved will put a great strain on individual mis-sionaries especially those who have reached middle-age. Keeping up morale in a very fragmented situation may be difficult. The Chapter of 1990 was aware of this. While it advocated mobility and flexibility it was concerned that the Society group in any particular diocese would be such that morale and mutual support would be assured.

St Patrick's Missionary Society faces the future with confidence, arising from sixty years of successful missionary work. The early years were marked by the struggle to survive. There followed a period of growth and expansion and remarkable success on the missionfield. Then came the major crises in Nigeria and Kenya during which the Society had to struggle to ensure the well-being of its members in dangerous and dif-ficult situations. More recently, mission work has progressed calmly and quietly in situations of great cultural and political change. The future will bring problems associated with an ageing membership and a Society which is for the first time beginning to decline in numbers. There may well be other unforeseen problems and difficulties as there will be new challenges and opportunities. It is for the Society to respond to these in a creative way as it has done to the problems and opportunities of the past.

Sources and Notes

THE titles of published works and academic dissertations are given in the 'Select Bibliography' and are referred to in specific notes. Primary sources—documents and interviews—are given under the heading 'Sources' in the notes to each chapter. Individual items are mentioned in the text but whenever a particular document, body of correspondence or interview forms a significant source for a chapter it is mentioned under 'Sources' below. Unless otherwise stated the items referred to are in the Kiltegan archives. For 'p.c.' read 'privately circulated'.

The following sources when drawn upon throughout the book but are not mentioned subsequently under 'Sources':

A series of interviews given by Bishop Moynagh are recorded by Fr Jim Sheerin SPS, in 1979. They were typed by Josie Dempsey and compiled by Fr Frank Morris SPS as a booklet entitled *Reminiscences of Bishop Moynagh* (82 pages). For reference purposes, they are regarded as a published work.

Correspondence between Bishop Moynagh and successive Superiors General and Vicars General from 1934 to 1957.

Correspondence between Bishop McGettrick and successive Superiors General and Vicars General from 1938 to 1957.

Interviews with the following cover most sections of the book: Bishop McGettrick, Fr J. Lane SPS, Fr J. Sheehan SPS, Fr J. Kelly SPS, Bishop W. Dunne SPS, Fr D. Newman SPS, Fr S. Meehan SPS, Miss Mary Campbell.

Chapter One, pp. 1–22
Sources
A notebook in which Fr P.J. Whitney kept a diary from 18 April 1918 to 29 December 1922. There are some entries for 1925 and 1926. It was kindly made available by Fr Ciaran Whitney.

Notes

1. Stephen Neil, *A History of Christian Missions*, 380.
2. Geoffrey Parrinder, *West African Religion*, 152–5.
3. E.A. Ayandele, *The Missionary Impact on Modern Nigeria* 1842–1914, 302.
4. H.J. Koren, C.S.Sp. *The Spiritans*, 531.
5. J.P. Jordan, C.S.Sp. *Bishop Shanahan of Southern Nigeria*, 82.
6. Colman Cooke, 'Irish Diocesan Priests in Southern Nigeria, 1920–1942', M.A. thesis, 48.
7. Jordan, *Bishop Shanahan*, 107–108.
8. Jordan, *Bishop Shanahan*, 179–80.
9. Denis Meehan, 'Maynooth and the Missions' in *Irish Ecclesiastical Record*, LXVI (1945), 224–37.
10. Scrutator, 'Jottings from Maynooth Records' in *Irish Ecclesiastical Record*, LV (1940), 496.
11. William E. Barrett, *The Red Lacquered Gate: the story of Bishop Galvin Co-Founder of the Columban Fathers*.
12. Hugh McMahon, 'John Blowick' in *The Furrow*, 39/10 (October 1988), 630–31.
13. R.F. Foster, *Modern Ireland, 1600–1972*, London: The Penguin Press 1988, 484–93.
14. Hugh McMahon, 'John Blowick', 634.
15. Francis A. Sullivan, SJ, *The Church we believe in*, Gill and Macmillan, Dublin 1988, 115.
16. P.J. Costelloe, 'Does the pagan think of God?' in *St Patrick's Missionary Bulletin IV/1* (January 1934), 16–17.
17. P.J. Whitney, *An Irish Missionary in Central Africa*, 27.
18. James Moynagh, handwritten Memoir.
19. Patrick Corish, *The Irish Catholic Experience*, 163.
20. Raymond Gore Clough, *Oil River Trader*, London 1972.
21. *Bulletin de la Congregation* (Annals of the Holy Ghost Fathers) 1922, 544–6.
22. Whitney, *An Irish Missionary*, 76–7.

Chapter Two, pp. 23–41

Sources

Memorandum entitled, *The Incident of Father P. Whitney as recalled by Mother Xavier O.P.*, 1954, in the Holy Rosary archives.

Memorandum entitled, *Our Relations with Bishop Shanahan*, 1969, by Sr Margaret Mary kindly supplied by Fr Ciaran Whitney (Holy Rosary archives).

A memoir written by Bishop Moynagh in April 1970, at the request of Fr Colman Cooke. Consisting of 26 pages of a writing pad it is a

remarkably frank and informative account of the development of St
Patrick's Missionary Society (referred to as 'handwritten Memoir').

Letter of Bishop James Fergus to Fr Paddy Hagan, 8 June 1982. (James
Fergus was a classmate of Pat Whitney in Maynooth.)

Interviews with Mrs Molly Whitney, Fr Kieran Whitney, and Archdeacon
Patrick Lyons of Limerick Diocese who was ordained in Maynooth
in 1920.

Notes

1. Colman Cooke, *Mary Charles Walker*, 32–58.
2. Mary Purcell, *To Africa with Love*, 26–35.
3. Mary Purcell, *To Africa with Love*, 39.
4. Desmond Forristal, *The Second Burial of Bishop Shanahan*, 179–81, 186–7.
5. Marian Keaney, *They brought the Good News*, 77.
6. Colman Cooke, 'Irish Priests in Southern Nigeria', 112.
7. James Moynagh, handwritten Memoir.
8. Colman Cooke, *Mary Charles Walker*, 113.
9. Brigid Ryan, *Bishop Shanahan and his Missionary Family*, published by the
   Holy Rosary Sisters, Vol. 1, 1967, 60.
10. Desmond Forristal, *Second Burial*, 251–9.

Chapter Three, pp. 42–63
Sources

A second notebook which contains 130 pages of notes written by Fr
P.J. Whitney between Christmas 1927 and Christmas 1928, kindly
supplied by Fr Ciaran Whitney (copy in Kiltegan archives).

Letters of Fr Tom Mulvaney to his brother Fr Patrick Mulvaney, in the
archives of the Diocese of Meath (copy in Kiltegan archives).

Memorandum entitled: *The Unanimous View of the Maynooth Nigerian
Priests expressed in 1927 at the request of the Vicar Apostolic, Most Rev.
Dr Shanahan.*

Declaration of Intent, signed by Bishop Shanahan, Fr Pat Whitney, Fr
Vincent Davey and Fr John Finegan in 1937; copy among the McCaffrey papers in the archives of St Patrick's College, Maynooth.

Letters of Archbishop Arthur Hinsley to Fr Pat Whitney with copies of
replies.

Letters of Monsignor Caesar Pecorari to Fr Pat Whitney (with replies).

Notes on his visit to Rome, 1929, by Fr Pat Whitney.

Notes on Fr Pat Whitney's visit to Mater Dei Convent, Rome, kindly
supplied by Fr M. Glynn S.P.S.

Notes
1. 1926: *Bulletin de la Congregation*, 1930, 842.
   1905: Jordan, *Bishop Shanahan*, 131.
2. This letter is quoted in Anon, 'Letter from the Grave' in *Africa*, 15/9 (November 1953), 10–12.
3. James Moynagh, handwritten Memoir.
4. Forristal, *Second Burial*, 212–13.
5. Brigid Ryan, *Bishop Shanahan and his Missionary Family*, Vol. II, 1977, 119–20.
6. The letter to Bishop McNamee is in St Michael's, Longford, while the letter to the Superior General is in the archives of the Holy Ghost Mother-house (555/B/IV).
7. Quoted by Colman Cooke in 'Irish Diocesan Priests', 97.
8. Roland Oliver, *The Missionary Factor in East Africa*, London, Longman, 275.
9. James Moynagh, handwritten Memoir.
10. Forristal, *Second Burial*, 228.

Chapter Four, pp. 64–91

Sources

Letters from Mr John Hughes to Fr Pat Whitney and to Fr Frank Whitney, 1927–1933 (with replies).

Correspondence between the Society and John Hughes, and the Society and Archbishop Byrne of Dublin, with regard to Aghavannagh, 1932.

Foundation documents, 1932.

Interviews with Archbishop T. Brosnahan C.S.Sp., who travelled to Nigeria for the first time with the 1920 group and later accompanied Monsignor Whitney on his journey to Nigeria in 1938; Sr Patrick Leydon M.M.M.; Fr Maurice Hayes S.P.S.

Notes
1. Fr Ignatius Murphy 'Westbys and High Park' in *Ad Invicem*, 2/27 (January 1967), 11–12; 'High Park and the 1798 Rebellion' in *Ad Invicem* 2/28 (February 1967), 9–10; 'High Park' in *Ad Invicem* 4/65 (June 1970), 12.
2. Notes on St Tegan were kindly provided by Fr Philip Magee S.P.S.
3. Colman Cooke, 'The Roman Catholic Mission in Calabar', 86.
4. Thomas McGettrick, *Memoirs of Bishop Thomas McGettrick*, published privately, 1988, 88.
5. James Walsh, 'Essene Parish' in *St. Patrick's Missionary Bulletin* 1/1 (June 1934), 12–13.
6. Moynagh, *Reminiscences*, 14–15. He refers to 'a very pagan play' because the members of the Eka Ekong went around as masked players.

7. McGettrick, *Memoirs*, 88.
8. Cooke, *Mary Charles Walker*, 144–6.
9. McGettrick, *Memoirs*, 81–82. Pat Kelly spent some time at Kiltegan awaiting word from Nigeria. As no decision was forthcoming, he went to Australia where he worked as a priest for 47 years. On retirement, he returned to Ireland and visited Kiltegan on several occasions and enjoyed a game of golf with some of the priests. He died in 1981. Two of his sisters had worked in the office in Kiltegan in Pat Whitney's time.
10. Moynagh, handwritten Memoir.
11. Thomas Ronayne, Memoir 1957.
12. Bishop McGettrick in an interview with the author given at Donamon Pastoral Centre, 14 October 1988.
13. A burse is a sum of money which is invested in order to provide an annual scholarship for one or more students.

Chapter Five, pp. 92–114
Sources
Minute book of General Council Meetings, 1932–1945.
Minute book which records three meetings with diocesan consultors, 1934–1938.
Notes of lectures given by Fr Pat Whitney to the priests in Nigeria, 1932.
Copy of agreement between the Society and the volunteers, 1932.
Documents of an inquiry conducted by Bishop Cullen, 1933.
Memoir written by Fr Tom Ronayne in 1957 explaining the circum–stances surrounding his decision not to join St Patrick's Missionary Society.

Notes
1. The term 'General Council' refers to the Central Administration of the Society viz. the Superior General and his four councillors. It is not a strictly accurate term. On all but a few occasions, the responsibility for decisions rests with the Superior General alone. In practice, however, the Superior General and the councillors live together in Kiltegan and partici-pate in the leadership of the Society to a greater or lesser extent, depending on the style of the Superior General. For convenience, I have used *General Council* to refer to the central team although it is not a constitutional term.
2. The students who came in 1932 were Daniel Creedon, Charles Fagan, Thomas Fitzgerald, Joseph B. Houlihan and Joseph Gilmartin, all from All Hallows; Thomas Vaughan came from St John's College, Waterford; those coming direct from secondary schools were Patrick Gannon, Carthage

Cantwell, Thomas Flanagan and Bernard McGuirk. All but Charles Fagan persevered and were admitted to the Society a year later; of these all except Thomas Vaughan, John Gannon and Thomas Flanagan were ordained for the Society by 1939.

3. Moynagh, handwritten Memoir.

4. McGettrick, *Memoirs*, 121.

5. Ronayne, Memoir, 1957.

6. All those admitted as probationers between 1932 and 1957 are listed in the Appendix.

7. Transcript of a journal kept in St Benedict's Mission, Ogoja, kindly supplied by Fr V. Dunne S.P.S. There is a copy in the Kiltegan archives.

8. Cooke, *Irish Diocesan Priests*, 152.

9. McGettrick, *Memoirs*, 95.

10. Cooke, *Mary Charles Walker* (contains the story of Sister Magdalen, an account of the coming of the Holy Child Nuns and a short history of the Handmaids of the Holy Child).

11. McGettrick, *Memoirs*, 96–7.

12. The 1933 volunteers were: Nicholas Cullen from Kildare and Leighlin, Peter Joe Duffy from Clogher and Patrick McDaid and Manus McClafferty from Raphoe. The 1934 group were: Thomas Reynolds from Ardagh, William Brodie from Minevia, Philip O'Connor from Derry, John Coffey from Cork and Martin Geraghty, Jarlath Canney and Thomas Rushe from Tuam.

13. Moynagh, *Reminiscences*, 8.

14. Moynagh, *Reminiscences*, 12.

15. Moynagh, *Reminiscences*, 18.

16. Moynagh, *Reminiscences*, 18.

17. Moynagh, *Reminiscences*, 18–19.

18. Moynagh, *Reminiscences*, 34.

19. Moynagh, *Reminiscences*, 32–3.

20. Moynagh, *Reminiscences* (extract from a letter to Fr Frank Morris), 82.

21. Moynagh, *Reminiscences*, 26.

Chapter Six, pp. 115–142

Sources

Audited Accounts prepared for the Society by O'Loghlen Gillic & Co. (1935 onwards).

Interviews with Mr Michael McShera and Mr Peter Cullen.

Notes

1. Bishop McGettrick spoke of Bishop Staunton's intervention in the 1988 interview. A number of Kiltegan priests interviewed spoke of Bishop Browne's support.

2. Moynagh, handwritten Memoir.
3. Cooke, 'Irish Diocesan Priests', 166.
4. The 1935 volunteers were: John Kearns of Ossory, Lawrence and Thomas Leavy of Ardagh, and Patrick J. McKenna of Derry. The 1936 volunteers were: James Savage of Cloyne, Michael McHugh of Tuam, Fintan Phelan of Ossory, Patrick McKee of Armagh and James B. McCartan of Dromore, Gerard Montague of Down and Connor came to teach in Kiltegan.
5. McGettrick, *Memoirs*, 106–7.
6. Moynagh, *Reminiscences*, 36.
7. Moynagh, *Reminiscences*, 36.
8. McGettrick, *Memoirs*, 108.
9. Archbishop Riberi uses this phrase in a letter written to Fr Pat Whitney on 2 March 1937.
10. Moynagh, handwritten Memoir.
11. The 'Bull' or *bulla* is a formal letter of appointment received from the Pope.
12. Moynagh, *Reminiscences*, 8.
13. The 1938 volunteers were: Noel Sandvoss of Ossory, Joseph Clarke of Meath, Martin McManus of Achonry, Dermot Higgins of Galway, Charles Smith of Kilmore and Thomas D. Slattery of Cork. Fr Slattery was appointed to Calabar and the other five went to Ogoja to join Manus McClafferty, Peter J. Duffy, Michael McHugh and J.B. McCartan. Four priests who volunteered in 1938 were retained in Kiltegan. They were Joseph Abbott of Meath, Michael Leahy of Waterford, Seamus McLoughlin of Elphin and Thomas Lavin, also of Elphin.

Chapter Seven, pp. 143–168

Sources

Letters from Manus McClafferty, Pro-Prefect of Ogoja to Fr Paddy Costelloe regarding Monsignor Whitney's illness, 1939.

Correspondence between Monsignor Whitney and Fr Paddy Costelloe, 1939–1942. There are also letters from other members of the Whitney family to Fr Costelloe.

A small number of letters from doctors relating to Monsignor Whitney's illness.

The death certificate of Monsignor Whitney.

Letter from Fr John McGuinness, in Nigeria, to the author giving details of the funeral of the Founder, 15 Dec. 1989.

Interview with Archdeacon Dermot Higgins of Galway (1938 volunteer in Ogoja), 1990; Fr Charles Smith S.P.S.

Consultation with Dr Tim Redmond re. Monsignor Whitney's symptoms.

Notes

1. 'Fr. Costelloe spoke on the Radio' in *Africa* 6/1 (Mar. 1939), 12–13.
2. Moynagh, *Reminiscences*, 25.
3. Moynagh, *Reminiscences*, 25.
4. James Moynagh to Paddy Costelloe, 19 Feb. 1939.
5. The 1939 volunteers who went to Nigeria were: Charles O'Hagan and Hugh Connolly of Dromore, Dan Ward of Clogher and Hugh McNelis of Raphoe. Those who went on to the college staff in Kiltegan were: Michael English of Cashel, James Kavanagh of Dublin and Patrick Crowe of Dublin.
6. Moynagh, *Reminiscences*, 49.
7. McGettrick, *Memoirs*, 105.
8. James Moynagh to Paddy Costelloe, 28 Jun. 1938.
9. McGettrick, *Memoirs*, 113, and Moynagh, *Reminiscences*, 38.
10. James Moynagh to Paddy Costelloe, 22 Jul. 1938.
11. McGettrick, *Memoirs*, 74.
12. Editor, 'Leprosy in Ogoja', in *Africa* 2/4 (May 1940), 3.
13. McGettrick, Memoirs, 127.
14. Manus McClafferty to Paddy Costelloe, 14 Feb. 1939.
15. The Jesuit Superior of Clongowes Wood College who had understood that Fr Hickey was a diocesan priest in retirement in Kiltegan returned the chalices to Kiltegan when he learned of Fr Hickey's significance for the Society. At that stage, the books had already been disposed of.

Chapter Eight, pp. 169–185

Sources

Documents relating to the renting of Humewood Castle, including a formal agreement.

Correspondence between Fr Paddy Costelloe and the diocesan consultors attached to the Council, Monsignor Delaney, Fr Brophy and Fr Browne.

A brief account of the 1944 Chapter printed as an Appendix to a Report of the 1950 Chapter—an 8-page pamphlet.

Notes

1. The Maynooth volunteers in those years were: in 1940—Martin Hannon of Tuam, Robert Mullally of Cashel, John Higgins of Clonfert, Eugene Lennon of Clogher, James Creaton from Elphin, James Tiernan of Elphin and Kevin Dodd of Elphin; all of whom went to Nigeria. An eighth volunteer, Daniel Duffy of Clogher joined the College staff in Kiltegan. In 1941 Denis Meehan was the only volunteer and he also joined the College staff. In 1942, the volunteers were Patrick Meenan of Down and Connor and Joseph Scott of Tuam. In 1943, Dominic Conway of Elphin went to

Calabar after spending a short time in Kiltegan. In 1945 John Corkery of Ardagh and Clonmacnois was the only volunteer. In 1946, Daniel Gallagher of Limerick, Patrick Quealy of Waterford and Humphrey Mulcahy of Cork volunteered. St Columban's Missionary Society gave Thomas Hanahoe for the College in 1942 and Hugh Markey in 1943.

2. Mark Girourd 'Humewood Castle, Co. Wicklow' in *Country Life*, 9 May and 16 May 1968, 1212–15 and 1282–5.

3. Joseph Moran of Tuam volunteered for College work in 1949. Then after a long break during which the Society depended on its own teachers, Maurice Dooley of Cashel volunteered in 1963; Ignatius Murphy of Killaloe in 1965, Anthony Conry of Elphin in 1966 and Eamonn Bredin of Kilmore in 1970. In the 1980s members of the teaching staff in St Patrick's College, Carlow taught particular courses in Kiltegan while members of the Kiltegan staff reciprocated from time to time.

4. Monsignor McGettrick, 'Steady Progress in Ogoja' in *Africa*, January 1946, 56–8.

5. Monsignor McGettrick 'Steady Progress'.

6. Fr Matt Magrath to Fr Paddy Costelloe, 14 November 1941.

7. A list of the lay medical personnel and lay teachers who served with the Society in Nigeria between 1930 and 1957 is given in the Appendix.

8. A General Chapter is a meeting of designated members which makes laws and elects Superiors. It consists of certain current office holders and some elected representatives. It takes place at intervals laid down by the Constitution.

Chapter Nine, pp. 186–202

Sources

Correspondence re. university hostel with auctioneers, with the Bishops of Dublin, Cork and Galway and with Fr Bastible, Chaplain at U.C.C.

Notes

1. McGettrick, *Memoirs*, 197–8.

2. McGettrick, *Memoirs*, 202.

3. McGettrick, *Memoirs*, 207.

4. Dr Godfrey Hinds, originally from Belfast, married Nancy Lee Bochin, a nurse with the American Catholic Relief Services, in 1970. He then opened a medical practice in Belfast. Two years later, the couple moved to Uganda where they spent four years. Eighteen months after their return to Strabane, Northern Ireland, Godfrey Hinds died, in March 1977, at the age of 53. His wife and three sons, Sean, Conor and Patrick, moved to the USA.

5. Mr J. Burke, 'Fr. Dominic's First Mass' in *Africa* 10/3 (Mar. 1948), 260.

6. Anon, 'A Most Impressive Occasion' in *Africa*, 10/8 (Sep. 1948), 365–7.

7. These figures are based on the Sacred Returns submitted to Rome in June 1949. They appear in *Africa* 12/6 (Jan. and Feb. 1950), 7, 8, 33. As the numbers for schools and teachers in Ogoja are not given, the figures for June 1950 which appear in *Africa* 12/12 (Dec. 1956), 226–8, are those given here.
8. James Moynagh to Paddy Costelloe, 30 Aug. 1946.
9. Those who volunteered in 1947 were: John Finn of Armagh, Liam Boyle of Dromore and Joseph Troy of Meath. The 1948 volunteers were: Joseph Young of Kilmore, J.P. Masterson of Ardagh and Michael Clancy of Killaloe. Those who volunteered in 1949 were: John Maher of Kerry, Edward Kennedy of Killaloe and Joseph Moran of Tuam, who joined the College staff in Kiltegan.
10. Cooke, 'The Roman Catholic Mission in Calabar', 186, 217.
11. Monsignor McGettrick, 'Mgr. McGettrick writes . . .' in *Africa*, 12/12 (Dec. 1950), 228. A Holy Child Sister had written of the slow progress in 'Letter from Ogoja' in *Africa*, Nov.–Dec. 1946, 210.
12. Moynagh, *Reminiscences*, 22.
13. Cooke, 'The Roman Catholic Mission in Calabar' treats this topic in depth in a section entitled 'Dissent from within; Religious Separatism', 186–200.
14. Rev. M. Magrath, 'With the African Pilgrims in Rome' in *Africa* XII/9 (Sep. 1950), 167–71. The Calabar/Ogoja pilgrims were: Monsignor T. McGettrick; Frs D. Ekandem, P.J. Costelloe, M. Magrath, J. Houlihan, D. Gallagher, J. Kearns, L. Walsh, D. Dolan; Srs Bridget, Oliver, Conlon and Elizabeth (M.M.M.); Mothers Teresa and Joachim (Holy Child); Srs St John and Lucy (Handmaids) and Michael Ekeng, Andrew Udo, Jacob Opala and Joseph Adiaha.

Chapter Ten, pp. 203–227

Sources

Minutes of 1950 Chapter and Minutes of 1956 Chapter.

Information on Fr J. Gilmartin supplied by Mrs P. Leydon and Mr Ultan McManus.

Draft document entitled 'History of the Diocese of Nakuru' by Fr D. Newman S.P.S. and the text of a talk given by Fr Newman at a meeting of Kiltegan priests in Eldoret in 1987 on the early days in Kenya.

Letters from Fr J. Houlihan in the USA, 1950–1954.

Correspondence with Archbishop Matthew, Apostolic Delegate, and Bishop F. Hall M.H.M., of Kisumu Diocese re. a new mission in Kenya, 1950–1953.

Interview with Fr V. Kiernan S.P.S., Fr D. Dolan S.P.S., and Fr P. Kittrick S.P.S.

Notes

1. Ex officio members were: P. Costelloe, C. Plunkett, J. Houlihan, J.F. Sheehan, J. McGuinness and C. Smith. Elected delegates were: M. Magrath, J. Gilmartin, W. Mullally and C. Cantwell from Calabar, V. Kiernan and L. O'Byrne from Ogoja and J. Kelly and W. Dunne representing the priests who were not on the missionfield.
2. Moynagh, *Reminiscences*, 63.
3. Archbishop Matthew's reply to Paddy Costelloe is in the Kiltegan archives, but it merely states that he intended to discuss the matter with Bishop Cavallera.
4. The phrase 'Whiteman's Country' is attributed to Sir Harry Johnston, Lord Salisbury's Lieutenant in Uganda.
5. J. Murray joined V. Farrell in Nakuru; W. Dunne went to J. van der Weyden in Eldoret; M. Brennan went to Nerkwo to J. Weech; D. Newman joined J. Kemper in Tartar and L. Doyle went to J. Molenaar in Kiminini. These Mill Hill priests stayed on for one year while John Hawes stayed in Kitale for two years because there was no one to take over from him.
6. These are the words of Sir Patrick Renison, Governor of Kenya, given at a press conference on 9 May 1960.
7. Four priests came at the end of 1952—Brian Cunningham, Leo Staples, Bill Tuohy and Paddy Cullen. Five came in 1953—Ted Smyth, Seamus Deignan, Gerry McCloskey, J.P. Bohan and Tom Grennan. Two came in 1954—Ned McElligott and Tony Prunty (Joe Houlihan the new Prefect Apostolic had arrived in July 1954). Six came in 1955—Christy Hannon, Donal Walsh, Celsus Heenan, Donald McDonagh and Vin Ambrose. Three came in 1956—Morgan O'Brien, Michael O'Dea and Pat Magee (to Kitui). Two came in 1957—Fintan McDonald (to Eldoret) and Harry Parkinson (to Kitui).
8. Bishop Hall to Joe Gilmartin, 11 February 1952.
9. Anon, 'The Race for the Schools' in *Africa* 18/1 (Jan. 1956), 6–10.
10. 'The Race for the Schools', 9–10.
11. Cooke, 'The Catholic Mission in Calabar', 234 (for Calabar statistics) and 'Ogoja Diocese, Sacred Returns 1954–55' in *Africa* 18/1 (January 1956), for Ogoja figures.
13. 'The Race for the Schools', 7.
14. Fr Patrick Laffey, 'Rosary Crusade', in *Africa* 14/5 (May 1952), 10–12.
15. Monsignor McGettrick, 'Report from Ogoja' in *Africa* 12/1 (Jan. 1950), 7.
16. Fr E. Fitzgibbon, 'The Catholic East of Nigeria' in *Africa* 23/8 (Nov. 1961), 5–10. Monsignor McGettrick, 'Report from Ogoja' in *Africa* 12/1 (Jan. 1950), 7. Fr Desmond O'Connor, 'Ogoja's Story' in *Africa* 17/7 (Aug.–Sep. 1955), 14, 15 (incorporates statistics for 1955). Statistics for Calabar and Ogoja are given in *Africa* 19/2 (Mar. 1957), 12, 13.
17. Moynagh, *Reminiscences*, 26.

18. 'Bricks and Mortar' in *Africa* 17/5 (May 1955), containing extracts from a letter sent to Kiltegan by Bishop Houlihan.
19. Anon, 'Safari by Air' in *Africa* 17/10 (Dec. 1955), 16.
20. P.J. McCamphill, *The Catholic Church in Kitui*, Kitui, 1989.
21. The delegates at the 1956 Chapter were: C. Cantwell, C. Donlon, W. Mullally, V. Brady, J. McGuinness, L. O'Byrne, W. Dunne, M. Grehan, K. Longworth, J. Mahon, Peter O'Reilly, S. Meehan and D. Newman.
22. Six Society members died in the 1950–57 period. Rev. Eamon Flynn, a deacon, died on 17 Mar. 1950 and was the first to be buried in Kiltegan. Fr Sean Casey (Calabar) was drowned while swimming at Afikpo during a visit to Ogoja on 20 Apr. 1952. Fr Alphonsus McKenna (Calabar) died in Ireland on 8 Oct. 1954. Brendan Bolger (Calabar) died at Enugu hospital on 3 Apr. 1955. Enda Davis (Ogoja) died in Ireland on 25 Apr. 1955, and Michael O'Sullivan, a member of the College staff, died on 25 Mar. 1957. The volunteers in the 1950–57 period were: 1951—Thomas Beirne of Elphin; 1952—Edward Looby of Limerick, John Conlon of Meath and Joseph Guiry of Limerick; 1953—Noel O'Donnell of Armagh; 1954—Raymond Browne of Elphin; 1955—Noel McIntyre of Kilmore; 1956—Michael Donovan of Cork, Celsus Heenan of Clonfert and Thomas McGeough of Armagh; 1957—James Casey of Elphin, Patrick Walsh of Cork and Daniel Simpson of Edinburgh.

Chapter Eleven, pp. 228–264

Sources

This chapter does not draw on archival material as the others have done. There are, however, a number of privately circulated (p.c.) publications and one unpublished draft which have supplied much of the information. They comprise:

James Good, *Mission to the Turkana*, p.c., 1988, 141 pp.

Rory O'Brien, 'My Personal Reminiscences of the Civil War in Afikpo', draft document, 64 typescript pp., 1986.

Frank Morris, *Calabar, a Diary of the Invasion*, p.c., 1968, 32 pp.

P.J. McCamphill, *The Catholic Church in Kitui*, p.c., 1989, 54 pp.

Interviews: Fr P. Moloughney S.P.S. (Brazil), Fr C. Napier S.P.S. (Minna), Fr P. Donnelly (Kitui), Fr Billy Feerick (Central Africa).

Notes

1. This letter was sent to Propaganda in the name of Monsignor Dominic Conway, Procurator of St Patrick's Missionary Society in Rome. The copy in the archives is undated.
2. The original five priests were: Kevin Brehony, Leo Traynor, John O'Callaghan, Joe Moran and Tony Barrett. The five from the 1968

ordination class, who came in September of that year, were Con Ryan, Gerry O'Carroll, Patsy Foley, Bill Pollard and Jim Brady.

3. Morgan O'Brien, whose brother Pat O'Brien is also a member of the Society and a missionary in Kenya, died in a car accident in Turkana on New Year's Day 1975. On 20 July 1975, Turkana was the scene of another tragedy for the Society when Fr Michael Gannon was drowned in a swollen river. His body was never recovered.

4. Rory O'Brien, 'My personal reminiscences of civil war in Afikpo', draft, 1986, 2.

5. Frank Morris, Calabar, *a Diary of the Invasion*, p.c., 1968, 21.

6. Rory O'Brien 'My personal reminiscences', 15, 17.

7. When Bishop Okoye was moved from Port Harcourt to Enugu after the War, Bishop Ekandem looked after Port Harcourt for a while and introduced Society priests there. The first to go was volunteer priest J.P. Masterson followed by Society priests Kevin Longworth, Eugene Bree, Tommy Browne, Roger Kinnane and Joe Rabbitt. In 1983, Bishop McGettrick resigned and was replaced by Bishop Michael Okoro. Bishop McGettrick stayed on at Abakaliki and did some parish work. He died in December 1988, having published his *Memoirs* shortly before that. He is buried in Abakaliki Cathedral. In 1990, Cardinal Ekandem was installed as Archbishop of Abuja, the new Capital City of Nigeria. He was replaced in Ikot Ekpene by Bishop Etukudo.

8. The following Society priests worked with St Paul's Missionary Society: Hugo McBride, Der Curran, Jim Sheerin, John Joyce, Paddy Duffy, Colm Clinton, Tom Ryan and Joe Rabbitt.

9. In September 1985, John Keenan and Jimmy Farrell joined the first group of Society priests in the Sudan.

10. Irish dioceses who have made a commitment to supply priests to missionary dioceses are: Limerick (Minna), Kerry (Nakuru), Ardagh and Clonmacnois (Chipata), Elphin (Kitui), Ferns (Sao Paulo), Galway (Chikwawa), Kilmore (Minna), Clogher (Kitui), Ardagh (Lagos).

11. This quotation is taken from a draft of the *Acts of the General Chapter*, 1990. The Chapter elected Kieran Birmingham as Superior General with Thomas Gillooly as his Vicar and Derek Byrne, John Marren and Oliver McHugh as councillors.

Appendix

1. *Probationers with St Patrick's Missionary Society 1932–1956*
Key: Names in italics indicate those who left the Society in the course of their studies either before or after taking the Oath of Membership. Names marked with an asterisk (*) refer to men who were subsequently ordained for a diocese. When a name is followed by the note '(Inc . . .)' it indicates an ordained member who left the Society and became incardinated in a named diocese or religious order. When the note '(d. . . .)' follows a name it indicates that a member has died and gives the date of his death.

1932 Joseph Houlihan (d. 4/12/75), Thomas Fitzgerald (d. 17/5/89), Joseph Gilmartin (d. 12/8/83), Daniel Creedon (d. 30/11/77), Carthage Cantwell (d. 19/1/81), Bernard McGuirk (d. 15/6/73). *Charles Fagan, Thomas Flanagan,* Patrick Gannon, Thomas Vaughan.**

1933 John Lavin (d. 22/6/71), Thomas Loughlin (d. 26/9/84), James Lane (d. 29/9/89), Michael V. Ambrose (d. 28/8/88), Michael Reilly (d. 12/4/80). *Edward Doorley, John Daly.*

1934 William Mullally (d. 28/9/90), Edward McElligott (d. 2/6/82), Vincent Kiernan, Patrick Doyle (d. 20/5/84), John Sheehan, James Byrne (d. 10/6/81), John Conway (d. 25/9/66). *Michael P. O'Reilly, Thomas Lorigan,* John Brennan,* Christopher Baxter, Patrick Reilly.*

1935 Joseph Kelly, Joseph O'Driscoll, Henry Bradley (d. 16/11/79), Thomas Mahoney (d. 20/4/60), Michael McDonald (d. 3/11/71), Edward McNamara, Cornelius Murphy (d. 27/7/45). *Eugene Sheerin, Vincent Reilly, John Browne.*

1936 Vincent Brady, Enda Davis (d. 25/4/55), Christopher Donlon (d. 28/5/80), John Lee (d. 27/1/82), John Moynihan, Patrick O'Reilly, *Thomas McGovern, Joseph Brady, Michael Gormally.**

1937 Maurice Hayes, Vincent Hannigan, John McGuinness, Timothy Carr (Inc. Miami, USA), Austin Gogarty, *James Duggan, Daniel Gorey, John Hoban.**

1938 Bernard Hughes (d. 1/1/82), William Dunne, Finbar Donegan (O.C.S.O. Mt Melleray), *Desmond Igoe, Liam Sandvoss.*

1939 Matthew Grehan (d. 29/2/76), Eugene O'Reilly, Joseph Murray, Laurence Walsh (Inc. New Orleans, USA), Kevin Longworth, Joseph Dollard, Liam O'Byrne, *Gabriel Kiernan.*

1940 Patrick Dorr (d. 18/11/85), Thomas Cafferty, John Brady, Sean McCormac, Thomas Grealy, Patrick Laffey (d. 7/7/89), *Maurice Daly, Noel Slattery.*

1941 Eamon Hannify (d. 7/1/84), Patrick Walsh (d. 2/4/73), Cathal McBride, Daniel Dolan, Liam McSorley, Patrick Quigley, Patrick Moore, Thomas O'Reilly (d. 2/1/73), Oliver O'Sullivan (d. 20/10/86), Michael Glynn, Peter O'Reilly (d. 26/9/88), Thomas Grennan (Inc. Wheeling, USA), Leo O'Sullivan, Ciaran Needham, Patrick Hannelly, John Mahon, *Anthony O'Malley, Patrick Brosnan, Edward Maxwell, James Kearney, James McEvoy, Austin Ruane, John Marron, John O'Neill, Noel Kelly, Hugh Daly, Fechin Murphy.*

1942 Sean Meehan, Nicholas Walsh, Kevin O'Doherty, John Deegan (d. 12/3/83), Thomas Gallagher, Patrick Kittrick, Patrick Hyland, Reginald Smyth, Liam McWey (d. 15/5/85), Donal O'Sullivan, Francis Morris (d. 4/1/80), Charles Napier, John Boylan, Denis Newman, William Dowling. *Thomas McVey, Patrick Glynn, Patrick Murphy, Brendan McDowell, Francis McAdam, Aidan Ryan, Francis O'Keeffe, John Fagan, Charles Carson, Seamus O'Connor.*

1943 Peter Ryan, Patrick Clifford, Sean Casey (d. 20/4/52), Michael Brennan, Alphonsus McKenna (d. 8/10/54), William Tuohy, Liam Doyle, Patrick Hannon, Edmond Fitzgibbon, Leo Sheridan, John Flanagan, Michael O'Sullivan (d. 25/3/57), Thomas O'Byrne, Desmond O'Connor, Eamon Flynn (d. 17/3/50), *Joseph Whooley, Thomas Wall, Michael Griffin, Timothy Curran, Christopher Kiernan, James Finnegan, James Devine, Henry Foy, Michael Kennedy, Patrick Friel, Liam McStay, Michael Lyons.*

1944 James P. Bohan, Eoin Lacey, Alphonsus Rushe, Patrick Prendergast, James A. Byrne, Sean Dillon, Thomas Lucey, Christopher Griffin (d. 14/12/85), Thaddaeus Smith, Brendan Bolger (d. 3/4/55), Joseph Griffin, Michael McCabe, Matthew Campbell, Terence Beagon, Daniel O'Kane, *Sean White, Patrick Kelly, Kevin Keegan, Michael Larkin,*

Thomas O'Donnell, * *Arthur Murphy, Philip Moore, Louis St John,* * *James Curry, Michael Toolan.*

1945 Joseph Lowney, Joseph Spillane, Patrick Cullen, James Kearns, Brian Cunningham, Christopher Hannon, Patrick Finnerty, *Ever McMahon, Eric Crotty, Joseph Lalor, Andrew McManus, Kevin Fitzmaurice.*

1946 Roger Kinane, Maurice Kerin, P.V. Flanagan (Inc. Portsmouth), Patrick McCormac, James Deignan, Anthony Prunty, Gerard McCluskey, Thomas Browne, Noel Bouchier (d. 21/2/90), Laurence Kearney, Owen Reid, Thomas McCracken, Henry Keogh (Inc. Galway), *Joseph Curran, Hilary O'Rourke, Peter Reynolds, Eugene Benson, Gerard Fay, Patrick Gilroy, Michael Tuohy, Charles McNaboe.*

1947 Leo Staples, James Murphy (Inc. Wheeling, USA), Vincent Cullen (d. 12/1/89), Donal Walsh (Inc. San Diego, USA), Joseph Pettit, Maurice Healy (d. 14/12/82), Patrick Scanlon, James Regan, *Murtagh McEvoy, Francis Kelly, Joseph Finneran.*

1948 Donald McDonagh, Stanislaus Connolly, Roderick O'Brien, James Sheerin, Patrick McGee (d. 3/4/72), James Reihill, Vincent McNamara, Philip Magee, Eugene Greene (Inc. Raphoe), Michael Gallagher, Michael O'Dea (d. 5/2/60), Maurice Kelly, Morgan O'Brien (d. 1/1/75), Michael Heenan (Inc. Rockville Center, USA), John Ralph (Inc. Wheeling, USA), Denis O'Hara, Denis O'Neill. *Patrick Doran, Patrick Cooke, John Lovett, Thomas Moore, Hugh Donnelly, Raymond O'Hagan, Thomas Maguire, John Ward, John Finnerty, Patrick Crotty,* * *Patrick O'Rourke, Henry O'Kane, Donal Doyle, Joseph McDonald.*

1949 Henry McCarney, Thomas Curran, Martin Dwan, Fintan McDonald, Peter Coyle, John Ryan, Dermot Curran, Henry Parkinson (Inc. Glasgow), Thomas Randles, Patrick O'Malley, *William Byrne, Brendan Swan, Michael Davern, Thomas McAlindon, Patrick Timmons.*

1950 Sean Weldon, Raymond Murtagh, John Counihan, William Fitzsimons (Inc. Meath), Liam de Veale, *Patrick McKeown, Thomas Flynn, Patrick McCarthy, Seamus Flanagan, John Moynihan, Aidan Gallagher, John Guckian, Ivor Quigley, John McCaul, John Gibbons, Michael McWey.*

1951 Thomas Ryan, Noel Cleary, Patrick Hagan, Patrick Kelly, Timothy Vaughan, Gerald Brady, Patrick Moloney, Stephen Donohue, Richard Brennan, Michael Golden, *David Slattery, John Durkin, Kieran Dodd,* * *Albert Parkinson, James Gould, John Verriker, Denis Harlow,* * *Thomas Madigan, Sean O'Donnell, Martin Hession.*

1952 Joseph O'Conor, Bernard Bohan, Neil Campion, Thomas O'Connor (Inc. Elphin), Aidan Surlis, Patrick Grey (d. 29/9/90), Desmond

Perry, Robert Kavanagh, Bartholomew O'Doherty, Edmond Grace, James Sharkey, Brian Twomey, James Barry, Noel Hayes, William O'Carroll, Francis McNabb, John Joyce, *James Forristal, Andrew O'Donnell,* * *William Sweetman, Noel Walsh, Brendan O'Keeffe, Sean Kelleher, Andrew Darmody.*

1953 Donal Dorr, Henry Farmer (d. 29/3/62), Seamus Whelan, Kevin Brehony (d. 19/1/85), Eugene Bree, Peter Gillooly, Brian Flanagan, Francis Lyons, Bernard Freyne (Inc. San Jose, USA), Dermot O'Connell, Leonard Forristal, *Sean Flynn, Joseph Hunt, Stephen McGarry, Anthony Cassidy, Richard Kennedy, Thomas O'Flynn, Peter Brett, William Joseph Quinlan, Eamon Lynch, Anthony Sharkey.*

1954 Patrick O'Brien, John Magee, Fiacre Ryan, Ciaran O'Flynn, Patrick Hamilton, Fintan Byrne, Leo Traynor, Brendan Kilroy, Michael Dillon, Francis Minogue, Joseph Taylor, *Michael Hearne, Eamon Mulrennan, Colm McAliskey, Desmond Brady.*

1955 Colm Hand, Thomas Greenan, Sean O'Dowd, Patrick Feeney, Sean Clyne (d. 14/8/58), Sean McTiernan, Terence Coughlan, Joseph Rabbitt, Patrick Flanagan, Sean Cullen, James Noonan, Francis Morgan, Dermot Nolan, John Jones, Raymond Reidy, Conor Moloney, Thomas Ryan, Anthony Terry, Peter Finegan, Eamon Hayden, Leo Flynn, *Owen Denneny, James O'Donoghue, Joseph Rodgers, Liam O'Brien, Desmond Lyng, Matthew McManus, Dermot O'Connor, Patrick Doyle, John McLoughlin, Joseph Glynn, Gregory Duffy, Anthony McDonagh, Colm Foyle, Seamus Byrne, William Ryan.*

1956 Jeremiah Kiely, Thomas Barrett, Thomas Gillooly, Dermot Connolly, Desmond McKeever, Thomas Naughton, Raymond McNicholas, Paul Hardy, Patrick Kelleher, James McAuliffe, Michael McNamara, Patrick Prunty, John Lalor, Laurence McElhill (Inc. Down & Connor), Patrick Hughes, Edward Lalor, Charles Ryan, Michael Kelly, Augustine Frawley, *Colm O'Liathain, Seamus King, Joseph McCausland, Michael Mulqueeney, Joseph Noone, Fergal McGuinness, Michael Hannon, Felim Maguire, Joseph Mullooly, John Keane.*

2. *Medical Personnel (1932–1957)*

Dr Lengauer (also spelt Leningar) Calabar, 1933; Miss Schallow, Calabar, 1933; Miss Daunt, Calabar, 1933; Dr Dufey, Calabar, 1937–1939 with Mrs Dufey; Dr Streyrath, Calabar, 1939; Nurse Angela D'Arcy, Calabar, 1936–37; Nurse Powell, Calabar, 1936–37; Dr Patrick Dunleavy, Calabar, 1937–38; Dr Gerald Connolly, Calabar, 1942–45; Dr Patrick Feeney, Calabar and Ogoja, 1944–51; John Turner, Calabar, Ogoja and Kitui, 1944–61; Dr Joseph Barnes, Ogoja, 1944–52; Dr Sean Flannery, 1945–49; Dr Tim Noonan, Calabar,

1946–49; Dr Eamon Corcoran, 1946–49; Dr Godfrey Hinds, Ogoja, 1949–69; Dr Eileen Barnes, Ogoja, 1950–52; Dr Bob Costelloe, Ogoja, 1949–57; Dr Denis Freeman, Ogoja, 1950–56; Dr Seamus Cronin, Calabar, 1950–53; Dr C.B. Burdett Smith, Calabar, 1951–56; Dr Jeremiah Twomey and Mrs (Dr) Emily Twomey, Calabar, 1953–55; Dr Frank Griffin and Mrs (Nurse) Jean Griffin, Calabar, 1953–55; Mrs (Dr) Rita Freeman, Ogoja, 1954–56; Nurse Helen Healy, Ogoja, 1954–55; Mrs (Nurse) C.B. Burdett Smith, Calabar, 1954–56; Dr Eilish Ridge (O'Brien) Ogoja, 1955–58 and 1960; Dr Bruno Troso, Ogoja, 1955–57; Dr Anthony Rodgers (dentist), Calabar, 1956–58; Dr & Mrs Brendan O'Farrell, Calabar, 1956–58; Dr Finbarr Murphy, Eldoret, 1956–59; Dr & Mrs (Nurse) P.J. Burke, Ogoja, 1956–57; Dr Eileen Fern, Ogoja, 1956–59; Dr & Mrs (Dr) Patrick Fahy, Calabar, 1956–57; Dr Eoin Leavy, Ogoja, 1956; Dr Joseph Stewart, Kitui, 1957–59; Dr Venanzio Marini, Ogoja, 1957–59; Dr Angelo Caroli, 1957–60; Dr Renato Zancelli, Ogoja, 1957–60.

3. Educational Personnel (1932–1957)
Patrick McLoughlin, B.A., H.D.G., Calabar, 1946–49;
James Burke, B.A., B. Comm., Calabar, 1946–49;
Lilian Murphy, Ogoja, 1950–67;
Patrick Bolger, B.Agr.Sc., Calabar, 1952–54;
Thomas Nunan, B.Sc., Calabar & Ogoja, 1952–58;
Desmond Flanagan, B.A., Calabar, 1953–55;
Seamus Flanagan, B.A., Eldoret, 1954–55;
Diarmuid O'Donovan, B.A., Eldoret, 1954–58 (also Legion of Mary Envoy to East Africa);
Sean Moynihan, B.A., Eldoret, 1954–57;
Patrick Connors, B.Agr. Sc., Calabar, 1956–58;
Joseph Hoade, B.Agr. Sc., Calabar, 1956–58;
Desmond Corcoran, B.A., Calabar, 1957–61;
Desmond Curran, M.A., B.L., Ogoja 1957–59.

Select Bibliography

Armour, M.A., *Cornelia: The Story of Cornelia Connolly 1800–1879*, Rome 1979

Ayandele, E.A., *The Missionary Impact on Modern Nigeria 1842–1914*, London 1966

Barrett, David B., *Schism and Renewal in Africa*, Nairobi 1968

Barrett, William E., *The Red Lacquered Gate* (Story of Bishop Galvin Co-Founder of the Columban Fathers), New York 1966

Baur, John, *The Catholic Church in Kenya*, Nairobi 1990

Burns, A.C., *History of Nigeria*, 5th edn, London 1955

Canning, Bernard J., *Bishops of Ireland 1870–1987*, Ballyshannon, Co. Donegal 1987

Clough, R.G., *Oil River Trader*, London 1972

Cooke, Colman, *Mary Charles Walker, The Nun of Calabar*, Dublin 1980

Cooke, Colman, 'The Roman Catholic Mission in Calabar 1903–1960' Ph.D. thesis, University of London 1977

Cooke, Colman, 'Irish Diocesan Priests in Southern Nigeria 1920–1942' M.A. thesis, University College Cork, 1971

Corish, Patrick J., *The Irish Catholic Experience*, Dublin 1985

Crowder, M., *The Story of Nigeria*, revised edn, London 1966

de Vaulx, Bernard, *History of the Missions*, London 1961

Forristal Desmond, *Second Burial of Bishop Shanahan*, Dublin 1990

Glynn, Michael, 'St. Patrick's Foreign Missionary Society' in *The Capuchin Annual*, XXIII, (1955), pp. 371–6

Glynn, Michael, 'St. Patrick's Missions' in *The Capuchin Annual*, XXIII, (1955), pp. 377–80.

Good, James, *Mission to the Turkana*, Lodwar, p.c. 1988

Heenan, J.C., *Cardinal Hinsley*, London 1944

Hogan, Edward, *The Irish Missionary Movement, A Historical Survey, 1830–1980*, Dublin 1990

Huxley, Elspeth, *Whiteman's Country*: Lord Delamere and the Making of Kenya, 2 vols., London 1935

Jordan, John P., *Bishop Shanahan of Southern Nigeria*, revised edn, Dublin 1971

Keaney, Marian, *They brought the Good News*, Dublin 1980

Koren, Henry J., *The Spiritans*, Duquesne 1958

Langley M. and Kiggins T., *A Serving People*, Nairobi 1974

Latourette, Kenneth S., *A History of the Expansion of Christianity*, vols. VI and VII, New York 1944 and '45 (reissued in paperback by Paternoster)

McCamphill, P.J., *The Catholic Church in Kitui*, Diocese of Kitui p.c. 1989

McGettrick, Bishop Thomas, *Memoirs of Bishop T. McGettrick*, p.c. 1988

McGlade, *The Missions: Africa and the Orient*, (vol. VI, A History of Irish Catholicism), Dublin 1967

McMahon, Hugh, 'John Blowick' in *The Furrow*, 39/10 (October 1988), pp. 627–35

Meehan, D., 'Maynooth and the Missions' in *Irish Ecclesiastical Record*, LXVI (1945), pp. 224–37

Morris, Frank, *Calabar, a Diary of the Invasion*, p.c. 1968

Moynagh, J., *Reminiscences*, Kiltegan p.c. 1979

Moynagh, J., 'The Society of St. Patrick for Foreign Missions' in *Irish Ecclesiastical Record*, LXIV (1944), pp. 107–14

Moynagh, J., 'St. Patrick's Missionaries in West Africa' in *The Capuchin Annual*, XXIII (1955), 382–8

Moynagh. J., 'The Church in Nigeria', in *The Furrow*, III, 1 (1952), pp. 3–16

Murray-Brown, Jeremy, *Kenyatta*, London, 1972

Neil, Stephen, *A History of Christian Missions* (vol. VI of The Pelican History of the Church), 1984

Obi, Celestine A., ed., *A Hundred Years of the Catholic Church in Eastern Nigeria 1885–1985*, Onitsha, 1985

O'Leary, Michael, *The Kitui Akamba*, Nairobi, 1984

Okwu, Augustine S.O., The Beginning of the Maynooth Movement in Southern Nigeria and the Rise of St. Patrick's Missionary Society, in Journal of Religion in Africa, X, (1980) pp. 22–45

Oliver, Roland, *The Missionary Factor in East Africa*, London, 1952

Parrinder, Geoffrey, *West African Religion*, London 1969

Purcell, Mary, *To Africa With Love* (Biography of Mother Mary Martin), Dublin 1987

Ramsford, Oliver, *Livingstone's Lake* (History of Malawi), London 1966

Ronayne, T., 'A Great Irish Missionary: Dr. J. Shanahan, 1870–1943' in *Irish Ecclesiastical Record*, LXIII (1944), pp. 228–36

Ryan, Sr M. Brigid, *Bishop Shanahan and his Missionary Family*, Holy Rosary Sisters, vol. I, 1967, vol. II, 1977

Sklar, Richard L., *Nigerian Political Parties*, New Jersey 1963

Todd, John M., *African Mission*, (A historical study of the Society of African Missions), London 1962

Turner, H.W, 'A Methodology for Modern African Religious Movement' in *Comparative Studies in Society and Religion*, VIII (1965–66), pp. 281–94

Wellbourne, F.B., *East African Christian*, London 1965

Whitney, P.J., *An Irish Missionary in Central Africa*, Dublin 1923

Index